ZULU
VICTORY

ZULU VICTORY

THE EPIC OF ISANDLWANA
AND THE COVER-UP

RON LOCK AND PETER QUANTRILL

Greenhill Books, London
Stackpole Books, Pennsylvania

Zulu Victory: The Epic of Isandlwana and the Cover-Up
first published 2002 by Greenhill Books,
Lionel Leventhal Limited, Park House,
1 Russell Gardens, London NW11 9NN
and
Stackpole Books, 5067 Ritter Road,
Mechanicsburg, PA 17055, USA

British Library Cataloguing in Publication Data
Lock, Ron
Zulu victory : the epic of Isandlwana and the cover-up
1. Isandlwana (South Africa), Battle of, 1879
I. Title II. Quantrill, Peter
968.4'045

ISBN 1-85367-505-9

Library of Congress Cataloging-in-Publication Data
A catalog entry is available from the library.

Edited and typeset by Donald Sommerville.

Printed and bound in Great Britain by
Creative Print and Design Group, Ebbw Vale, Wales.

Contents

	List of Maps	6
	List of Illustrations	7
	Authors' Note	9
	Acknowledgements	10
	Glossary	12
	Foreword *by Prince Mangosuthu Buthelezi*	13
	Prologue	15
Part One	**The Conflict**	17
Chapter 1	The Ultimatum	19
Chapter 2	Lord Chelmsford's Army	36
Chapter 3	King Cetshwayo's Army	51
Chapter 4	Into Zululand	66
Chapter 5	The Armies Converge	86
Part Two	**The Battle**	143
Chapter 6	The Game of Chess	145
Chapter 7	Descent of the Whirlwind	183
Part Three	**The Cover-Up**	233
Chapter 8	Web of Deception	235
Chapter 9	Horse Guards' Interrogation and Verdict	264
	Epilogue	284
	Notes	303
	Appendices	
Appendix A	Chronology	315
Appendix B	Regiments of the Zulu Army	320
Appendix C	The Ammunition Controversy	322
	Bibliography	328
	Index	331

List of Maps

Map No. 1   page 18
Natal and the Zulu kingdom, showing Lord Chelmsford's invasion
plan, mid-January 1879

Map No. 2   88–89
Movements of the opposing armies, 21–22 January 1879

Map No. 3   152–153
Movements of the opposing armies. 7.00 a.m. to noon,
22 January 1879

Map No. 4   156–157
Map copied from the original made by Captain Anstey, RE,
and Lieutenant Penrose, RE, dated 13 November 1879

Map No. 5   197
Deployment of Cavaye's and Mostyn's companies of the 1/24th on
the Tahelane Ridge.

Map No. 6   200–201
Final phases of the battle, 1.00 p.m., 22 January 1879.

Map No. 7   207
Reproduction of Sergeant-Major Jabez Molife's map, one of the few
surviving maps actually drawn by a participant in the battle.

Map No. 8   234
A map copied from the original drawing by Inspector Mansel, NMP,
which he sent to Edward Durnford.

Map No. 9   258–259
A copy of the map of the battle situation at 1.00 p.m. drawn by
Lieutenant Walter James, RE, and dated 18 March 1879.

Map No. 10   260–261
A reproduction of Gerald French's map from his book *Lord
Chelmsford and the Zulu War*.

Map No. 11   286
Wolseley's division of Zululand into thirteen 'chiefdoms', which
effectively destroyed the Zulu kingdom.

List of Illustrations

(pages 97–128)

1. Isandlwana Hill, as seen from the vicinity of Rorke's Drift.
2. The area of the wagon park, looking towards the Nqutu Ridge.
3. One of the many massive *dongas* that criss-cross the Isandlwana plain.
4. The Mangeni Falls.
5. The Kwa Mahamba Drift.
6. iThusi's rocky crest, shaped like a cock's comb.
7. The view from the top of iThusi.
8. Looking down from the Tahelane Ridge.
9. From Magaga Knoll.
10. Looking down on the position of Durnford's encounter with the Zulu left horn.
11. The trail of white cairns leading to Fugitives' Drift.
12. Looking down on the Buffalo River.
13. Fugitives' Drift at low water.
14 & 15. Members of the Isandlwana Zulu community painted and embroidered these quilt panels depicting scenes from the battle of 1879, as this is remembered in local oral history.
16. The British ultimatum being delivered to Cetshwayo's representatives.
17. Lieutenant-General Lord Chelmsford.
18. Sir Bartle Frere.
19. Mfunzi, Cetshwayo's messenger.
20. A Zulu warrior and his girlfriend.
21. Cetshwayo at the time of his coronation.
22. A young warrior ready for battle.
23. A group of Zulu dignitaries.
24. Imperial infantry on parade at Pietermaritzburg.
25. Lord Chelmsford as drawn by Lieutenant-Colonel Crealock.
26. Fynn, Dartnell and a group of Border Guard officers.
27. Coate's Ferry Hotel on the Tugela River.
28. Lieutenant Horace Smith-Dorrien, transport officer.
29. Commandant Rupert Lonsdale, Natal Native Contingent.
30. Mr Paul Brickhill, interpreter.
31. Thousands of oxen and hundreds of wagons were needed to move Chelmsford's army.
32. Captain Walter James, RE.
33. Major John Dartnell, Natal Mounted Police.
34. Trooper (later Colonel) William Clarke of the Natal Mounted Police.

35. Veterans of the Natal Native Horse and Natal Native Contingent.
36. *Donga* in the Magogo Valley.
37. British infantry on the march.
38. Lieutenant-Colonel Henry Pulleine, 24th Regiment.
39. Lieutenant Alfred Henderson, Natal Native Horse.
40. Colonel Anthony Durnford, RE, Commander of No. 2 Column.
41. W. Edwards, W.W. Barker and a group of Natal Carbineers.
42. Lieutenant Charlie Raw, Natal Native Horse.
43. Lieutenant-Colonel J.C. Russell, Imperial Mounted Infantry.
44. Captain George Shepstone, Natal Native Horse.
45. Quartermaster-Sergeant John Bullock, Natal Carbineers.
46. Quartermaster William London, Natal Carbineers.
47. Lieutenant Henry Curling, RA.
48. An officer of the 80th Regiment.
49. The Durban Volunteer Artillery.
50. The summer of 1879 was an exceptionally wet one with rivers and streams often in flood.
51. The Last Stand of the 24th.
52. Prince Shingana kaMpande, half brother to King Cetshwayo.
53. Sigcwelegewele kaMhlekehleke, commander of the Nkobamakosi.
54. Colonel Pulleine's message advising Lord Chelmsford that the Zulus were advancing on the camp.
55. Prince Ndabuko kaMpande, younger full brother of Cetshwayo.
56. The commander of the Zulu Army, Ntshingwayo kaMahole.
57. Chief Zibhebhu kaMaphitha, hereditary chief of the Mandalakazi.
58. Men of the amaNgwane tribe, taken in 1883.
59. Zulu warrior.
60. Lieutenant-Colonel Crealock, assistant military secretary to Lord Chelmsford.
61. Lt Wyatt Vause, Natal Native Horse.
63. Captain William Eccles Mostyn, 24th Regiment.
63. Lt Charles Walter Cavaye, 24th Regiment.
64. The Natal Hussars.
65. Lieutenant Roberts, Natal Native Horse.
66. The remainder of No. 3 Column departs the devastated camp.
67. Lieutenant Edwards Hopton Dyson, 24th Regiment.
68. Lieutenant Charles Pope, 24th Regiment.
69. Captain Reginald Younghusband, 24th Regiment.
70. Melvill's and Coghill's grave.
71. Private Samuel Wassall, Imperial Mounted Infantry.
72. Cornelius Francis Clery, principal staff officer to Colonel Glyn.
73, 74, 75. Three views of the Isandlwana ammunition box in the Warriors Gate Museum, Durban.

Authors' Note

In some of the contemporary quotations reproduced later in this book the words 'kaffir' or 'caffre' are used. It has often been said that 120 years ago these expressions did not carry derogatory connotations. Not so, their use was offensive, then as now. In November 1878 Lord Chelmsford issued his *Regulations, Field Forces South Africa* which contained advice on the management of the Natal Native Contingent.

> 'No. 7. Never use epithets of contempt such as niggers, kaffirs etc. Call them "abantu" (people), "amadoda" (men), or "amabuti" (soldiers).'

This was excellent advice which in the main was regrettably ignored.

Arthur Konigkramer, a person wise in the ways of the Zulu people and their history, has pointed out to the authors that the use of the word 'enemy' in the pages that follow, when the British refer to the Zulu and vice versa, is wrong. He correctly maintains that the Zulu people were never enemies of the British, who brought about the war, and should not be described as such. We considered our options in the light of this sensible suggestion and, in the context of the violent story that follows, we decided that it would be confusing to replace the word 'enemy' by any other. For this we apologise.

Rather than interrupt our narrative with numerous footnotes we have decided to collect these together at the end of the book. Sections in the text which are amplified in this way are shown by the symbol ◊ and the notes have page references indicating which section of the book they refer to.

Parts One and Two and Appendix C of the book were written by Ron Lock; Part Three was written by Peter Quantrill. All other sections are a 'joint effort'.

Acknowledgements

Numerous individuals and organisations have generously given their assistance in providing the authors with primary source material without which a subject as complex as Isandlwana would be difficult to comprehend. In no particular order we wish to offer them our thanks.

An immeasurable debt of gratitude is owed to our friend Peter Robinson of Gerrards Cross, who undertook the difficult task of researching and collating a plethora of primary source material from various parts of the UK. Without his unsparing help this book would not have been possible.

The authors would like to acknowledge the help given by Lady de Bellaigue, formerly Registrar, The Royal Archives, Windsor, and to Mrs Jill Kelsey, Deputy Registrar. All quotations and photographs originating from materials in the Royal Archives are reproduced by gracious permission of Her Majesty Queen Elizabeth II. Beverley Williams, the Assistant Curator, Royal Engineers Museum, Chatham, helped immeasurably by allowing us access and permission to quote from the Durnford Papers, Major Martin Everett, the Curator of the Regimental Museum of The Royal Regiment of Wales, also kindly allowed us access to primary source material.

In South Africa, we acknowledge the help given by Carol Leigh of the Brenthurst Library, Johannesburg, for allowing us to quote from the Harness, Crealock and Clery letters, part of the Brenthurst Library, Anglo-Zulu War manuscript. Thanks are due to Jack and Kay Churchill Simpson for their interest and encouragement; to Charlie van der Merwe, curator of the Warriors Gate Museum, Durban, who, at short notice, made available documents and artefacts; to Di Matheson and Marise Bauer of Pietermaritzburg for patience and skill in drawing the maps, and to Brian Thomas for sharing his knowledge on the VC awards to Melvill and Coghill.

Much assistance was given by the Killie Campbell Africana Library, Durban, and Mark Coghlan of the Natal Carbineers' Museum, Pietermaritzburg. The Natal Archives, Pietermaritzburg, gave unrestricted access to its wonderful collection of photographs and documents and the African Museum, Johannesburg, supplied a number of illustrations.

In the UK we thank: Lee Stevenson who, at short notice, was ever willing to help out and research some character or event; John Young of the Anglo-Zulu War Research Society who generously made available his knowledge and his collection of photographs and illustrations; Lt Colonel Ian Bennett for his interest and advice regarding several survivors of the battle; Bill (W.W.) Race for his illustrations and Denis Montgomery for details of the eclipse. In America Ron Sheeley kindly allowed the use of his photograph of Lord Chelmsford.

Special thanks go to many individuals who are acknowledged experts on the subject, in particular: Arthur Konigkramer, Chairman of Amafa aKwaZulu-Natali, the body responsible for all heritage matters in kwaZulu-Natal including the curatorship of battlefield sites, for his continued interest and for sharing his knowledge of Zulu culture and history. The authors were privileged by his being instrumental in introducing them to Prince Mangosuthu Buthelezi. Other to whom we are grateful are: Professor John Laband for his continued patient response to the many queries he fielded; Lieutenant-Colonel S.B. Bourquin, the doyen on matters Zulu, for sharing his knowledge and anecdotes, and for allowing us to research his extensive library and collection of photographs; Colonel Joe Williams, the representative of The Royal Regiment of Wales in South Africa for his continued encouragement; Robin Stayt of the Vause family for allowing us access to the original Vause diaries and papers; members of the Raw, Vause and Henderson families, all of whom generously helped. We also thank Des Watkins who bequeathed to the authors his great-great-grandfather, James Lloyd's original album of 220 contemporary photographs. When restored, this album will be presented to AMAFA and housed at the Ulundi Museum.

Taking cognisance of the military maxim that time spent on reconnaissance is never wasted, the authors made numerous visits to Isandlwana Lodge, an ideal setting for research with its dramatic views of the battle site. Pat Stubbs, the gracious American co-owner, welcomed us with hospitality and kindness. To Rob Gerrard, the resident historian at the Lodge, we offer our thanks for the time he set aside on numerous occasions and the many happy hours spent traversing the ground from all angles.

Our gratitude also goes to: our helicopter pilot, Eugene 'Dog' Kalafatis, remembered for a hair-raising day spent contouring the entire battlefield, finishing with a sweep at ground level to simulate the movement of the Zulu right horn – a fearsome experience; Laura Courtney-Clarke who typed the manuscript, for her efficiency, smiling calm, humour and in particular her patience in revising the text more often than we care to remember; Nicki von der Heyde whose knowledge of Zulu and military history, plus a degree in English Literature was invaluable in the role we thrust upon her, that of chief corrector and critic of the text; Miriam Vigar for her interest and advice; 'Chelmsford' Ntanzi whose grandfather fought with the Nkobamakosi Regiment, for his companionship and for sharing his knowledge of the battle. The people of Zululand earn a special vote of thanks for their cheerful disposition and great white-toothed smiles which they constantly bestow on passing travellers.

The final appreciation has been reserved for our wives. Jacquie Quantrill for her tireless energy in typing the portion of the text relating to the cover-up and for her unstinting love and support for the project; Brenda Lock who bravely taught herself to operate a laptop whilst coping with the despatch and receipt of numerous emails – a tricky business. Without the patient and loving attention of our dear wives this book would not have been possible.

Glossary

amabutho	Age group regiments.
amakhosi	In the context of 1879, chiefs of the Zulu nation.
Boer	Dutch speaking white settler from the Cape.
donga	An eroded watercourse.
drift	A ford or shallow river crossing.
hlanza	To vomit.
ibutho	Warrior.
iklwa	Broad bladed stabbing spear.
impi	Zulu fighting force or army.
indaba	An important meeting or discussion.
induna	A commander or headman, a person of authority.
inkatha	Sacred coil formed of a python skin, symbolic of the Zulu nation.
inkosi	King, chief – a person of importance.
isicoco	A head ring worn by married men.
isigodlo	The accommodation or harem occupied by the King's wives.
isihlangu	Large war shield.
iZigqoza	The political faction of Prince Mbuyazi, Cetshwayo's rival brother, who was slain at the Battle of Ndondakusuka, 2nd December 1856.
iziMpisi	Hyena men, nickname given to executioners.
iziNyanga	Healers and witchdoctors.
kloof	A cliff or small ravine.
kop or *koppie*	A hill.
kraal	A cattle enclosure or group of huts (*kraal* is a term frowned upon by the Zulu people when used in reference to a group of huts).
laager	A defensive position usually formed of wagons but can also refer to a permanent position such as a fort.
Makolwas	Christian Zulus.
nek	A saddle between two hills.
Ondini	The royal homestead of King Cetshwayo burnt by the British after the Battle of Ulundi, 4 July 1879.
pont	Flat bottomed boat used as a ferry at river crossings.
spruit	A small stream.
trek	To make an overland journey.
udibi	Teenage Zulu boy. Baggage carrier to the army.
umkhosi	First Fruit Ceremony. An annual Zulu event performed on gathering the harvest.
uSuthu	King Cetshwayo's political faction. Later used as the national war cry in the war of 1879.
Voortrekker	Boer pioneer journeying overland.

Foreword

by Prince Mangosuthu Buthelezi

I am pleased to introduce the work of Ron Lock and Peter Quantrill who have researched the history of the battle of Isandlwana, in order to tease out the truth of an event which remains emotional for my people and myself. This is a very personal issue for me, as my own grandfather, Mkhandumba Buthelezi, fought in this battle and survived, while his half-brother, Mntumengana, sadly lost his life to the same. During the reign of my maternal great-grandfather King Cetshwayo, my paternal great-grandfather, Mnyamana Buthelezi, was Commander-in-Chief of all operations and imbued his warriors with the same valour that strengthened his own heart. The strategic genius of men such as my great-grandfather, matched with the fearlessness of the Zulu warriors, won a victory that has been, and will be, remembered down the generations.

This book offers a new insight into the history of Isandlwana which is both valuable and welcome. It is significant that there are few treatises on the Anglo-Zulu War of 1879 which do not refer to the defeat of Lord Chelmsford's invading army at Isandlwana on January 22 as a 'disaster.' Similar adjectival nouns punctuate the vocabulary of the majority of those who recollect and interpret these events to the thousands of visitors who come to the battlefield each year.

I feel that, in a sense, such language demonstrates a somehow superficial approach to events which require the scrutiny of more careful historical critique. In fact, the facts reveal that those colonial officials within South Africa who engineered this war committed grave injustices against the Zulu people and their King, the effects and legacy of which are still with us to this day. A more critical approach such as that employed in this book questions how the defeat of an invading army moved by destructive intent can be depicted as a 'disaster.'

Even these days it is salutary to consider the arrogance of individuals like Sir Garnet Wolseley, the chief architect of the disintegration of the Zulu State that brought about untold suffering to my people. His personal diary of July 19, 1879 has an entry which shows how deeply he misread and misunderstood the Zulus, their *amakhosi* and their needs and aspirations. Concerning his remarks to *amakhosi* he noted:

> 'that the great Queen who ruled in South Africa desired to see the Zulu people rich and happy as those Zulus who resided in Natal. They expressed themselves highly pleased with what they had heard.'

It is thus refreshing to note that authors Ron Lock and Peter Quantrill have now, for the first time, described the battle of Isandlwana for what it is: a magnificent Zulu victory against an invading army with superior arms. On the basis of meticulous research, they have demonstrated that the British generals and their intelligence departments were simply no match for the commanders of the Zulu army and its people-driven intelligence of that day.

Undoubtedly, some may find the dispelling of long-held myths uncomfortable and even unpalatable, but that should not unduly concern those of us who believe that it is high time that the writing of African history sheds the legacy of colonial romanticism. While it might be a truism that the truth is the first casualty of war, history itself should not be debased by sacrificing the truth.

It is equally important that those who provided weak leadership, albeit for a questionable colonial cause, should be hauled from behind their scapegoats and be exposed to the critical light of history. The book shows how even though Anthony Durnford cannot be described as a friend of the Zulu people, he was a true gentleman and did not deserve to be used as a scapegoat for Lord Chelmsford. His exculpation in this book is a fitting vindication for those greatest of friends of the Zulu people, the Colenso family, who fought a long and debilitating battle to restore Durnford's honour against a manipulative military establishment.

Isandlwana was indeed a victory for Zulu generals. But the war of which it formed part was a miserable affair, not only for my people, but for the many individuals who paid with their lives for the folly of allowing themselves to be misled by Lord Chelmsford and others into joining the war, with dubious offers of farms in the Zulu Kingdom.

Destruction on a grand scale followed the events of 1879 and the dignity of our Kingdom has not yet been fully restored in the new South Africa we are building. It is my hope and prayer that this will happen in a spirit which the Zulu people have nurtured from their founding roots and which persists to this day – that of universality. This book may be another stepping stone in that process and, with this fond hope, I wish to thank Ron Lock and Peter Quantrill for a job excellently done.

Prince Mangosuthu Buthelezi, MP
Traditional Prime Minister to the Zulu Nation,
Minister for Home Affairs of the Republic of South Africa.

Prologue

Zululand, mid-afternoon, 22 January 1879

———

Lieutenant-General Lord Chelmsford, the General Officer Commanding Her Majesty's forces in southern Africa, sat astride his horse, straining his gaze to the north-west whilst struggling to conceal the dread that had suddenly come upon him, an awful apprehension that the camp, containing all the equipment and transport for his entire column of 5,000 men, was now in the hands of the enemy. Hamilton-Browne, close at hand, a colonial and thus in Chelmsford's estimation less reliable than an imperial officer, had been almost belligerent a few minutes earlier when he had imparted the shattering news. He claimed that he and his contingent of native levies had stood by, helpless in their inadequacy, and had witnessed the fall of the camp as long as two hours before. Chelmsford had been sharp with the man for his outrageous tale, which could only be an exaggeration spawned of panic and rumour!

It was the culmination of a number of messages that had irritated the ordered schedule of Chelmsford's day – a day that had been full of frustration. As early as 9.30 that morning a note, written one and a half hours before, had arrived by messenger riding a sweat-streaked horse, stating that 'the Zulus' were advancing in force on the camp. It was a brief note – too brief. How many Zulus were there? Lieutenant-Colonel Henry Pulleine, who had written the message, had taken command of the 1st Battalion, 24th Regiment, only a few days earlier, and was more of an administrative officer than a fighting soldier; he had yet to hear a shot fired in anger. Other than sending two of his aides to a nearby hilltop from where the men would have a good view of the camp (where they saw nothing amiss), Chelmsford had ignored the report. At the time he had been trying to get to grips with an elusive enemy; there seemed to be Zulus everywhere but none closer than half a mile or so. Chelmsford's worst fear seemed to be proving well founded, a fear that the Zulu, like the tribes of the Eastern Cape whom he had recently fought to submission, would not 'come on' – that is, fling themselves against the shattering volley fire of his infantry, and thus terminate hostilities in a quick and conclusive conquest for Britain.

Only a few weeks earlier Chelmsford had written to a colonial official, 'I shall strive to be in a position to show the Zulus how hopelessly inferior they are to us in fighting power', and now, only eleven days into his campaign against the Zulu, he was being asked to believe that a native army not only had the gall to take the initiative, but had achieved the unthinkable by conquering half a British column.

As Chelmsford peered at the camp, three and a half miles away, he could see moving figures amongst a cloud of smoke, and some of the tents still standing. Many miles further on, almost lost in the haze and jumble of the distant Biggarsberg Mountains, he could just discern the outline of the Oskarberg at Rorke's Drift, across the Buffalo River on the Natal side of the border. He dare not think what might be happening there if this nightmare were indeed reality.

Moments passed in silence, neither Chelmsford's staff nor escort wishing to make comment. Then, not far distant, a lone figure came into view, a tired, slouching figure, leading an equally tired pony, frequently glancing behind, clearly apprehensive of pursuit.

Chelmsford rode forward to meet the man, familiar to them all, another colonial but previously an imperial officer, Commandant Rupert Lonsdale, who had ridden to Isandlwana earlier in the day to organise rations. However, as Lonsdale spoke, whatever fragments of optimism there may have remained were brutally dispelled. Lonsdale had, by a miracle, survived his visit to the camp. There was nothing left there but chaos, death and destruction. In the stunned silence that followed Lonsdale's brief testimony, Chelmsford finally spoke, perhaps more to himself than anyone else; in a whisper of disbelief he said, 'But I left over 1,000 men to guard the camp!'

Isandlwana! How could it have happened? Over 120 years later, and after hundreds of thousands of written words on the subject, we are still unsure. We hope that this book will not only provide some of the answers, but will justly apportion blame for the defeat as, hardly had the blood dried on the battlefield, than those who were responsible were plotting to cover up their own inadequacies and blunders, and to shift the blame elsewhere...

PART ONE

The Conflict

'The Zulus have been very kind to us... They must be thoroughly crushed to make them believe in our superiority.'

Lord Chelmsford to Sir Theophilus Shepstone, July 1878

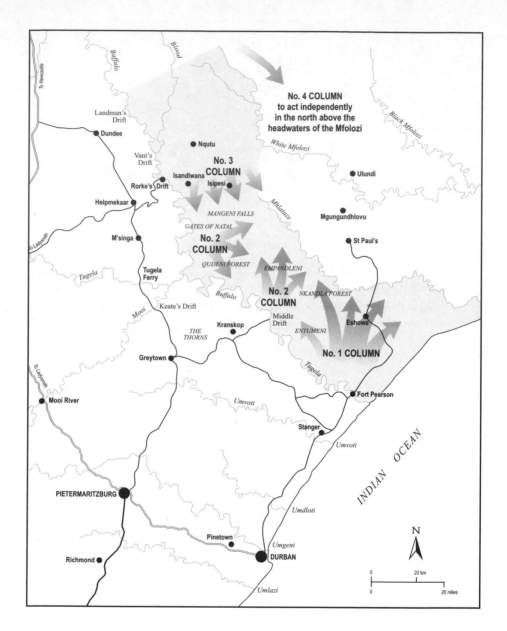

Map No. 1

Lord Chelmsford originally intended to invade Zululand with five separate columns. However, he soon reduced the number to three: No. 5 Column was completely disbanded and No. 2 Column disbanded after the Battle of Isandlwana. The above map reflects Chelmsford's intention, of mid-January 1879, to clear an enemy-free buffer zone (indicated by the shaded area on the map) on the Zululand side of the Tugela and Buffalo Rivers. This was prior to the disbandment of No. 2 Column.

Chapter 1

The Ultimatum

Natal bank of the Tugela River, 11 December 1878

'My reports from Natal breathe nothing but peace...'

Lord Chelmsford to Sir Bartle Frere, July 1878

>=•=<

It was an extremely hot afternoon, a little more than a week away from mid-summer's day. A white canvas sailcloth had been rigged in the branches of a wild fig tree, close to the riverbank, providing a wide area of welcome shade for the assembled dignitaries.

On the instructions of the British High Commissioner in southern Africa, Sir Bartle Frere, officials of the Natal government had requested the Zulu King, Cetshwayo kaMpande, and his councillors to attend an *indaba* (an important meeting or conference) at which the findings of a long awaited land claim, involving 1,800 square miles of territory, would be disclosed – hopefully, as far as the Zulu were concerned, in their favour. In fact it had been, more or less. Yet, unbeknown to the Zulu, the British had a far more sinister reason for calling the *indaba*. The real purpose, ominous and threatening, was yet to be revealed.

Before noon, the land dispute, in which Britain had acted as arbitrator between the Transvaal Boers and the Zulu – who both claimed sovereignty over the property in question – had been settled and the Zulu, not exactly pleased with the outcome, but nevertheless satisfied, had enjoyed a midday repast of beer and beef. Now, somewhat drowsy in the warm and humid cloak of the afternoon, the delegation hoped that whatever the white man had planned for further discussion would not take long and that they could shortly return across the river, bearing good tidings to their king.

King Cetshwayo had not attended the *indaba* in person, likewise, on the British side, neither had Sir Bartle Frere. Relations between the Colony of Natal and the Zulu kingdom had been somewhat tense for several months – more so than at any other time during the last forty years.

The British had taken possession of the territory in 1842 and had proclaimed the Colony of Natal in 1856. This had been in the time of Cetshwayo's father, King Mpande kaSenzangakhona Zulu, once described as a peaceful but crafty monarch – indeed he would have needed to be crafty to retain peace in such potentially lawless territory. In those days Mpande had three sets of neighbours: the British to the south, their colony separated from his kingdom by the Tugela (Thukela) River; the Boers to the west, along a border partly defined by the Pongola (Phongola) River and partly by vague treaties; and, somewhere amongst the mountainous terrain to the north, the border again ill-defined and contested from time to time by fierce warrior neighbours, the Swazi Kingdom. Only the surf-pounded shore of the Indian Ocean provided a permanently tranquil border.

Although Mpande, keeper of the peace, did not die until 1872, his impending death had long since triggered a war of succession amongst his many sons born of different mothers. The heir apparent was Cetshwayo but he was not his father's favourite; Mbuyazi, a younger son, would have been Mpande's choice. Prompted by the royal mothers of possible successors to the throne, the kingdom erupted in a tragic civil war contested by two factions: Cetshwayo's *uSuthu* and Mbuyazi's *iZigqoza*.

On 2 December 1856 the two contestants finally met in battle at a hill called nDondakusuka, situated only a few miles upstream from the location of the *indaba* site. Mbuyazi's clan, including all its women and children were pursued by Cetshwayo's numerically superior, and unhampered warriors, numbering some 15,000, against Mbuyazi's 7,000 fighting men. There was even a scattering of white men on both sides, notably an English settler named John Dunn, who had crossed the river from Natal bringing with him, without the consent of the Natal authorities, a number of the colony's Border Police. Dunn unwisely took the side of Mbuyazi, he and his musketeers for a time wreaking destruction amongst the advancing *uSuthu*. Led by Cetshwayo, then about 30 years of age and looking fearsomely magnificent in his crane-feathered head-dress and kilt of silver jackal skins, the *uSuthu* finally turned the retreat of the *iZigqoza* into a rout. The fleeing thousands of women and children were overtaken by their own *iZigqoza* warriors and together the whole panicking mass of humanity, John Dunn amongst it, was pushed to the banks of the Tugela River which was pumping along in full flood. There was no mercy and, as Dunn who survived, later wrote, 'the uSuthu moved with great earnestness, in their work of slaughter.' Only those who successfully hid amongst the reeds, faked death or swam the river lived on. The number who perished will never be known – perhaps 10,000 would not be an exaggeration. And amongst them was Mbuyazi.

Three years after the battle of nDondakusuka, Cetshwayo was still deeply uncertain of his succession despite the death of Mbuyazi. Mpande, though close to senility and of so great a bulk that he had to be conveyed about in a wheelchair made by a missionary, was still king. Yet he had sired three sons by his latest and much beloved young wife – with whom he became quite besotted as only old men can – and it was the eldest of these sons, Mthonga, that Mpande would now have as future king.

Cetshwayo, aware of his father's doting affection for Mthonga and his brothers, commissioned a loyal *induna* to murder them. What was required was a clandestine doing-away-with, carefully planned and discreetly executed. However, Cetshwayo's *induna*, on discovering the mother and boys absent from their village, threw discretion to the winds and, with a company of warriors at his back, flagrantly broke Zulu custom by surrounding the ageing king himself and demanding that the family be surrendered. The youngest boy was with Mpande and the *induna*, losing all self-control, had the weeping child wrenched from Mpande's arms and put to death. The young mother was then tracked down and also murdered, but Mthonga and his brother escaped and found temporary refuge amongst the Boers across the border. Twenty years later in the war of 1879, Mthonga, still an exile, would join the British invasion columns.◊

Thus Cetshwayo established his succession before his father died, being finally acknowledged as successor by Mpande in 1861, but his ruthless acquisition of power was regarded with alarm by his colonial neighbours. Nevertheless, when the time finally came in September 1873 to 'crown' Cetshwayo before the Zulu nation, official British approval of the new monarch was expressed by sending Theophilus Shepstone, ('on behalf of Queen Victoria' as he put it), the Secretary for Native Affairs, to perform a European-style coronation. And to impress the Zulu nation, Shepstone was escorted by about 120 mounted soldiers, drawn from an assortment of local colonial regiments, including a contingent from the Durban Volunteer Artillery with two cannons which, at the appropriate moment, fired a seventeen-gun salute.

It was a ceremony far from Cetshwayo's liking or desire, but for him it was a necessary one, as just below the seemingly tranquil surface of the Zulu nation there still ran a current of civil war. Mbuyazi was dead but there remained the other royal half brothers, with influential backers, awaiting an opportunity to contest the throne. Thus, the placing of his crown by British hands sent a potent message to would-be rivals: their powerful white neighbours were on his side. It also afforded the Natal government an opportunity to impress the Zulu people with its own importance and the hold it had upon their king and, consequently, upon the whole nation.

Having become king, Cetshwayo set about revitalising the Zulu army, which again raised waves of apprehension in the colony but, by and large, there were no significant signs of Zulu aggression against the whites. True, Cetshwayo had committed many killings amongst his own people, only recently executing several previous servants of his father in order that they might accompany the royal body to the grave and, in Zulu belief, wait upon the dead king in the realms of the ancestors. There were other recent killings, mostly servants of the royal household who, having committed trivial offences – or having been accused of witchcraft – had been given over to the 'bewhiskered men', or the *iziMpisi* ('hyena men') as the executioners were nicknamed, taken to the rock of execution and clubbed or strangled to death. To make his own position as king more secure Cetshwayo killed Masiphula kaMamba who had not only been his father's chief councillor but had formerly supported Mbuyazi and of late had tried to promote the cause of another of Cetshwayo's half brothers. However, Masiphula was too powerful a man to be done away with publicly, so he was poisoned. The lethal draught, so it was said, was supplied to Cetshwayo by none other than John Dunn, who, having made amends with the king, had become an almost indispensable advisor and favourite. Cetshwayo had made Dunn a chief in his own right, providing him with a large tract of land, close to the Natal border where, having taken some 40 Zulu wives, he eventually fathered a tribe of his own. His many descendants still populate the area today.

At his royal homestead at Ondini, which had a circumference of over one and a quarter miles, and where he had built a European-style home with doors and windows, Cetshwayo continued to order the killings of his subjects, as was his prerogative by Zulu custom. Although these killings were abhorred by the many white missionaries living in Zululand, they were of little concern to the average white settler across the Tugela; the hunters and traders continued their journeys in and out of the kingdom where they were welcomed by every level of Zulu society. In truth the Natal settlers were in greater fear of the Zulu population within their own borders than of Cetshwayo's warriors. Due to defectors, deserters and refugees who had fled the Zulu kingdom during the reigns of previous and more fearsome monarchs, and during such times as the civil war between Cetshwayo and Mbuyazi, the number of 'colonial Zulus' (for want of a better description) living in Natal under the protection of the colonial government had grown. These amounted to some 6,000 at the time of the British occupation in 1842. By 1867 they numbered about 170,000 and by 1878 the figure would have been over 250,000, outnumbering the whites by eight to one.

There had been the greatest alarm only a few years earlier in 1873, when a local Natal chief, Langalibalele kaMthimkhulu, of the amaHlubi tribe, refused to register the firearms that his young warriors had received as wages for their labour on the Kimberley diamond fields. Rather than comply, fearing he would never see his arsenal again, Langalibalele attempted to take his people and cattle out of Natal, over the Drakensberg Mountains and into what was then called Basutoland. A force of volunteers was sent in pursuit. Finally, high up in the mountains at Bushman's Pass, a small contingent of the Pietermaritzburg and the Karkloof Carbineers, led by Major Anthony Durnford, RE, an imperial officer, confronted an overwhelming number of warriors. Three of the young carbineers were killed, Durnford was badly wounded and his force ignominiously defeated. The result was the declaration of martial law by the Natal government and near panic in the colony, followed by a ruthless pursuit of Langalibalele and the harshest chastisement for his tribe, many of whom, including women and children, were killed in the months that followed. Langalibalele himself was eventually captured, and after a trial devoid of justice, was sentenced to exile and imprisonment in the Cape. He became one of the first inmates of Robben Island, a prison that Nelson Mandela's incarceration would make famous a century or so later. The greatest fear amongst the settler population was that tens of thousands of colonial Zulu residents would rise up in support of Langalibalele, followed by 30,000 warriors pouring in from Zululand intent on the rich plunder to be had, and the prospect of retaking the land lost to their kingdom forty years earlier.

It never happened. But the shadow of its possibility remained.

⸺⸻⸺

In most things Cetshwayo appeared to value the friendship of his British neighbours. He also believed that the British were his champions in the land dispute that festered on between the Zulu kingdom and the Boers of the Transvaal Republic. That seems to have been the case until 1877 when Britain, pursuing an ambitious imperial vision of the confederation of all the territories in southern Africa, annexed the Transvaal Republic which formed much of the northern border of Zululand. Shepstone, who led the coup, had been knighted and appointed Administrator of the Transvaal. Thus, in one stroke, the interests of the Transvaal Boers, since they were now British subjects, became more important than those of Cetshwayo and the Zulu. Shepstone, who had always been a paternal, if patronising, figure to the Zulu, now loomed as a potential enemy.

Yet, despite the new circumstances prevailing, the three British arbitrators in the land dispute were forthright and incorruptible, as were many British officials throughout the Empire, and had found in favour of the Zulu – much to the displeasure of Sir Bartle Frere, the champion of confederation. In the event, Sir Bartle suppressed the findings of the commission, keeping them secret whilst he plotted the invasion of Zululand. (On 28 January 1879, six days after the Battle of Isandlwana, Sir Bartle reneged on the land award. He informed Chelmsford that, 'the boundary award is torn up'.)

Nevertheless, there would have to be some justification for an invasion as there was no authority from the British government for such action. Reasons would have to be contrived. There were, of course, Cetshwayo's executions, but these were comparatively few, and, despite the killings, Cetshwayo was regarded by many of his subjects as a just, if rather stingy king – and furthermore, despite his power, Cetshwayo was not an absolute monarch by any means, his councillors having an immense influence in the affairs of the nation.

However, there was, in addition, the question of the treatment of the missionaries. Cetshwayo had decided that their activities undermined his authority and by April 1878 had expelled them all from Zululand. The missionaries now demanded reinstatement and freedom from harassment. They might well have also requested Cetshwayo's removal as king, for there was no doubt he had made their chosen work extremely difficult to perform – converts to Christianity were few and far between, it being most perilous for any Zulu to accept that there might be a greater king than Cetshwayo. Also, with the decision of the land dispute remaining undisclosed, some Zulu residents in the disputed area, far distant from any restraining authority that Cetshwayo might have imposed, now proceeded to harass the white settlers, most of whom were Boers, forcing them to flee their homes and farms. Yet, these were insufficient reasons to invade.

Thus, Sir Bartle Frere, in the middle months of 1878, looked around for more compelling causes and found one on the Zululand border at a place called Rorke's Drift. In July of that year, two adulterous wives of Sihayo, a powerful Zulu chief and favourite of Cetshwayo, departed Zululand with their lovers, one wife already pregnant, and established themselves just across the Buffalo River on the Natal side. Adultery was a capital offence in Zululand and Sihayo's sons, incensed by the affront to their family in general and their cuckolded father in particular, decided to seek retribution.

In July the eldest son, Mehlokazulu kaSihayo, accompanied by two younger brothers and a large force of warriors, all armed with spears and shields, crossed the Buffalo River into Natal. Close by Rorke's Drift were the barrack huts of a small contingent of Natal Native Border Police, commanded by Field Cornet Robson, and it was here the adulterous wives were living, one at least having now taken a Native Border Police lover. Mehlokazulu and his many warriors found the women at home and, forcing down any resistance, took them back across the river and put them to death. The Border Police, greatly outnumbered, came close to opposing the abduction. Had they done so their action would have undoubtedly led to a great deal of bloodshed and even more serious consequences. Even so, having the Zulu king executing his subjects was one thing, but having hot-headed young warriors kidnapping and murdering on colonial territory was not to be tolerated. The perpetrators would have to be handed over to the Natal courts of law and put on trial.

Early in August the Governor of Natal, Sir Henry Bulwer, sent two separate messengers to Cetshwayo demanding the surrender of Mehlokazulu and other ring-leaders, but Cetshwayo replied that the incident was the result of boyish excess and offered a sum of money, or cattle, as restitution for the violation, which was refused. And there the matter rested unresolved.

In September there was another incident that outraged Sir Bartle even more. A few years previously, a wagon route had been constructed from a point close by the abandoned Fort Buckingham, about twenty miles out of Greytown on the main road leading to Stanger and the Tugela Drift. This new route plunged from the heights of Kranskop in a series of perilous hairpin bends, through awesome scenery, to the Tugela River 3,000 feet below and, finally, to a crossing which became known as Middle Drift. The effort expended in its construction provided little in the way of economic benefit, but as its nickname, 'Sir Garnet's Road' (after Major-General Sir Garnet Wolseley) suggested, it was of military significance, giving the colony a further point of entry into Zululand. Sir Garnet had arranged its construction during his governorship of Natal in 1875, believing that war between the colony and Zululand was inevitable. With the collaboration of

Bishop Schreuder of the Norwegian Mission, whom Wolseley considered to be half Zulu in outlook, and who was an opponent of Cetshwayo's reign, the route was explored and a road built at a cost of £300 that Sir Garnet paid from the Native Reserve Fund – a rather unlikely source of finance for a military road.

Now, with Sir Bartle intent on war, the road was of some importance and in September two civilian officials, Messrs. Smith and Deighton, of the Colony Engineer's Department, were sent to inspect its condition. Whether ordered to or not, having got down to the drift, they crossed over to evaluate the lie of the land on the Zulu side. There they were apprehended by a group of patrolling warriors who were astute enough to suspect the purpose of their crossing into Zululand. The white men were subjected to the indignity of being manhandled – some reports say they were even stripped naked. However, they were not harmed and after a few hours were released. Such was not to be tolerated and Sir Bartle set about hammering home what, he believed, would be the last nail in King Cetshwayo's coffin.

Nevertheless, the commencement of hostilities would require careful timing. Much had to be taken into account: sufficient troops for the job; transport and supplies; weather conditions and the state of the roads; many arrangements had to be made whilst retaining at least an element of surprise. The number of imperial (rather than local) troops available was as great as it was ever likely to be. The Ninth Frontier War in the Eastern Cape had just been fought to a satisfactory conclusion and the conquering regiments of British infantry were continuing their march north into Natal. With no prospect of orders from London to open hostilities with Zululand, it was likely that a good portion of the army would soon be whisked off to other trouble spots around the Empire, and thus the opportunity to annex Zululand would be lost.

The month of January would be a good time for invasion. Although heavy rain could be expected at that time of the year, there would be sufficient grazing for the thousands of oxen required to haul the transport. Furthermore the Zulu nation as a whole, including the men who made up its army, would all be pre-occupied with the gathering of the harvest and the performance of the First Fruits ceremony (*umkhosi*). This was the most important event of the Zulu year, when all the regiments, male and female, young and old, would assemble at the royal homestead: a time for the revitalising of the nation. The days preceding the actual ceremony would be filled with the rehearsal of ancient dances and songs, the brewing of vast quantities of sorghum beer and the production of regalia. On the appropriate day, festivities would begin in the late afternoon, when the assembled regiments, comprising thousands of warriors and young women attired in ceremonial war dress or traditional finery, would commence their rhythmic dancing, swaying in unison in front of the royal residence, and in song imploring the appearance of the king:

'You mighty elephant,
Give us war'

would be a prominent refrain among their songs. As darkness fell, great fires would be lit and the dancing and tumultuous singing would continue.

Throughout the night lights would burn in the hut containing the sacred *iNkatha*, an heirloom which had been handed down in the Zulu royal family since the reign of Shaka sixty years before. It was comprised of many things: the body dirt of Cetshwayo and that of his ancestors, straw from the floor of the royal house, teeth and hair, the whole being sown into a python skin and shaped into a coil. It reputedly held a mystic strength that protected and unified the Zulu nation.

Not until sunrise would the king appear, clad from the neck downwards in a cloak of green fibre, his face ghoulishly painted: the right cheek white, the left black and the forehead red. In his right hand he would carry a sacred tribal spear with a crescent shaped blade. He would be received with thunderous adulation and the earth would shake as the warriors thudded the ground acknowledging the king with stamping feet.

Then the test of bravery would be performed. The biggest and fiercest bull amongst the herds would be released and those brave enough would fall upon it to kill with their bare hands. It was a game of deadly teamwork and before the beast's neck was broken, dead and wounded bodies of gored warriors would litter the arena. Finally dead, the bull's carcass would be burnt and its ashes added to the magical contents of the sacred *iNkatha*, thus revitalising the nation.◊

The First Fruits ceremony having been concluded, a new year would be proclaimed and the King would give his permission for the newly harvested grain to be eaten. It was an important event and, as Sir Bartle anticipated, the core of the Zulu army would be participating in it at far off Ondini, leaving the Natal border virtually unguarded.

There was nothing new about the idea of war with the Zulu kingdom. Sir Theophilus Shepstone had been musing on the prospect for years; Sir Garnet Wolseley, during his time as Governor of Natal, thought it inevitable and described it as, 'the best solution to all our native difficulties here'. He had urged such a course on Lord Carnarvon, the Secretary of State for the Colonies, but finding Carnarvon unenthusiastic, Wolseley confided to his diary, 'our ministers are such cowards that they are afraid of the word annexation.'

Whether war was, in fact, inevitable is difficult to say. Whether a white South African civilisation, fast becoming a copy, albeit a backward one, of its industrialised parent, Britain, could proceed side by side with its warlike neighbour as equals into the twentieth century, was most unlikely. And to achieve the submission of the proud Zulu people by diplomatic means was even more unlikely.

However, Sir Bartle, led on by Sir Theophilus, had convinced himself that his quarrel was not with the Zulu people but with their monarch alone; and Sir Bartle began to believe that once war commenced, many of the Zulu clans would, with alacrity, defect to the invaders. At one stage of his governorship Sir Garnet Wolseley almost convinced himself that with 1,000 redcoats behind him, he could stride into Zululand, announce the dethronement of Cetshwayo, and start shaking hands with grateful and surrendering chiefs. Some months later, when about to board ship in Cape Town on his departure from southern Africa, Sir Garnet confided to some officers of the 1/24th Regiment that, with the slightest encouragement from the British government, he would have attacked Zululand.

Unfortunately for Sir Bartle, Wolseley's assessment of the likely course of events, once the ultimatum had been delivered to Cetshwayo, was unrealistic. The number of troops required to subdue Zululand would be many more than just 1,000 redcoats.

Lieutenant-General Lord Chelmsford, commander of Her Majesty's forces in southern Africa, who enjoyed the confidence of Sir Bartle, began active preparations for invasion almost six months before the ultimatum was delivered. In July 1878, whilst still in Cape Town, he wrote to Sir Theophilus Shepstone:

> 'The Zulus have been very kind to us in abstaining from any hostile movements during the time we were so bitterly engaged [with the Ninth Frontier War] in this colony. If they will only wait until next month, I hope to have the troops somewhat better prepared than they are at present... if we are to have a fight with the Zulus, I am anxious that our arrangements should be as complete as it is possible to make them – half measures do not answer with natives – they must be thoroughly crushed to make them believe in our superiority.'

During the same month he wrote to the Duke of Cambridge, Commander-in-Chief of the British Army, advising him of the successful conclusion of the recent campaign, and went on to remark that it is, 'more than probable that active steps will have to be taken to check the arrogance of Ketywayo [Cetshwayo], chief of the Zulus.' (This was prior to the Sihayo raid across the Buffalo and the harassment of the colonial surveyors at Middle Drift). Yet, only a few days earlier, he had confided his disappointment in the tranquillity prevailing along the Zulu border, writing to Sir Bartle:

> 'My reports from Natal breathe nothing but peace, and I cannot discover that they [presumably the colonial authorities] have as yet organised, even on paper, any native contingent [to fight the Zulu].'

It seems, then, that as far as the Natal colonists themselves were concerned, they, like their Zulu neighbours, were unaware of any need for war – and such was the opinion of the Governor of Natal, Sir Henry Bulwer. Nevertheless, Chelmsford, pushing his concern that Natal was virtually defenceless against a sudden Zulu attack (and here it must be admitted there was a cause for concern, the total strength of the part-time volunteer units throughout the colony totalling only 755 men), began to assemble an army and to request further reinforcements from more peaceful outposts of the Empire, such as Mauritius and Malta. Still vastly short of men, especially horsemen, who would be needed for such an ambitious campaign, he planned to put the settler volunteer cavalry units on to a full-time basis and to conscript 'colonial Zulus' in vast numbers, forming them into battalions, each of approximately 1,000 men, which were to be named the Natal Native Contingent (NNC).

In all this he was strongly opposed by Bulwer, whose consent would be required before any 'colonial' natives could be conscripted. But, if Bulwer could see no reason for war with the Zulu kingdom, and was therefore uncooperative, Chelmsford was well aware that Frere would back him up, and Frere, as High Commissioner in southern Africa, was one step above Bulwer on the bureaucratic ladder.

By late August Chelmsford had drawn the outline of his invasion plan under the heading: 'Invasion of Zululand; or Defence of Natal and Transvaal Colony from Invasion by the Zulus' His plan provided for: a five pronged invasion route (later to be described in detail); immediate steps to ascertain military resources; each of the five invasion columns to be of sufficient strength to take care of itself; commissariat, transport and medical requirements to be prepared in anticipation of hostilities; an immediate increase in the number of Natal settler (volunteer) mounted regiments; every available native (in Natal) to be enrolled in the NNC 'so as to avoid any possibility of anxiety within the Colony as regards the loyalty of the native population'; the recruitment of white officers and NCOs to staff the NNC. Chelmsford also offered the proposal, which would be well received by the white population, that:

> 'If all the young blood amongst the Natal Zulus is separated into three
> distinct Corps, and mixed up with the European parties of our army, any
> danger of their rising against us, which by some is considered not only
> possible but probable, would be at once removed.'

By the end of the month Chelmsford, now in Pietermaritzburg, was writing to Frere requesting his presence in the colony:

> 'The result of our conversations [those between himself and Bulwer] has
> been to impress me more fully than ever that your Excellency's presence
> in Natal is absolutely essential in the interests of South Africa.'

Two days later Chelmsford wrote again, 'Sir Henry has high notions of subordination and will, I feel sure, be only too glad to recognise your Excellency as his chief in your capacity as High Commissioner.'

Chelmsford, with Frere's support, finally had his way. However, the terms of recruitment governing the white colonial volunteer units specified that their duties only required them to defend the colony, not to cross its border into Zululand and, if they were to do so, each man's consent would be required.

To make the prospect of war more attractive to the colonists, Chelmsford made rash promises of free land for farms as an added incentive. Who gave him authority to do so, and where such land would be acquired, remains unclear, yet the inference was that land in Zululand would be parcelled out to the volunteers once the kingdom had been conquered. Carl Müller, an officer of the Stutterheim Mounted Police in the Eastern Cape, had met Chelmsford during the Ninth Frontier War, and in the latter part of 1878, was requested by him to recruit a mounted unit for service in Natal. Müller recorded that he was instructed to:

'"recruit young men who were strong and who could ride and shoot well."
They were promised five shillings a day and uniforms. If they were successful in quelling the rebellion [*sic*] they would also receive a farm of 3,000 morgan [approximately 6,350 acres]. I was to recruit 100 men immediately and they were to be equipped in Natal.'

Alfred Knox, a trooper in the Durban Mounted Rifles and part time news correspondent for the *Natal Colonist*, a Durban daily newspaper, recalled how, in December 1878, his unit had been paraded one Sunday morning at Potspruit, and how Lord Chelmsford had addressed the men, promising each volunteer who crossed the border a farm in Zululand. And Wally Stafford, who was destined to be one of the few survivors of Isandlwana, when he was reminiscing, many years later, on his terms of recruitment as an officer of the NNC, recalled that he was offered fifteen shillings per day, and after the war, a farm in Zululand. Later in his reminiscences, he ended his story, remarking wistfully:

'In conclusion I would like to add that the gift of farms to those who took part in the Zulu War never materialised.'

———⟶•◦•⟵———

During the early part of 1878, Lieutenant-Colonel Durnford, who it will be recalled had fought in the unsuccessful skirmish with Langalibalele's warriors in 1873, had sat as one of the three arbitrators in the land dispute between the Zulu and the Transvaal Boers. Notwithstanding his martial spirit, which was far from lacking, he had an empathy with the black people of southern Africa and had, at times, despite the disapproval of his superiors and the scorn of the colonists, been outspoken against what he saw as injustices inflicted on them by the colonial authorities and settlers. It was probably due to his presence that the outcome of the arbitration had been in favour of the Zulu – despite Durnford being well aware that such an outcome would find disfavour with Sir Bartle and possibly jeopardise his own career.

It is rather ironic then that Durnford, having only concluded his work as arbitrator in June, would immediately, at Lord Chelmsford's request, enthusiastically set about drawing up a memorandum containing proposals for the conscription of the thousands of 'colonial' Zulus to be used in the invasion of the Zulu kingdom. Durnford was, in fact, the architect of the formation of the NNC and the Natal Native Horse (NNH).

Chelmsford approved Durnford's memorandum. However, the white male population of Natal was insufficient in number to supply the men for the mounted units and, in addition, those required to serve as NCOs and officers in the NNC. They would have to be found further afield and, conveniently, not far away there was a plentiful supply of men who had commanded native levies during the recent Ninth Frontier War. Rupert Lonsdale, who had successfully led the M'fengu Levy, was commissioned by Chelmsford to put out the word to old comrades that lucrative employment was available up north. Lonsdale arrived in Natal on 23 November with 180 white followers who would soon be enlisted as either officers or NCOs of the NNC. Ultimately, before British forces crossed into Zululand, the native troops would amount to approximately 5,500 NNC, 250 NNH and 1,400 auxiliaries led by almost 600 white officers and NCOs.

In September, heeding Chelmsford's plea for his presence, Sir Bartle sailed up from the Cape and, on arrival in Pietermaritzburg, settled himself and his staff into quarters at Government House. It was an occurrence worthy of the 'Grand Ball' that the settlers organised shortly thereafter at the exorbitant price of fifty shillings (£2.50) a ticket – half a month's pay for a colonial horseman and almost two months' pay for a British soldier.

Things were coming together nicely and throughout the military there was an air of expectation and excitement. The majority of the 1/24th Regiment was on its way up from King Williams Town in the Cape, the men having marched to the local railway station, en route to Port Elizabeth, with the regimental band playing, and with the men lustily singing the chorus of a popular music hall song:

> 'We don't want to fight,
> But by jingo if we do,
> We've got the ships, we've got the men,
> And we've got the money too.'

They were full of bounce and pride as they climbed aboard the train; not knowing that within weeks most of them would be disembowelled corpses lying on the bloodstained battlefield of Isandlwana.

Other troops, who would be luckier than the men of the 1/24th, would soon be on the move. The 3rd Foot (The Buffs), with a contingent of sailors and marines, would be marching to the newly constructed fort on the Tugela River (Fort Pearson). The local volunteer cavalry units of the Stanger

Mounted Rifles and Natal Hussars would make their way to Thring's Post, thirty miles inland in higher and healthier country for horses; the Victoria Mounted Rifles, the Durban Mounted Rifles and the Alexander Mounted Rifles would ride to Potspruit, a farm adjacent to abandoned Fort Buckingham. The 1/24th Regiment, having arrived in Durban, would make their way to Helpmekaar, a hamlet in the hills above Rorke's Drift, and, from various points of departure, the mounted men of the Natal Carbineers, the Natal Mounted Police, the Buffalo Border Guard, the Newcastle Mounted Rifles and a squadron of mounted infantry, would also rendezvous at Helpmekaar.

The 1/13th, 80th and 90th Foot, with the mounted men of the Frontier Light Horse, having either marched their way up from the Cape, or down from the Transvaal, would be assembling at various points about 150 miles or more inland from the coast, in the area disputed by the Zulu kingdom and the Transvaal. The various battalions of the NNC, still being rushed through their basic training by impatient and often brutish NCOs, were also about to be deployed, whilst Chelmsford, still recruiting heavily for horsemen in the Eastern Cape and the Transvaal, would soon be rewarded with the arrival of scores of adventurers, rovers and ruffians riding under their unit names of Baker's Horse, Raaff's Rangers and the Border Horse. Even better news for Chelmsford was the granting of his request for more imperial infantry. Alarmed by his description of a virtually defenceless Natal, the British government had sanctioned the despatch of the 2/4th and 99th Foot, but with the proviso that these regiments were to be employed in the defence of the colony only. This was a hindrance, but only a slight one, as Chelmsford would deploy them to guard the depots and lines of communications within the colony, leaving his other regiments of infantry, which were unencumbered by such orders, to cross into Zululand.

So, by 11 December 1878, the day of the ultimatum, Frere and Chelmsford were well pleased with their preparations. A month previously Bulwer had informed Cetshwayo, via John Dunn, that the findings of the arbitrators, known as the Boundary Commission, would be disclosed at a place convenient to both the kingdom and the colony, the Natal bank of the Tugela River at Lower Drift. Here there was a ferry service, operated by the colonial border agent, which would be an essential communication if the river happened to be in flood, as indeed it would, the long drought of the last two years having at last been broken.

The Lower Drift was an idyllic spot. When not in flood, the wide river meandered slowly by, revealing here and there flats and islands of golden sand protruding from the shallows. The Natal bank was steep, and hard by the drift, a turret-shaped hill, resembling a Rhineland castle, offered the ideal site for the newly constructed Fort Pearson. Around this hill the coastal road from Durban made its way down to the drift from whence the rolling hills of Zululand could be seen, range after range that grew into a blue haze of distant mountains. Two miles to the east, from the vantage point atop the hill, a surf-pounded coast and a wide expanse of the Indian Ocean could be seen, with a warship riding the swell to impress the Zulu delegation. And close by the drift, the wild fig tree with its canvas awning would provide a pool of shade for the delegates.

The colonial officials arrived two days before the appointed date and set up camp. Their leader, John Wesley Shepstone, had stepped into his brother's shoes as Secretary for Native Affairs (although only in an acting capacity), on Sir Theophilus being appointed Administrator of the Transvaal. John Shepstone was not a good choice for the job at hand. Although he had also served on the Boundary Commission, he had neither the imposing appearance nor the charisma of his brother and, almost as if he wished to compensate for his lacklustre presence, he wore a vast moustache which, even in an era when it was fashionable for men to grow outlandish facial hair, could only be described as bizarre. Furthermore, he had a reputation with the Zulu of being a man not to be trusted.◊

There was also Frederick Fynney, the Natal border agent, who was fluent in the Zulu tongue. It would be his task to translate the findings of the Boundary Commission and the terms of the ultimatum. As long ago as April, he had, at Lord Chelmsford's request, compiled an astonishingly comprehensive description of the Zulu army, which must have been of inestimable value to Chelmsford and his staff. *(See Appendix B: Regiments of the Zulu Army)*

Another delegate of similar calibre was Henry Francis Fynn, the magistrate of M'singa Division, an area along the west bank of the Buffalo River incorporating Rorke's Drift. Fynn's father, also Henry Francis, was not only the first white settler in Natal but had also held the highly esteemed position of advisor, physician and true friend to the mighty King Shaka, and was, consequently, revered by the Zulu people. His son, one of the first white children to grow up amongst the Zulu and who would, no doubt, have been cared for by a Zulu nanny, spoke the Zulu language with utter fluency and had an encyclopaedic knowledge of Zulu custom and law. Like his father, he was revered and completely at ease amongst the Zulu on both sides of the border. We shall hear more of Fynn, who was destined to accompany Lord Chelmsford to Isandlwana.

The military were represented by Colonel Forestier Walker of the Scots Guards, Sir Bartle's military secretary. He was accompanied by a number of sailors from the Naval Brigade in Durban and twenty colonials of the Stanger Mounted Rifles. The mariners and horsemen were ordered to keep a low profile. Finally, from the Cape Colony, acting as Sir Bartle's representative, there was the Honourable Charles Brownlee, that colony's resident Commissioner for Native Affairs. All in all it was not an overly impressive delegation.

The Zulu visitors duly arrived on the 11th and by mid-morning had been ferried across the Tugela. They, too, were of unimpressive appearance, wearing no regalia. Their warrior escort was also unadorned and unarmed; their weapons had been left on the other side of the river. The delegation were not men of the king's inner council, they were officials of lesser stature. Nevertheless, they were described as being amongst the most venerable and trusted elders of the Zulu nation. Amongst them were several chief *indunas* and captains of great regiments: Mabilwana, *induna* of the regimental barracks situated at Gingindlovu, not far away across the river; Mahubulwana, a chief of the abaQulusi clan located in the disputed territory far to the north; Vumandaba kaNtati, commander of the 2,500 strong uMcijo regiment, a crack unit of young warriors, and Gebule, who had previous experience in negotiating with colonial officials. The day following the delivery of the ultimatum, a Natal newspaper wrote of Gebule:

> 'Very remarkable was the keen and ceaseless attention paid by this wiry little Zulu to every word that was uttered.'

The complete Zulu contingent, including escort, numbered fewer than fifty. They were trusted messengers, but with no power to negotiate; their responsibility was to remember, clearly and precisely, and to relay the news to their king. Ironically, the only white man amongst them was by far the most influential person of the Zulu delegation: John Dunn, a great chief in his own right, presiding over a chieftainship as big as an English county, where he held power over a retinue of followers, dozens of wives (several of whom were not only gifts from the king, but his royal sisters) and scores of children. Indeed, Cetshwayo regarded 'Jantoni' (Dunn's Zulu name) as a brother-in-law, and during Dunn's visits to the royal residence, which often lasted for a month or more, the king would listen for hours to Dunn's stories of the white man's world. Now forty-six years old, Dunn had become rich as a middleman between the colony and the kingdom, supplying goods to the Zulu (not least amongst them the firearms which would shortly be used against Chelmsford's army), and, as the colony's representative to the kingdom, receiving the handsome salary of £300 per annum. (Fynney, the border agent, received only £80 per annum). Sir Garnet Wolseley, who had met Dunn in 1875, and who usually had little praise for anyone, thought Dunn 'a very fine looking fellow' with a 'very determined face.' It would be left to Dunn to deliver the bombshell of the ultimatum.

The officials of the colonial delegation seated on chairs, no doubt provided by Fynney, had an advantage in height over their Zulu counterparts who squatted on the ground, whilst a fair crowd, made up of retainers, servants and hangers-on, sat outside the pool of shade provided by the canvas awning. At about 11.00 a.m. the findings of the Boundary Commission, largely in favour of the Zulu, were made known to the satisfaction, and perhaps to the surprise, of the Zulu delegation who were then informed that there was yet further business to be discussed and that the proceedings would resume after lunch.

Mystified, and somewhat alarmed, the Zulu delegates reassembled and at once John Shepstone, with Fynney slowly and with great care interpreting every word, began a long tirade, citing numerous misdemeanours that the colonial government declared the Zulu had committed. Then followed the reading of the ultimatum which demanded, amongst other things, that both Sihayo's sons be surrendered as well as those warriors who had manhandled the surveyors, Smith and Deighton; that all warriors be allowed to marry whenever they so wished (currently they could only do so with the king's permission); that a resident British official be installed at the Zulu capital; that the missionaries and their converts be allowed to return to Zululand without harassment; that in the event of a white man being involved in a dispute, he might not be expelled from Zululand without the consent of the proposed British resident; and, most shattering of all, that the Zulu army be disbanded immediately and only reassembled with the consent of the British government. Furthermore, Cetshwayo had thirty days to comply with all the conditions, failing which the British forces would invade and enforce submission. It was not an ultimatum that had been designed with any thought of possible acceptance; indeed, it had been deliberately designed for rejection.

Stunned with the enormity of the ultimatum, and the about-turn from the friendly events of the morning to the truculent demands of the afternoon, the Zulu delegation, silent and apprehensive, crossed back over the Tugela. They were not only apprehensive of the drums of war that could be clearly heard amongst the words of the ultimatum, but also of the malevolent displeasure that Cetshwayo might discharge on the harbingers of such news. However, Dunn, armed with both English and Zulu transcriptions of the ultimatum, set out for Ondini. In the furore that followed his disclosure of the ultimatum to the king and the great council, Dunn was blamed, as the king's advisor, for not predicting events and, worse still, there were veiled accusations of treachery. Dunn, a survivor of precarious situations, unobtrusively made his way back to his territory close by the Tugela where he gathered together his vast family, hundreds of retainers and 3,000 head of cattle. He then prudently crossed the river into Natal where he enlisted the younger of his retainers into a corps of scouts to fight against his former friend and king. Dunn's people had brought with them weapons of every description including breech-loading rifles of both British and Prussian manufacture.

War was now inevitable and Sir Bartle Frere, having decided to open Pandora's Box, would find inside 40,000 'black devils', disciplined and courageous, of whom a British general was shortly to write:

> 'Nowhere in southern Africa or central Africa, did such a powerfully organised, well disciplined and thoroughly trained force of courageous men exist as lay at the disposal of Ketchwayo.'

In little more than a month from the delivery of the ultimatum, the

British invasion plans, like Sir Bartle's career, would be in tatters, and Lord Chelmsford, with his confidence destroyed, would admit in a memorandum to the Duke of Cambridge:

> 'We have certainly been seriously underrating the power of the Zulu Army... The Zulu have no fear whatever of death... The crisis is a very serious one and I am in daily dread of hearing that some [additional] misfortune has happened.'◊

There would indeed be further misfortune, but none as shattering as that which would occur at Isandlwana.

Chapter 2

Lord Chelmsford's Army

'They [Zulu warriors] though big and strong do not have the martial spirit of an Englishman.'

Private Goatham 1/24th Regiment

———◦◦———

Lord Chelmsford's original intention was to invade Zululand with five separate columns: however, hardly had the invasion got underway when he reduced the number to three by attaching Column No. 2 to No. 3 and disbanding Column No. 5. Thus, the pattern of invasion would be a three pronged attack:

- No. 1 Column, commanded by Colonel Charles Pearson, 3rd Regiment of Foot, to follow the coastal road from Durban across the Tugela and into Zululand at Lower Drift.
- No. 3 Column, commanded by Colonel Richard Glyn, 24th Regiment of Foot, via Pietermaritzburg, to Helpmekaar, eventually crossing the Buffalo River at Rorke's Drift.
- No. 4 Column, commanded by Colonel Evelyn Wood, 90th Light Infantry (LI), via Pietermaritzburg, Utrecht and across the Blood (Ncome) River, thirty-five miles above Rorke's Drift.

The total number of fighting men set to cross into Zululand would be approximately:

Cavalry*	1,040
Royal Artillery	260
Imperial Infantry	5,120
Native levies, including white officers & NCOs	8,700
Approximate Total	15,120

* comprising Imperial Mounted Infantry (IMI), Natal Mounted Police (NMP) and
   numerous units of locally raised volunteer horsemen including the Natal Native
   Horse (NNH)

In addition a small contingent of sailors and marines from HMS *Active* would accompany No. 1 Column. Engineer, transport and hospital units would also support each column. Chelmsford and his staff would accompany No. 3 Column into Zululand, the backbone of the column being the 1st and 2nd Battalions of the 24th Regiment of Foot (also known as the 2nd Warwickshire Regiment).

By late 1878 the 1/24th had been serving in South Africa for over three years, during which time it had marched several thousand miles, had skirmished with the enemy on a number of occasions and, at Centane in the Eastern Cape, had fought a pitched battle when the battalion, using the new breech-loading Martini-Henry rifle for the first time in action, effectively brought to an end the Ninth Frontier War. The battalion received much local praise, with the Colonial Secretary being informed that, 'the 24th are old, steady shots whose every bullet told.'

Prior to its arrival in South Africa the 1/24th had spent eight years in various parts of the Mediterranean; thus by the close of 1878 it had been out of England for over a decade with the men having become hardened soldiers, heavily bearded and tough. One man who had joined the battalion at the age of seventeen wrote home to his siblings in 1878, 'I don't suppose any of you would really know me now as I have grown much stouter and whiskers as well!' whilst another, no doubt to impress his family, wrote:

> 'I have been marching nearly all over Africa and have not known what it is to sleep in a bed for this time. My clothes are worn to rags and I have not a boot to my feet and God knows when I shall get any!'

Lieutenant W.W. Lloyd, an accomplished artist, also of the 1/24th, left testimony to the plight of the regiment's apparel, his drawings recording bearded men dressed in tatters.

Having been recruited before the regimental depot of the 24th was established at Brecon, the men of the 1/24th were far from being predominately Welsh as is usually supposed; they were, in fact, mainly of English and Irish birth. Such was not the case with their comrades of the 2/24th, many of whom were indeed Welshmen, generally younger and less experienced in the trade of soldiering than the 1/24th. They were 'Johnnies come lately' to Africa having only arrived at the Cape in February 1878 when, on disembarking from their troop ship, they were described by one newspaper correspondent as, 'Stout, healthy, well built lads with plenty of beef in their muscles.' They had enlisted under the new short service system, having been required to sign on for only six years whereas the men of the 1/24th were serving out their time of twenty-one years. Strangely, there was little or no fraternising between the two battalions.◊ However, both were excited by the prospect of a campaign against the Zulu, the successful conclusion of which, every soldier seemed firmly to believe, would result in his immediate return to England. This yearning for England was the dominant thought in most letters home despite the knowledge that the civilian population generally regarded 'Tommy Atkins' – a contemporary nickname for the ordinary British soldier – with a degree of contempt –

except, of course, in times of national emergency when he became everyone's hero.

Apart from the lowest of the working class, the British soldier at that time was regarded as little better than a convict, and for any parent of a higher social order, it was a disgrace to have a son enlist – so much so that many a young soldier who had 'followed the drum' for adventure rather than for the usual reasons of hunger and poverty, might well find himself disowned by his family. One educated young private, seven years after enlisting and only months before he was killed at Isandlwana, was still seeking his father's forgiveness when he wrote:

> 'Dear Father, I can't find out the reason that you do not write to me and answer to my letter... you must write a letter to me as I wish to hear from you if it is only your signature on a sheet of paper.'◊

When reading those lines one can still feel the young man's hurt and frustration.

And if the British soldier was regarded as being little better than a convict, he was frequently treated worse than one. In 1879 he was the only person who could, within British law, be sentenced to be flogged, a punishment abolished in the Royal Navy ten years earlier – and, in fact, already abolished in the army in times of peace but, on active service still permitted though seldom used. At least that seems to have been the case prior to Chelmsford's army crossing into Zululand. In 1879, a correspondent of *Truth* magazine wrote, 'I cannot conceive how anyone can support that respectable men will enlist so long as they know they may be flogged after a very perfunctory trial for some breach of discipline.' Yet flogged they were and for such offences as drunkenness, absence from duty, theft, or disobeying an order. Early in 1879 a Natal newspaper sombrely recorded:

> 'On Monday morning the troops in the garrison [Durban] were paraded at 7 a.m. ...to witness the carrying out of sentences of corporal punishment awarded by districts Court Martial [*sic*].'

And a soldier of the 1/24th writing home from Helpmekaar in November 1878 told his family:

> 'I am sorry to state we have had to see a very painful sight – that is corporal punishment to one of our men for gross insubordination... The colonel said... he could certainly make an example of some more and hopes that no such thing will occur in the regiment again.'

Unfortunately it would, and with increasing frequency after the Battle of Isandlwana. There would be over 500 instances of corporal punishment before the campaign closed in July.◊ Hard liquor was the root cause of most breaches of discipline – liquor being the only relief for most soldiers from the harsh life and grinding monotony. And if the soldiers' fate for consuming too much grog was a cruel one, the illegal supplier often justly received similar punishment. One such camp follower who had been warned that the sale of whiskey and gin to the troops was strictly prohibited, but who continued to ply his wares, was caught red-handed in the midst of a transaction. He was brought before Colonel Wood at Kambula camp and sentenced to 'receive twenty four lashes, his hair and whiskers cut close and expelled from the camp.' This sentence was carried out with immediate effect. And Lieutenant-Colonel Baker Russell, writing a few months later, informed a subordinate of the punishment he intended to inflict on a camp-following liquor tout:

> 'If he follows us up with it [liquor] I will make a prisoner of him, tie him
> up to a cartwheel and have him flogged... You may tell him that I do not
> care one damn for the consequences.'

With liquor being difficult to obtain and, in any event, the consequences of being drunk so severe as to make any level headed soldier think twice before imbibing, there was little to break the monotony of his life or give comfort. On campaign there was rarely the chance of female companionship and at any other time the likelihood of finding romance was equally remote. One of the ironies of the campaign against the Zulu was that the British soldier was supposedly fighting to deliver the Zulu warrior from a harsh system, which, amongst other things, would not allow him to marry without his king's consent. However, the Zulu warrior enjoyed a far more benign life, and had far greater prospects of happiness with the opposite sex than a British soldier could ever hope for. Indeed, it was probably the soldiers' rare encounters with women that were partly responsible for the disdain with which the civilian population held the British soldier. With but a pittance to purchase affection, they associated with the lowest of prostitutes which led to approximately thirty per cent of Britain's private soldiers being infected with venereal disease each year. Rough humour and the camaraderie of fellow soldiers – his mates – were the core of the ranker's comfort. Furthermore his regiment, with its ancient traditions, history and the protection it afforded against those elements which had forced him to join up in the first place, gave solace in the absence of family. And, like most families, each regiment had its feuds and rivalries – so much so that one regiment, due to some long forgotten slight or provocation, might be on fighting terms with another, the men of both being eager to brawl with fists, belts and buckles at the first sight of their rivals. A wise administration would keep such regiments far apart.

Even the soldiers' uniform, one of the few attractions the army had to offer, was uncomfortable and anything but suitable for the climate of South Africa. It does not take much to imagine the distress of wearing a suit of thick serge material during the height of a Zululand summer. And it would have been the same uniform that the soldiers would have worn had they been serving in Alaska. The only concession to climate was the white tropical helmet which, on issue, was immediately dyed with tea or some other mixture to make it less of an enemy target. Worse still, in Zululand there would come a time when both officers and men would be required to keep themselves fully dressed at all times for weeks on end – the consequent odour and discomfort can only be imagined.

On campaign his food was generally appalling, made up of boiled meat and hard-tack biscuits that the wise man thoroughly soaked to avoid broken teeth. Fresh bread was a luxury. And for his soldiering he was paid a shilling a day – less deductions. However, if there was fighting to be done, the British soldier could take comfort from the fact that the weapon he had been issued, the Martini-Henry .577/450 Mark II rifle, was probably the best of its kind in the world. It had been specifically designed to halt mass attacks by primitively armed and numerically stronger foes, with bone shattering volleys of 480-grain bullets – a function it performed well. The weapon fired one shot at a time and was loaded by lowering a lever, situated beneath the stock, which action exposed the breech ready for the cartridge to be inserted. As the lever was raised to close the hinged breech-block, the rifle was simultaneously cocked and made ready to fire. Once fired, lowering the lever again ejected the spent cartridge clearing the breech to receive the next round. The Martini-Henry weighed nine pounds unloaded and, with its 22-inch bayonet attached, was a formidable, yet cumbersome weapon which, in length, with bayonet fixed, exceeded the height of the average British soldier. Its recoil when fired was vicious and could break the collarbone of a careless or inexperienced marksman. Although its negative points of weight and recoil must have been cursed at times, Victoria's soldiers regarded it as their friend and best insurance for a safe return to England. Rudyard Kipling would have some homely advice to offer young soldiers regarding their rifles:

> 'When 'arf of your bullets fly wide in the ditch,
> Don't call your Martini a cross-eyed old bitch;
> She's human as you are – you treat her as sich,
> An' she'll fight for the young British soldier.'

She would indeed. Within a few weeks, at Isandlwana and Rorke's Drift, the Martini would be put to the test in a manner far beyond the limits of its perceived capabilities. In fact, prior to those battles, its firepower had created such feelings of superiority and complacency in Chelmsford's army that, paradoxically, these would be partly responsible for the British defeat. Chelmsford himself revealed his over-confidence in the weapon when he wrote to Colonel Evelyn Wood in November 1878:

> 'I am inclined to think that the first experience of the power of the Martini Henrys will be such a surprise to the Zulus that they will not be formidable after the first effort.'

The men of the other imperial units, and the conditions under which they served, were much the same as those of the infantry except that some rode instead of marching. Such was No. 1 Squadron Imperial Mounted Infantry (IMI), which accompanied No. 3 Column. At the time mounted infantry was a new concept in warfare, the very first unit having been raised in the Northern Cape only four years earlier from officers and men of the 1/24th. Since then the IMI had operated under several different titles including Carrington's Horse and the Transvaal Mounted Infantry. Brown corduroys and button-up gaiters had replaced blue infantry trousers, and a bandolier of ammunition was carried slung over the left soldier. Of all the men in Chelmsford's army, none had experienced tougher service and extremes of climate than had the men of the IMI. They had ridden and skirmished over much of southern Africa from Hopetown in the Cape to Sekhukhune's stronghold in the Northern Transvaal, and then back again to Natal, probably covering as many as 2,000 miles in the process. The IMI now numbered 120 and included not only men of the 24th amongst its ranks but also intakes from almost every other regiment serving in South Africa. However, it was not a particularly happy unit, many of the men wishing to return to their parent regiments. The severity of the conditions that they had endured was reflected in their appearance – one officer wrote of them:

> 'A more ragged crew was perhaps never got together, except for professional beggars on a stage'

and an even less sympathetic description was:

> 'Their uniform was a redcoat, more or less tattered, trousers and leggings ditto, with a battered helmet. They looked like a cross between a groom out of place and a soldier after a night in the cells and a big drink.'

N Battery of Number 5 Brigade Royal Artillery had accompanied the 1/24th in much of its marchings in the Eastern Cape and had endured the same conditions of service. The battery consisted of six 7-pounder guns and 130 men of all ranks. Horses drew the guns and limbers whilst other equipment was carried in mule carts, and for an arsenal it had a stock of 600 rounds of ammunition: a mixture of shrapnel shell and canister shot. The latter, rather like an enormous shotgun cartridge, contained scores of lead balls about half an inch in diameter – a deadly missile when fired into the packed ranks of a charging enemy. The battery was also equipped with two rocket-launching troughs, weapons of dubious efficiency and effect. The rocket when fired was intended to scream through the air, the noise of its flight striking terror into the hearts of a primitive foe, then to explode causing death and destruction. However, as the events at Isandlwana would show, this was not to be the case. In fact, as one officer was to remark, the person firing the contraption was in greater peril than those at which it was aimed.

In addition there were various other small detachments of imperial troops: the Royal Engineers (5th Field Company), the Army Service Corps (Commissariat) and Army Hospital Corps.

Apart from the IMI all mounted units were colonial, but their exact numbers are a little uncertain. Most official sources give the total number of cavalry as 320 but, as far as can be ascertained, the number was slightly higher:

Imperial Mounted Infantry	120
Natal Mounted Police	134
Natal Carbineers	60
Newcastle Mounted Rifles	32
Buffalo Border Guard	20
Total	366

Major John Dartnell had raised the Natal Mounted Police (NMP) in 1874 at the request of the Natal government. In peacetime it was the colony's only full time force of a military nature. The troopers were recruited in Britain from young men of good education and on arrival in Natal were given a rigorous cavalry training. Uniformed in black corduroy with a white helmet topped with a brass spike, armed with the breech loading Swinburne-Henry carbine, and astride an equally well trained horse, they manned the many little police outposts around the borders of the colony. In the grand tradition of the numerous para-military police forces scattered around Queen Victoria's Empire, they were expected to solve problems and keep the peace using their own initiative whilst incurring a minimum of expense. Having local knowledge, the NMP formed the vanguard of Chelmsford's column. In terms of their enlistment however, they, like the other colonial cavalry units, were only required to serve within the borders of the colony and before they could be ordered to cross into Zululand, the consent of every trooper had to be obtained. Thus the status of all the colonial mounted units was that of volunteers – an important condition of their service which the men would shortly flaunt in a confrontation with Lord Chelmsford when he attempted to replace their commanding officer with a man of his choice.

The Natal Carbineers had been in existence since 1855. They were 'week-end' soldiers raised mainly from the upper classes of the commercial and farming communities. Every man was required to finance from his own pocket his uniform, horse and equipment, whilst the government supplied carbine and ammunition. It was a Pietermaritzburg-based regiment, and although well disciplined and efficient, one gets the impression from surviving correspondence and diaries that the main attractions for most of the young volunteers were the dark blue cavalry uniform and the prospect of adventure.

Incorporated with the Natal Carbineers were the Karkloof Carbineers, who had suffered an ignominious retreat in 1873, during the pursuit of Langalibalele and his amaHlubi warriors (an incident which had earned Durnford the nickname of 'Don't Fire Durnford'). Now, five years later, several of the young carbineers who had retreated in disorder from the amaHlubi, would be present at Isandlwana – as would Durnford himself.

The Buffalo Border Guard (BBG) was the smallest unit to accompany No. 3 Column, its total strength numbering only twenty-three men of all ranks. Although small in number, they were smartly turned out wearing a black Bedford cord uniform with a silver buffalo head as their cap badge. Recruited from the scattered settler population along the Buffalo River, they were well aware that their homes and farms would be the first to bear the brunt of any Zulu attack and, in consequence, were serious about the role they played in guarding the frontier. James Rorke, the trader who had given his name to the drift where his home had been sited, had commanded the unit until his death a few years earlier. Of the twenty men of the BBG who volunteered to cross into Zululand, only four would survive the Battle of Isandlwana.

The Newcastle Mounted Rifles (NMR), also formed from the settler population, numbered forty of whom thirty-two volunteered to cross into Zululand. Although their base at Newcastle was forty miles west of the Zululand border, the boundary became ill defined further to the north as it entered the 'disputed territories'. Recruited from traders and men of the remote farming areas, they were a tough, bearded, mature unit and were well mounted. They would have better luck than their comrades of the BBG as all but three of their number would survive the events of the coming weeks.

One of the commonly held concepts of the Anglo-Zulu War is that Lord Chelmsford's army was comprised almost solely of British soldiers and a small number of colonials. In fact, as far as No. 3 Column was concerned, white soldiers amounted to less than forty per cent – the rest were black men, the conscripts who formed the NNC. It was as if Frere and Chelmsford, more than confident now that so many imperial troops were to hand, believed that the calibre of the local native regiments was unimportant and that mere numbers would suffice.

The 'colonial Zulus' of Natal had responded well to the call of Sir Henry Bulwer, their Supreme Chief and their substitute for a hereditary Zulu king. He had ordered that each native location conscript a percentage of its able bodied men for military service. Thus the conscripted recruits for the NNC had come from the four corners of the colony. No fewer than twelve different Zulu sub-tribes contributed men.

Chief Phakade of the amaChunu, who had sought sanctuary in Natal many years earlier, sent over 600 of his men to swell the ranks of No. 3 Column. The tribe occupied a large area of thorn scrubland alongside the Tugela River, bordering on the main invasion route between Greytown and Helpmekaar. By descent the amaChunu were as Zulu as any of their kin across the river. Because Phakade was now an old and corpulent man, his son, Gabangaye, would lead the amaChunu. But Gabangaye was almost as rotund as his father and already of middle age, so although he would accompany the tribe the actual leadership would devolve upon his son, Mbonjana.

At the Inanda location,◊ close to Durban, Chief Umqwe of the Maqatini clan said his young men would not go to war alone and that he, personally, would lead them. Good to his boast, he accompanied over 1,000 men to the front. The amaThembu, neighbours to the west of the amaChunu, set out to register their young recruits with Fynn, the magistrate at nearby M'singa. On the way they met some equally young amaChunu, drinking at a stream, where a Chunu warrior trod upon a Thembu shield, a calculated insult. A fight immediately broke out and sticks and stones flew in all directions until the elders of both sides, lambasting the youngsters' heads with swinging sticks, brought the battle to a close.

The survivors of Mbuyazi's *iZigqoza* faction, who had escaped into Natal in 1856, had now become a tribe, bearing the name iZigqoza. They were led by Sikhota who, by all accounts, was as imposing as any Zulu king. Men of royal Zulu blood were not lacking in the NNC.

These then, with the addition of men from other smaller clans, would fill the ranks of the 1/3rd and 2/3rd Battalions of the NNC, each numbering approximately 1,000 men. Both battalions would be assigned to No. 3 Column.

⟶•◦•⟵

For almost forty years the men of the NNC and their forebears had been discouraged, indeed forbidden, from indulging in any martial activities; they had been encouraged to live in peace and neither to be a threat to the white settlers of Natal nor to incite their Zulu kin across the river. Now, however, like some Rip van Winkle warrior race, they were to be awakened from a long, peaceful slumber, given a few days of confused training, then with their rusty spears and moulting shields, to take on the highly trained and motivated warriors of the Zulu king. They had been ordered to bring their own weapons, whilst the government would issue one man in ten with a musket or rifle of some kind, and ten rounds of ammunition. Their pay, twenty-two shillings (£1.10) per month, was almost generous bearing in mind that the trained British infantryman, with perhaps fifteen years service, received only nine shillings (£0.45) a month more. A ration of maize meal, one and a half pounds of meat a day. and a free blanket concluded the government's side of the contract. A black *induna*, or leader, received £4 per month. Unlike the rest of the column, which would be housed in tents, the NNC, during the rainy season that was just about to break with all the vengeance that follows a two-year drought, would have to make their own shelters as best they could. In appearance all but naked, there was little to distinguish them from their Zulu kin apart from a crimson rag worn around the head.

The white officers and NCOs of the NNC had also arrived at the front, and although many of the former were competent – and a few even spoke the Zulu language – hardly a good word has ever been written about the NCOs. Nevertheless, the lowest corporals were paid six shillings (£0.30) a day, which, in comparison with the meagre pay of the British soldier, should have been sufficient cause to incite mutiny amongst the imperial troops.

Although Lord Chelmsford's regulations had been couched in the paternalistic jargon of the time, he had taken trouble to ensure that his black troops would be treated well and not abused: Appendix H of his *Regulations for Field Forces South Africa 1878* read in part:

> 'The Natal Zulu may be looked upon as an intelligent, precocious boy, with the physical strength of a man... he is very sensible of justice and equally sensitive to injustice. A firm, kind rule is what he understands and appreciates... if you look after his personal comforts, and take an interest in his welfare, you will certainly gain his confidence... never use epithets of contempt such as niggers, kafirs, etc. Call them "abantu" (people) "amadoda" (men), or "amabuti" (soldiers)... an intimation that they are behaving like common kafirs (amakafula) and not like royal soldiers (amabuto wenkosi) is certain to produce an effect... teach them slowly, quietly and good humouredly... do not weary them by too long drills... never punish a man for disobedience of an order until you have clearly ascertained that he understood it; nor for disrespect, unless you are certain of having understood what he said.'

The men to whom this advice was mainly addressed were the white NCOs who were later described by one of their own officers (he himself frequently given to kicking and abusing his men as though it were a bit of a lark), as:

> 'A motley crowd, a few of them old soldiers and ex clerks, the majority of them runaway sailors, ex marines and East London boatmen. They were an awful tough crowd.'◊

It is hardly surprising then that Chelmsford's well-intended advice was ignored. Conscripted from a rural life that by European standards was virtually eventless, the black NNC recruit suddenly found himself a soldier in a foreign army, commanded by foreign officers and under orders given in a foreign language.

There were clans and tribes amongst the NNC who, although in exile, had continued the *ibutho* tradition, the forming of age group regiments from amongst the young men. Such clans were in a position to offer the colonial government organised bodies of warriors familiar with their own system of fighting, but when the offer was made it was rejected. Instead the government formed the young men into companies structured on identical lines to those of the British Army.

The white officers and NCOs of the NNC had been recruited as early as November and had received two weeks' intensive training. However, the majority of the black rank and file only started to arrive at Sand Spruit, near M'singa, their training base, between 28 November and 6 December, leaving no more than a few days before they crossed into Zululand at Rorke's Drift.

During that time they were expected to have assimilated dozens of orders, drill movements and regulations, all given in English. Yet, it seems, Frere, Chelmsford, Durnford, and all those responsible for putting the NNC into the field, were under the delusion that the rabble which they had created was a match for the Zulu army. Properly trained and led, they might well have been but, as it was, the British expectation of their ability was an example of imperial over-confidence and underestimation of the enemy.

John Shepstone was to condemn the military system of training that had been imposed on the NNC by concluding that it had placed:

> 'the men at a decided disadvantage; having no confidence whatsoever in the presence of an enemy, either in their new leaders, new drill or themselves.'

These then, the imperials, the volunteer colonials and the conscripted blacks were the fighting men who made up Chelmsford's column. But in order to fight they had to be supported by hundreds of tons of equipment, provisions and ammunition carried by an assortment of wagons, drawn either by horses, mules or oxen depending on the type of conveyance and the load to be pulled. The equipment of each imperial infantry battalion weighed nine tons, the tents alone weighing four and increasing to five and half tons when wet, whilst a battalion's ammunition reserves weighed a further two tons. Thus the speed of Lord Chelmsford's advance into Zululand would be determined by the speed of the slowest vehicle.

At the time there was no establishment for commissioned officers in the Army Service Corps (ASC), it being manned only by warrant officers and other ranks. Commissariat officers, frequently recruited from the civilian population, were responsible for the supply of all that was required. The ASC had little to do with the actual physical transportation of such supplies as the vast variety of wagons, carts and omnibuses were either purchased or hired from the local settler population. Later in the campaign this would change, with the ASC bringing out draft horses from England.

The Boers, who had been traversing southern Africa for almost 200 years, were the masters both of wagon construction and of the handling of the great spans of oxen which were required to haul the heavy vehicles. Their wagon technology for local conditions was unrivalled. The wagon they contrived, and which would be the means of transporting Chelmsford's supplies and equipment, was 20 feet long and 6 feet wide, with rear wheels as tall as a man and hooped with half-inch-thick iron tyres. The teams of oxen, greatly prized by their owners, were colour matched, the favourite combination being beasts with hides of red and white, or black and white. They required no fodder other than a reasonable amount of good grazing. But the oxen were desperately slow eaters – the time taken for them to graze their fill caused rage and despair amongst those anxious to get on. Yet to hurry them and deny them a full intake could result in loss of condition or even death. No reins were used: the lead oxen (the oldest or most experienced) were guided by a *voorlooper* ('leader'), usually a teenage boy, who would prod the oxen in the right direction, whilst the driver, standing upright, wielded with great dexterity a long whip, which he could crack with the sound of a rifle shot above the ear of a laggardly beast.

Such transport was not cheap and when the invasion plan became known, and the demand for transport of all kinds skyrocketed, the cost or hire of wagons followed suit. After Isandlwana, where most of No. 3 Column's transport, amounting to over 130 wagons and 2,000 oxen, was lost and, with few exceptions, the wagon personnel killed, the cost of wagon hire spiralled again.

There were no army personnel with the training or experience needed to take control of the concourse of transport attached to each column. When in convoy and on the move, the wagons could be strung out over a distance of five to six miles. Again, civilians were employed for the task and given the title of 'conductors'. There were a dozen or so per column, patrolling the moving convoy on horseback, ensuring wherever they could that there were no undue hold-ups.

Senior in authority to the conductors, and again a civilian, was the 'laager commandant' whose job was to allocate within the camp a place for every wagon – and, if required, to have the skill to construct with all speed, a wagon *laager*. Such men were rare and in great demand. Colonel Glyn, No. 3 Column commander, had tried in vain to employ several; Mr Edmond Dubois and a Mr Woodruffe had both indicated to Glyn that they would accept the position but, to their good fortune, declined at the last moment. (However, Dubois' brother, Robert, engaged as a conductor and was killed a few days later.) Thus the column took the road to Isandlwana devoid of the skills of a *laager* commandant. Nevertheless, armed and equipped as the column was, it still had not only to find its way into the interior of Zululand but also to find the Zulu army.

Accurate maps of Zululand were non-existent, although Colonel Durnford and the Honourable William Drummond, a local civilian resident of Natal attached to Chelmsford's staff, had both produced rough sketch maps. But these were based on scant first-hand knowledge plus hearsay. As Chelmsford was later to explain to the Duke of Cambridge:

> 'I have already pointed out to Your Royal Highness how impossible it has been to obtain really reliable information regarding the country even from those who ought to know it well. They have never been accustomed to look at any of the roads from any but a trading point of view, and are therefore quite unable to give the detailed information which is so important where movements of troops are concerned.'

Quite who 'they' were is unclear, but it is likely that Lord Chelmsford was referring to the local civilian guides and interpreters that each column had employed as intelligence and political officers, men such as John Dunn, now attached to No. 1 Column, who, though a trader, had an unrivalled knowledge of Zululand and was acquainted with every Zulu personality of any importance. Similarly, No. 4 Column had acquired the services of Llewellyn Lloyd and Charlie Potter – both young men and fluent Zulu linguists.

No. 3 Column was fortunate in having the services of three local men: Henry Francis Fynn, Henry Longcast and William Drummond.

Chelmsford had brought pressure to bear on the civilian administration to have Fynn relieved of his magisterial duties at M'singa and attached to his own staff. Fynn was not only fluent in Zulu, but also in Dutch, and had been present at the coronation of King Cetshwayo. As an indication of the esteem with which he was held by the Zulu people on both sides of the border, he had been given the name of Gwalagwala, 'the red feathers of the lourie bird', adornments which were the preserve of royalty or a distinction awarded for heroic deeds performed in battle.

Longcast, an orphan brought up in Zululand by missionaries, and who might well have spoken Zulu as his first language, was twenty-nine years of age and had lived in Zululand all his life. He would be described by a senior British staff officer as, 'a constant companion for eight months, resourceful and unwearying, with the cunning of the Zulu and the feelings of the Englishman.' Longcast was also credited with the ability to throw an assegai with all the skill of a Zulu warrior.

The Honourable William Drummond appears to have fulfilled a destiny typical of second sons of Victorian nobility, his father being Viscount Strathallan. Drummond was thirty-four years of age at the time of the invasion and had been following a hunting career in Zululand for some time. Brave to the point of recklessness, one of his claims to fame was the shooting of twenty-three 'Sea Cows' (hippopotami), in a single morning. (A photograph of this 'achievement' is still displayed in the Eshowe Museum, kwaZulu-Natal.) He was destined to die in the last battle of the Anglo-Zulu War at Ulundi. A fellow Scot, writing to the future MacLeod of MacLeod, would record:

> 'We were sent to burn one [section of the Royal homestead] and were
> nearly cut off. Drummond, who was drunk that morning, rode right into
> the Zulus alone, nothing has been seen of him since but his pistol.'

These men of the frontier were to be the eyes and ears of Chelmsford's army, keeping it supplied with the latest intelligence. Unbeknown to them they were to serve another purpose, for there is little doubt that it was from men such as these that H. Rider Haggard, then an impressionable twenty-three-year-old poorly paid clerk in the service of Sir Theophilus Shepstone, would later sketch the character of Allan Quartermaine.

The commander of the juggernaut-like No. 3 Column, Colonel Richard Thomas Glyn, was little more than 5 feet 2 inches in height; in the correspondence of acquaintances he was frequently referred to as 'Little Glyn.' He was forty-nine years of age and, with a rather pugnacious face glaring from behind a grey beard, looked ten years older. Glyn came from a British Raj background, being the only son of an official of the Honourable East India Company. He had joined the 24th Regiment over twenty years previously in 1856 and had seen active service in the Crimean War and the Indian Mutiny. Slowly climbing the tree of army promotion, he attained by purchase the lieutenant-colonelcy of the 1/24th in 1867 and in 1872 had been promoted to full colonel. His wife and four daughters had followed the battalion on its odyssey up from the Cape and, perhaps as a means to escape from female domination at home, Glyn had formed a regimental pack of fox hounds. He was elected master of the pack, whilst his adoring and exuberant subalterns performed the role of huntsmen as they pursued the Cape jackal, which substituted for a fox. Whilst Glyn got on well with his subalterns, he was often at odds with his more senior subordinates and with his superiors. Difficult to motivate and inclined to obstinacy, he had, nevertheless, been a key figure in the successful conclusion of the Ninth Frontier War for which he had been made a Companion of the Bath. Glyn was, no doubt, looking forward to the independent command of No. 3 Column and his reaction to Lord Chelmsford's decision to accompany it, thus effectively usurping his command, was one of irritation and disappointment.

Lieutenant-General the Honourable Frederic Augustus Thesiger had inherited the title Lord Chelmsford, a mere three months prior to the invasion of Zululand. Having fought the Ninth Frontier War – which had been dragging on under the previous commander – to a successful conclusion, he was held in high esteem by his superiors. Chelmsford was as tall as Glyn was short, and at the age of fifty-one, was still full of the vigour that he would have required in his younger days in order to become the accomplished boxer that he had been.

He had originally been commissioned into the Rifle Brigade, but soon purchased a commission in the Grenadier Guards. After twelve years service with the Guards he exchanged into the 2/95th (Derbyshire) Regiment, becoming its colonel which, according to a biographer, caused 'a great outcry and much heart burning'. Chelmsford had served in a number of campaigns including the Crimean War, the Indian Mutiny and, in 1867, the lesser known Abyssinian Expeditionary Force which had fought its way from Massowah on the East African Coast, 300 miles inland to the capital Magdala. King Theodore of Abyssinia had imprisoned and put in chains the British consul and some missionaries, whom the expeditionary force set out to rescue, a task which it accomplished with exemplary aplomb, suffering only twenty-nine casualties out of a force of 14,000 men. It then razed Magdala to the ground, marched to Massowah and departed. Chelmsford was awarded the Companionship of the Bath for his 'great ability and untiring energy' in this undertaking. However, until taking command of the Ninth Frontier War, Chelmsford had never led troops in action; all his previous duties had been as a staff officer. Before Chelmsford left for South Africa, General Sir John Mitchel, who had commanded troops at the Cape during earlier campaigns, wrote to him giving some very good advice:

'My dear Thesiger,

I wish you joy. The best climate in the world... no plan of operation of yours can in any way circumvent the caffre [a derogatory term for a native warrior or person]. He is your master in everything. He goes where he likes, he does what he likes, he moves three miles whilst you move one, he carries no commissariat or only a day's supply... you will scarcely believe that I who had always commanded about half the army, who was everywhere and saw everything, never saw thirty caffres together in my life... I am of the opinion that you cannot too carefully instil in your commanding officers and their juniors, that in no case are they to move without their flanks fairly covered... Officers should carry revolvers, not swords... I recommend that you do not try night surprises... I have spoken of lots of trifles, but the world is made of trifles... Yours, my dear Thesiger, is a command of great danger to your reputation... '

Chelmsford would find these to be prophetic words indeed.

Chapter 3

King Cetshwayo's Army

'The Zulus travel nearly as fast as men on horseback. They are reckless of death.'

Miss Mary Frere writing to General Sir Henry Ponsonby, 27 January 1879

Southern Africa 1819. The Ndwandwe army of Chief Zwide, numerically superior by far than their Zulu opponents led by Shaka, the bastard son of Senzangakhona, began to form up on the sides of a thickly wooded hill, which the Zulu army had chosen to defend, south of the Mhlatuze River.

This would be the second battle between these rival clans of Nguni people – the first, fought the previous year, though indecisive, had been hailed as a victory by the outnumbered Zulu. Now, Zwide was determined to kill his usurper opponent and to destroy his entire clan. But Zwide and his warriors would find to their cost that the time-honoured method of combat in southern Africa was about to change. No longer would it be a matter of opposing sides standing back and casting abuse and spears at each other, a form of warfare in which most of those involved would live to fight another day, for Shaka had devised a new spear and a revolutionary method of delivering it to an enemy. It would not be thrown and lost; the new spear was to be hand delivered and retained. The throwing spear, in order to perform efficiently, had a light blade attached to a slender wooden shaft, and obtained its impact through flight. As a hand-to-hand weapon it was too flimsy and lengthy to be effective. What Shaka had devised was a heavy, broad blade, about eighteen inches long, mounted on a stout, short shaft fluted outwards at the end to prevent a hand, wet with blood, sliding off with a backwards pull. It was a stabbing spear, little different in basic design from the short bladed sword of the Roman legions. Shaka had also enlarged the Zulu buffalo hide war shield to protect efficiently against a rain of throwing spears as his warriors closed with the enemy.

As Chief Zwide's Ndwandwe warriors encircled the hill containing Shaka's smaller army they believed that none would escape. To their surprise they were met not with a shower of throwing spears but by a mob of Zulu warriors racing towards them, dodging through the trees as they came. Hardly had a Ndwandwe spear been thrown when the Zulu were upon them. Using a single sweeping movement, the Zulu warriors thrust their shields behind those of their opponents, yanking them forward and away. Shaka's broad bladed invention was thrust into the exposed armpit, killing almost instantly. The weapon was to be called an assegai by other races but to the Zulu it would be known as the *iklwa*, an onomatopoeic word for the sucking noise made by the blade as it was withdrawn.

As one stunned and dying Ndwandwe warrior was felled by a Zulu *iklwa* the next was engaged with the same devastating result.

Shaka's victory that day was to be repeated many times in the years ahead, Shaka and his army forging a kingdom of extent and power unknown before in black Africa. What had been an insignificant Nguni clan became the Zulu nation. Their territory, although not always inhabited entirely by Zulus, but nevertheless conquered and suppressed by them, began in the north at the Swazi border and the precincts of Delagoa Bay, then continued south along the coast for over 450 miles to the Mzimvubu River and the land of the amaPondo. Inland, it extended over 150 miles to the foothills of the Drakensberg Mountains.

Various conquered tribes and clans lost their former identities to become 'Zulus'. On one occasion Shaka was taken to task by an old comrade in arms, who asked how it was that a warrior of a newly conquered tribe could be given rapid promotion in the Zulu army – albeit that he had performed with exemplary ability in his first battle under Shaka's command. Shaka is reputed to have retorted that:

> 'Any man who fights in the Zulu army becomes as much a Zulu as had he been born a Zulu.'

To rid the nation, and in particular the army, of any tribal or clan loyalties which might linger in those newly subjugated, Shaka formed his warriors into age group regiments (*amabutho*), each with its own name (and often a nickname), uniform-like apparel, shields of a distinctive colour, barracks and traditions – remarkably similar in many respects to things held dear by British regiments.

Thus with pride a warrior grew to give his first loyalty to his regiment which might contain men gathered from many other clans or tribes, but who would all be of a common age. So, if a warrior were asked who he was, he would likely answer in the vein, 'I am Mtuzwa, son of Nhlaka, of the Mbelebelele [regiment]', he would need no other qualification of identity.

With knowledge of their king's fearless example in battle, and his imposition of savage discipline, including certain death for disobedience and cowardice, Shaka's regiments became the most efficient and the most feared army south of the Sudan. Over half a century later Shaka's nephew, Cetshwayo, would inherit the Zulu army, but it would have to pass through hands less appreciative of its worth before it would be his to command.

Shaka reigned for only twelve years before his half brother Dingane and his accomplices murdered him. Dingane was no soldier. He preferred a life of indolence, giving much of his time to the company of his harem (*isigodlo*) women. With them assembled by the score, ululating their approval, he, adorned in a costume of beads, would dance before his subjects, whilst his warriors, magnificently attired, chanted and stamped their feet, 'until the earth trembled', giving rhythm to their king's performance. But fortunately for his army, its commanders did not allow it to degenerate into a military chorus line and saw to it that the *amabutho* system continued to be practised, the young men of the nation forming new regiments as they became of warrior age.

Dingane reigned for ten years before the Zulu fought their first battle with the white man. The dissatisfied Boer farmers (*Voortrekkers* or trekkers), emigrating from the Cape to be rid of British rule, seeking a territory in the vast hinterland of Africa where they could establish an independent republic, reached the Drakensberg Mountains in 1837.

Gazing on the rolling green hills of the Zulu kingdom they believed they had been guided by their God of the Old Testament, to their 'Promised Land'. Making their way down the precipitous passes, some 10,000 feet above sea level, they reached the sylvan foothills. Whilst their leaders set out to parley for land with King Dingane, the rest established themselves in camps, taking up makeshift farming amongst the valleys where streams flowed crystal clear. Dingane received the *Voortrekker* emissaries with false goodwill, but in reality he was greatly concerned by their numbers, the speed of their horses and the power of their firearms and could see no peaceful conclusion to their demands.◊ He therefore decided to destroy them all. The seventy emissaries were brutally murdered in early February 1838 whilst Dingane's regiments spread out towards the Drakensberg. Within days a bloody massacre ensued when, without warning, his warriors descended on the scattered wagon camps of the sleeping Boers. Throughout the night and the whole of the following day, the warriors slaughtered men, women and children wherever they could be found. When the *impi* triumphantly withdrew, taking with it thousands of cattle and sheep, a few whites still survived. Retribution would follow.

When the handful of English settlers living at Port Natal (later to be called Durban) had heard of the intended assault upon the Boers, they had set out to aid their white kin. A force of seventeen Englishmen, supported by several hundred mixed-race and black retainers, had crossed the Tugela River only to be ambushed by a large *impi* just below nDondakusuka Hill, the very place where Cetshwayo would establish his succession eighteen years later. Only four Englishmen and a few of their auxiliaries survived to re-cross the river.

Dingane, outraged at what he considered to be English treachery, immediately sent an *impi* to destroy the fledgling town of Port Natal, appointing his half brother, Mpande, to command the expedition. Port Natal, such as it was, was razed to the ground. The population, forewarned of the approaching army, escaped either by sea or by retreating south.

In those first encounters with the white man, the Zulu had the advantage of surprise and overwhelming numbers. Yet they had not killed all the *Voortrekkers* and those who had escaped had seen the Promised Land. Soon the news of its paradise-like qualities, and Dingane's treachery, would be relayed to the long wagon trains of Boers still on their way north. It was decided to avenge Dingane's treachery and to take the Promised Land by conquest.

The Zulu had been familiar with the ox-drawn wagons of the traders and the firearms of the white hunters for a number of years; now they would encounter both, ingeniously combined into a mobile fortress. Ten months after the massacre, a convoy of 64 wagons, 468 *Voortrekkers* – most with two horses apiece – and as many as 300 servants, under the command of elected Commandant-General Andries Pretorius, descended from the Drakensberg and slowly made its way north-east, seeking a confrontation with the Zulu army. Dingane was not slow to respond and by the time the convoy was half way to his capital of Mgungundlovu, the *Voortrekker* scouts were able to report that a vast *impi* of 10,000 warriors was advancing rapidly towards them.

From the Boer point of view, the battle that followed on 16 December 1838 can only be described as miraculous for several reasons, the foremost being the advantageous terrain that the Boers happened upon when news of the approaching *impi* was received. Had Pretorius searched the whole of Zululand, it is doubtful if a better site could have been found for a defensive position. The convoy was close by the Ncome (later to be called Blood) River, a tributary of the Buffalo, at a spot where a wide deep *donga* entered the river at right angles, forming a natural moat. Thus the Boer wagons were arranged with a water bastion on two sides, with each outer corner being linked together by a convex line made from the remaining wagons. The Boers had come fully prepared for battle; not only had they brought with them three small cannon, they had sewn their musket ammunition of gunpowder and shot into easily loaded individual bags, and had made numerous 'fighting gates' to block the gaps between and under the wagons.

The engagement, well known to history as the Battle of Blood River, is regarded by the Boers as perhaps their nation's greatest military triumph – yet it holds no momentous place in Zulu oral history. One cannot help but wonder whether or not the Boers, in their euphoria of victory, and in the retelling of their miraculous success, did not exaggerate. Boer history tells us that the 468 *Voortrekkers*, supported by their servants, defeated the Zulu army, slaying 3,000 warriors, at a cost of three Boers slightly wounded.

One Boer leader described the victory in farming terms that his kin would find easy to understand: 'They [the Zulu dead] lay on the ground like pumpkins on a rich soil that had borne a large crop.' Yet, whatever the statistics, the Zulu army had been defeated in a manner that would only be surpassed by Lord Chelmsford's victory at Ulundi forty years later. The Boer triumph would also influence Chelmsford's assessment of Zulu prowess and, to a degree, be responsible for his own defeat at Isandlwana.

Dingane, full of apprehension for the future of his kingdom south of the Tugela, which he correctly anticipated would be taken by the hated Boers, decided to expand his territory by seizing the land of the amaSwazi. So, whilst Dingane's emissaries commenced tentative negotiations with the victorious Boers to the south, two large armies, one after the other, marched north on Swaziland.

Both in turn were defeated. It was not a good season for the previously invincible Zulu war machine. Dingane could sense the destruction of his kingdom to be close at hand.

Then, into the potential battleground of Natal, marched a small contingent of 100 redcoats. They built a fort at the entrance to the harbour at Port Natal and settled in under the command of Captain Henry Jarvis. Britain now had a military presence in the territory where previously its only representation had been a scattering of hunters and traders.◊

Jarvis had been ordered by the Governor of the Cape to placate both Boer and Zulu and, if possible, broker a boundary between them. This the talented Jarvis most ably did, the Tugela and Buffalo Rivers eventually being accepted by both sides as the demarcation line between Natal and Zululand.

A peace treaty was signed and Jarvis, with the satisfaction of a job well done, stayed on at Port Natal, determined to see that both parties honoured the terms of the treaty. With his company of redcoats he believed he could even enforce compliance if necessary. To underline his authority as the representative of the British government, he delivered a formal protest to the Boers, 'regretting the slaughter of the Zulu and the unwarranted invasion of their country', and, as instructed by the Cape government, further warned that any similar aggression in the future would receive Britain's marked displeasure. Yet, strange to relate, within three years the land that the Boers had taken from the Zulu, Britain would take from the Boers, not with the intent of returning it to the Zulu, but in order to establish its own crown colony of Natal. Indeed, forty years later, Sir Bartle Frere would strive to justify Britain's unwarranted invasion of what was left of the Zulu kingdom.

In the meantime, Dingane was still determined to replace the land lost to the Boers, and once again set about rallying his warriors to conquer the amaSwazi. He had still to resolve with the Boers the return of 40,000 head of cattle that the Boers claimed Dingane's army had taken during the time of the massacre the previous year. As Dingane set about assembling a new army to march north, he sent orders throughout the kingdom instructing every homestead to contribute cattle towards the Boer demands. In particular, he sought out his half brother Mpande, insisting on being given hundreds of men to fight and thousands of cattle with which to satisfy the Boers. However, many were reluctant to respond to Dingane's orders. Shaka, his predecessor, had been regarded with immense fear by the Zulu – but also with respect. Dingane was feared to the same degree but was also loathed and hated. He had no heir and was forever fearing the assegai of some avenging usurper – his suspicions of late focussing on Mpande, a favourite with the people, and, apart from himself, the last surviving royal son of Senzangakhona.

Mpande was sent warning of Dingane's growing hysteria of suspicion and feared that, once he had handed over his cattle, he and his entire household would be put to death. Mpande therefore decided to flee and in doing so brought the inheritance of the Zulu army one step closer to his son, Cetshwayo.

At the time Mpande's homestead was located no more than ten miles north of the Tugela River, the only direction in which he could escape. It was a mark of his popularity that, when he crossed the Tugela into Natal, taking Cetshwayo with him, he was followed by 17,000 of his kinsmen. Mpande was supposedly a simpleton, yet he had survived the bloody purges of both Shaka and Dingane; it was almost as if he had been anointed with the blessing of survival. Now, by the force of circumstance, he would again survive and, what is more, become king of the Zulus.

The Boers, sick of bloodshed, had but one desire, to live in peace and prosper in their Promised Land. But knowing that they could no more trust Dingane than he could trust them, they saw Mpande's arrival in their midst, with his great following, which included some of the ablest commanders in the Zulu army, as yet another miracle. A deal was struck; the Boers and Mpande would join forces, pursue and kill Dingane, recover the 40,000 head of cattle and then crown Mpande king – albeit to rule as a puppet king of the Boers.

As news spread of Mpande's uprising against his hated brother, more and more Zulus pledged their allegiance to him. But nothing could be done all the while Jarvis and his soldiers remained at Port Natal. Then another miracle occurred. The Governor of the Cape, believing that all was calm and peaceful to the north, decided to withdraw the British garrison. So a few weeks later, on Christmas Eve 1839, Jarvis and his men set sail for Cape Town. Free of the fetters of British surveillance, the gleeful Boers at Port Natal triumphantly raised their flag over Fort Victoria, declared their independence, and named their Promised Land the Republic of Natalia.

In less than three weeks following Jarvis' departure, a combined Boer-Zulu army had been assembled, comprising over 800 Boers and their mixed-race retainers, with almost as many horses, and thousands of Zulu warriors led by Mpande's acclaimed commander, Nongalaza. It was planned that the Boer contingent would march north-west into Zululand by way of Blood River, whilst Nongalaza's *impi* invaded directly north over the Tugela at Lower Drift.

Mpande did not accompany his army; indeed he was unable to do so as the wily Boers had taken him and Cetshwayo hostage as insurance against any possible treachery. Legend has it that the Boers, in order to prevent any clandestine substitution of some other youth for Cetshwayo, had his ear snipped as a means of identification.

Dingane, with his army melting away as many of his warriors defected to Nongalaza's advancing *impi*, eventually stood to do battle. It was a battle fought as of old. There were neither firearms nor horses to give either side advantage. It was warrior against warrior in close fought combat. The Boer contingent, deliberately or otherwise, had marched many miles in the wrong direction. They were still several days' journey away and would take no part in what was to become an icon battle in Zulu history. In a fight that lasted many hours, and in which 10,000 warriors fought, Mpande's forces finally won the day, but not before both armies had suffered over 1,000 casualties. Eventually, Dingane and a small following fled north pursued by Nongalaza, crossing the Pongola River into the Lebombo Mountains where he found temporary sanctuary. However, he was too close to the territory of his old enemies, the amaSwazi, and it was inevitable that his presence would become known. It was also inevitable that, in his vulnerable state, he would be tracked down and killed. In a sudden night raid the Swazi, most likely guided by defecting Zulu warriors, mortally wounded Dingane who died a few days later. To his credit, with his dying breath he beseeched those still about him to carry his last request to his defeated warriors, that they pay homage to Mpande and thus make the Zulu a nation once again.

The Boers had played no part in Dingane's defeat and death except for the intimidating menace of their advance into Zululand. They had kept a safe distance from the action, rounding up all the cattle they could find. Later they would herd them back to Natal. They would also ensure that their outstanding claim of 40,000 beasts was paid in full – and, for the ineffectual part that they had played in the campaign, they would make a further demand. They chose the moment well for the Zulu casualties on both sides exceeded 2,000, the nation was in disarray and Mpande was still their hostage. The Boers demanded and got a further chunk of the Zulu kingdom: all the land between the Tugela and Black Mfolozi Rivers and as far inland as the Drakensberg Mountains, over 7,000 square miles of territory. The seaboard of the Zulu kingdom that had once measured 450 miles was now reduced to little over 100 miles in length.

On 10 February 1840 the Boers performed a mock coronation proclaiming Mpande 'King of the Zulus' and their 'great ally' (a ceremony that the British would copy thirty-three years later at Cetshwayo's enthronement). The Boers then departed back to Natal, leaving Mpande to heal the wounds of his divided nation. One can imagine the smouldering fury of the young Cetshwayo as he witnessed the humiliation of his father and the theft of the land which would have been his to inherit.

Exultant in their triumph, which they believed had been brought about by the hand of God, the Boers now looked south for further expansion and commenced raiding the amaPondo. However, news of the mayhem in

Zululand and other disturbing Boer activities finally reached the Governor of the Cape who decided that the Boers, who were deemed by Britain to be subjects of Queen Victoria, should again be brought under British authority. Consequently, in April 1842, a small detachment of the 27th Regiment, under the command of Captain Thomas Charlton Smith, marched north.

What followed is an epic story in itself. Suffice to say that Captain Smith, after a confrontation with Pretorius, was besieged with most of his men in a makeshift fort for almost two months before a warship of the Royal Navy arrived carrying six companies of redcoats. In view of the bravery, tenacity and religious fervour shown by the Boers in various earlier confrontations, often against overwhelming odds such as at Blood River, it is extraordinary that they hardly put up a fight, never seriously opposing the bloodless victory of the British landing which resulted in the loss of their Promised Land. Within a relatively short time Natal was declared a crown colony and, no doubt to Mpande's extreme satisfaction (and grudging admiration for the British), the earlier boundary between Natal and Zululand, that of the Tugela and Buffalo Rivers, was recognised and the 7,000 square miles of territory that the Boers had taken were restored by Britain to the Zulu kingdom. Mpande could now go about the unification of his kingdom in peace – and perhaps he would also have to give thought to the restoration of his army.

⸺ ❖ ⸺

Soon after daylight on 30 March 1879, Sergeant-Major F.W. Cheffins of Raaff's Rangers, walked the battlefield of Kambula. He was fascinated by the magnificent physique of the Zulu warriors who had been killed the previous day and now lay scattered in their hundreds around the British camp. Later, Cheffins was to write in his diary:

> 'Without denial the Zulus are the finest race in South Africa. Well built and possessed of bodily strength, they can endure all manner of hardship. Every Zulu that was killed was about six feet in height and had limbs on them that completely throw Europeans in the shade.'

Even Sir Bartle Frere had been impressed with the enemy having described the Zulu, just prior to the invasion, with the awesome phrase, 'celibate, man-slaying gladiators'. And Lieutenant Carl Müller, of the Stutterheim Mounted Police, who survived several battles against the Zulu, was moved to write at the conclusion of the war: 'May happier times come to the people who are superstitious pagans, yet they are a superior people.' Most white men, especially those recently arrived from Europe, were struck by the near perfect physique, strong white teeth, and powerful eyesight of the Zulu.

Bertram Mitford, who travelled throughout Zululand in 1882, wrote of two warriors who had fought the British:

'[they are] from five foot ten inches to six feet in height, broad and well proportioned, their countenances straight featured and bearded, with good humoured yet dignified expression and splendid foreheads.

Where had they come from, this warrior race who so impressed their enemies? There are several theories: some believe the Nguni originally came from the forests of Central Africa; others believe they originated in the great lakes region of Uganda, whilst some hold that the Nguni came from much further north, perhaps beyond Ethiopia, and that ancestrally they had been in contact with the outposts of Rome. It is possible that the Nguni travelled south from their country of origin, passing through the present-day territory of Kenya and Tanzania, since many words in the Zulu tongue and the kiSwahili of the east coast, close on 2,000 miles to the north, are identical or close to being so.[◊]

There is evidence that the Nguni became a warlike people during the 17th century, but it had taken Shaka to weld the numerous clans and tribes into a nation and institute the *amabutho* military system. However, the details of the system are not all entirely clear. Historians seem to agree that it is not possible to identify all the Zulu regiments that had been formed from the time of Shaka to the commencement of the Anglo-Zulu War; for instance some regiments became known by two different names, their official one and, perhaps in addition, a nickname or the name of their barracks.

The detailed list of regiments compiled by Fynney, the border agent, in November 1878, at the request of Lord Chelmsford, and his revised second edition of April 1879, published in booklet form, is certainly the most detailed account available (an abbreviated copy of Fynney's 1878 list appears as *Appendix B, pages 320–1*). Another list can be found in Dr Eileen Krige's book *The Social System of the Zulus* published in 1974. Fynney lists twenty different regiments as being raised by Mpande, whilst Krige mentions twenty-two. Both list the more famous regiments of the Anglo-Zulu War, but with slightly different spellings, for instance: Tulwana Regiment or uThulwana; Umbonambi or uMbonambi; Iowa or iQwa; Nkobamakosi or nGobamakhosi. However, generally it is difficult to reconcile the regimental names shown on one list with those of the other. On occasion, instead of raising a new regiment, recruits were drafted into an existing one thus perpetuating the regimental name. It also became common practice during Cetshwayo's reign to embody two or three regiments together into a corps comprising several thousand warriors. Eventually there were twelve such corps, the most famous being the Undi.

By 1879 the regiments raised by Dingane had been depleted by time and it is doubtful if more than one, the Umkusi, manned by a few hundred veterans in their late fifties, took an active part in the war. All the effective regiments, amounting to between 37,000 and 40,000 men, would have been formed during Mpande's time with the exception of the two regiments, the

Nkobamakosi and uVe, 9,500 men in total, raised during the five years of Cetshwayo's reign. As the average age of the uVe, the youngest regiment, was twenty-three it is likely that further units were due to be formed, and probably were, either just prior to or during the course of the war. In fact Paulina Dlamini refers to 'the recently raised Falaza Regiment' as belonging to the same junior age group as herself. However, Fynney makes no mention of this unit.

It would seem that, although Mpande had his British neighbours to protect him against the Boers, he nevertheless, as one of his first acts as monarch, raised a new regiment naming it the Ngwekwe, no doubt in the hope that its formation would do much to bring about the reunification of the Zulu nation. Most likely, Mpande, the man of peace, and his warriors also, had had enough of war. Mpande did not enforce conscription with the vigour of previous kings and the young men took advantage of his lenient attitude, many evading call up. Traditionally, the *iziNyanga* (healers and witchdoctors) of the nation were not subject to military service and the ranks of this profession swelled as young men joined to ensure their exemption from conscription. And because of the numerical strength of the *iziNyanga*, their power became a force to be reckoned with. But all this was destined to be changed.

At last Mpande died and Cetshwayo inherited the kingdom, and with it the command of the Zulu army which he was determined to restore to the proud and fearsome force that it had been in the days of Shaka. Henceforth malingerers would not be tolerated. Every Zulu male would be a warrior, and to thwart the *iziNyanga*, Cetshwayo ordered them into a regiment of their own, to be kept apart from other warriors, and to be subject to strict discipline. Soon the Zulu blacksmiths would be as busy as any European munitions factory in time of war, forging assegais by the thousand; the clandestine acquisition of firearms would be urgently pursued; new barracks built, shields and regalia manufactured and gunpowder procured. And it would not only be men who would be subject to this military renaissance. The maidens of Zululand would again be formed into guilds or regiments, loosely affiliated to those of the newly formed warrior units.

In Shaka's day there had been a number of maiden regiments, all of them with female officers and commanders. Henry Francis Fynn (Snr.) recorded:

> 'The isigodlo of Shaka contained not less than 5,000 girls. The whole of these girls was divided into regiments (one of these being attached to each regiment of soldiers).'

Shaka, for his own mischievous amusement, and out of his friendship for Fynn, actually raised a female guild, which he named the *Mkisimana* (Englishman). Fynn dryly noted in his diary that the girls, 'were employed for his amusement more than any other purpose.' Cetshwayo would see to it that the duties of his girl soldiers were strictly military, going so far as to issue firearms (which he had obtained via John Dunn) to the ladies of the three senior units. Paulina Dlamini, a member of a junior regiment later recalled:

> 'The idea was that while the army was in the field, these young women would defend the royal residence... how we laughed when we watched them shoot. The King also watched but got very cross... '

The training of the Zulu soldier began early in life, casually and almost unintentionally, as at about five or six years of age, in the domestic surroundings of his home village, he was given the daily task, with other local boys, of guarding and herding the community cattle. Out all day in all weathers, the boys had to be tough to survive; in daily pursuit of roaming cattle, up and down the steep and broken hills of Zululand, they became possessed of great physical fitness and acquired an astounding agility that allowed them to cover, barefooted, the roughest terrain at racing speed without a stumble. They carried sticks, which they learnt to throw with accuracy, being able to bring down birds in flight – birds whose feathers might provide the adornment for an elder brother's regimental head-dress. They also used their sticks in mock battles between themselves – but under the eye of an elder, and woe betide the boy who lost his temper or shed unwarrior-like tears. These were the youngsters who would grow to become the black gladiators of the Zulu king.

At about twelve years of age, before reaching the status of warrior, a boy would become an *udibi* (baggage carrier) a sort of cross between a medieval knightly page and a British public schoolboy fag. The *izindibi* (the plural of *udibi*) accompanied the army conveying items of kit for a father or elder brother: a sleeping mat, wooden headrest, food and, probably, at times the awkward burden of a shield. During the Zulu Civil War of 1888, a white man witnessed a Zulu army on the march supported by *izindibi*:

> 'After the fighting men trotted the mat boys, few more than ten or twelve years old, carrying food and sleeping mats for their masters, these boys were an invariable adjunct of Zulu warfare.'

The *izindibi* stayed with the army until the enemy was sighted, then at a safe distance, watched in excited apprehension the outcome of the battle, poised to rush in and claim a trophy if their side were victorious. The Zulu army that would march to Isandlwana, vast in numbers, would be accompanied by numerous *izindibi* whose role in the closing moments of the fight would be far from passive.

On reaching manhood, and having received notice to report to the barracks of a new regiment that had been formed around his national age group, the warrior recruit would be subject to a period of service not unlike that of the British compulsory national service system after World War II. The requirement was initially two years' full-time service and, thereafter, part-time duty with annual camps. It is likely that, on arrival at his depot, the recruit would find little other than fellow recruits, his instructor and hard work. There would probably be no accommodation – he and fellow recruits would have to construct their own – and by their labour not only achieve a barracks, but also the beginning of a regimental esprit-de-corps. Only part of their time would be spent at military training as they would also become a labour force for the king, constructing barracks and fences, hoeing the royal fields and at times forming hunting parties seeking wild pigs, antelopes and, on occasion, fiercer game that would provide skins for regalia. They were also taught to dance in regiments, keeping them fit and agile.

At the annual First Fruits ceremony each regiment would attempt to outperform its rivals, the warriors becoming trance-like and aggressive as the throbbing rhythm of the dance took hold of body and mind. The elders, well aware of regimental rivalries and potential conflict, banned spears from the ceremony, sticks alone being permitted, which, perhaps, encouraged rather than prevented rival violence. There had been a most serious incident at the First Fruits ceremony of 1877, when a newly raised draft of young warriors, the nDluyengwe, who were to be amalgamated with Cetshwayo's prestigious uThulwana, were attacked by the Nkobamakosi Regiment who started to lay about both the young and elderly warriors in a most violent manner, forcing them back to their barracks where the uThulwana immediately seized their assegais. Dunn, who was present, reported that, in the battle that followed, over sixty men were killed and many more were taken to a nearby Norwegian mission station where their gaping wounds were tended.◊

Cetshwayo had been outraged, ordering the execution of Sigcwelegcwele, the commander of the Nkobamakosi who wisely disappeared for a few months until his monarch forgave him – subject to the payment of a large fine of cattle. The cause of the dispute had been due to Cetshwayo giving permission to the uThulwana Regiment, at the age of forty-three or thereabouts, to marry young women of a guild that the Nkobamakosi themselves had coveted – a hopeless infatuation as the Nkobamakosi would have to wait many years before they could expect the award of the *isicoco* (the head ring of elder status) and permission to marry. Ultimately, rival regiments, like those of the British army, were best kept well apart.

When John Shepstone (nicknamed 'Misjan' by the Zulu), as Acting Secretary for Native Affairs, was asked to describe some features of the Zulu warrior and his training, he wrote:

> 'Equipment: Each man carries his shield and assegais, and a kaross or blanket if he possesses one, he may also have a war dress of monkey skins or ox tails, this is all. Discipline: Is maintained by the free use of a knobkerrie or stick.'

Drill instruction formed part of the recruit's training, such as forming a circle of companies, (usually sixty men to a company) breaking into companies, forming up into marching order and other simple movements. Early in the war, Colonel Evelyn Wood witnessed, from a distance, 4,000 Zulus at drill and later recorded: 'they formed in succession a circle, triangle and square, with a partition, about eight men thick, in the centre.'[0] But it was at skirmishing that the Zulu warriors excelled; their speed and determination as they advanced would later receive the admiration of many a British officer.

Regimental uniforms differed slightly one from another, the main feature being the shield colour and head-dress. War shields were the property of the king and usually remained at the regimental barracks. Traditionally, the darker the shield the younger the regiment, with the most senior warriors eventually graduating to shields white in colour.

Regalia played an important role in the performance of ceremonies and each warrior had to provide his own. The head-dress, made of animal skins and feathers, was the most elaborate item, often fantastically barbaric in conception. It is astounding to contemplate the industry and the volume of material that would have been required in providing the head-dresses alone for the Zulu army. According to Fynney's list, almost 10,000 warriors wore otter skin headbands and 28,000 those of leopard skin. Calculating four headbands to one otter and ten to a leopard, the number of slain beasts required to provide regalia would have been 2,500 otters, 2,800 leopards, and 30,000 sakabull birds. Regalia, however, was expensive and encumbering and by 1879, except for a modified head-dress, was no longer worn in battle. Fynney wrote:

> 'it is to be noted that during the present war [1879] no ornaments or distinguishing marks of any kind, save the difference in shields, have been made use of by the Zulus.'

And the correspondent of the *Times Weekly*, commenting on the scavenging souvenir hunters of the British Army after the Battle of Kambula, wrote:

> 'Few curiosities or ornaments reward the searchers who are anxious to preserve souvenirs of their Zulu foe. For the first time in their history, these Black warriors have discarded the usual fantastic costumes in which it has hitherto been their habit to fight.'

And whilst the British soldier, quite rightly, groused about his meagre pay of one shilling a day, his Zulu equivalent received no pay at all and little thanks.

There are other comparisons to be made between the British and Zulu armies. The British, with the exception of the NNC, were far better armed with modern weaponry than their Zulu foe. However, by 1879, over thirty per cent of Cetshwayo's warriors were armed with a firearm of one sort or another – a much higher average than the ten per cent of the NNC, who made up sixty per cent of Chelmsford's army. In mobility the British army, requiring some nine tons of equipment for each imperial battalion, was a tortoise in comparison to the Zulu army's baggage train of fleet footed *izindibi* boys.

In communications the British should have had an advantage with the availability of the heliograph which, depending on weather conditions and terrain, was capable of flashing messages over twenty-five miles or more. However, there is no record of this device being used to communicate between Helpmekaar, Rorke's Drift and Isandlwana despite the terrain being ideal and the weather often likewise. Apart from the heliograph, the Zulu had the advantage since a warrior-messenger could travel as fast as a horseman over rough terrain. In addition the Zulu were able to throw their voices from one hilltop outpost to another, thus eliminating the need for a courier to traverse the kloofs and valleys below. In this way messages could be passed with a speed that seemed supernatural and completely mystified the white man.

There are several well documented examples. John Eustace Fannin, the border agent at Middle Drift, claimed that he had been the first white man, other than those who were actually at the battle, to have heard of the reverse at Isandlwana, picking up the news long before it reached Pietermaritzburg, from 'natives shouting from hill to hill.' L.H. Samuelson, shortly after the Anglo-Zulu War, wrote:

> 'The Zulus are celebrated for being marvellous news carriers... during the recent wars we often heard from natives of attacks which had taken place, even before special editions of the paper had been established... particular arrangements for forwarding news were made by them in times of war... and lines of communications were established from hill to hill.'

Rider Haggard was in Pretoria on the morning of 24 January 1879, when an old native woman told him that away in Zululand there had been a great battle with hundreds of redcoats being killed. Alarmed, Haggard asked when this had occurred and was told about thirty hours previously. Immediately cynical, Haggard asked, 'Where is the man who can run, or the horse that can gallop over 200 miles of veld in thirty hours?' His question was not answered but twenty hours later an exhausted horseman rode into Pretoria with the news of the British defeat. Paulina Dlamini, who was at Ulundi with Cetshwayo on 22 January, confirmed that the news of the Zulu victory arrived that evening, a distance of fifty miles.

And it was not only Zulu communications that could travel faster than those of the British columns; the speed and agility of the Zulu warrior, against that of his booted and kit-laden foe, would be telling factors in the battle to come.

Such was Cetshwayo's army in the closing months of 1878. A fighting machine without an enemy. His warriors desired to wash their spears, not only to establish manhood, but also to confirm by doing so, as required by tradition, Cetshwayo as their monarch. There had been a prospect of battle with the Boers over the disputed territories, but Britain was arbitrating on that score. There were the amaSwazi to the north, the kingdom's traditional enemies, but Britain had denied Cetshwayo that warpath a year or so before. Out of courtesy he had sent a letter, via John Dunn, to the Governor of Natal, informing him of the Zulu intention to raid the Swazi, and had immediately received a reply reading:

> 'The Lieutenant Governor sees no cause whatever for making war, and informs Cetshwayo that such an intention on the part of the Zulus meets with his entire disapproval… and trusts what he has said will be sufficient to deter Cetshwayo and the Zulu nation from entertaining such a project.'

Legend has it that Cetshwayo, thwarted and enraged, replied by delivering a sack of millet to the Natal government with the message:

> 'If you can count the grains in this sack then you may also be able to count the number of my warriors.'

Not to be outdone or intimidated, Theophilus Shepstone, then the Natal government's Secretary for Native Affairs, responded by sending a large ox hide with the retort:

> 'If you can count the hairs on this hide, then you will know the number of British soldiers with whom you will have to contend.'

So, by 1878, Cetshwayo and his army were boxed in: Swaziland was a no-go area; his dispute with the Boers was currently under British arbitration; and a war with Britain, the nation that had restored 7,000 square miles of kingdom to his father, was out of the question. Therefore the problem of his warriors being able to wash their spears seemed to be insoluble. However, it was a problem that Sir Bartle Frere would shortly solve. Had the findings of the Disputed Territories Commission been made known without the accompanying ultimatum, perhaps Cetshwayo would have accepted that it would no longer be possible for his warriors to wash their spears in blood in order to obtain the status of manhood and the right to marry. With as much territory as his kingdom was ever likely to achieve, Cetshwayo might have seen the wisdom of diluting the traditional belligerent militancy of his army, and of diverting the energy of his warriors into peaceful pursuits.

Chapter 4

Into Zululand

'[The Zulu king] believes that he is being surrounded and that it is the intention of the English to attack him – an intention which is without foundation.'

The Colonial Secretary, Natal, to the resident magistrates at Greytown, Stanger, Verulam, M'singa and Lower Tugela, 30 October 1878

Lord Chelmsford, having decided to accompany Colonel Glyn's No. 3 Column into Zululand, was advised that Helpmekaar would serve as a satisfactory assembly point for the thousands of men and animals, the tons of equipment and hundreds of wagons which would shortly have to cross the Buffalo River.

The name Helpmekaar, Dutch for 'help one another', or 'pull together', gives some indication of the difficulties the early *Voortrekkers* found in surmounting the tortuous terrain of its approach. Helpmekaar itself was little more than a featureless, treeless plateau high up on a ridge of the Biggarsberg Mountains. Altitude had led to its selection, for at 5,000 feet the cavalry would most likely be free of horse sickness, the scourge of the African lowlands, a disease that could strike a horse without warning; first the hollows above the eyes would swell, with the nose pouring mucus, followed by coughing, extreme distress, fever and death. A visitation of this sickness could leave a cavalry unit with half its horses dead within forty-eight hours.

Apart from its altitude, Helpmekaar had other advantages. It was situated, more or less, at the junction of three roads: the main invasion route via Pietermaritzburg and Greytown, the road from Ladysmith and that from Dundee – the latter two being important highways (if muddy tracks can be so described) for local volunteers, transport and commissariat. Helpmekaar was also situated just twelve miles from Rorke's Drift, 1,200 feet below, where it was planned that No. 3 Column would cross the Buffalo River into Zululand.

Due to its air of desolation, Helpmekaar was an unwelcoming place and its climate was savagely inhospitable. A blazing sun could be replaced within the hour by a greenish-black sky, laden with hailstones 'as big as goose eggs' and heavy enough to break skin or dent a tin roof; the hail being followed by icy rain. (The writer's present-day weather experiences of the place include a mini-tornado, and a snowstorm at eleven o'clock in the morning that left the Helpmekaar plateau looking like a cheerless Christmas card.) However, when the weather is fine, during the clear days of winter, at a particular spot just short of the plateau, it is possible to see, between the sea of hills to the west, the snow-covered peaks of the Drakensberg a hundred miles away. Then a few miles further on to the east, far below, almost as an aerial view, there is a magnificent vista of Zululand, the hills rolling away from the Buffalo River on towards the blue outline of the distant Babanango escarpment which, in 1879, sheltered the approaches to the White Mfolozi River and King Cetshwayo's capital of Ulundi.

The weather in January 1879 was not kind. The incessant rain, the cold of high places, the mud and flooded rivers were the foremost topic in almost every diary or letter written by Lord Chelmsford's forces. The rains had come as early as November. Trooper William James Clarke of the NMP, making his way to Helpmekaar recorded:

'We commenced the ascent of the Biggarsberg where we [toiled with] the wagons in black soil which clogged our feet and in some places reached the top of our boots... By pulling the wagons [with the oxen] up every rise, we managed to get to Helpmekaar, wet and tired out... the cold was bitter.'◊

By late December a Natal newspaper was predicting:

'It is feared that the rains will retard operations. Ox wagons are apt to stand still when rain is pouring down, and roads are deep in mud. Many days of heavy rain and never ending reports of flooded or impassable rivers have made the exact period of our departure uncertain.'

Charles Norris-Newman, the special correspondent of the *London Standard*, left Pietermaritzburg for Helpmekaar in heavy rain and 'thick fog' and on reaching his destination several days later found, 'the cold during the night was intense, and we all suffered from the want of sufficient blankets.' And twenty-six-year-old Lieutenant Nevill Coghill, who until a day or so earlier, had been aide-de-camp to Sir Bartle Frere, encountered foul weather whilst hurrying to the front to rejoin his regiment, the 1/24th. He had been eager to show Colonel Glyn the fine horse that he had chosen and purchased on Glyn's behalf. Coghill was successful in crossing the Mooi River by means of a *pont* which was being supervised by twenty-year-old Horace Smith-Dorrien, a special service officer (that is an officer from a regiment not involved in the campaign who had been seconded or had volunteered to take part), who would, within the month, be one of only five imperial officers to survive Isandlwana. However, on approaching a small stream in torrents of rain, Coghill was told that the stream had suddenly become a river and that a wagon, pulled by thirty-two oxen, had just been 'swept away into the Tugela and thence to the sea.'

Whatever advantages Chelmsford may have seen in commencing the invasion of Zululand at that particular time, he must later have questioned the wisdom of doing so in the middle of the summer rains.

The condition of the main invasion route presented the biggest problem. From Pietermaritzburg to Greytown the road climbed continuously through green fields of settler cultivation, and beyond Greytown it continued to climb, not steeply but almost endlessly. Then quite suddenly it descended into countryside so different that it was like passing in a moment from a land of plenty into a desert. The green of cultivation was replaced with tired dun-coloured soil, strewn with rocks and giant boulders, in which little grew except aloes and thorn trees. Aptly, it was a transit known as 'The Thorns', baking hot by day and cold at night. Continuing, the road clung to the sides of massive cliffs, in places perilously steep as it descended to the Mooi (Pretty) River, and the crossing at Keate's Drift. It then climbed steeply into the Biggarsberg only to descend again, in less than ten miles, to the Tugela itself and the crossing known as Tugela Ferry. Further along, going north-east, it followed the Tugela Valley, the border of Zululand, only twelve miles distant, before climbing again, affording the traveller panoramic views away to the east and north. Hereabouts, the Buffalo River replaced the Tugela as the Zulu boundary, closer now, across broken country, seven miles away. Between Lower Drift on the Indian Ocean and Rorke's Drift, there were no fewer than twenty-six named drifts across the river boundary between the Natal colony and the kingdom, each providing the possibility of an invasion route.

Nearing Helpmekaar the road passed close to Sand Spruit – where the NNC was being subjected to its inadequate training. Further on it passed M'singa where Francis Fynn's magistracy had been fortified in anticipation of Zulu attack. Finally, seventy miles from Greytown, the road reached Helpmekaar. It was along this rain-sodden highway of potholes, landslips, swollen rivers and precarious pontoons that No. 3 Column laboured its way, not in one gigantic convoy, but piecemeal, one company of infantry at a time, perhaps days ahead of the next, the soldiers heaving and pulling the heavy wagons, and putting in as much effort as the oxen themselves. There were troops of cavalry, their horses soaking wet, heads down and ears back in their dejection. Civilian transport riders also played a part, many of them Boers, dour, bearded men, seemingly impervious to the weather, muffled in capes and wide brimmed dripping hats. All were making their way to the ultimate discomfort of Helpmekaar.

———◆———

The NMP had been the first to arrive as early as November.◊ An advance party of seventy-four men had marched up from Estcourt, the untrained oxen with which they had been lumbered being unable to pull the wagons up the steeper slopes nor pull them through the many drifts encountered on the way. The men, attaching their picquet ropes to the wagons, laboured with the oxen, but frequently the best the convoy could achieve was eight miles a day. On reaching the hamlet of Dundee, the NMP found the impending war, and anticipated shortages, had already sent the price of food and liquor soaring: a half-pound tin of jam cost three shillings and a pint of beer two shillings and sixpence.

The commanding officer of the NMP, Major John Dartnell, age forty-one, was also the designated commander of all the mounted volunteer units accompanying No. 3 Column. Dartnell, born in Canada, was a talented and experienced soldier. Having joined the British Army at the age of seventeen, he had been commissioned into the 80th Regiment, later serving with distinction during the Indian Mutiny. Retiring from the army in 1869 he had settled in Natal and at the request of the Natal government had raised the NMP five years later. His second-in-command, Inspector George Mansel, also with a military background, had been with the force since its inception and, like Dartnell, had a distinguished career ahead of him.

The men of the NMP arrived at Helpmekaar in the dark, and had no option but to picquet their horses in the mud and rain, and were unable to feed them until 9.00 p.m. that night. The horses, disgusted with this treatment, on being turned out to graze the following morning, with their guard dismounted, decided to bolt back the way they had come. Sixty of the seventy-two mounts made good their escape and, wisely it would seem, split up to confuse their pursuers. It took weeks to recover them in various parts of the colony, the furthest escapees being finally captured over 100 miles away at Harrismith in the Orange Free State.

The Natal Carbineers had a more stylish send-off when they departed for the front. They were drawn up on parade in the market square at Pietermaritzburg where they were admired by the populace, inspected by Lord Chelmsford (who reiterated the promise of a farm in Zululand for every man who crossed the border),◊ and finally rode out of town in pouring rain, led by the band of the 1/24th playing 'Let Me Kiss Him For His Mother' and 'The Girl I Left Behind Me'. Unfortunately their supply wagon was hindered by the weather with the result that the carbineers went supperless to bed. On reaching Greytown they received a rousing reception and were again led out of town by the band of the 24th. Their passage through 'The Thorns' was made on one of the rare dry days and in 'overpowering heat'. On arriving at the Tugela River, the men were eager to plunge in for a swim.

One of the young troopers, Fred Symons, who kept an informative account of his experiences, and who came from settler farming stock – and was thus a man familiar with the ways of the wild – was amused by two of his 'townie' comrades who had gone upriver looking for clear water in which to bathe:

> 'but as the shadows fell, weird sounds (to the city ears) and the gloomy look of the place, filled them with terror and they hurried back and were fain to content themselves with the thick pea-soup of the River Tugela.'

The various companies of the 24th followed in due course. Some had arrived at Helpmekaar in November, but by later the following month much of the column was still at Greytown, or on its way through 'The Thorns' and the Tugela Valley. A day or so before Christmas, strong rumours came from a border agent claiming that the Zulu army was assembling on the other side of the river and causing Colonel Henry Degacher, commanding the 2/24th, to send four companies hurrying out of Greytown en route to the front.

At Helpmekaar the plateau was now covered by the tent lines of the various units and, according to Norris-Newman, the newly-erected iron and wooden storehouses already contained enough forage for a year's campaigning. However, Christmas at Helpmekaar was a dull affair with the rain continuing to pour remorselessly from a low grey sky hung with swirling mist. The NMP were worse off than most. As they were responsible for the payment and procurement of their own commissariat, they had ordered a wagon load of luxuries for Christmas dinner, only to have their vehicle swept away in the Mooi River taking six of the oxen with it to a watery grave.

Morale at Helpmekaar was given a boost on 4 January with the arrival of Lord Chelmsford, more men of the 24th, the IMI and later the six guns of N Battery, No. 5 Brigade, RA. Soon the Union flag was flying from its staff set in front of Chelmsford's tent.

On Sunday 5 January Chelmsford attended a church parade of all the mounted colonials and once again reminded every volunteer that a farm awaited those who crossed into Zululand. Trooper Clarke recalled that:

> 'He [Lord Chelmsford] complimented us on our appearance and said we should have hard work in Zululand where the enemy would outnumber us by more than 20 to 1, but that if we were victorious those men who wanted to settle in the country would be given the choice of farms.'

It is likely that the offer of free farms was a clandestine scheme agreed between Chelmsford and Sir Bartle Frere as it is doubtful that Sir Henry Bulwer would have been party to it and certainly the British government had no knowledge of the scheme.

The arrival of Lord Chelmsford at Helpmekaar caused 'unusual activity' throughout the camp and a general inspection was ordered.◊ His manner was affable to everyone, but he was a stickler for punctuality. The General 'set an example for all to follow by rising at dawn, shunning any form of luxury, and even assisting with the pitching of his own tent.' However, Colonel Glyn, as column commander, did not welcome the presence of Chelmsford and his staff.

As frequent reference will be made to various staff officers in the pages ahead, and in order to avoid confusion, the staffs of Chelmsford and Glyn are set out opposite.

Lord Chelmsford's staff

Assistant Military Secretary	*Lieutenant-Colonel John North Crealock, 95th Regiment*
	Crealock had previously served in India and in the Eastern Cape. Self-opinionated and described by Bulwer as a waspish military man and not pleasant to deal with. A talented water-colour artist.
Aides-de-camp	*Major Matthew Gosset, 54th Regiment*
	Self-opinionated and haughty.
	Captain Ernest Henry Buller, Rifle Brigade
	Not to be confused with Lt-Col Redvers Buller.
	Lieutenant Berkeley Milne, RN
	Attached to Chelmsford's staff as a courtesy to the Naval Brigade
Civilian aides	*Henry Francis Fynn, political*
	William Drummond, intelligence
	Henry William Longcast, interpreter and guide

Colonel Glyn's staff

Principal Staff Officer	*Major Cornelius Francis Clery, 32nd Regiment*
	Formerly an instructor in tactics at Camberley Military Staff College, Clery had been involved in the Sekhukhune Campaign of 1878. Vindictive and a gossip.
Aides-de-camp	*Captain Alan Gardner, 14th Hussars*
	A varied career as a cavalry and artillery officer. Also served in the Intelligence department and had successfully passed Staff College.
	Captain Henry Hallam Parr, 13th Light Infantry
	Hallam Parr had been ADC to Sir Bartle Frere who had recently released Parr from duty in order that he might take part in the campaign.
Orderly Officer	*Lieutenant Nevill Josiah Coghill, 1/24th Regiment*
Civilian	*J.A. Brickhill, interpreter*

In the weeks following the defeat that would shortly befall No. 3 Column, it would become a matter of great controversy as to who had been responsible for the catastrophe, the column commander or the general? Glyn was already resentful that his role had been usurped, and Chelmsford seemed either oblivious or indifferent to Glyn's piqued frustration, keeping him and his staff uninformed of what was planned or intended. Instead of initiating the column's invasion of Zululand, Glyn and his staff found themselves supervising the placing of the camp guards and ensuring that the camp was clean.◊

Both Clery, Glyn's principal staff officer, and Crealock, Chelmsford's military secretary, had an entrée to correspond with Major-General Sir Archibald Alison⁰ (and also with his wife, Lady Jane) who was responsible for intelligence at the War Office. The private letters of both Clery and Crealock were often disparaging when commenting on their peers, or those senior in rank. Several other officers who served in Zululand had the same facility of direct and secret contact with Alison who would undoubtedly have shown selected correspondence to the Duke of Cambridge, the Commander-in-Chief. For instance Crealock wrote to Alison from Helpmekaar thanking Alison for his assistance in his appointment as Chelmsford's military secretary. Later he went on to deride Glyn, the column commander, writing:

> 'Clery is out here with Colonel Glyn and high time too; do not expect anything from the latter. He is purely a regimental officer with no idea beyond it.'

And Clery writing later, laying the blame for Isandlwana, reported that:

> 'Crealock acted as adjutant-general to the General, and all patrols, reconnaissances, etc, were detailed by the General himself.'

One is left wondering whether or not the intelligence department had in fact recruited these gentlemen for the specific purpose of reporting on their fellow officers.

Amongst the orders that were issued by Crealock and his staff immediately on arrival at Helpmekaar was a directive that brought about unexpected consequences. Apart from the IMI, the remainder of Chelmsford's cavalry, including the NMP, were colonials who had volunteered to cross into Zululand under certain conditions which included such considerations as their rate of pay and their acceptance of the officer who would command them. In other words they had a contract, and any enforced changes to its terms could result in the volunteers withdrawing their commitment. Major Dartnell, who by then could also have been regarded as a colonial, had been accepted by all the volunteers as their commander. However, Chelmsford had a friend, a special service officer and former ADC to the Prince of Wales, Captain John Cecil Russell of the 12th Lancers. Russell had seen service in the Ashanti War under Wolseley in 1873, and now Chelmsford unwisely decided to promote him to the rank of brevet-major and to give him command of the volunteers over the head of Dartnell.

Months earlier, when Russell had newly arrived from England, resentment had been caused by his superseding Lieutenant Edward Browne of the 1/24th as commander of the IMI, Browne having led the unit almost since its inception. While the IMI could do nothing about that then, now the colonials could react and did. The Biggarsberg correspondent of a Natal newspaper (almost certainly Norris-Newman) reported that as soon as Captain Theophilus ('Offy') Shepstone, son of Sir Theophilus ('the most powerful family in Natal') commanding the Natal Carbineers, heard of the order on 5 January, he rode to the volunteer camp, now located some distance from Helpmekaar on the way to Rorke's Drift, where he ordered the call 'fall in' to be passed from tent to tent. Once they were assembled, Shepstone wheeled the men around him and read Chelmsford's directive and asked the volunteers for their comments. The Biggarsberg correspondent reported:

> 'Can you wonder that the volunteers stood amazed... for a short time there was complete silence. Shepstone spoke again "Now is your time to speak... once you enter under the command of Captain Russell, no murmurings or complaints of any kind must be heard or made... Do you accept Captain Russell as your commander or no?" They answered in one accord, "No" ...and Shepstone rode away to impart the news to Dartnell and Chelmsford.'[◊]

Mutiny? If it was, it was permitted in terms of the volunteers' contract, and Chelmsford was now faced with a situation as unlikely as ever confronted a British general commanding British troops. He could not lose face by countermanding his order, so he proposed Dartnell's promotion to his staff as cavalry adviser. Dartnell accepted the unexpected elevation, asked the volunteers to serve under Russell, and the crisis was over. Russell's ascendancy would continue but not for long; Chelmsford shortly promoted Russell again, to the acting rank of lieutenant-colonel, but due to his questionable behaviour when confronting the enemy, Russell would, within a few months, be relegated to the rank of major and put in charge of a remount depot at Pietermaritzburg.

—————⊷•⊶—————

During the first week of January the troops began moving down into the valley of the Buffalo River to the crossing at Rorke's Drift. The volunteers were the first to go, making a temporary camp at a lonely settler homestead situated on a terrace of the Biggarsberg. The spot offered a splendid prospect of the river below and the Zulu country beyond. Keen eyed volunteers noticed that every time a body of troops moved down the escarpment, smoke signals were emitted from a nearby village. On investigation it was found that the occupants were men of the notorious Chief Sihayo, whose sons' conduct the year before had provided Sir Bartle Frere with an excuse for making war. Soon the first Zulu prisoners-of-war were taken into custody.

There was an air of gaiety abroad in the ranks of No. 3 Column. At last they were leaving boring and detestable Helpmekaar. (Yet, within the month, to many of the men present, Helpmekaar would become a haven – albeit a haven rife with fear, disease and privation, where heroes who had by some miracle survived Isandlwana would die of fever, diarrhoea and neglect.[◊]) It was going to be a great adventure. If only the rain would stop it would be perfect. There had been inter-unit cricket matches; the men of the 24th had been taken for a run each morning; the carbineers' mounted drill now surpassed that of the NMP – so the carbineers said; and the imperial officers speculated on their chances of advancement and glory. One correspondent predicted that a 'large concourse' of tourists would arrive to witness the battle between the redcoats and the Zulus which would immediately follow the crossing of the river, and the *Natal Mercury* predicted that the Zulus would never stand the fire of regular troops. Chelmsford himself being:

> 'inclined to think that we may possibly induce him [Cetshwayo] to attack us, which will save a great deal of trouble.'

However, a feeling of gloom spread throughout the camp with the death of Trooper Arthur Dixon of the NMR, the first British casualty. The Buffalo River, when not in spate, had become a great attraction for bathers in the sullen heat and humidity that followed days of rain. Dixon, who could not swim, missed his footing on the treacherous river bottom, stepped out of his depth and drowned.

One evening the officers of the 1/24th invited those of the 2nd Battalion to join them for dinner and to drink the last few bottles of wine remaining in their mess. During the course of the evening it was remembered that the date was close to the thirtieth anniversary of the Battle of Chillianwalla, a particularly disastrous engagement of the Second Sikh War of 1848–49 where, badly led and in confusing terrain, the men of the 1/24th had emerged from the jungle to find themselves facing Sikh cannon and entrenched infantry. The battalion had been immediately ordered to charge with the bayonet, which it did most gallantly, and was all but annihilated, losing 21 officers and 503 other ranks dead and wounded. Now, Captain William Degacher, the senior officer present of the 1/24th, proposed a toast, 'that we may not get into such a mess, and have better luck this time.' It was a toast that challenged fate, for all the officers of the 1st Battalion that drank it were dead before the month's end.

On 9 January Lord Chelmsford moved down to Rorke's Drift where he inspected the property of the Swedish Mission, once the home and trading store of James Rorke. Immediately behind the buildings, between the mission and the river, rose the hump of Shiyane ('eyebrow') Hill, so called by the Zulu because of its arched shape. Otto Witt, the Swedish missionary in charge, had recently renamed the hill Oskarberg in honour of his king. Chelmsford entered into negotiation with Witt to acquire the buildings, which he intended to put to use as a hospital and commissariat store. Despite the threat of war, Witt and his young family were still in residence, and Witt knew how to haggle, demanding £14 per month for the lease of the house alone. Chelmsford, a man of thrift, could also haggle and, threatening expropriation, finally got Witt to agree to £14 a month for all the buildings including the use of the ferryboat. Nevertheless, it was not a bad deal for Witt, considering that since 1860, and until his death in 1875, Rorke had been paying a quit rent of only £3 3s 5d (£3.17) per annum for the 3,000-acre property.◊ The lease, granted by the Natal government, was still in effect with Witt continuing to pay the same low annual rental. The lease required the tenant to be in occupation for at least half the year and that travellers be permitted to outspan (rest draft animals) on the property for twenty-four hours without charge. There were further conditions, none of which were unreasonable, except perhaps, that no one being of 'any barbarous tribe' be allowed to occupy the land. Witt had purchased the lease on behalf of the Swedish Mission for £1,800. Alas for Witt, before a contract could be signed with Chelmsford, the mission station was a smouldering ruin.

Chelmsford's original intention for No. 3 Column – most likely before he had decided to accompany it – was that the column would cross the Buffalo at Rorke's Drift. Chelmsford believed it to be the same crossing that the Boers had used in their pursuit of King Dingane forty years earlier. In December 1878, Chelmsford had written to Wood:

> 'I find on reading Chase's History of Natal, that in 1838 Andries Pretorius, with a commando of 400 men, took only six days to march from Rorke's Drift to the hill where Retief and his party were massacred [twelve miles from Ulundi]. They entered Zululand on 13 December during the rainy season… the road Pretorius took is the same as Glyn's column will move along.'

Chelmsford then went on to say that he had spoken to an ancient Boer who had actually accompanied Pretorius, and who confirmed that the proposed route was 'hard and open all the way until it reached the White Mfolozi River.'

However, Chelmsford had misread, or misunderstood, Chase's account as Pretorius had entered Zululand by crossing the Buffalo and Blood Rivers some distance above present day Dundee, over twenty miles further upstream from Rorke's Drift. It seems that Chelmsford never realised his error and was still under the impression that the column, once across the Buffalo River at Rorke's Drift, would soon be bowling along over firm going and would likely be at Ulundi within a week. However, it would take six months, rather than six days for Chelmsford and an army to reach the Zulu capital.

Francis Fynn, who now accompanied Chelmsford, had received crucial and reliable information from his spies, and later wrote:

> 'It was planned for this column to proceed northwards to central Zululand. In such case however, I pointed out the Zulu plan [which his

spies had reported] to descend the Mange [Mangeni] Valley of the Nhlazakazi [Hlazakazi] Mountain and there shelter until they [No. 3 Column] had moved forward sufficiently to enable the Zulu army to creep round from the Mange Valley, up the Buffalo River, and so cut off the column in the rear and close in upon them.'◊

In other words, Fynn believed that the Zulu intended to get behind the British column and to attack it from the rear. It may well be that it was only because Chelmsford acted on Fynn's advice that No. 3 Column was headed towards Isandlwana – otherwise it would have turned north, following the left bank of the Buffalo, until it eventually got onto Pretorius's old road somewhere near present day Nqutu.

By 8 January a pontoon had arrived, brought up in sections from Durban, and a unit of Royal Engineers had commenced its assembly ready for launching. The same afternoon there was a moment of excitement when several horsemen were seen approaching along the Zulu bank. They turned out to be an adventurous scouting party from Wood's column: Captain Robert Barton of the Coldstream Guards and Baron von Steitencron, a soldier of fortune, with a small escort of four men of the Frontier Light Horse (FLH). They had ridden thirty miles through Zululand that day, receiving hospitality and gathering information from the local population, hardly the warlike reception that had been expected from the Zulu people! Nevertheless, it was considered dangerous for the horsemen to return at so late an hour and so they stayed the night, arriving back safely at Wood's camp the following day.

———❖———

At 2.00 a.m. on 11 January, as the terms of the ultimatum had threatened, British troops commenced the invasion of Zululand. Reveille was sounded throughout the various camps of No. 3 Column and, in darkness and heavy drizzle, the great concourse of men, animals and wagons began to converge on the river. The artillery deployed on rising ground, commanding the opposite bank, to protect the *pont* and drift.

Captain Mainwaring of the 2/24th, who had been detailed for outpost duty that night and was some distance from the camp, later recalled how some of his weary men had tried to sleep lying in pools of water, and how he had kicked them up, telling them they would be crippled with rheumatism by morning if they did not move.◊ In the early hours there was a false alarm that sent the whole column scurrying to action stations. Some of the sentries taking over from Mainwaring's company, peering through the drizzle and mist, believed that they saw Zulus on the opposite bank and commenced shouting, 'there are four of the enemy on the right!' As this warning was passed by sentry to sentry down the line, it somehow changed to, 'enemy in force on the right!' The company cook who was about to return to the main camp with empty coffee pails, was ordered to double to headquarters and raise the alarm with the message, 'Mr Mainwaring says the enemy in force on the right!' which prompted the whole camp to fall in at battle stations, including Lord Chelmsford and his staff, and which caused Mainwaring to get into 'no end of trouble'.

The cavalry were the first to cross, but before entering the river they deposited their carbines and haversacks on the pontoon to give their weapons and kit a dry crossing, the infantry and guns covering the cavalry's unarmed landing on the opposite bank. Almost simultaneously, the 3rd Battalion NNC plunged into the swirling river, neck deep in places and running at about six knots. Twenty-seven-year-old Lieutenant Henry Harford of the 99th Regiment, a special service officer attached to the NNC, led the way on his pony with the river lapping the top of his saddle. Harford was unusually accomplished in that, having spent all his teenage years in Natal, he could speak the Zulu language with some fluency. He later described how the NNC had linked arms and formed two human chains across the river, allowing their comrades to wade safely through the human corridor, whilst all the while the entire battalion uttered a weird, high pitched humming sound, similar to a swarm of furious bees, that not only kept up morale, but was designed to put fear into potential enemies – including any loitering crocodiles.

The sound was a typically Zulu one – a battle cry in fact – for the men of the NNC were as Zulu as the men they had come to fight. Indeed, serving with the NNC and acting as advisors on Glyn's staff, were two of Cetshwayo's half brothers: Mthonga kaMpande who, it will be remembered, had escaped assassination and had fled Zululand in 1861, and Sikhota kaMpande of the *iZigqoza*.

The men of the 24th were detailed to cross on the pontoons but not before a search of their water bottles had been made for concealed grog; in the pre-dawn the 24th had looted the tent of a camp-following liquor tout, stealing all his wares. The tout was thrown out of camp and the grog raiders, with so many other distractions to concern their officers, went unapprehended into Zululand.◊

Once over the river, the cavalry rode out to reconnoitre, carbines at the ready, whilst the infantry and NNC deployed skirmishers as far as two miles distant from the drift. The remainder of the 24th formed into squares, guarding their regimental bands and colours, in the traditional formation taken up by infantry when threatened by cavalry. Then came the tedious task of ferrying the laden wagons over, one at a time. Finally at three o'clock in the afternoon the rearguard and the artillery crossed; No 3 Column had made it into Zululand without a shot having been fired.

It had been anticipated that the Zulu army would pounce on the column when it crossed the Buffalo. The Biggarsberg correspondent had earlier told his readers that the crossing, 'would be disputed by the Zulus and the first battle would be fought there.' He now wrote: 'Crossing the river at this point, without any resistance, is a moral victory as if a battle had been fought and won.'

Back in Durban, a local editor, referring to the successful crossing of the Tugela by No. 1 Column, imperiously thundered:

> 'I have seen... the red and blue uniforms of men who have gathered... to vindicate the just cause of an offended civilisation, and to assert the outraged authority of the British Crown; I have seen the climax of a policy which must end in the undisputed supremacy of British rule over all the native tribes that live south of the Limpopo.'◊

In No. 3 Column there were feelings of euphoria that they were at last in enemy territory, and disappointment that there had been no resistance. The open plain before them would have made an ideal battle ground and although no battle was fought, the plain is still known today as *Masotsheni*, 'The Place of the Soldiers'.

When half the column had yet to cross the river, Chelmsford, assertive and full of vigour, had ridden north, accompanied by his staff and a strong mounted escort, eventually meeting up with Colonel Wood of No. 4 Column at a rendezvous between Bemba's Kop and Rorke's Drift. Whilst the commanders conferred, Chelmsford's mounted men had off-saddled and rested. At that time, the column commanders were supposedly under orders to act within the bounds of Frere's pretence that the war was not aimed at the Zulu people, but at their tyrannical king alone. However, this did not deter Chelmsford from offering Wood, in the name of the High Commissioner, and in anticipation of conquest, the political office of Resident of Zululand, which offer Wood refused.

Nor did Frere's pretence deter Wood's escort of the FLH. Rather than off-saddle and rest, they spent the time profitably scouring the countryside for any cattle that could be 'lifted' from the local population. Cattle were the common currency of Zululand – indeed much commerce was transacted throughout southern Africa using cattle as cash – and within a few days of Wood's column crossing into Zululand, his horsemen had captured over 7,000 beasts, with 2,500 of them being sent for sale to the Orange Free State.

The disposal of captured cattle seems to have been both devious and dubious. In his *Field Force Regulations*, Chelmsford had set out a scale for the distribution of prize money (paragraph 145 'Cattle and Other Prize') but many of the troopers complained of the unequal distribution – or complete absence – of prize money, asserting that the cattle they had captured were sold to the prize agents (often butchers), at 30 shillings (£1.50) a head, who in turn resold them to the column's supply contractors at £8 per head and that they who had done the capturing, 'did not get a sovereign as their share [of the booty] at the end of the campaign.'

Chelmsford conferred with Wood for two hours and then made his way back to Rorke's Drift, his flankers of the NMP skirmishing ahead and, taking an example from the FLH, visiting several Zulu homesteads on the way to seize 300 head of cattle:

'Lord Chelmsford explaining to the people that he was making war against Cetshwayo and that the Zulu who joined the British would receive back their cattle and weapons.'

Prior to crossing the Buffalo, Chelmsford had been genuinely concerned that the local people should be treated well by his invading columns, and had included in his *Regulations* instructions not only on the manner to be adopted by his white troops in their handling of the NNC, but also the manner in which all his troops, both white and black, must behave towards the Zulus themselves. Paragraph 9 of 'General Regulations, under the heading 'Treatment of the Natives', stipulated:

'Natives will be treated with kindness. Commanding officers will exert their influence with all ranks to prevent their being in any way molested or oppressed.'

There can be doubt that initially Chelmsford intended to see that his compassionate orders were obeyed, as two weeks prior to the invasion he issued a further memorandum:

'Officers commanding columns are requested to have it clearly explained to the native portion of the force under their command that any native convicted of wilfully killing a woman or child or a wounded man, will render himself liable to be hanged. No huts in Zululand are to be burnt except under the special orders of the officer commanding the column. Any soldier, European or native, transgressing this order will render himself liable to a flogging.'

However, once into Zululand, these high flown ideals were soon disregarded; not only was the looting of thousands of cattle condoned, but Chelmsford himself decided to attack forthwith a Zulu village close to Rorke's Drift. From Chelmsford's point of view there was good reason for doing so, for it was Sokexe, the stronghold of Sihayo, and if anyone should be set an example it was he and his sons. Chelmsford wasted no time. By 3.30 a.m. on the 12th, he was ready to direct an attack against Sihayo, whose rocky habitat formed part of the Nqutu range and dominated the landscape four miles east of Rorke's Drift. It was a good British showing: a hundred horsemen each of the IMI and NMP, with detachments of all the other mounted units; and for infantry the 1/3rd NNC plus four companies of the 1/24th; the whole nominally under the command of Colonel Glyn, the column commander. There was also a reserve force of NNC and 2/24th, in total some 300 cavalry and 1,800 footmen.

Sihayo's homestead Sokexe, a natural, flat-topped fortress, rose over 1,000 feet from the valley floor. Its approaches were boulder-strewn, steep and seemingly impregnable – which they might well have been, if defended by adequate numbers – but most of the fighting men of Sihayo's clan, including Sihayo himself and most of his sons, had already departed to join the king at Ulundi.

The British force, advancing in skirmishing order, was halted whilst Chelmsford and Glyn determined their plan of attack. After a lengthy pause, the cavalry, under Russell's command, were ordered forward, the IMI to the left, and the colonials to the right where it appeared possible to gain the table-top heights, and so cut off any enemy attempting to escape to the east. The main attack was to be delivered to the centre of a cleft-shaped ravine, which seemed to lead to the heart of the labyrinth, by the 1/3rd NNC led by colonial Commandant 'Maori' Hamilton-Browne. He was a man who had knocked about the world, attracted by the trouble spots of the Empire, and who would with alacrity, and for little cause, knock about the natives he commanded. The commander of the 3rd Regiment NNC, Commandant Rupert Lonsdale, from the Eastern Cape, was not present. Having taken a bad fall from his pony several days before, he was suffering from concussion and still confined to the hospital at Helpmekaar. Major Wilsone Black of the 2/24th, seconded to the NNC for the day, had taken his place.

Before the British force made its final advance Chelmsford reiterated that no women or children were to be harmed. Then, as the troops moved forward, the eerie sound of Zulu chanting and singing could be heard echoing around the rocky walls ahead, whilst the silhouettes of warriors, stark against the skyline of the bright African morning, could be seen taking up position amongst the boulders. Suddenly the chanting ceased and a deep Zulu voice called a challenge, asking by whose orders the white *impi* had come?◊ Hamilton-Browne's interpreter, Captain Dunscombe, immediately shouted 'By orders of the Great White Queen!' which, whilst a stirring reply, was completely untrue as neither Queen Victoria nor the British government had any knowledge of what was taking place.

For the few defenders high above the plain, it must have been an awesome sight: horsemen galloping to the left and right, whilst the NNC, 1,200 strong, each man distinguished by a red headband, jogged forward, supported by scarlet-coated white soldiers.

As Dunscombe's reply carried to the stronghold, its defenders opened fire with a variety of ancient weapons, mainly old British Tower pattern muskets, scoring a few casualties as Hamilton-Browne's NNC entered the bush- and rock-strewn clefts. Then it was a mad dash forward with shots from unseen marksmen whistling through the air. Hamilton-Browne related that when his charge stopped for a moment, only his No. 8 Company was still close behind him, the majority of the battalion having gone to ground amongst the boulders further back whilst his officers vainly endeavoured to get the men to face the enemy fire – not a good start for the NNC. The only company that had performed well was comprised of the young warrior-refugees from the Zulu army who had fled to Natal after the bloody fight that had taken place during the First Fruits ceremony of the previous year.

Further on, Harford, the Zulu speaking imperial officer, had recklessly, but gallantly, stormed a cave not only single-handed but also empty-handed for in the excitement of trying to reload his jammed revolver, he had cast it from him down a cliff. Thereafter, like some present day negotiator in a siege situation, he had cajoled the defenders to surrender, and then, triumphantly, led his captives down to the valley where, now in the presence of an admiring Lord Chelmsford, he had handed them over as prisoners-of-war.

Finally, Hamilton-Browne's men, in a series of rushes, reached the Zulu marksmen and after a brief but fierce hand-to-hand engagement, all resistance was overcome. Some of the warriors, led by one of Sihayo's sons, escaped up to the tableland, where they joined the remaining defenders, who had been keeping pace with the carbineers and NMP. As the horsemen rode up the valley, the warriors jeered and taunted them with all the dramatic talent with which the Zulu nation is gifted.

Close to the top, Russell ordered four of the carbineers to ride forward in order to 'draw the enemy's fire' and obtain some idea of their number. This was the first time that the young volunteers had been in action, yet they rode forward without hesitation despite 'cumbros' missiles flying overhead.◊ Then the line of mounted men, with Dartnell somewhere in their midst, advanced in skirmishing order and opened fire all along the line at anything that might conceal a Zulu, 'a frightful waste of ammunition' as Trooper Fred Symons was to recall. Yet it was enough for the defenders, who quietly made their escape. The drama was not quite over; one group of carbineers was suddenly faced with forty armed warriors charging towards them and the order was given to fix bayonets. As the first volley was about to be delivered the charging 'foe' threw up their hands shouting for the carbineers to hold their fire. It was a group of disorientated NNC who, believing they might encounter the enemy at any moment, had prudently, but dishonourably, removed their red head bands, thus to all appearances becoming Zulus themselves.

The battle was over and the reserve force of NNC and 2/24th, coming forward to complete any mopping up that might be necessary, found further on along the hill top a fortress-like building with loop-holed walls. It had been abandoned but within its defences there was found, 'a wagon belonging to a European with all the implements for repairing guns of every description.'

Over thirty Zulus had been killed, several wounded and a number of prisoners taken – all old people or children – against which two men of the NNC had been killed and twenty wounded. It was a British success. In fact it had been a walk over. Fynn, who had predicted a stiff fight once across the river, was 'twitted upon' by the imperial officers. That Sihayo's stronghold had been held by only a handful of warriors was, in the flush of victory, overlooked. Finally, all Sihayo's huts were put to the torch. Later the same day Chelmsford wrote to Sir Bartle Frere:

'I am in great hopes that the news of the storming of Sirayo's [*sic*] stronghold and the capture of so many of his cattle [about five hundred] may have a salutary effect in Zululand and either bring down a large force to attack us or else produce a revolution in the country.'

Thus the British, already rashly over-confident, became even more scornful of the Zulu. The military virtues of prudence and vigilance were soon to be exchanged for negligence and folly.

———→-0-←———

Fifty miles due east from Sihayo's homestead thousands upon thousands of warriors had been assembling for many days past. By this time Cetshwayo had begun to despair of a negotiated settlement and had accepted that the British had every intention of carrying out their threat of invasion unless he complied with their demands to the letter – and that was impossible – so he set about assembling the Zulu army. As it happened, this was a relatively simple matter as the approach of the full moon heralded, as it did every year at that time, the First Fruits ceremony when all warriors throughout the kingdom were duty bound to report to their respective regimental barracks at Nodwengu, on the Mahlabathini plain, a short distance from the royal residence at Ondini (adjacent to Ulundi).

Cetshwayo and his councillors, through numerous spies in Natal and observers located along the Tugela and Buffalo Rivers, were well aware of the strength and disposition of the British columns. The days following the ultimatum had been a time of great stress for Cetshwayo; the threat of war had caused division within his inner council, and throughout the Zulu nation. There were those who would hand over the sons of Sihayo – and Sihayo himself if necessary.◊ Some declared that, even though Sihayo was a great favourite of the king, he was, in fact, not a true Zulu and therefore not worth the catastrophe that threatened; they would also have the fines in cattle paid in the belief that the two submissions would satisfy the British.

At about this time, John Dunn, although now safe in Natal and collaborating in the invasion of his former friend's kingdom, declared in an interview with the *Cape Argus*, that it was not possible that Cetshwayo could comprehend what was being demanded of him:

> 'Dunn states that Cetywayo [*sic*] does not, even now, know fully the contents of the ultimatum... the document was read over once [to the delegates at the Tugela] and its length was such that the messengers could not possibly fix the whole in their memory.'◊

Dunn went on to say that the copy of the ultimatum that he had undertaken to deliver to the king had been passed over to messengers whilst he, fearing for his life, departed for Natal. Dunn further confided that an angry and accusatory message from Cetshwayo had later been delivered to him in which the king declared that he had been deceived:

> 'The English had thrown the bullock's skin over his head whilst they had been devouring the titbits of the carcass.'

Dunn, remorseful it seems that he should have taken up arms against Cetshwayo, then attempted to vindicate the king by challenging the tyrannical image that Frere and others had created for him: The *Cape Argus* went on to quote:

'Dunn makes this apology for Cetshwayo: "that he is not by any means so black as he is painted... Compared with Chaka and Dingaan, he is a prince of humanity... " Dunn has a very high notion of the king's natural sagacity.'

This all amounted to a nice gesture by Dunn, but it was too late to be of any use.

The royal messengers that Cetshwayo had sent into Natal in an endeavour to clarify what was required of him – and also to plead for more time to assemble the cattle fine – were treated with indifference. Bulwer informed the final royal messenger, coming by way of Lower Drift, that henceforth any negotiations should first be proceeded by Cetshwayo's unconditional acceptance of all the terms contained in the ultimatum, and thereafter be conducted direct with Lord Chelmsford who was, of course, many miles away.

Yet, for days after the invasion had commenced, Cetshwayo clung to the hope that there still might be an opportunity to negotiate and was at pains not to provoke war, going so far as to give orders that those of his men guarding the drifts were not to attack an invading force as, unbeknown to them, last minute negotiations might be in progress. This may explain the Zulu lack of resistance at the crossing of No. 3 Column and Chelmsford's unmolested ride through Zululand on the day he conferred with Wood. But there were to be no last minute negotiations and Cetshwayo, reluctantly accepting that war with the British seemed inevitable, sent orders to his assembling warriors that their regalia should be left at home.

If many of his councillors had resisted the thought of war, there was no such notion amongst his *amabutho*. Fired by rumours currently rife in Zululand that the British would ship all the young men to England as slaves, and force all Zulu girls to marry red soldiers, the warriors, boastful, vain and impatient to display their courage, were particularly eager to get to grips with the invaders – as equally eager to fight as the cocksure British soldiers who, fifty miles away, were already marching towards Isandlwana.

Ritual preparations for war had been performed; a maddened black bull had been killed; mock battles between the regiments had been fought, and in addition – and unlike other years – the whole army had marched fifteen miles west to the emaKhosini Valley, the sacred burial place of the Zulu kings. There, in the presence of Cetshwayo, the war doctors had beseeched the ancestral spirits to accompany the army into battle and to give blessing to the enterprise of war. All night the warriors had prayed or slept in the moonlit valley of the dead, whilst the war doctors continued to entreat the shades by the ceremonial slaughter of cattle. At some time in the pre-dawn, by way of a ghostly bovine lowing, the ancestors spoke their approval.◊

Only the ritual of doctoring the army remained.◊ The wizards of the Basuto, the nation that inhabited the bleak and windswept summit of the Drakensberg mountains, were known to possess powers that could render harmless the spears and bullets of an enemy. But such magical formulae had to be ritually applied; the whole army would need to be 'doctored' before it marched.

Two such men of magic were at hand, having made haste from their high homeland in response to Cetshwayo's summons. Yet many warriors would in addition have taken their own precautions to enhance their chances of success and survival;◊ it was well known that hedgehog skin, cut into round pieces and attached to a leather thong worn around the head, would both confound an enemy and protect the wearer. It was also wise to carry a small pouch of amabophe roots (a red coloured climbing plant) to chew when going into battle; spitting the juice at an enemy would undoubtedly cause him to blunder. Furthermore, it was risky to consume the flesh of birds or fish for both flinched and fled at danger, and to eat them – or the wild potato whose leaves trembled in the slightest wind – might well bring similar cowardly manifestations upon the consumer. However, these were precautions and taboos of a minor nature. The forthcoming ceremonies of doctoring and cleansing by the war doctors were the rituals that would ensure victory for the nation.

It had been the warriors' task to collect many of the ingredients that comprised the war doctors' magical brew:◊ herbs; roots; the body dirt of the nation scraped from any object, such as a gateway, fence or seat that, due to constant contact with human skin, had built up a patina of human grease and dirt; the flesh of brave animals such as the lion and buffalo; scrapings of dried blood from a hunting spear; and, best of all, certain body parts of an enemy. During the course of the war that was to follow, body parts from many British soldiers would be carried away to provide powerful *muti* (medicine) for future doctoring.

During the early morning of the final day, the regiments were called upon to perform *hlanza* (vomit), to cleanse the inner body.◊ Vomit pits, six feet deep, had been dug earlier at the direction of the war doctors who now brought to the boil a steaming concoction made from ingredients gathered previously. As the regiments filed past the pot, each man was ladled a mouthful of the emetic brew, causing a spontaneous eruption into the vomit pit. Many young warriors, disregarding the dire penalties for heresy, rather than taste the contents of the cauldron, pretended to sip and vomit, but the war doctors, wise to such pretence, beat the offenders with sticks until a good mouthful was gulped down and a genuine contribution made to the contents of the pits. Once the ritual had been performed, the pits were covered lest an enemy obtain a portion of the contents and with it work counter-magic against the Zulu nation. Inner cleanliness achieved, the warriors went to bathe to ensure that their outer bodies were likewise pristine.

It was then time for the climax. The carcass of the great black bull, having been roasted and cut into tiny pieces, was doctored with secret powder. The warriors then formed into a massive semi circle and began to shuffle past their *induna*s and, as they went, the war doctors flung morsels of the bull's meat amongst them. These they caught, sucked, and tossed on to their comrades who, likewise, sucked and passed the morsels on. If a piece fell to the ground, there it was left. Finally there was the sprinkling of the army. The warriors, accoutred and armed, assembled in their regiments then passed before the war doctors who stood beside large cauldrons of the strongest mystic substance, and with tails cut from the wildebeest, flipped and sprinkled the shuffling throng with an indemnity from harm. The Zulu army was now ready to march. It was the 17th day of January 1879.

Chapter 5

The Armies Converge

'We are about to capture all the cattle belonging to the
Zulus and also burn all their kraals.'

Private Owen Ellis, 1/24th Regiment

'March slowly, attack at dawn and eat up the red soldiers.'

King Cetshwayo's instructions to his army

No. 3 Column, after successfully crossing the Buffalo, had made little
progress into Zululand. Shortly after Chelmsford had returned from his
meeting with Wood, Colonel Durnford arrived at Rorke's Drift having ridden
in from Kranskop, a distance of over ninety miles. Presumably he had been
bidden by Chelmsford who, knowing that it was his intention to confer with
Wood that day, would also wish to meet with the commander of his No. 2
Column.

Durnford reported that all was quiet along his section of the frontier, a
statement that might have prompted Chelmsford to consider a new plan of
action. Despite having yet to score his victory at Sihayo's stronghold,
Chelmsford had determined – due to the absence of Zulu opposition – to
occupy a corridor of enemy territory on the Zulu side of the Buffalo and
Tugela Rivers, which would form a buffer against any possible Zulu counter-
invasion of Natal. To implement this plan he had decided to break No. 2
Column into three units: one battalion of the NNC was to remain at
Kranskop, poised to cross into Zululand via Middle Drift; the other two
battalions were to move to M'singa from whence they could ford the Buffalo
at a place called the Gates of Natal, whilst Durnford, accompanied by all his
mounted men, a mule-carried rocket battery and a company of NNC, was to
make his way to Rorke's Drift, there to await orders. Pearson's No. 1
Column, close on 4,500 strong, advancing along the coast, was to strike
inland to Eshowe while No. 3 Column proceeded on towards the Zulu
capital, assisting Durnford and Pearson as required *(see Map 1, page 18)*.

On 16 January Chelmsford expounded his new plan of campaign in a memorandum to Sir Bartle Frere. He began by pointing out that a rapid advance into Zululand at that time of the year was:

> 'absolutely impossible: the present condition of the roads in Natal will be sufficient to bring home to the mind of everyone what difficulties must stand in the way of those who are endeavouring to move forward into enemy country, over tracks which have never been traversed except by very few traders' wagons... No. 3 Column... cannot possibly move forward even eight miles until two swamps, into which our wagons sink up to the body, have been made passable.'◊

He went on to explain that, without attempting to push forward faster than his means would allow, he intended to subjugate all the territory between the Buffalo, Tugela and Mhlatuze Rivers. He planned that No. 1 Column, having reached and occupied Eshowe, would then clear the Nkandla Forest, a thickly wooded land of hills and gorges, covering hundreds of square miles. The single NNC battalion at Kranskop would descend into even more inhospitable country that Chelmsford had previously described as being:

> 'so rugged and broken on the Zulu side as would entail a very great exertion, which, combined with the heat, would inevitably knock off young soldiers – the difficulties of transport and hospital arrangements would be very great.'

No less difficult a place in which to operate was the Qudeni Forest, where the remaining two NNC battalions of No. 2 Column were to search. As mentioned, they were to ford the Buffalo at the so-called Gates of Natal. It was a name so inappropriate that perhaps it was wrongly recorded. A more likely name would have been the 'Gates of Hell', as anyone looking down at the river, as it twisted its way through a wilderness of rock-strewn razor-backed ridges, cut with defiles and gorges, would have been aghast at the prospect of entering there.

Thus the central thrust of Chelmsford's operation was to be borne by the three battalions of Durnford's column, consisting of, at the most, 3,000 untrained, poorly armed and badly led men of the NNC. The odds were, that on crossing into Zulu territory, they would never be seen again.

Chelmsford, wrongly believing that many Zulu chiefs would submit as he made his advance, confided to Frere:

> 'These combined moves will, I hope, have the effect of removing any dangerously large body [of Zulus] from the Natal border... From a military point of view, I am convinced that it is the only practical one at this time of the year... We shall oblige Cetshwayo to keep his army mobilised, and it is certain that his troops will have difficulty in finding food. If kept inactive, they will become dangerous to himself; if ordered to attack us he will be playing our game.'

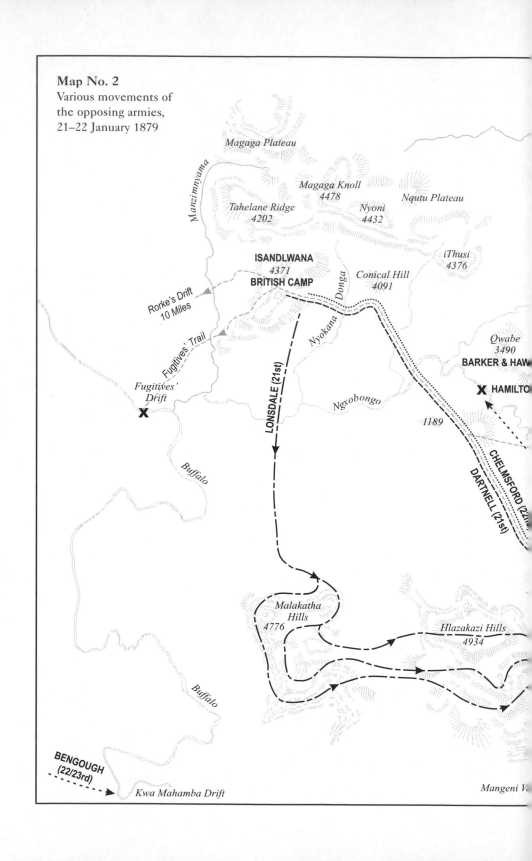

Map No. 2
Various movements of
the opposing armies,
21–22 January 1879

Magaga Plateau

Manzimnyama

Magaga Knoll
4478

Tahelane Ridge
4202

Nyoni
4432

Nqutu Plateau

iThusi
4376

ISANDLWANA
4371
BRITISH CAMP

Donga

Conical Hill
4091

Rorke's Drift
10 Miles

Nyokana

Qwabe
3490
BARKER & HAW

Fugitives' Trail

X **HAMILTO**

Fugitives'
Drift

LONSDALE (21st)

Ngxobongo

1189

X

CHELMSFORD (22n
DARTNELL (21st)

Buffalo

Malakatha
Hills
4776

Hlazakazi Hills
4934

Buffalo

BENGOUGH
(22/23rd)

Kwa Mahamba Drift

Mangeni V

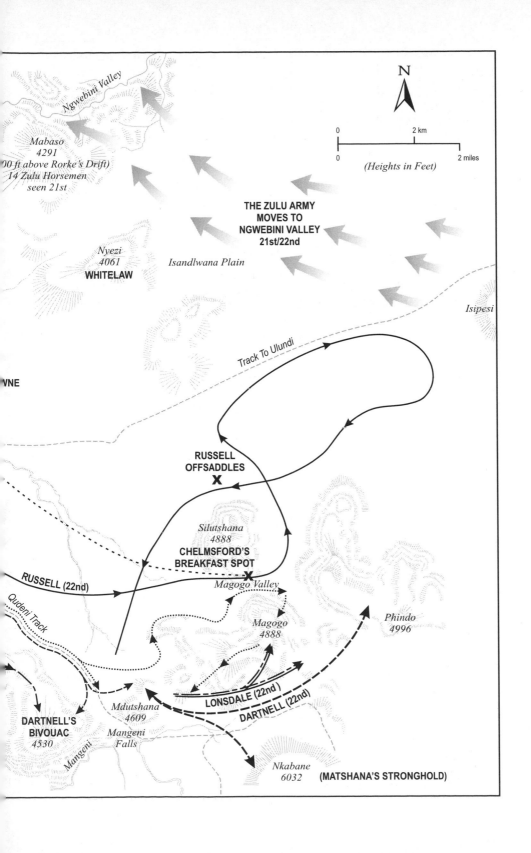

However, the game Chelmsford intended to play was a dangerous one indeed. With little more than 11,000 men, of whom almost 8,000 were NNC, he intended to invade, subdue and occupy some 3,500 square miles of virtual wilderness (120 miles long, and in places over 35 miles wide), leave behind an army of occupation and, with what remained of his scattered forces, push on to seek out the Zulu army. Nor did he consider it necessary to include Wood's column in his invasion plan, having already instructed Wood to act independently in the north.[◊]

Such was Chelmsford's confidence that he concluded his memorandum to Frere by stating:

> 'When Cetywayo has either surrendered or been defeated, which can only take a few more days to decide, Colonel Wood will take up a position covering Utrecht and the adjacent Transvaal border.'

Before Durnford left Rorke's Drift, Chelmsford had ordered him to implement the new troop disposition, but on his arrival at Kranskop, exciting news awaited Durnford. A messenger from Bishop Schreuder, the same cleric who had connived with Wolseley in the building of the military road to Middle Drift, brought news of an impending Zulu attack. The impulsive Durnford, without seeking corroboration of Schreuder's intelligence, decided to disobey Chelmsford's orders and, having sent a messenger to advise Chelmsford of his intention, prepared to advance into Zululand at Middle Drift.

There must have been some very hard riding between Kranskop and Rorke's Drift over the next couple of days. On receipt of Durnford's message, Chelmsford flew into a fury and immediately despatched a reprimand to Durnford at Kranskop, instructing him to follow the orders given to him at Rorke's Drift. To make matters worse for Durnford, Schreuder's intelligence turned out to be a false alarm. On 14 January Chelmsford committed his reprimand to writing:

> 'Unless you carry out the instructions I give you, it will be my unpleasant duty to remove you from your command, and to substitute another officer for the command of No. 2 Column. When a column is acting separately in an enemy's country [Chelmsford's emphasis] I am quite ready to give its commander every latitude, and would certainly expect him to disobey any orders he might receive from me, if information which he obtained, showed that it would be injurious to the interests of the column under his command. Your neglecting to obey my instructions in the present instance has no excuse. You have simply received information in a letter from Bishop Schroeder [*sic*], which may or may not be true and which you have no means of verifying – if movements ordered are to be delayed because report hints at a chance of an invasion of Natal, it will be impossible for me to carry out my plan of campaign. I trust you will understand this plain speaking and not give me any further occasion to write in a style which is distasteful to me.'

Fortunately, Durnford had yet to reach Middle Drift and his battalions were recalled. The upshot of this stormy incident was recorded by the Kranskop correspondent of the *Natal Witness*:

> 'On the 16 January the whole of the 2nd Battalion, NNC, and two companies of the 1st Battalion Natal Native Contingent, the mounted contingent and the rocket battery [all of No. 2 Column] are ordered off at an hour's notice to Helpmekaar.'

Despite most of the draft oxen of the column having 'died like flies' of red water fever,◊ Durnford, his horsemen and the rocket battery, travelled fast. Within three days they had reached Vermaak's farm just below Helpmekaar, and a few miles above Rorke's Drift. Durnford vividly described the journey in a letter to his mother:

> 'You would have been pleased at seeing us in the night, marching, dark night, water course roads, self leading, with an orderly and lantern, then cavalry, each man leading his own horse, rocket battery next, then infantry, the wagon train straggling over some five miles of road. Crossing rivers in large boats in the night, horses swimming, then cattle killing, cooking on the red embers, horses feeding, men eating and sleeping, etc. All the sights and sounds of camp life that I love.'

The mundane life of an engineer officer, inspecting fortifications, building roads and the like, must have been irksome to such a man as Durnford; his cavalier spirit would have undoubtedly been better satisfied at the head of a cavalry squadron.

The two battalions of NNC, following Durnford on foot and under the command of Major Bengough, an imperial officer, would later arrive at M'singa in preparation for crossing the Buffalo at the Gates of Natal: it was their good fortune that circumstance would prevent them from doing so.

Little has been mentioned of the horsemen who formed such an important element of Durnford's force.◊ Apart from a handful of white officers, all were black including the senior NCOs. There were about 250 of them in all, divided more or less equally into five troops, each troop bearing its own tribal associated name. Although all black, there was great diversity in both their origins and religions; some were heathen and others devout Christians. Durnford had cultivated their friendship and had sought their loyalty ever since a number of them had accompanied him into the Drakensberg Mountains during the abortive pursuit of Langalibalele six years earlier. There can be little doubt that Durnford had seen to it that they were given basic military training and had somehow equipped them with firearms – on the quiet perhaps for, had it been known, there would have been a clamour of protest from the settler population. It is unlikely that, denied the prior benefits of training in drill and marksmanship, Durnford's horsemen would have been able to perform with the skill which they would shortly display during the battle of Isandlwana.

In common with all of Durnford's mounted men, the Christians (the *Makolwas*) had, in years gone by, been displaced from their original homeland by the Zulu. At that time they had been known by their tribal name of amaNgwane. They had eventually found sanctuary in Natal, establishing themselves close to Pietermaritzburg. There they prospered as small farmers, eventually taking up the ways of the white man, including European dress and devout worship of God. In the eyes of the Natal government they were a shining example, a people transformed from barbarism to a life of pious purpose. Yet, within their demure exteriors, there still beat the hearts of warriors. They had responded immediately to Bulwer's call for volunteers and, in addition, had supplied their own horses, saddlery and uniforms. Proud men, they were armed with Swinburne-Henry carbines and fifty rounds of ammunition. For their military title they had adopted the name of their mission settlement, calling themselves the Edendale Troop, NNH. Their leader, Sergeant-Major Simeon Kambule, was the son of Elijah who, acting as the column guide and interpreter, had been killed at Durnford's side during the fight at Bushman's Pass. The departure of the troop to the front, and their ride through Pietermaritzburg, was later described by a member of the Edendale congregation:

> 'We were all proud of them as they marched through the city. Sober, clean, and well-made men in the fullness of their strength. Their equipment was of the best and perfect in every particular.'

Yet they would be unjustly treated by the very government they were willing to defend. They received only half the pay of their white equivalents, one of whom wrote of them:

> 'They [the NNH] were courageous and possessed the merit of being cheap, providing their own horses and getting three pounds a month.'

It was not only the Edendale blacks who had cantered off to volunteer their poorly paid services. Along the foothills of the Drakensberg men of various clans, riding their sturdy ponies, had reported for duty. From the beautiful valley of the Polela River came volunteers of the amaXimba tribe, calling themselves Jantee's (or sometimes Jantzi's) Horse. They wore no uniform but were similarly dressed in old coats, cord trousers and wide brimmed hats bound around with a red cloth. Apart from the government issued carbine, they carried weapons of their own: knobkerries and quivers of throwing spears. The amaXimba were a mixture of people who had bound together in the 1820s in order to survive the depredations of the Mfecane Horde, a marauding mass of 50,000 uprooted people, forced by hunger into cannibalism, who were laying waste to the interior of southern Africa. Having established themselves as a tribe, the amaXimba had fought with the Boers against Dingane and had later accompanied Durnford in 1873.

Similarly, the Hlubi Troop of the NNH came from a people who in earlier times had been harassed and decimated by the Zulu. Although their leader bore the name of 'Hlubi', it was merely a commemorative one given to him by his father in remembrance of a past victory over the amaHlubi tribe. Because of their many wanderings, which had taken place over several generations, Hlubi's people had acquired a number of different clan or tribal names: baSotho, Hlongwane and Batlokwa or Tlokwa. Hlubi himself was special to Durnford; he had stood fast at Durnford's side at Bushman's Pass. Later, in 1877, Durnford had displayed his gratitude by employing Hlubi as the commander of his black mounted guides during the British annexation of the Transvaal.

The Zikali Troops took their name from a former chief who had died in 1863. They too were of the amaNgwane and had an ancient score to settle with the Zulu. Their home had once been in central Zululand, along the banks of the White Mfolozi River, until Shaka, the chief who would be king, attacked them.◊ Led by Matiwane, Zikali's father, the amaNgwane had fled west and crossed the Tugela River to settle at Ntenjwa, in the foothills of the Drakensberg Mountains. Years later, when Dingane had become king, Matiwane had attempted to return to Zululand. He put himself at the mercy of the king but Dingane, having first put out Matiwane's eyes, then had him cruelly executed on a little hill adjacent to his capital. To this day the hill is known as kwaMatiwane. It was the very same hill on which Piet Retief and his followers would also die some years later.

After Matiwane's death the tribe was forced to wander far over southern Africa, into Basutoland and the Cape. Eventually, the amaNgwane found a home in the Drakensberg, a domain reaching to the very mountain tops. Zikali's brother, Sergeant-Major Nyanda, led the NNH contingent. He and Sergeant-Major Kambule of the Edendale Troop would become the first black soldiers to receive the Distinguished Conduct Medal (DCM).

In appearance the NNH, oddly clothed and with their persons and ponies festooned with weapons, bandoliers, haversacks and feed bags, looked more like brigands than soldiers of the queen – Durnford was no less a robber-chief in appearance with his long drooping moustache. He took delight in his unorthodox attire, writing this to his mother:

> 'I wonder whether you would admire my appearance for the field? Boots, spurs, dark cord britches, serge patrol jacket, broad belt over the shoulders, and one around the waist – to the former a revolver, and to the latter a hunting knife and ammunition pouch. A wide-awake soft hat with a wide brim, one side turned up, and a crimson turban (puggaree) wound round the hat – very like a stage brigand!'

Despite the wide diversity of race and culture, a bond existed between Durnford and his wild horsemen. He appreciated their worth and admired their courage. Consequently the troops of the NNH had two things in common: their devotion to Durnford and their hatred of the Zulu.

Whilst Durnford and the NNH had made good time along the road from Kranskop, No. 3 Column had all but rooted itself in the dark alluvial soil of

Zululand, a short distance from Rorke's Drift. The men, working in shifts of 2,000 at a time, black and white, laboured like navvies breaking rock, moving boulders and digging trenches in an endeavour either to drain or fill in the swamps that held the column in their grip. The white NCOs of the NNC were particularly put out and objected strongly to performing manual labour; their curses and protests were accompanied by threats of resignation. Chelmsford's well-intended order that no Zulu dwelling be destroyed was ignored; every hut along the way was torn down and trampled into the boggy track.

Some three miles from Rorke's Drift the road to Ulundi crossed the Batshe River shortly before it flowed into the Buffalo. Here an advance camp had been set up guarded by four companies of the 2/24th, one battalion of the NNC and some black pioneers, all under the command of Major W.N. Dunbar. In compliance with Chelmsford's standing order that all camps be entrenched,◊ an attempt had been made to fortify this vulnerable position by the construction of a low walled redoubt (the remains of which can still be seen). However, this work was not undertaken until 19 January. No attempt was ever made to *laager*, or entrench, the main base established close to Rorke's Drift.

The various delays were particularly galling to Chelmsford and on 15 January, whilst most of his command sweated and toiled at road building, he ordered Russell, with a strong escort of mounted infantry, to scout the countryside ahead. The road passed Dunbar's camp then crossed the Batshe, pushing on over broken, rising ground towards a strange shaped hill that seemed to crouch, sphinx-like, on the horizon, a landmark that could be seen for miles around. It was known locally as Isandlwana.◊ At the southern end it was joined by a wide, stony saddle to a flat-topped koppie (or small hill) which would later be named Black's Koppie (and which will be referred to as such for the remainder of this narrative). Russell, having crossed the saddle, found the country ahead opened into an undulating plain, five miles wide and twice as long, surrounded by hills and mountains on all sides. Further out on the plain there was another landmark, not as big as Isandlwana but being perfectly conical in shape, a very distinctive hill.

As the IMI rode further east towards Ulundi, they found additional landmarks: low ridges – one ending in a conical, rocky turret – and many deep *dongas* concealed in the undulations of the plain, all running with shallow streams. Much of the plain itself was strewn with rocks and boulders, causing the horsemen to have to pick their way. It would be difficult terrain for wagons and artillery. Some distance on, the track split, the right fork leading to the Qudeni Forest and the left to Ulundi. Way beyond the left fork, twelve miles away from Isandlwana, the great hump of Isipesi Hill rose out of the heat haze, dominating the route to the Zulu capital.

It was an empty land, devoid of people – or so it seemed – but there would have been watching eyes up in the hills. Russell and his men, scarlet-coated specks out in the vastness of the plain, would not have gone unobserved by local Zulu scouts stationed in the hills above, men who had the ability to see further with the naked eye than a white man could see with the aid of a telescope.

Although now devoid of life, the many empty homesteads bore witness to a land that had long been occupied by the Zulu people. Large gardens of mealie plants, some with stalks still heavy with lush green cobs, adjoined each gathering of huts. Out of curiosity, the horsemen dismounted and inspected a group of dwellings and were surprised at the complexity of their construction. However, it is unlikely that they appreciated that an average of 500 saplings was required to build one hut.[◊] In a land largely treeless, the value of such raw material is hard to assess. It is even harder to assess what the destruction of 20,000 huts over the next seven months would mean to the Zulu nation.

Eventually the IMI neared Isipesi Hill, the limit of their patrol, and the closer they got the more the *dongas* increased in size and number. They had now become giant erosions, jaggedly crossing the plain in all directions; in depth many were the height of a two-storey house and in width as wide as a modern day highway; all were bounded by crumbling, perpendicular walls. The way ahead would not be easy. This would be depressing news for Chelmsford.

The following day, 16 January, Chelmsford and his staff, with an escort of fifty IMI, rode as far as Isandlwana, Chelmsford seeing for himself the appalling condition of the route ahead.

───────◆───────

During the days when the column stagnated, unable to move, several well-wishers, eager to offer advice and satisfy their curiosity, paid their respects to Chelmsford. J.J. Uys, who had fought the Zulu forty years earlier at Blood River, dropped by and advised: 'Be on your guard and be careful. Place your spies out, and form your wagons into a *laager*.' Willem Landman and Gert de Jager, old hands at fighting Zulus, offered similar warnings. Chelmsford, ever a courteous man, no doubt listened but dismissed their wise counsel. *Laagering* took time.

A more welcome visitor by far had been Sir Theophilus Shepstone who, with his entourage, had been making his way from the Transvaal to Durban. Later, Chelmsford was able to report to Frere that he had been delighted at Shepstone's approval of the action taken against Sihayo.

Rather than being concerned over defensive precautions, Chelmsford's obsession was to get on into Zululand, and to do so he needed to chase up delays in the arrival of the column's essential supplies. He blamed these hold-ups on laggardly commissariat officers. His irritation was plain in the letter he wrote to Commissary-General Strickland, who was stationed in Pietermaritzburg:

'I have been across the Buffalo river today to see how the depot [at Rorke's Drift] was going. I find there is absolutely nothing there and this column cannot move until there is a month's supply in hand over and above the fifteen day's regimental supply with the column... You must send up one of the new Assistant Commissary-Generals who are on their way out [from England], at once to Helpmekaar, or we shall have a breakdown. There is no one here like Colonel Wood [a dig at Colonel Glyn?] to keep everyone up to the mark and Helpmekaar appears to me to have been sadly neglected... This column will advance shortly, and it will be a sad disgrace to the Commissariat, if it is obliged to halt short of its destination for the want of supplies.'

Chelmsford was also determined to have Fynn permanently attached to his staff. Having accompanied the column across the Buffalo on 11 January, Fynn had been ordered back to M'singa. On the 16th, Chelmsford requested Frere to put pressure on the Governor:

'I wish Sir H. Bulwer would allow Mr Fynn to be with me. I have no-one to consult with as regards my duties as Resident in Zululand [it seems that it had been agreed with Frere that Chelmsford be appointed Resident once Zululand had been conquered, Wood having already refused the position] and I am afraid that unless I am allowed his services, I shall not be able to deal satisfactorily with any chiefs who are anxious to tender their submission... I do not think it is right I should be left without one representative of the Natal Government at my headquarters as the disposal of prisoners and refugees has already cropped up and Mr Fynn is twenty five miles distant.'

On reflection, Chelmsford decided that he was not prepared to await Bulwer's co-operation, and so summarily ordered Fynn to Rorke's Drift. A few days later Chelmsford wrote to Frere:

'I hope you will be able to pacify Sir H. Bulwer with regard to my annexing Mr Fynn. It was only after seeing how essential it was in the public interest that he should be with me that I decided to summons him to headquarters.'

On 19 January Fynn duly arrived at Rorke's Drift, at the same time as Captain George Shepstone, a son of Sir Theophilus, and Durnford's staff officer. He and Durnford had been acquainted for a long time, Shepstone having been a corporal in the Carbineers at Bushman's Pass. A barrister by profession, he was also a fluent Zulu linguist – which Durnford was not – and wise in the ways of the frontier. He had the distinction of having attended King Cetshwayo's coronation. The purpose of his visit was to inform Chelmsford that the NNH had arrived at Vermaak's farm and to ask for further orders. He stayed the night, returning to Durnford the next day, just as No. 3 Column finally freed itself from the bog that had held it captive. At dawn on 20 January the wagons began to move towards Isandlwana.

Isandlwana Hill, as seen from the vicinity of Rorke's Drift.
(All colour photographs copyright Ron Lock)

The area of the wagon park, where the severest fighting took place, looking
north-east towards the Nqutu Ridge. In the centre far distance, the outline
of Isipesi Hill, twelve miles away.

Left: Hills overlooking the Magogo Valley, where Lord Chelmsford and his staff had breakfast on the morning of the battle. Chelmsford and his men were under continuous observation from the Zulu army.

Below: One of the many massive *dongas* that criss-cross the Isandlwana plain and the Magogo Valley.

Right: The Mangeni Falls with the little pointed hill in the background used as an observation point by Chelmsford and his staff at about 1.00 p.m.

Below: The Kwa Mahamba Drift where Bengough's NNC spent the day of the battle.

Bottom: iThusi's rocky crest, shaped like a 'cock's comb'. A feature noted by Francis Fynn.

Left: The view from the top of iThusi. Conical Hill is to the left and Isandlwana right of centre, both in shadow.

Right: Looking down from the Tahelane Ridge along one of the re-entrants that would have been used during Cavaye's and Mostyn's retreat.

Below left: From Magaga Knoll. Cavaye's and Mostyn's position on the Tahelane Ridge is below and to the right.

Below: Looking down on the approximate position of Durnford's encounter with the Zulu left horn. Right to left along the skyline: iThusi, the Nqutu Ridge, Conical Hill and finally Isandlwana Hill.

Above: Just beyond the Nek, the trail of white cairns, marking British graves, leads to the Buffalo River and Fugitives' Drift.

Above right: Looking down on the Buffalo River with Fugitives' Drift in the middle distance. The Natal bank is on the right and the tip of Isandlwana Hill can just be seen on the skyline to the left centre of the picture.

Right: Fugitives' Drift at low water. On the day of the battle the river was in flood and most of the rocks would have been submerged. Many fugitives entered the river from above the low cliff on the left.

Members of the Isandlwana Zulu community recently painted and embroidered these quilt panels depicting scenes from the battle of 1879, as it is remembered in local oral history. The artists provided the following captions for their work:

(Top) 'This is the time of the great battle that took place between the blacks and the whites. The gun fell as the black stabbed the white. He did not even get a small time to shoot. He was stabbed once and died.'

(Above) 'I show the whites riding on their horses after the battle. They went across the Mzinyathi River. "I'm the last one, the last from the fight", he calls.'

The original photograph of the British ultimatum being delivered to King Cetshwayo's representatives. James Lloyd, a professional Durban artist and photographer, took the picture and many others during the Anglo-Zulu War. *(James Lloyd album; copyright R. Lock and P. Quantrill)*

Lieutenant-General Lord Chelmsford, commander of HM Forces in southern Africa, 1879. *(Ron Sheeley)*

Sir Bartle Frere, the British High Commissioner for southern Africa, largely responsible for the Anglo-Zulu War of 1879. *(KZN Archives)*

Above: Warriors of a senior Zulu regiment, possibly the uMbonambi, a 32-year-old age group. *(KZN Archives)*

Below: Mahubulwana (wrapped in blanket). A chief of the abaQulusi clan, he was one of the Zulu representatives at the Ultimatum Tree. *(KZN Archives)*

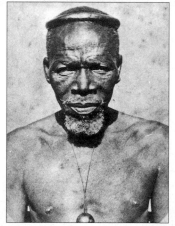

Left: Mfunzi, the king's messenger. Cetshwayo sent him to Natal in an attempt to prevent the war. *(KZN Archives)*

Below: Zulu warriors were only allowed to marry with their king's permission. This picture of a warrior and his girlfriend is unique. *(KZN Archives)*

Above left: King Cetshwayo at the time of his coronation in 1873.

Above right: Although a studio picture, this photo correctly depicts a young warrior, uncluttered with finery, stripped for battle. With his spotted black and white shield, he could be of the uVe Regiment. *(Africa Museum, Johannesburg)*

Below: A group of Zulu dignitaries including some of the king's royal brothers, *circa* 1880/81. Men of similar standing and appearance represented their king at the Ultimatum Tree. *(KZN Archives)*

A battalion of imperial infantry on parade at Pietermaritzburg, *circa* 1879. The 'parade ground' is now occupied by the pavilion and cricket ground which formed one of the settings in the film *Zulu Dawn*. *(Africa Museum, Johannesburg)*

A mixture of colonials in camp. A Natal Carbineer, several troopers of the Natal Native Horse and the bearded man in the foreground most likely an NCO of the Natal Native Contingent. *(KZN Archives)*

Lt-General Lord Chelmsford as drawn by Lt-Colonel John North Crealock. Crealock later modified the sketch by removing the mounted infantryman in the background and replacing him by a drawing of himself. *(Sherwood Foresters Museum)*

Second from the left, back row, Henry Francis Fynn, Chelmsford's political officer and interpreter. To the right of Fynn, Major Dartnell who commanded the Natal Mounted Police. The rest of the group are Border Guard officers. *(KZN Archives)*

Top far left: Coate's Ferry Hotel on the Tugela River, one of several makeshift hotels on the invasion route. *(James Lloyd album; copyright R. Lock and P. Quantrill)*

Top left: Lt Horace Smith-Dorrien, attached to No. 3 Column as an assistant transport officer. *(John Young)*

Top right: Commandant Rupert Lonsdale, Natal Native Contingent. *(John Young)*

Above: Mr J.A. Brickhill, interpreter on Lord Chelmsford's staff. *(KZN Archives)*

Left: Thousands of oxen and hundreds of wagons were needed to move Chelmsford's army.

Lieutenant Walter James, RE, of the Intelligence Department, was sent to South Africa by the War Office to investigate the British defeat at Isandlwana. *(Africa Museum, Johannesburg)*

Major John Dartnell, Natal Mounted Police, rose to the rank of major-general in the British Army. *(KZN Archives)*

Trooper William Clarke of the Natal Mounted Police, later rose to command the force. Colonel Clarke seated centre front row. *(KZN Archives)*

Veterans of the Anglo-Zulu War. Men of the Natal Native Horse and Natal Native Contingent. *(KZN Archives)*

The Magogo Valley today, showing one of the many *dongas* that criss-cross the landscape and which, in 1879, frustrated the progress of Colonel Harness' guns. Co-author Peter Quantrill leads the horse. *(Ron Lock)*

Above: Hot work for British infantry as they march into Zululand at the height of summer.

Below: Lieutenant-Colonel Henry Burmester Pulleine was in command of the British camp at Isandlwana on the day of the battle.

Below: Lieutenant Alfred Henderson, a former gold miner and transport rider commanded No. 4 Troop of the Natal Native Horse. *(Henderson family)*

Right: Colonel Anthony Durnford, RE, Commander of No. 2 Column.

Below: A unique photograph of Natal Carbineers who were involved in the Battle of Isandlwana. W. Edwards (3rd from left, back row) and W.W. Barker (sitting far right, front row) fought in the battle itself and later escaped across Fugitives' Drift. Barker was recommended for the Victoria Cross. Of the remaining eight Carbineers, five were with Chelmsford and one of those five lost a brother in the battle. *(KZN Archives)*

Above right: Lieutenant Charlie Raw, commander of No. 1 Troop NNH, second from the right. The picture was taken at the time of King Cetshwayo's coronation. *(Paul Raw)*

Above left: Lieutenant-Colonel J.C. Russell, 12th Lancers, commanded No. 1 Squadron Imperial Mounted Infantry. *(Regimental Museum 9/12th Royal Lancers, Derby)*

Left: Captain George Shepstone of the NNH, Colonel Durnford's staff officer. *(Local History Museum)*

Right: Quartermaster-Sergeant John Bullock and *(far right)* Quartermaster William London of the Natal Carbineers; both lost their lives at Isandlwana. *(KZN Archives)*

Above: Lieutenant Henry Curling, RA, the only imperial officer to survive from the firing line, in later life. *(Royal Artillery Library, Woolwich)*

Top: An officer of the 80th Regiment, part of No. 4 Column. Note the souvenir skull displayed on his table. *(James Lloyd album; copyright R. Lock and P. Quantrill)*

Top left: The Durban Volunteer Artillery guarded the approaches to Durban in 1878. *(KZN Archives)*

Left: The summer of 1879 was an exceptionally wet one with rivers and streams often in flood.

The Last Stand of the 24th, one of the most famous pictures of the Anglo-Zulu War. *(National Army Museum)*

Prince Shingana kaMpande, half brother to King Cetshwayo. Shingana fought at nDondakusuka as well as Isandlwana. *(KZN Archives)*

Sigcwelegewele kaMhlekehleke, commander of the Nkobamakosi regiment. Cetshwayo ordered his execution after the brawl at the First Fruits ceremony in 1877. He was later forgiven and led the Nkobamakosi at Isandlwana. *(S.B. Bourquin)*

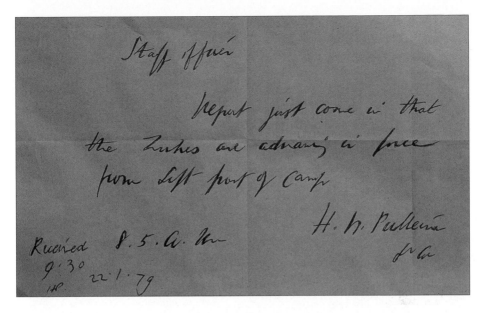

Above: A copy of Colonel Pulleine's famous message advising Lord Chelmsford that the Zulus were advancing on the camp. *(Museum of Royal Regiment of Wales, Brecon)*

Below left: Prince Ndabuko kaMpande, younger full brother of Cetshwayo, fought at Isandlwana. *(KZN Archives)*

Below right: The commander of the Zulu Army, Ntshingwayo kaMahole. After the war Sir Garnet Wolseley awarded him one of the thirteen chiefdoms of the divided Zulu kingdom.

Chief Zibhebhu kaMaphitha, hereditary chief of the Mandalakazi, who was wounded at Isandlwana. *(KZN Archives)*

Men of the amaNgwane tribe, taken in 1883. Many of Colonel Durnford's black horsemen and infantry were recruited from the amaNgwane. *(James A. Murray)*

Above: This magnificent warrior predates the Anglo-Zulu War of 1879. *(KZN Archives)*

Right: A latter day photo of Lt-Colonel John North Crealock, assistant military secretary to Lord Chelmsford. *(The Royal Archives, Windsor)*

Above: Lt Wyatt Vause, No. 3 Troop, Natal Native Horse. *(By kind permission of Robin Stayt)*

Below left: Captain William Eccles Mostyn, 24th Regiment, killed at Isandlwana.

Below: Lt Charles Walter Cavaye, 24th Regiment, killed at Isandlwana.

Above: The Natal Hussars. To guard the colony, the settler population raised volunteer units, often with colourful names and uniforms, but seldom amounting to more than twenty men. The Natal Hussars joined the Coastal Column and fought at the Battle of Nyazane. *(KZN Archives)*

Left: It is probable that Lieutenant J.A. Roberts, who commanded No. 2 Troop Natal Native Horse, was killed by artillery fire. *(Lieutenant-Colonel Justin Hulme)*

Above: In the dawn after the battle, the remainder of No. 3 Column departs the devastated camp. An eye witness sketch by Trooper W. Nelson of the Natal Mounted Police. *(KZN Archives)*

Below: Lieutenant Charles Pope, 24th Regiment, killed at Isandlwana.

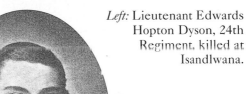

Left: Lieutenant Edwards Hopton Dyson, 24th Regiment, killed at Isandlwana.

Below: Captain Reginald Younghusband, 24th Regiment, killed at Isandlwana.

Above: A photo taken *circa* 1880 of Melvill's and Coghill's grave. Fugitives' Drift and the Buffalo River can be seen lower left middle distance. The dotted line indicates the flight of the fugitives. It is interesting to note that the hill down which they fled is now covered with thick thorn scrub and is impenetrable to a man on horseback. *(James Lloyd album; copyright R. Lock and P. Quantrill)*

Left: Private Samuel Wassall of the 80th Regiment, attached to No. 1 Squadron Imperial Mounted Infantry, was awarded the Victoria Cross for saving a comrade's life at Fugitives' Drift. *(The Royal Archives, Windsor)*

A photograph taken later in the career of Major Cornelius Francis Clery,
32nd Regiment, principal staff officer to Colonel Glyn.
(The Royal Archives, Windsor)

The ammunition box, reportedly recovered from Isandlwana, now in the Warriors Gate Museum, Durban. The initials RL, between the government broad arrow, show that this box and its former contents were issued from the Royal Laboratory, Woolwich. The 'V' indicates that the box is a Mark V version and 1878 gives the year of manufacture.

The intricate dovetail joints, thick mahogany planking, and metal bands are indicative of anticipated rough handling and long service.

The wedge shape of the sliding lid can be clearly seen, as can its tongue and groove slides. The hollow at the top of the lid is a thumb slot to facilitate opening. Beyond the thumb slot is the counter-sunk hole for the 2-inch securing screw.

Chelmsford, following his new plan of action as earlier outlined to Frere, instead of leading his column eastwards towards Isipesi, the direct route to the Zulu capital, concentrated his attention towards the Malakatha and Hlazakazi hills which rose between the Isandlwana Plain and the Mangeni Valley to the south-east. Not only did he wish to clear this area as part of his enemy-free corridor, he was still concerned by Fynn's assertion that it was the intention of the Zulu high command to descend the Mangeni and attack No. 3 Column in the rear.

At 9.00 a.m. on 20 January, with Fynn as his guide and accompanied by Glyn and various staff officers, plus a small escort, Chelmsford rode east from Rorke's Drift, pausing on Isandlwana Nek for breakfast. He intended to confront Matshana kaMondisa, a Zulu chief who, whilst having an aggressive reputation, had in fact previously indicated to Fynn that he would consider joining sides with the British. Chelmsford was now eager to secure submission, but on arrival at Matshana's stronghold, a maze of cliffs and caves nearby the precipitous descent of the Mangeni River, he saw no sign of the chief or his followers.

The patrol rode to the very edge of the basin from where they could see range after range of hills disappearing into the blue haze of the Biggarsberg. Below, looking 'no bigger than ants', they could just discern cattle and herders. Colonel Crealock, indulging in his favourite hobby, found time to sketch and water-colour the scene – perhaps increasing Chelmsford's frustration and impatience. If people like Matshana were to be elusive and unwilling to parley, it would be almost impossible for Chelmsford to achieve his objectives. He was most concerned, and would have been even more so had he known that Matshana was at that time conferring with the commanders of the Zulu army, 20,000 strong, not nine miles away behind Isipesi Hill.

The Zulu army had not suffered the transport problems plaguing the British invaders. Once the war doctors had completed the various rites and ceremonies on 17 January, Cetshwayo had addressed his army. His speech had been short and to the point. He had told his warriors that they were being sent to fight the whites that had not only invaded the kingdom, but had already stolen many Zulu cattle. The whites had entered Zululand at Rorke's Drift and must now be thrown back across the Mzinyathi (Buffalo) River, and right over the Drakensberg mountains (the original route of entry by the Boers forty years earlier). Cetshwayo had instructed his army to march slowly, preserving its strength, to attack at daybreak and to 'eat up' the red soldiers.

With bellows of adulation for their king, the immense array of warriors had left the royal barracks of Nodwengu and had made its way, regiment by regiment, downhill and westward to the nearby White Mfolozi River, through which the men waded waist deep.◊ It was already late in the afternoon but the army had fed well. The king had ordered the slaughter of 120 prime cattle to ensure his warriors did not depart hungry. It would require a similar number of beasts each day in order to keep his army reasonably fed before it fought the red soldiers.

Once across the river the regiments spread out, each bivouacking for the night in a place allocated by the Zulu commander. Sixty-six-year-old Mnyamana kaNgqengelele Buthelezi was Cetshwayo's chief *induna* and commander-in-chief, but it seems that on this occasion he stayed behind with his king. Instead the Zulu army was commanded by Ntshingwayo kaMahole, a stout man, already in his mid-sixties. His hooded eyes, grim mouth and greying beard conveyed a countenance that was stern indeed. Despite his corpulent waistline and heavy thighs, he would march with his warriors, disdaining to ride, unlike many young *induna*s who had, in recent years, acquired equestrian skills. Ntshingwayo was not only a renowned warrior but also Cetshwayo's close friend. He had as his second-in-command Mavumengwana kaNdlela Ntuli, a man twenty years his junior, but equally well connected, his father having been a favourite of both the previous kings, Dingane and Mpande. Mavumengwana was not only a confidant of Cetshwayo but was also the commander of the royal uThulwana Regiment. Yet, despite both the Zulu commanders' close friendship with their king, Cetshwayo had sent along his special confidant, Ntuzwa kaNhlaka, to act as his 'eyes and ears.' Ntuzwa's duty was to report on the performance of both commanders and the way in which the campaign was conducted.

Amongst the Zulu army there were a number of mounted scouts, most of whom had been recruited by Chief Sihayo who, accompanying the force, was making his way back to his homestead which now lay in ruins.

The Zulu army was capable of covering thirty miles a day with ease if called upon to do so. However, there was no urgency and the second day's march, like the first, was leisurely, covering only nine miles to the Isixepi military barracks. There the column slept. Sightseers, women, small boys and old men who had accompanied the army so far, giving its march a carnival air, now mostly departed. Some women remained, a number of whom would stay with the column until the day of the battle. Yet, apart from the women, it was not an army composed solely of men. For every three or four warriors there would have been one *udibi* boy accompanying a father or brother. The boy would be loaded down with as much paraphernalia as the haughty warriors could expect him to stagger along with: cooking pot, sleeping mat, dismantled shield; and at times perhaps, the boy would have been given the honour of hefting the warriors' weapons. On top of all this, an *udibi* might well have carried a small spear of his own – those who did so would soon have an unexpected opportunity to wash their blades in the blood of red soldiers or, at least, in the blood of their kin now serving in the NNC.

The third day's march was again performed at a gentle pace, the column ascending slowly westwards towards the tableland south of Babanango.

About midday the more senior warriors were able to point out the location of Dingane's old capital, where Piet Retief and his followers had been put to death forty-one years earlier.

The Zulu army was now gradually closing with the British and, despite the scouts' reports that the red soldiers were still at Rorke's Drift many miles away, precautions were taken against the remote possibility of a surprise attack. The army split into two columns, marching three or four miles apart, but still within sight of one another. Mounted scouts rode miles ahead whilst between them and the main column, parties of 200 to 400 fully armed warriors patrolled, unencumbered by *udibi* boys and the like, ready to double forward and intercept the enemy. Their task would be two-fold: first to draw the foe away from any possible sighting of the main column, thus keeping its whereabouts unknown, and second, should the terrain and strength of the opposition present a fighting chance, to seek concealment and lure the enemy into a trap.

As the Zulu army reached the summit of the heights, the land formed a broad ridge gently sloping on either side to the vast pasture lands of the Zulu kingdom. Dotted here and there family homesteads of beehive-shaped huts and herds of grazing cattle could be seen. The ridge formed a natural highway to the west in which direction, beyond Babanango, the great hump of Isipesi Hill, which four days earlier had been the limit of Russell's patrol, could be seen twenty miles away. The army had fed well, the scouts, apart from their military duties, had been busy throughout the countryside commandeering cattle, goats and corn. Many warriors originated from the district through which they now marched. They must have had mixed feelings, their loyalty torn between their king and their kin, as they witnessed family cattle being driven in to provide part of the army's evening meal.

On the fourth day, now conscious that they were drawing within striking distance of the red soldiers, the columns proceeded with great caution until late in the afternoon of 20 January, the army set up camp in the shadow of Isipesi Hill. Some warriors were permitted to clamber up its northern face from whence, gazing towards the setting sun, they could see the white bell tents of Chelmsford's column against the black backdrop of Isandlwana Hill ten miles away.

Messengers, forging ahead of the main army, had visited Matshana at his Mangeni stronghold earlier in the day, and had later escorted him to Isipesi where he now conferred with Ntshingwayo. Matshana was not to be trusted.◊ Rumour had it that he had negotiated with the British. Twenty years earlier Matshana, then resident in Natal, had been involved in a dispute with John Shepstone.◊ The two parties and their respective followers had agreed to parley unarmed, but it was alleged Shepstone and his men had carried concealed weapons, and at a given signal opened fire killing fifteen of Matshana's supporters. Matshana himself fled into Zululand where Mpande had provided him with sanctuary at the place where he now lived.

Nevertheless, it seems that Matshana hankered after Natal; Cetshwayo had once petitioned Theophilus Shepstone, on Matshana's behalf, that he be allowed to return to his former home. Fynn was also considered to be Matshana's friend. With such aspirations and acquaintances, it is hardly surprising that he was regarded with suspicion. However, if the Zulu army were to advance unseen upon the red soldiers, Matshana's knowledge of the local terrain would be indispensable.

It was getting dark by the time Lord Chelmsford and his reconnaissance party returned from Matshana's country. It had been a particularly uncomfortable ride back for Lieutenant Coghill who, in the pursuit of a local fowl for supper, had stumbled, hurting his knee – not a serious injury but one that caused dire consequences forty-eight hours later. They found the camp at Isandlwana neatly laid out, even though it sprawled across the eastern slopes of the hill for over half a mile. No comment was made regarding the lack of defensive precautions.

Chelmsford also learned that, despite days of road repairing, there had been much difficulty in getting the convoy through. At the Batshe River, a dreadful pile-up of wagons had occurred, the *Times of Natal* correspondent reporting:

> 'The drivers and leaders were in a most helpless state of confusion and had they been left to themselves would not only have entirely blocked up the road for hours, but most probably smashed up several wagons and their contents completely.'

The day had been saved by Captain Krohn of the 3rd NNC, a master wagon driver, who, with two NNC lieutenants to assist him, drove each wagon across the river 'enabling the whole convoy to pass through without accident.'◊

The NMP had acted as advance guard and Trooper Clarke later recalled:

> 'I was one of the left flank skirmishers and never have I ridden over such appalling country. At no time was I in sight of the column, which stretched for miles.'

Since Dartnell had been transferred to Chelmsford's staff, command of the NMP had devolved on Inspector George Mansel. On reaching the *nek* of Isandlwana, where the NMP had taken a brief rest, Mansel had been approached by Major Clery, who asked for Mansel's assistance in selecting a place to pitch camp.◊ They had ridden together to the eastern slopes of the hill where the ground began to level with the plain. There Clery remarked, 'I think this will do' and asked Mansel for his opinion. Mansel replied that he 'did not like it one bit', pointing out that the site was commanded at a distance of 300 yards by Black's Koppie, and also by the shoulder of the hill itself. Clery, irritated at Mansel's remark, replied, 'No, this will do.' Clery then ordered Mansel to post vedettes (cavalry outposts usually comprising two to three mounted men) in front of the camp. Fynn was also asked for his opinion on the camp site, and had pointed out the flat open ground two miles further on as a more suitable place.

At about 10.00 a.m. Mansel rode off with his troopers towards the Nqutu Ridge, the range of hills that rose from the plain to the north, about half a mile from the north extremity of the camp site and he placed four vedettes there, the closest two miles from the camp, and the furthest five miles out. They were situated on the highest points of the range, where their silhouettes could be clearly seen from the camp itself. Their method of communication, should the enemy be sighted, was to circle their horses round and round at a spanking pace, before retreating on the camp. Mansel also placed vedettes to the rear of Isandlwana Hill.

Trooper Clarke was amongst those chosen for vedette duty. He had been up since as early as 3.00 a.m. and had been constantly on the go for days. Consequently, in the hot sun and in the quietness of the high ridge, the desire to sleep became overpowering. He and his companion, Trooper Green, succumbed. They were awakened by the noisy approach of an inspecting staff officer who, not knowing that they had been sleeping, remonstrated with them for lying down. Quick-witted Clarke replied that they had done so in order to render themselves less conspicuous! Later, after the disgruntled officer had passed on, the two troopers saw a few Zulu herding cattle about two miles off. They started in pursuit but, 'rode into such vile country that we could not find them.'

By about 2.00 p.m. Mansel had just finished placing his men when he received another order to report to Clery who complained that the vedettes were too far out, and that those placed to the rear of the camp were of no use.⁰ Mansel pointed out that the latter guarded broken ground, ideal for concealment, but Clery would not have it, retorting, 'My dear fellow, those vedettes are useless there, the rear always protects itself.' Clery insisted that the distant vedettes be brought in closer. Reluctantly, Mansel set out to comply. When he got to where his second-in-command, Sub-Inspector F. L. Phillips, was posted to the south, a man was seen running in the distance. Mansel and a couple of troopers gave chase and on catching up with the fugitive, found him to be a very old Zulu.⁰ He was taken back to Phillips for questioning and indicated that a big *impi* was on its way from Ulundi. The incident was reported to Clery but there is doubt as to whether or not Chelmsford was informed. Mansel then returned to the task of bringing in the vedettes closer to the camp, but he managed to leave the outposts on the Nqutu Ridge undisturbed until darkness fell.

Infantry picquets of the NNC were placed closer to the limits of the camp: No. 4 Company 2/3rd NNC on the high ground to the north, and No. 9 Company 1/3rd NNC, on the knob-like height of Magaga Knoll to the north-east. The duty of guarding the south-eastern approaches leading towards the Mangeni Valley, the direction from which Fynn had predicted the Zulu army would attack, was entrusted to picquets of the imperial infantry.

Sub-Inspector Phillips (who had commanded Sir Theophilus Shepstone's escort of twenty-five NMP troopers during the audacious annexation of the Transvaal) was also deeply troubled at the defenceless state of the camp, especially the unguarded rear of Isandlwana Hill. Later in the day he approached Crealock direct, expressing his concern. Chelmsford, overhearing the conversation, called to Crealock:

> 'Tell the police officer my troops will do all the attacking but, even if the enemy does venture to attack, the hill he complains about will serve to protect our rear.'

It was not only the colonials who were concerned, Major William Dunbar, 2/24th, also complained to Crealock about the absence of picquets to the rear of Isandlwana and received the sarcastic reply 'Well, Sir, if you are nervous, we will put a picquet of pioneers there.' Lieutenant Teignmouth Melvill, adjutant of the 1/24th, also thought the precautions being taken to defend the camp were inadequate remarking:

> 'These Zulus will charge home, and with our small numbers we ought to be in laager, or, at any rate, be prepared to stand shoulder to shoulder.'

Glyn himself was seen shaking his head in disapproval of the sprawling camp which one officer was later to describe as, 'defenceless as an English village and with the air of a racecourse on a public holiday.'

A few months later, in describing the camp Mansel wrote:

> 'The 1/24th Regiment had their camp pitched right on the Black's Koppie... and from the top of the koppie to the nearest tents was certainly considerably less than 100 yards... I am certain of my distances... The koppie was a rough stony place looking right down into the camp and giving excellent cover to anybody occupying it. This koppie was not occupied by picquets during the two nights the camp was occupied. From the shoulder of the hill [Isandlwana] the distance to the camp varied from 200 to 300 yards at most and the shoulder of the hill was covered with stones and boulders affording excellent cover and thoroughly commanding the camp. Neither was this place occupied by a picquet at night.'

However, Chelmsford and his staff were unconcerned; the camp would be on the move again within a couple of days and trying to dig entrenchments in the stony ground around Isandlwana would be a futile exercise. As for *laagering* the wagons, they would be required bright and early on the morrow to move additional supplies up from Rorke's Drift. Indeed, some of the wagons had not yet arrived.

Despite all the efforts of the drivers and road makers, a number of vehicles were still in difficulties in the vicinity of the Manzimnyama Stream. A tired and disgruntled detachment of the 2/24th was ordered back to guard them and, on arrival, found that Captain William Mostyn and his F Company 1/24th had just arrived. They had left Pietermaritzburg on

9 January and had been marching for twelve days. Mostyn was heard to exclaim, 'Thank goodness we are here at last!'

―――――――❧―――――――

A contemporary sketch of the Isandlwana camp, presumably made on 21 January, shows rows and rows of bell tents aligned with military precision. The physical laying out of such a large encampment was a mammoth task – to dismantle it was only marginally less so. Needless to say there were rules and regulations, down to the finest detail, as to how it should all be done. As the tents play a passive but key role in the battle of Isandlwana, it is worth studying for a moment the complexity of setting up and striking a camp. The following are extracts from contemporary army regulations:

> 'Tents
>
> The 'Bell' tent is the universal pattern for home and colonial service…
>
> For pitching and striking the Bell tent. One NCO and six men are told off as follows:- one file as polemen, one as packers, and one as pegmen.
>
> The NCOs in charge of squads will be extended sixteen paces from the left by officers commanding companies in prolongation of their arms and turned to the right.
>
> The senior major will dress the NCOs of the first row of tents, along the front of the column, so that they will stand exactly on the line marked out as the front of the camp and the captain of each Company will, from them, dress the NCOs of his squads who, whilst being so dressed, will stand at attention.
>
> After being dressed, No. 7 of each squad will drive a peg in between the heels of his NCO, who will after turning about take eighteen paces to the front, when another peg will be driven in, in a similar way. He will then turn to his left and take five paces measuring the depth, when another peg will be driven in. He will again turn to the left and take eighteen paces (being the length in rear) when another peg will be driven in at his heels.'

More regulations in the above vein continue for several pages and include the following:

> 'Striking Tents
>
> On the order being given to strike tents, all ropes except the corner ones will be quickly undone and hanked up close to the flies; walls will be unlaced and packed in the bags.
>
> The corner ropes will then be loosened and the tents dropped on the bugle sound 'G.' No's 1, 2, 3, 4, 9 and 10 will remove poles, bank corner ropes, fold up flies, and lace them carefully up… while No's 5, 6, 7 and 8 take out pegs, count them and pack them in the peg bag.'

There was much more.◊

By the time all the stragglers had arrived, accommodation would be required for over 4,500 men of whom 2,000, the rank and file of the NNC, would have to find their own. Harford recalled:

> 'Plenty of wood [small trees] being close at hand behind the hill, the natives [NNC] soon set to work to run up shelters for themselves on the other side of the road, clear of the camp. A queer looking place they made of it, being packed like sardines, the space allotted to them being limited.'

Nevertheless, close on 300 tents would be needed to accommodate all the white troops, and provide shelter for stores, hospital, messes and headquarters. By the time the cursing redcoats had aligned the tents to the perfection required, a veritable canvas town had been constructed.

Although Chelmsford had usurped Glyn's position as column commander – Chelmsford deciding where, when and how the column would proceed – he expressed little interest in the camp's layout and no concern regarding its lack of defensive precautions. His concentration and energy were focused elsewhere.

Having failed to secure Matshana's defection, Chelmsford determined to achieve either the submission or the destruction – preferably the former – of all the local chiefs, thus eliminating any hostile force within his proposed enemy-free corridor and, at the same time, ensuring that the Zulu army did not get behind him via the Mangeni Valley. To accomplish these objectives, Chelmsford decided to make a reconnaissance in strength through the jumbled terrain south-east of Isandlwana. Almost half the column would be committed to this operation.

At daybreak on 21 January, sixteen companies of the NNC, comprising approximately 1,600 men under the command of Commandant Lonsdale (who had been discharged from hospital the previous day), accompanied by several of Chelmsford's staff officers, and Drummond, the civilian chief of intelligence, marched off towards the turret-shaped outline of the Malakatha Hills. Lonsdale's force had been ordered to carry one day's rations, but believing they would be back before nightfall, did not bother to do so except for pots of porridge, still smoking hot, which they carried with them. It was an omission they would regret in the days to come. Theirs was to be a particularly arduous march through some of the most rugged country in Zululand. Scrub and thorn trees hindered movement, precipitous ravines compelled frequent changes of direction, and the stony valleys became 'as hot as furnaces' as the day wore on. The white NCOs, many unfit for such activity, suffered the most. Fortunately, there was no lack of fresh running water, which tumbled in streams down from the hills. Nor was the country completely devoid of habitation. In pockets of level land there were homesteads, grazing cattle, and gardens full of mealies. Wherever possible the cattle were confiscated. Old men, women and young girls made appearances, and when questioned as to the whereabouts of the Zulu army they naively pointed to the north-east, in the direction of Isipesi. All the young men, they said, had already gone to the king.

Hamilton-Browne, commanding one of the battalions, stumbled upon two young warriors (whom Browne later admitted to having tortured). They confessed that they had left the Zulu army that day in order to visit their mother. On being instructed to point out the whereabouts of the army, they too indicated the direction of Isipesi Hill.◊

In the late afternoon, having swept through the southern slopes of the hills above the Mangeni River, Lonsdale's force reached the eastern end of the flat-topped Hlazakazi Mountain. There it was decided to drive all the captured cattle back to the camp, about seven miles away, and at the same time to inform Chelmsford of the information extracted from the young warriors. Captain Orlando Murray and Lieutenant Pritchard, with two companies of the NNC, were given the task and departed for Isandlwana.

In addition to Lonsdale's NNC, the colonial mounted troops, mostly carbineers, police and a few NMR, under the command of Major Dartnell, had also been sweeping the Malakatha and Hlazakazi range. Their task had been to clear the northern slopes, combine with the NNC at the eastern end of the range, and march back to camp. However, the troopers' day, unlike that of the NNC, had been most eventful. They had paraded at daybreak and, on hearing that Dartnell was to be in overall command of the operation, had let out a spontaneous cheer expressing their approval of his leadership rather than that of the newly promoted Russell. One young trooper of the NMR, S.B. Jones, had been even more elated. Because he was credited with having the finest horse in the column, Dartnell had ordered him to act as his trumpeter for the day.

The mounted troops had followed the wagon track east taking the right hand fork towards Mangeni. Further on the force separated, the carbineers, under Captain 'Offy' Shepstone, taking a footpath leading towards the summit of Hlazakazi. The path being too steep and rocky to ride, the carbineers dismounted and led their horses. On reaching the crest they rode again and, after a short march, reached the precipitous basin of Matshana's stronghold, the spot where Crealock had sketched the previous day. Trooper Symons remembered: 'The country might well have been a desert, for the only sound was the howling of a dog in the distance and no sign of humanity.'

The NMP had kept to the wagon track on the plain below. But neither they nor the carbineers had gone unobserved. They had all been under the scrutiny of scouts of the Zulu army since daybreak. Now, hundreds of warriors, accompanied by Matshana and his followers, were hurrying south from Isipesi, concealed by the Phindo and Magogo hills, to intercept the horsemen. During the late morning, close to where the Mangeni River crossed the Qudeni track, the opposing forces met (*see Map 2, pages 88–9*).

Dartnell found it difficult to ascertain the Zulu strength and deemed it wise not to engage. Trooper Parsons of the NMP, who had decided it was high time to load his revolver, fired one shot, unintentionally. His accidental round caused his horse to shy and to throw him off, just the thing to exasperate an already edgy Dartnell who immediately ordered Parsons – either under arrest or in disgrace – back to Isandlwana camp, where he was to lose his life the following day.◊

The shot was heard by the carbineers who had off-saddled and had been resting on Hlazakazi summit. They quickly made ready and rode off to make contact with the NNC whom they knew to be behind them. Symons found this strange, riding away from the sound of gunfire instead of towards it. He wondered to himself what the NMP would think of such a manoeuvre! The carbineers had not gone far when more pistol shots greeted them. It was, however, only Mr Drummond trying to gun down, at the gallop, a fleeing antelope!

Dartnell, keeping a valley between the NMP and the Zulu, who were steadily increasing in number 800 yards away on the Magogo hills, sent messengers off to bring up the carbineers and the NNC. It was particularly bad news for the NNC – especially so for the weary and disgruntled white NCOs who were impatient to return to camp. Now they were being ordered to march in the opposite direction. It was too much for two young officers, Lieutenants Avery and Holcroft. They had had enough and, 'went off without leave, evidently to ride back to Isandlwana but were never seen or heard of again.' In fact they arrived safely at the camp but were slain there the following day.

Eventually, Dartnell's scattered forces combined, the NNC taking up a position on the reverse slope of a small plateau with all the horsemen below confronting the enemy. Dartnell, now together with Lonsdale, tried to estimate the strength of the opposition. Finally he called for volunteers to ride forward, and so force the enemy to show his hand. Up to this point, although well within range, neither side had fired a shot. At a signal from Dartnell, a small force of volunteers from both the NMP and carbineers, commanded by Mansel, trotted away towards the enemy-held hill where now hardly a man could be seen. As they approached, as if by magic, the hillside became alive with warriors. Trooper Symons remembered:

> 'From one end of the ridge to the other… rose a long line of black warriors advancing at the double in short intervals of skirmishing order. It was a magnificent spectacle, and no British regiment could excel in keeping their distances in skirmishing at the double. They uttered no sound. On reaching the brow of a hill their centre halted, while the flank came on, thus forming the noted horns of the Zulu impi.'

The horsemen almost got caught. Mansel later wrote:

> 'Immediately they [the Zulu] saw us come up, they came out again and throwing out their flanks they tried to surround us. In my anxiety to see

their numbers, I stayed almost too long and very nearly got caught. The Zulus must have received orders not to fire as they never fired a shot, but they tried to catch us. If they had tried, I think they must have shot us.'

The reluctance of the Zulus to open fire mystified Dartnell and his command. Yet the reason for their not doing so was simple enough. Although Cetshwayo had sent his army on its way with blood-stirring oratory, 'to eat up' the red soldiers, he still clung to the forlorn hope of a negotiated peace. Thus the Zulu facing Dartnell were, at that moment, more intent on capture than on killing.

Dartnell, full of uncertainty, finally decided not to return to camp as ordered but to bivouac the night on the plateau occupied by the NNC. Major Gosset, who had accompanied the column, decided it would be prudent to appraise Chelmsford of the situation and, together with Captain Buller and Mr Drummond of the staff, set off for Isandlwana.

Meanwhile, Chelmsford had experienced another disappointing day. After the early morning departure of Dartnell and the NNC, Chelmsford, guided by Fynn and accompanied by Glyn and a number of staff officers, had set off along the same track as the NNC had taken only a few hours earlier. It led past the homestead of Gamdana kaXongo, a brother of Sihayo, and a man with whom Chelmsford, with Fynn's aid, had been discussing submission. It had been Chelmsford's intention to turn Gamdana's formal defection into a public ceremony of sorts but, on arrival at his village, he found that Gamdana had vanished. The sight of Lonsdale's NNC battalions tramping past his home, and the news of the Zulu army's arrival, had been too much. He had gone off to the Buffalo valley, taking his women and cattle with him. It must now have seemed obvious to Chelmsford, that his plan to achieve the submission of local chiefs was not going to work. He would have to move with more aggression.

As Chelmsford's party was about to leave Gamdana's homestead, George Shepstone arrived requesting orders for No. 2 Column. Chelmsford's last instructions had been issued on 19 January and had read:

'No. 3 Column moves tomorrow to Isandlwana Hill and from there, as soon as possible to a spot about ten miles nearer the Indeni [Qudeni] Forest.

From that point I intend to operate against the two Matyanas [Matshanas – there was another chief by the name of Matshana whose village was situated in the Qudeni Forest]. If they refuse to surrender then Bengough ought to be ready to cross the Buffalo R. at the Gates of Natal in three days time, and ought to show himself there as soon as possible.

I have sent you an order to cross the river at Rorke's Drift tomorrow with the force you have at Vermaak's. I shall want you to operate against the Matyanas, but will send you fresh instructions on the subject. We shall be about eight miles from Rorke's Drift tomorrow.'

Chelmsford, having changed his mind, now had fresh instructions for Shepstone. Bengough was no longer to cross the Buffalo at the Gates of Natal, but was to join Durnford at Rorke's Drift. Fynn recorded: 'It was the last time I saw my old school fellow G.P. Shepstone alive.'

Chelmsford and his followers returned to camp with the intention of reconnoitring the Nqutu Ridge to the north immediately after lunch. Just as they were about to depart, Gamdana arrived, accompanied by another old chief. Both brought an assortment of weapons signifying their unconditional surrender. For Chelmsford it was at least a step in the right direction, but not good enough. The arms they proffered were of poor quality and vastly insufficient to represent the total armoury of Gamdana's people. Obviously the young warriors had departed with the best of the weaponry. An argument ensued and, perhaps to placate Chelmsford, and also underline his own risk in the matter, Gamdana reported that, 'Cetshwayo had sent an impi to eat him up, for surrendering his arms to the English, he had expected the impi that morning [21st] but it had not arrived.' (It was in fact making towards its new place of concealment, the Ngwebini Valley five miles away). Chelmsford, however, appeared to be unimpressed by this news. Gamdana was dismissed, he and his companion having had the opportunity of sighting the layout of the camp and its poor state of defence. After the battle, many, including Crealock, would infer that Chelmsford was responsible for allowing 'spies', such as Gamdana, the opportunity to view the camp's defences and to report to the Zulu high command.

⟶•⟶

It was late in the afternoon before Chelmsford with his staff, finally set out to reconnoitre the Nqutu Ridge. Along the way, at about 4.00 p.m., they met Gosset, Buller and Drummond, who informed Chelmsford that Dartnell was confronting a strong force of Zulus. Major Clery, who was accompanying Chelmsford, later testified:

> 'They informed the General that Major Dartnell had come up with the enemy in considerable force... furthermore, that it was Dartnell's intention to... attack the enemy in the morning.'

Lieutenant Milne, Chelmsford's naval staff officer, wrote:

> 'Major Dartnell sent in for instructions as to what he was to do; in the meantime if no orders were sent, he intended to bivouac on the ground he had taken up and watch the enemy. Orders were immediately sent to Major Dartnell to attack if and when he thought fit. Food was also sent for his force.'

Whilst orderlies rode off to organise the NMP packhorses that would carry Dartnell's supplies, Chelmsford continued with his reconnaissance, eventually reaching the crest of iThusi Hill, which appeared to be the highest point of the Nqutu Ridge. There the party paused to gaze out over the undulations of the plain below. To the south Hlazakazi could just be discerned where, at that moment, Dartnell and his command were preparing to sit out a night of discomfort, cold and apprehension; to the east, a few miles away, the hump of Isipesi Hill, purple in the gathering twilight, marked the road to Ulundi. The packed ranks of the Zulu army that had slept around its base the previous night were mostly gone. During the day they had moved on, concealed by the undulations of the plain, to where they now lay hidden in the Ngwebini Valley in the broken ground less than four miles away to the north-east of iThusi Hill. On a plateau above the valley, a group of Zulu horsemen stared back at Chelmsford and his staff; the rival armies had met at last. Milne later recorded:

> 'On reaching the summit of the highest hill I counted fourteen Zulu horsemen watching us at the distance of about four miles; they ultimately disappeared over a slight rise. There were two vedettes at the spot from where I saw these horsemen; they said they had seen these men several times during the day, and had reported the fact. From this point the ground was nearly level; there were slight rises, however, every now and again, which would prevent our seeing any men who did not wish it.'[◊]

Apart from Dartnell's skirmish, a small element of each army had fought an engagement earlier in the day. Lieutenant Browne, IMI, had led a reconnaissance of four mounted infantry towards Isipesi and had not only 'seen several bodies' of Zulu moving west but had also encountered a Zulu flanking patrol.[◊] Browne failed to grasp that the latter was a decoy and was skilfully led away before he could sight the main army. Shots were exchanged and Browne returned to camp claiming that he and his men had either killed or wounded several of the enemy. Clery had reported this incident to Chelmsford at about the time he returned from his visit to Gamdana's village.

As the only intelligence department in No. 3 Column was 'entirely at the disposal and under the control of' Chelmsford and his staff, the department would have received at least five reports during the course of 21 January of Zulu presence between Isipesi and the Nqutu Ridge: the statements of the Zulu villagers on the Malakatha and Hlazakazi hills; the young warriors' admission extracted by Hamilton-Browne; Gamdana's report; the vedettes' sighting of the mounted Zulus; and finally Browne's encounter with the Zulu decoy, all seemingly ignored by Chelmsford.

By the time Chelmsford reached camp, the night picquets were being posted. Lieutenant Mainwaring, 2/24th, had been on outpost duty with his company to the south-east since 6.00 a.m. that morning. During the afternoon, Lieutenant-Colonel Henry Pulleine, the newly promoted commanding officer of the 1/24th, had ridden up to Mainwaring's position. Pulleine had been with the column for only a few days, having previously held the post of Garrison Commander, Pietermaritzburg. Mainwaring had been about to fall in his men, but Pulleine had told him not to bother, as he was merely riding around inspecting the lie of the land. It was to be the first and only time that the two would meet.

By rights, Mainwaring and his company should have remained on duty until the next morning; however, for some reason which was never explained, they were relieved at 6.00 p.m. by a party led by Lieutenant Charles Pope, also of the 2/24th.◊ The NNC picquet on the Nqutu Ridge was also brought closer in, to be followed in the gathering dusk by the forward scouts of the Zulu army.

Throughout the camp itself there was an air of excited anticipation. Supper that night was a 'merry affair'. Dartnell was engaged and things were about to happen; the campaign was under way. There was a spirit abroad of aggressive superiority. Private Owen Ellis wrote home:

> 'We are about to capture all the cattle belonging to the Zulus and also burn all their kraals; and if they dare to face us with the intent of fighting, well, woe be to them!'

Through the long grass, the Zulu scouts on the Nqutu Ridge above watched as the soldiers, silhouetted against the glow of the cooking fires, moved about the camp. During the hours of darkness, the scouts daringly drew closer, so much so that they were able to call and talk to the lone NNC picquet on Magaga Knoll, only one and a half miles distant from the centre of the British tent lines.◊

PART TWO

The Battle

'We have certainly been seriously underestimating the power of the Zulu army.'

Lord Chelmsford to the Duke of Cambridge, 27 January 1879

Note

One of the problems in tracking the progress of the Battle of Isandlwana is the discrepancy in times given by different people for the same occurrence, a difference of a couple of hours in some instances. And the longer the time from the actual day of the battle to that when the occurrences were related, the more the discrepancies increase. In his *The 24th Regiment at Isandlwana*, the late Frank Emery, an authority on the Anglo-Zulu War, wrote, 'Few, very few, passages of arms remain so clouded with uncertainty.' And the uncertainties in times given by those who did survive and those who witnessed events obscure what evidence there is still further. Therefore a pertinent question must be, 'By what source was the time established to begin with?' As there were no modern aids, the time was most likely set by the orderly officer's watch and thereafter, until 'lights out', by the bugle calls that marked the passage of the military day. We have endeavoured to corroborate times from as many sources as possible and, on occasion, have adjusted times to a probability.

The contemporary habit of giving directions as left or right, instead of north, south, east or west also adds to the confusion, as does the lack of names for important topographic features. We mention that there are two landmarks with similar names which may cause confusion: the Magogo Hills and the Magaga Knoll; the former can be found towards the south-east corner of Map 2 (pages 88–89) and the latter in the north-west.

The Authors

Chapter 6

The Game of Chess

'It is not Lord Chelmsford only who has found out that
the Zulus are a match for us in generalship, and more
than a match for us in cunning.'

*East London and Eastern Province Standard, 14 February
1879*

———⋙⋖———

Ten lonely miles south-east of Isandlwana camp with its air of gaiety, its
campfires, cooking pots and tented comfort, Major Dartnell's command
prepared itself, reluctantly, to sit out a cold and hungry night. Lonsdale had
shepherded the NNC onto a small plateau above the Qudeni track where the
mounted men had joined them. As darkness began to fall it was easy to
discern that the Zulus on the opposite hill were steadily increasing in
number. As the warriors finally merged into the gloom, they were still
shouting taunts at the British bivouac, taunts that mostly described in
graphic detail what they proposed doing to the mothers and sisters of their
apprehensive enemies.

Since the departure of Gosset and his fellow staff officers during the early
afternoon, carrying Dartnell's message that it was his intention to attack the
Zulu at first light, the situation had changed, as had Dartnell's confidence.◊
The enemy was now estimated to number several thousand◊ and, as matters
stood, Dartnell was disobeying orders in that he had not returned to
Isandlwana before dark as directed. Furthermore, he had yet to receive
confirmation that Gosset had appraised Chelmsford of his intentions and
that Chelmsford had fully approved of them. Consequently, at about
6.30 p.m., Dartnell selected Lieutenant Davey of the NNC to ride back to
Isandlwana, there to seek Chelmsford's authority for the proposed dawn
attack.◊ Davey, with no more than the light of the stars by which to see his
way for much of his journey, departed for the British camp. The 1,600-
strong NNC and the mounted men were formed into a square two deep, the
NNC making up three sides and the troopers the fourth. A string of picquets
was posted out in the darkness to give early warning of any approaching
enemy. Horses of the NNC officers were held individually in the centre of
the square, while the troopers ringed their mounts together. Six troopers
were placed on duty to keep the horses calm.

As the temperature fell and darkness descended, so did the morale of the

NNC.◊ The night held many fears, not least of which was the opposite hillside which now, sparkling with campfires, seemed to be invested by thousands of the enemy.◊ Clearly they were not just a local *impi* made up from Matshana's men since his warriors numbered no more than 700.◊ To bolster their sagging spirits, the NNC fell upon some nearby abandoned huts and, tearing them to pieces, built huge bonfires in the middle of the square, thus illuminating all as targets. The white officers and NCOs seemed to have little control over these activities and it was only at this juncture that many of the NCOs admitted to being without their rifles; they had been left behind at Isandlwana camp, 'as a burden too heavy to carry'. Now those NCOs, unarmed and consequently scared, commandeered the rifles of the NNC gunmen. Many officers and NCOs huddled down in the square, intent on sleep and oblivion. Commandant Hamilton-Browne later recalled:

> 'As soon as the square was formed, I lay down and strange to say, I fell asleep. I had loosened my revolver for a moment, meaning to buckle it again, but went to sleep without having done so. I do not know how long I slept when I felt myself brushed over and trampled on. I tried to get to my feet, but was knocked down again. I then tried to find my revolver but was unable to do so. I never let go of my horse's bridle which I was holding in my hand, and I at last staggered to my feet.'

The square had been broken. One of the outlying picquets had mistaken some sound for an advancing enemy and had fired at the unknown. Immediately three sides of the square had erupted in panic. Leaping to their feet, the NNC, losing all self-control, began firing their guns and hammering their shields, making a din that might have been heard ten miles away at Isandlwana camp. Creating their own terror, they broke ranks and began rushing to and fro. Likewise the NNC horses, mad with fear, went careering about the camp.

The horse guard of the police and carbineers, with soothing voices and reassuring hands, managed to prevent a stampede. Yet the rifle butts of several troopers were required to keep the demented NNC from colliding with their mounts. With the rest of the troopers standing to with loaded carbines and fixed bayonets, it was fortunate that no one was shot. Trooper Symons recalled in admiration the calm and reassuring voice of the NMP sergeant-major as he ordered his troopers not to fire. Symons wrote: 'I liked that man's voice. It inspired confidence and courage.' It was a minor tragedy of life that the nameless sergeant-major of mounted police never knew of the high esteem in which a young trooper of carbineers held him.

Trooper Clarke later wrote:

> 'Without food or blankets, and living in fear of an attack by overwhelming numbers, we spent a very uncomfortable night... Had the Zulus attacked, not a man would have escaped, for our natives were panic stricken and would have caused the greatest confusion in the dark.'

Before the night was out, there was another false alarm during which Lieutenant Harford witnessed the horses and men of the NNC in a 'terrific stampede', with Lonsdale and Norris-Newman turning a somersault as the NNC 'bounded over them'.

———▶◦◀———

Several hours earlier, shortly after Gosset had told Chelmsford and his staff of Dartnell's situation, Major Clery had issued orders for blankets and food (for the white troops) to be taken out to Dartnell's position (the NNC had carried their blankets with them). Lieutenant Henry Walsh, 13th Light Infantry, attached to the IMI, with a small mounted escort, had set out with four loaded police pack horses at about 5.00 p.m., arriving at Dartnell's camp as dusk was falling. On the way he must have passed Davey going in the opposite direction. The blankets, tea, sugar, biscuits and tinned meat, limited in quantity to what four pack horses could carry, were insufficient to go around the white troops, and the little they got only seemed to increase their hunger. The rations that had been issued to the NNC earlier that morning, and which had mostly been left behind, were deemed to be sufficient for their needs.

Walsh carried the reassuring news for Dartnell that he had Chelmsford's full support for an attack at daylight. But this was only reassuring up to a point. Dartnell, full of unease at the number of the enemy confronting him, and now dubious of the NNC's fighting ability, deemed it unwise to attack without support. He ordered Walsh back to Isandlwana post-haste and gave him a pencilled note requesting two or three companies of the 24th as reinforcements.

Meanwhile, Davey had arrived at Isandlwana, delivering Dartnell's earlier request for clarification of his orders. At about 9.00 p.m. Gosset, on Chelmsford's orders, visited Glyn's tent. What transpired is contained in Clery's subsequent report:

> 'Major Gosset came to Colonel Glyn's tent to say that Lieutenant Davey had brought information that led the General to fear that Major Dartnell was under the impression that he would not be at liberty to attack the enemy in the morning without instructions, and that the General therefore wished that Lieutenant Davey would be found and directed to start as early as possible in the morning, and inform Major Dartnell that he was at complete liberty to act on his own judgement as to whether he should attack or not.'[◊]

Davey, after an exhausting day and a long nerve-racking ride in the darkness, had wisely gone to bed. It took Clery a considerable time to locate his tent at the other end of the camp. Having found him, Clery gave Davey Chelmsford's instructions, making Davey repeat them to Clery's satisfaction. There is no record of when Davey accordingly returned to Dartnell but, as he survived the events of the coming day, it can be assumed that he either left the camp immediately or in the early hours of the morning.

Having given his orders, Clery too made his way to bed, only to be awoken at 1.30 a.m. by Walsh's arrival with Dartnell's pencilled note requesting reinforcements and stating that he, Dartnell, would not attack without them.

Clery, now wide awake, made his way to Glyn's tent where, correctly in accordance with military protocol, he first gave the note to Glyn, the column commander, rather than to Chelmsford. It was but a gesture. Glyn, well aware that it would be Chelmsford who would make the decisions and give the orders, wearily directed Clery to take the note 'to the general'.◊

In the dim light of a lantern, Clery, squatting close to Chelmsford's bed, had difficulty in deciphering Dartnell's pencilled note. Milne later recorded the incident:

> 'At 2 a.m. …a dispatch was received from Major Dartnell that the enemy seemed in much stronger numbers than had been supposed, and he would not attack them unless two or three companies of infantry were sent out to support his natives.'◊

Eventually both men fully understood the implications of the message. Chelmsford's reaction was immediate and decisive. There was no discussion – least of all with Glyn, the column commander. The enemy had been found in exactly the direction that Fynn had predicted. No doubt their intention was to link up with Matshana, descend the Mangeni Valley, and take the column in the rear. With sufficient force, and hopefully with the good fortune that the Zulu army would stand, a decisive battle could be fought and won. Chelmsford at once ordered the IMI, four of the Royal Artillery 7-pounder guns, six companies of the 2/24th, and a detachment of NNC pioneers to be made ready to march. There was not a moment's contemplation that this force might be of insufficient strength to deal, in the open, with a Zulu army 20,000 strong, no more than there had been any misgivings in sending Lonsdale's NNC, 1,600 strong, blundering into the hills, equipped with fewer than 200 firearms, where they too might well have found the Zulu army. Chelmsford's decision was, no doubt, influenced by his past experience of African campaigning: of the virtually bloodless victory over King Theodore of Abyssinia eleven years earlier; the recent 'Promenade' (as Clery called it) of the Ninth Frontier War of 1878 with its final battle at Centane; the steadiness of his campaign-hardened infantry; the fire power of the Martini-Henry rifle; the failure of the Zulus to oppose his crossing of the Buffalo River; and the recent victory at Sihayo's stronghold. These experiences, coupled with memories of the Boers' legendary victory over the Zulu at Blood River forty years earlier, compounded to create in Chelmsford an unshakeable over-confidence in himself and an unwarranted disdain of the Zulu army.

Chelmsford had given Dartnell complete 'liberty' as to whether or not he should attack. Yet, later, as the dramas of the day began to unfold, Chelmsford and Crealock would conspire to divert blame to others for their own shortcomings and blunders. They would need to find a reason compelling enough to justify the splitting of No. 3 Column in order to attack a perceived Zulu army. Chelmsford, in attempting to justify his actions and, in spite of having ordered the reconnaissance, was later to make this extraordinary statement:

> 'The two native battalions were very raw and the colonial troops under Major Dartnell had never been under fire – I felt certain therefore that they could not be expected either to attack any large force of the enemy, or to retire from in front of it with any chance of success.'

Chelmsford would contrive to make his fateful decision appear to be a necessary one designed to extricate Dartnell who, it would be alleged, had placed his command in a 'critical position' by disobeying Chelmsford's orders.◊ It was the first distortion of the truth; many more would follow.

The decision having been made to attack the force opposing Dartnell, the sleeping troops were aroused and ordered to fall in, attired in light marching order of rifle and bayonet, seventy rounds of ammunition, water bottle and light pack; greatcoats and blankets were to be left behind.

As the grumbling, sleepy men began to parade in the darkness and chill of the pre-dawn, further orders were being issued. Durnford and his column must be brought up from Rorke's Drift; and Bengough's battalion must move up through the Mangeni Valley, via Elandskraal, to Mangeni Falls. Lieutenant Horace Smith-Dorrien, the twenty-year-old special service officer of the 95th Regiment, attached to No. 3 Column as a transport officer, was selected to carry the dispatch to Durnford.

Although Glyn and his staff would accompany Chelmsford, leaving Lieutenant-Colonel Pulleine in charge of the camp, Glyn had never been consulted in the deployment of his column. However, before setting out that morning, Glyn asked Chelmsford two pertinent questions. The first was whether reserve ammunition was to accompany the column as stipulated in *Field Force Regulations*? The reason for querying such a basic order was that ammunition would have to be conveyed by ox wagon which, due to the state of the track ahead, would delay the progress of the column, causing it to take hours to cover the ten miles to Dartnell's bivouac. Chelmsford, impatient to press ahead with all speed, ordered the ammunition wagon to remain behind but to be kept ready to depart at a moment's notice. Furthermore, the ox wagon was to be replaced by his own speedier, mule-drawn cart. It was a compromise that might have given comfort to those apprehensive of an ammunition drought, but in reality it was a useless gesture. There would be little chance of such a laden conveyance making a safe and timely passage to a beleaguered force ten miles distant. The column would have to manage with whatever ammunition the men carried about their persons.

Glyn's second question concerned the many transport wagons kept in camp. A number of them were due to return to Rorke's Drift that day to bring up the supplies that Chelmsford had been demanding from the commissariat, but this might be unwise when the camp would be depleted of manpower. Chelmsford decided the wagons should stay put until further notice. Glyn may have had one further question: should a light wagon containing rations for Dartnell's ravenous troops be taken? However, the question was never posed and on Glyn's orders a ration wagon accompanied the column, bumping along in the rear, getting further and further delayed at each *donga* and becoming a graphic example of the transport problems that plagued the movement of Chelmsford's troops.

At about 4.30 a.m. the column began to march. The dawn in Africa is always a dramatic event and that day, at just about mid-summer, it was particularly so. Long streams of thick mist hung from the mountain crests on both sides of the wide plain and as the sun, a great crimson ball, rose to the left of Isipesi, eleven miles away, it turned the spindrifts of cloud above the troops into a blood red canopy, a phenomenon of nature that many would remember as an ominous prelude to the day.

George Mainwaring and most of his fellow officers were subjected to a somewhat perplexing and unwelcome order just as the column was about to move off. It was customary for officers to ride whilst the men marched. However, on this occasion all officers were informed that the 'commanding officer' had issued very strict orders that no man in the ranks was to be permitted to hold an officer's horse. As Mainwaring and several others had no servant to act as groom, their horses were sent back to the wagon lines.

The column was in high spirits in anticipation of some 'real fighting', and light-hearted banter was exchanged as it passed through the sentries of Lieutenant Pope's outposts. Pope's picquet was three-quarters of a mile out from the camp and his men, in sections of four, extended in a line half a mile long to the south-east of the camp. Pope's was the only company of the 2/24th that would remain at Isandlwana that day and jocular commiserations were called to the unfortunates left behind. Also remaining in camp were the 2/24th's regimental colours, its bandmaster and four drummer boys. It was originally intended that the whole of the 2/24th's band should stay behind, but at the last moment they were ordered to accompany the column as stretcher-bearers.

Captain Hallam Parr, either because he had a groom or because he was a staff officer, was permitted to ride. He recalled the difficulties of getting the four 7-pounder guns of Lieutenant-Colonel Harness' artillery along the road and how the pioneers of the NNC, the only blacks to be issued with red tunics, would double ahead with the advance guard in order to pick and shovel a passage for the guns. Nevertheless, at the steepest *dongas*, the artillery had to be lowered in and pulled out with drag ropes.

The Qudeni wagon track, along which the column marched, was better than most roads of recent experience as it had been used for some time by traders carting timber from the Qudeni forest into Natal. Yet it took most of the column three and a half hours to march the ten miles to Dartnell's bivouac. The exceptions were Lord Chelmsford and his staff. With an escort of only twelve mounted infantry (six days earlier he had deemed an escort of fifty to be a wise precaution) he cantered ahead of the column to where Dartnell – as far as Chelmsford knew – was facing thousands of the enemy. Milne, who accompanied Chelmsford wrote:

> 'We rode on quickly and at 6 a.m. had arrived at the ground taken up by Major Dartnell [over an hour ahead of the main column]. The enemy had retired from their former position and was not in sight. No patrols had been sent out by Major Dartnell, so in what direction they had gone was not known.'◊

How strange that the thousands of Zulus had vanished. Chelmsford's irritation and disappointment must have been acute, yet it did not occur to anyone, except in retrospect, that the British commander had been duped and outmanoeuvred by his enemy. The thousands of Zulus of the night before had been a decoy.◊ But many were still there, hidden in the folds of the hills. They would reappear on the arrival of the main column which they would lure further and further away from Isandlwana camp.

———◆◦◄———

In order for the events of the day to unfold as they did, it had been necessary for Ntshingwayo, commander of the Zulu army, to make two momentous decisions, both within the last few hours. He had decided, contrary to the instruction of his king, to discontinue any attempt to negotiate with the British and to ignore the implications of a deep spiritual belief, held sacred by the Zulu, that it was inauspicious to fight on the 'day of the dead moon' (the day before the first appearance of the new moon in the night sky). And, in all likelihood, if Fynn's predictions were correct that the Zulu army planned to attack via the Mangeni Valley, Ntshingwayo had also decided to change his plan of battle.

When news had come of Dartnell's reconnaissance, Ntshingwayo had sent a detachment to distract Dartnell from returning to the camp, whilst the remainder of the main Zulu army had made its way unseen to the shelter of the Ngwebini Valley (*see Map 4, pages 156–7*). From there, despite it being the 'day of the dead moon', it would launch its attack on the camp whilst 1,800 of the enemy were distracted ten miles away to the south-east. That was probably as far as Ntshingwayo's plan had evolved on the night of 21 January. Then, as dawn broke on the 22nd, the Zulu lookouts, already in the hills above the camp, had sent messengers racing to Ntshingwayo with the news that another column, greater still than the one at bay above the Qudeni track, was seemingly marching to its support. It was a glorious opportunity, one that no general worthy of the name would not seize, and no doubt Ntshingwayo recalled King Shaka's famous exclamation when he

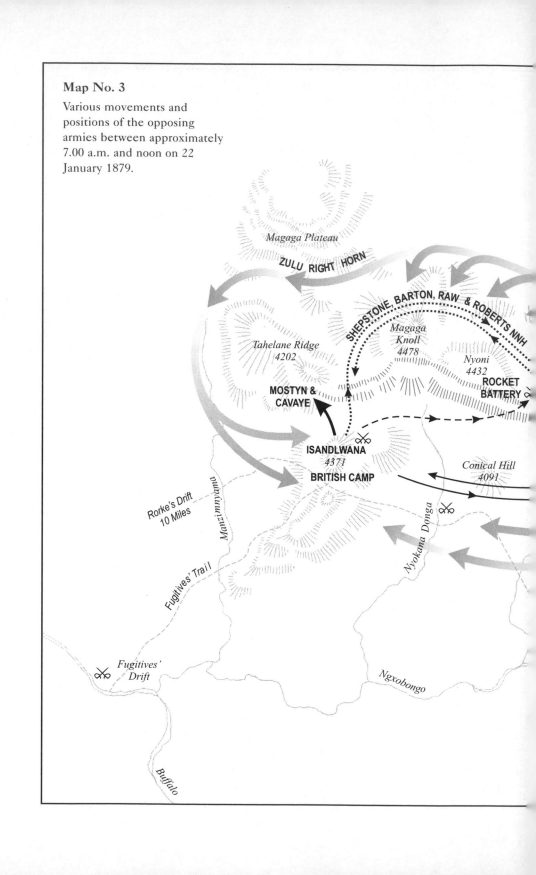

Map No. 3

Various movements and
positions of the opposing
armies between approximately
7.00 a.m. and noon on 22
January 1879.

Magaga Plateau

ZULU RIGHT HORN

SHEPSTONE, BARTON, RAW & ROBERTS NNH

*Tahelane Ridge
4202*

*Magaga
Knoll
4478*

*Nyoni
4432*

**ROCKET
BATTERY**

**MOSTYN &
CAVAYE**

ISANDLWANA
4371

BRITISH CAMP

*Conical Hill
4091*

*Rorke's Drift
10 Miles*

Manzimnyama

Nyokana Donga

Fugitives' Trail

*Fugitives'
Drift*

Ngxobongo

Buffalo

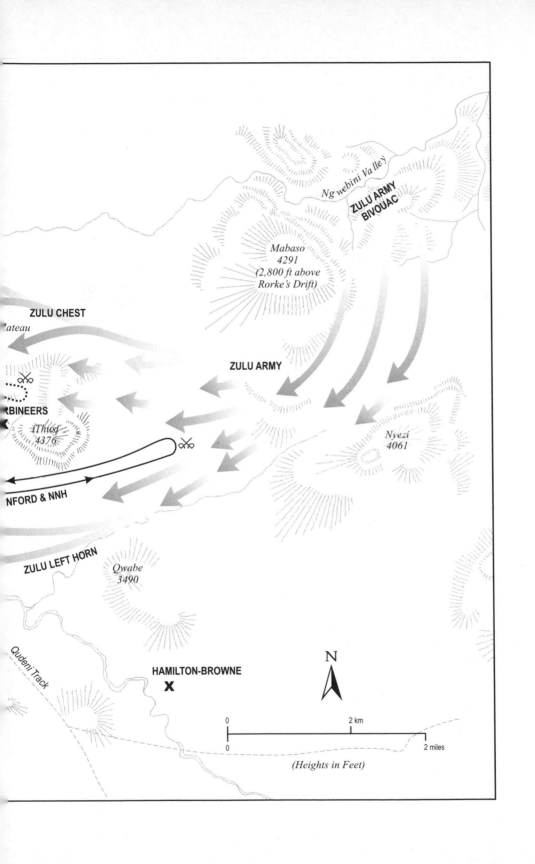

Ng'webini Valley

ZULU ARMY BIVOUAC

Mabaso
4291
(2,800 ft above
Rorke's Drift)

ZULU CHEST

lateau

✄

ARBINEERS

ZULU ARMY

iThusi
4376

Nyezi
4061

NFORD & NNH

ZULU LEFT HORN

Qwabe
3490

Qudeni Track

HAMILTON-BROWNE
X

N

0   2 km

0   2 miles

(Heights in Feet)

had outmanoeuvred the Ndwandwe army: 'A partridge is about to settle in my hand.'

The British camp, with its rows of tents resembling a great herd of white cattle on the plain below, and containing immense riches in arms and ammunition, would be theirs for the taking. Thus the battle of Isandlwana was to be fought over a far greater area than the mere surrounds of the camp; the Isandlwana Plain would take on the semblance of a giant chess board, over 100 square miles in extent, on which the Zulu forces would out-manoeuvre the enemy.

Lieutenant Harford, after a mostly sleepless night amongst the stampeding NNC, saw the approach of Chelmsford and his staff on the Qudeni track below. They were a welcome sight. He rode down to meet them and, as they made their way up to the plateau, he was bombarded with questions.

There is no record of whatever conversation took place between Chelmsford and Dartnell when they met that morning. It must have occurred to Chelmsford that he had been brought out on a wild goose chase, but he failed to look beyond it for a motive. It was one and a half hours after daybreak and Dartnell had made no move to attack. He could not even indicate the direction in which the 'thousands of Zulus' had gone. Harford was able to placate Chelmsford somewhat by pointing out, 'a few Zulu hanging about on the opposite hilltop, as well as some of their fires still smoking.'

It must have been a period of indecision as Chelmsford, surrounded by Dartnell's officers and his own staff, awaited the arrival of the column. Crealock spent time sketching a water-colour of the scenery below, adding to his picture as they arrived the lines of red-coated infantry and horsemen, over 2,000 fighting men with no one to fight. Then, as the column drew near, a large group of Zulus, a number of whom were mounted, appeared in the east towards a red coloured, rock-strewn hill, on the further side of the Mangeni stream.

Inspector Mansel was at once ordered to take the mounted contingent and confront the enemy. At the same time other groups of warriors appeared further to the north, covering much of the Magogo and Silutshana hills on the other side of the Qudeni track, to the north-east of Dartnell's position. The Zulu were now estimated to number several thousand.

The position taken up by the enemy was immensely strong. The Magogo and Silutshana hills rise to over 1,000 feet above the plain and, although separated by the Magogo Valley, both are identical in height, with their summits protected by precipitous cliffs and ledges. It was on the slopes and crests of these hills that the Zulu now arose in thousands. It was exactly what Chelmsford had hoped for. From Dartnell's plateau it appeared possible that the enemy's position could be outflanked by the cavalry working around the hills to the east and west, whilst the NNC made a direct assault across the Qudeni track and up the slopes of Magogo. The police and carbineers were already riding towards the eastern side of the hills and Chelmsford, taking charge, sent a dispatch to Glyn, who was still with the column, but some distance away, ordering him to send Russell, commanding the IMI, around to the western side of Magogo. Shortly thereafter, to Glyn's frustration and chagrin, he learned that Chelmsford had once again usurped his position as column commander. After Glyn had given Russell his orders, he saw him riding in a different direction and on enquiring the reason, was informed, 'that Lieutenant-Colonel Russell had received fresh instructions direct from the Lieutenant-General.'

The infantry and artillery had now caught up and they too received instructions direct from Chelmsford. Four companies of infantry and the guns were first to follow in the wake of the IMI and then turn up the Magogo Valley. There they would form a stop-line and await the retreating enemy who, it was anticipated, would be pushed over Magogo, into the trap, by the advancing NNC and the remaining two companies of infantry. As the fleeing Zulus came into range, murderous volleys of Martini-Henry fire would meet them. Lieutenant John Maxwell of the 2/3rd NNC, who had been recruited in the Cape the previous November, later recalled seeing the long line of skirmishers start off, the British infantry in the centre and the NNC companies on either side.

However, this manoeuvre would involve the troops in a rugged climb and march of over four miles, while facing an enemy of unknown strength. The war correspondent of the *Natal Witness* was in awe of the ground held by the Zulu: 'A stronger position than that held by the enemy would be hard to imagine,' he was to tell his readers. The four companies of the 2/24th and the guns would be faced with a march of similar length around the western face of Magogo, much of it rock strewn and cut by deep *dongas* that would frustrate the passage of the guns.

Chelmsford decided to lead this force but proceeded far ahead accompanied by the IMI, to penetrate the Magogo Valley.◊ He eventually arrived at a shoulder of land that opened into a further valley running directly across his front below the barrier of the Phindo Hills. This valley petered out to a dead end to the south whilst to the north it broadened out on to the Isandlwana Plain. Both valleys were criss-crossed by *dongas* that would make the going difficult for cavalry and impossible for the guns. It was an isolated spot; the infantry were still far behind and out of sight.

Chelmsford and his escort were closely pressed in by hills and, eerily, the Zulu who until a few moments earlier had been seen to the north, had suddenly vanished only to be replaced by many more directly above on the Phindo Hills. They too vanished almost as soon as they were seen. Hallam Parr recalled that:

> 'The morning was spent in endeavouring to get to close quarters with an enemy who could, and did, avoid us at [his] pleasure.'◊

Map No. 4

A map copied from the original surveyed by Captain T.H. Anstey, RE, and Lieutenant C. Penrose, RE, dated 13 November 1879. It is the only contemporary map that shows the bivouac position of the Zulu Army on the night of 21/22 January 1879. The army is shown as *a a a a* at the south-east end of the Ngwebini Valley above and to the right of the letter *F*.

A. The British camp at Isandlwana.
B. Conical Hill.
C. Nqutu Plateau.
D. iThusi Hill.
E. Qwabe Hill
F. Mabaso Hill above the Ngwebini Valley, where the fourteen Zulu horsemen were seen on the evening of 21 January 1879.

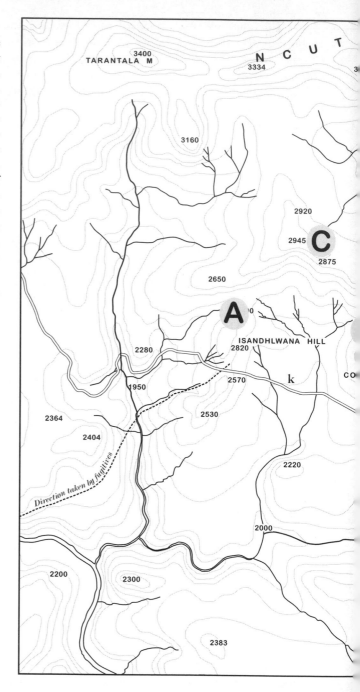

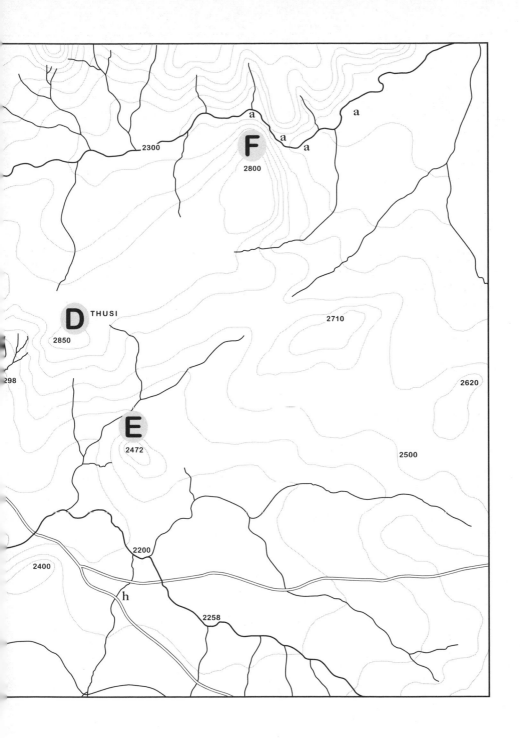

The *Natal Witness* reported similarly:

'Although they showed themselves in very considerable form all along the hill tops, they kept retiring, according to what, as after events taught us, must have been their preconceived plan. The General, however, did not, of course, at this time, imagine that the Zulus were carrying out a concerted scheme, but thought they were probably falling back on their supports.'

With the infantry a mile behind, and the surrounding heights harbouring thousands of Zulus, Chelmsford and his immediate command remained oblivious of their peril.

Shortly a dispatch arrived from Lieutenant-Colonel Harness: the *dongas* were proving to be too difficult an obstruction to overcome.◊ This news seemed to trigger a mercurial change of mind in Chelmsford.◊ He immediately abandoned his plan to encircle Magogo. In fact, after being drawn on in a will-o'-the-wisp pursuit for the past three hours, without a shot having been fired by the imperial infantry, he abandoned the chase. Norris-Newman later wrote:

'The idea did not seem to have occurred to anyone that the enemy were carrying out a pre-constructed plan.'

Chelmsford now set about salvaging some advantage from what had, so far, been a wasted day. The site of the next camp would be decided upon. Orders were sent back to Harness, instructing him to retire with his guns to the Mangeni Falls, taking with him two of the four companies of infantry, there to await further orders. The remaining two companies of infantry were to continue their march and join up with Chelmsford. By this time Inspector Mansel, in pursuit of the elusive enemy, had ridden the whole length of Magogo. He found himself looking down on Chelmsford and his staff in the valley below. Mansel decided to ride down and report. Having done so, he was ordered to guide Harness and his infantry escort around to Mangeni Falls.

Meanwhile, on the eastern side of Magogo, a number of troopers and a section of the NNC had actually come to grips with the enemy. The NMP had pursued a large body of Zulu as far as Nkabane Hill,◊ known also as Matshana's stronghold, which harboured a labyrinth of caves.

Harford, following up with the NNC and having traversed the ground previously held by the enemy, attempted to storm a particularly inaccessible and well defended position. His NNC, now full of courage in the light of day, lost thirteen men, one after the other, before Harford put a stop to an 'impossible undertaking.' Harford himself displayed the same nonchalant bearing that he had shown during the attack on Sihayo's stronghold. Norris-Newman informed his readers:

'Lieutenant Harford… again distinguished himself by going in alone under a nasty crevice… shooting two men and capturing another.'

Eventually the NNC were credited with killing eighty of the enemy, most of whom were of Matshana's clan.

Norris-Newman was also enraptured over the marksmanship of the galloping carbineers. This was the sort of copy the Natal settler population would eagerly devour. A body of mounted Zulu had stood jeering at the carbineers and were greatly surprised when the horsemen opened fire, bringing down one or two. The Zulu then turned and fled but:

> 'not fast enough to escape the men of the carbineers, who putting their horses to full speed, gained upon them and shot many running. Indeed I was told by an eyewitness that dead shots were made in this manner at over 600 yards.'

Trooper Symons recorded a far more realistic account of carbineer marksmanship when he joined up with some of his comrades. They were busy shooting at a Zulu moving at a walk across the hillside:

> 'It seemed cruel to fire at him, but no one hit him. There was one boulder on the hillside, and he took cover behind this and aimed several times at us, but his gun misfired... he had a nice little rest and then stood up and walked quietly over the brow of the hill amidst a shower of dust sent up by our bullets.'

The most spectacular event performed by the carbineers was the mounted pursuit by 'Offy' Shepstone of a fleeing Zulu chief, reputed to have been Matshana himself. Perhaps Shepstone was trying to accomplish what his uncle 'Misjan' Shepstone, had failed to achieve all those years before. In any event Matshana, if it was indeed he, successfully escaped death by dismounting and leaping into a *kloof*. The total tally of enemy dead in these running skirmishes was reported to be 140, plus several prisoners.

The first sounds of the NMP and carbineer rifle fire had carried over the hills to Chelmsford's position, causing speculation amongst the officers who now included Glyn and his staff. Shortly thereafter Captain Buller arrived, closely followed by the remaining two companies of infantry, with the news that the cavalry and NNC were engaged on the eastern side of Magogo.

Chelmsford's reaction was almost one of indifference. He merely ordered the infantry, in their sweat-drenched, thick red tunics – for the sun now shone from a clear sky – to march back to Mangeni Falls, though not by the direct route, but via the top of Magogo, in the hope of aiding the NNC and taking the enemy in the rear.

Private John Price of the 2/24th later complained to his father in Brecon that he had marched thirteen miles out and back but had not seen one Zulu. However, Captain William Penn Symons, 2/24th, thought the invasion was:

> 'going as smoothly as an autumn manoeuvre in pleasant but hot weather in England.'

At about this time a carbineer arrived at Chelmsford's position riding a horse covered in a froth of sweat.◊ He had galloped the ten miles from Isandlwana carrying a half sheet of pale blue paper bearing a brief note. Captain Hallam Parr took delivery of the message, noting its time of arrival as 9.30 a.m. The message read:

> 'Staff Officer – Report just come in that the Zulus are advancing in force
>   from the left front of the camp. (8.5 a.m.)
>   H.B. Pulleine, Lt Col.'

Hallam Parr handed the note to Clery who, again to Glyn's chagrin, gave it straight to Chelmsford instead of, correctly, first giving it to Glyn. Chelmsford glanced at the note, said nothing and handed it back to Clery who asked, 'Is there anything to be done on this?' to which Chelmsford replied, 'There is nothing to be done on that.'◊ Less than a month later, Clery would write to an old military acquaintance of Chelmsford's, suggesting that he, Clery, would normally have had something to say to such a dismissive remark and adding:

> 'I said nothing more; the fact is that, whether from overwork or other
>   causes, the General has got rather irritable since we knew him, and
>   particularly touchy about suggestions being made to him.'

The special war correspondent of the *Natal Witness*, who was undoubtedly none other than William Drummond, Chelmsford's chief of intelligence,◊ questioned the carbineer as to what the enemy being 'in force' meant. He replied 'some 500 or six hundred men.' The carbineer then added a third piece of crucial information. Many of the mounted men who had been left at Isandlwana, and there were over 100 of them, had left the camp in the direction of the enemy.◊

Lieutenant Smith-Dorrien, having been woken in the middle of the night and ordered to carry Crealock's despatch to Durnford, set off on his lonely ride to No. 2 Column camp. Durnford had moved his wagons across the Buffalo at Rorke's Drift the day before and was now established on the Isandlwana road two miles on from the river.

Smith-Dorrien had little to guide him except for the outline of the hills against the night sky and, as transport officer, his knowledge of the track. At that moment he felt completely at ease riding alone in the darkness. The possibility that there might have been Zulus around did not occur to him, but he was later to write:

> 'It ought to have been a very jumpy ride, for I was entirely alone and the
>   country was wild and new to me... but the pride at being selected to carry
>   an important dispatch and the valour of ignorance... carried me along
>   without a thought of danger.'

His only weapon was an unloaded revolver. As he neared the camp he could see the Oskarberg caught in the early sunlight, further up the river, where it marked the position of the drift. It was just before 6.00 a.m. when he rode into Durnford's camp, only to find that Durnford had left at 5.30 a.m. to cross back into Natal. He was on a foraging expedition, seeking additional wagons for No. 2 Column. George Shepstone took the message and, as senior staff officer, immediately read it. It contained the news that every officer in the column had been waiting for. They were to move at once and join Chelmsford who, it seemed, was about to engage the enemy.

Shepstone, in a flurry of excitement and activity and on his own initiative, immediately ordered the camp to be dismantled, packed and loaded onto the wagons. At the same time, he gave Crealock's despatches to twenty-five-year-old Lieutenant Alfred Henderson and sent him off to find Durnford.◊ Henderson, although a man of education who had attended Heidelberg University, also knew how to rough it on the frontier; he had held his own with the toughs of the Kimberley diamond fields and the diggers of the Transvaal gold reefs. Henderson rode hard, at a gallop for most of the way, and within thirty minutes caught up with Durnford on the Natal side of the Buffalo. On reading the dispatch, a delighted Durnford exclaimed:

> 'Just what I thought. We are to proceed at once to Isandlwana camp. There is an impi eight miles from the camp which the General has moved out to attack.'

Only the previous evening in a letter home to his mother, Durnford had written, 'I am down because I am left behind but we shall see.' Now it would appear that he was in favour again after Chelmsford's stern admonishment following Durnford's impulsive move to invade Zululand. He and his command were not to be left behind, as he had feared. He must now hurry lest he incur Chelmsford's displeasure again.

Valuable time had been wasted – or so Durnford thought – whilst Henderson had ridden to find him. However, on arrival at camp he was gratified to find the camp had been dismantled and packed; the rocket battery with its loaded mules, mounted gunners and NNC escort was ready, and the five troops, amounting to 250 horsemen, were already in the saddle. Shepstone had done it all. It was the sort of flying column that any officer, in any army, would have been elated to command in action. Nevertheless, it was a strange mixture of fighting men and weaponry. The black horsemen, in their assortment of garb and with their quivers of throwing spears, could have been from another age. Yet they would ride with one of the more modern – if least effective – weapons of the time, the rocket battery; and the NNC, the majority armed with only spear and shield and all but naked, would not have looked out of place in some colonial Roman legion.

But Durnford was still fearful that he might be missing out, for it was now five and a half hours since Crealock had dispatched Smith-Dorrien with his orders. The urge to gallop on was almost overpowering. Yet he was well aware of an addendum to *Field Force Regulations*, issued by Chelmsford a month earlier (23 December 1878) which, amongst other things, stipulated:

> 'The leading troops must not be allowed to out march the baggage wagons. The latter must be kept together as much as possible, and should one break down, or stick fast, those in front must not be allowed to leave it behind.'

However, in the exhilaration of the moment Durnford refused to be restrained by the millstone of his wagons and marching NNC. He chose to disregard Chelmsford's recent instruction and, with 250 horsemen behind him, he rode ahead leaving the rest of his column to make the best speed it could. Had Ntshingwayo continued with his plan to descend the Mangeni Valley and get behind the British, Durnford's unguarded convoy would have been strung out across the Zulu line of advance.

⟹◆⟸

There was also the other portion of No. 2 Column, Major Harcourt Bengough's 1,200-strong 2nd Battalion, 1st Regiment NNC. Crealock's dispatch, however, had arrived too late to divert Bengough from crossing the Buffalo in the region of Elandskraal, an area containing several missions and scattered settler farms.

Bengough's outdated orders required him to collaborate with Chelmsford's plan to force the submission of the two Matshanas. He was unaware that circumstances had changed and that the forces of No. 3 Column were not about to combine with him in the encirclement of the Matshanas, but were instead in pursuit of a Zulu army in the Magogo and Phindo Hills.

Bengough was a special service officer seconded from the 77th Regiment, who had been in southern Africa for little more than a month. He had been joined the day before, 21 January, by twenty-eight-year-old William Beaumont, who was both the Resident Magistrate of Newcastle Division and the newly appointed civilian District Commandant of the region.◊ Although Sandhurst-trained and a man of considerable ability, Beaumont spoke neither Dutch nor Zulu and would have been as ignorant of the territory that Bengough was about to invade as Bengough was himself. In fact, Beaumont probably had no business crossing into Zululand. Both men would have to rely heavily on their subordinates for local knowledge.

Some time on the 21st Beaumont had received intelligence from a Mr Woodroffe, a local levy leader (and possibly the same man Glyn had tried to recruit as *laager* master) that a large *impi* had been seen across the Buffalo and that it intended crossing into Natal by the Kwa Mahamba Drift.◊ Confrontation with this *impi* would have been within the scope of Bengough's orders, so having dispatched his wagons and equipment to Rorke's Drift, he pressed ahead through rough terrain towards Kwa Mahamba *(see Map 2, pages 88–9)*.

At about the same time as Lonsdale's NNC had stampeded above the Qudeni track on the night of the 21st, so Bengough's NNC reached the Buffalo about nine miles due west of Dartnell's position and 2,050 feet below. There, like Dartnell's command, Bengough's men sat out a cold and uncomfortable night. But, unlike around Dartnell's camp, there were no Zulus to be seen. At 8.00 a.m. the following morning, the 22nd, just about the time Durnford was well on his way to Isandlwana, Bengough and his battalion forded the Buffalo and breakfasted in Zululand.

———※◦≺———

After he had delivered Crealock's dispatch to George Shepstone, Smith-Dorrien had ridden on to Rorke's Drift, a fairly pleasant place now that the main column had moved out. Rorke's old storehouse that Witt, the Swedish missionary, had converted to a church had, on Chelmsford's orders, been turned into a store again. Part of its commissariat housed tons of maize corn bundled into sacks, and hundreds of heavy wooden boxes containing army hard tack biscuits. The old family house, with its odd configuration of little rooms, was full of sick and wounded men, the latter having received their injuries during the attack on Sihayo's stronghold the previous week. The post was under the temporary command of Major Henry Spalding of the 104th Regiment, a special service officer, and was guarded by B Company 2/24th commanded by Lieutenant Gonville ('Gonny') Bromhead. The men of B Company had little to do and their inactivity gave the post a tranquil air. There was also a small contingent of Royal Engineers still working on the *pont*. Their officer Lieutenant John Chard, who had been in the country for little more than two weeks, had left earlier in the day for Isandlwana camp hoping to clarify instructions issued to him.

It had occurred to Smith-Dorrien, after Shepstone had read Crealock's dispatch aloud, that his ride to Rorke's Drift could have been a hazardous one. He now thought it prudent to find some ammunition for his empty revolver. However, there were a few chores requiring his attention as a transport officer, and he gave some time to a gallows-like construction on which he intended to make rawhide trek tows (rough harness for ox-drawn wagons). He then sought out his friend Gonny Bromhead to cadge a few rounds but found that revolver ammunition was in short supply. Eleven rounds were all that Bromhead could spare.

Just as Smith-Dorrien had not been told that a Zulu *impi* was in the vicinity, so he had not been informed, despite his being a transport officer, that the wagons at Isandlwana camp were staying put that day. So, having loaded his revolver and pocketed the remaining spare rounds, he set off back to Isandlwana, believing his presence there to be urgently required.

———※◦≺———

At the time that Chelmsford's column had left Isandlwana, and Chelmsford with his escort had pushed on towards Dartnell's bivouac, there had been over an hour to go before the night picquets of the camp were to be relieved. Drawn mostly from the colonial volunteers, the cavalry vedettes had marched out to their distant posts of vigilance at daybreak. Initially they rode a parallel course a mile or so from Chelmsford's column, hugging the slopes of the Nqutu Ridge. This took them to the landmark of Conical Hill, one and a half miles east of the camp. There Lieutenant Frederick Scott, who was in charge of the vedettes that day, had established a command post.◊ To Scott, the Natal Carbineers were something of a family institution; two younger brothers also served with the regiment, one as the regimental trumpeter and the other as the carbineers' sergeant-major. Both had spent the night with Dartnell.

Conical Hill provided a splendid lookout. From its summit there was a 360 degree view of the Isandlwana Plain. To the south-east were the Magogo and Silutshana hills with Isipesi in the east beyond; to the west the white tents of the camp showed against the dark hump of Isandlwana Hill; ten miles beyond the camp the outline of the Oskarberg could be seen against the haze of Biggarsberg Mountains; to the south the barrier-like Malakatha and Hlazakazi range below which Chelmsford's column was marching. Between every landmark there was distance and space except to the immediate north where the Nqutu Ridge, only half a mile distant, dominated Conical Hill by over 300 feet. It was from the high point at the east end of the ridge, iThusi Heights, that Chelmsford had observed the fourteen mounted Zulus the previous evening, their ominous presence since forgotten by Chelmsford in his enthusiasm to 'rescue' Dartnell. Immediately beyond iThusi, the Nqutu Ridge fell away, its slopes concealing the entrance to the Ngwebini Valley, just over two miles further to the north where the Zulu army, still undetected, waited.

Scott gathered his carbineers and other volunteer horsemen around him at the bottom of Conical Hill, and gave them their orders.◊ He allowed them to choose their own partners for the day before splitting them up into vedettes, of two troopers each. They were then directed to various elevated points out on the plain, forming a bowed line of observation posts about three miles north-east of the camp. Two or three vedettes were also sent up onto the Nqutu Ridge, forward and east of the NNC night picquet position on Magaga Knoll.

The work of a vedette in enemy territory was both boring and dangerous. Scanning empty countryside in the glaring African sunlight, and in the heat of the day, became a constant strain. It induced an overpowering desire to snooze; yet constant vigilance was necessary if a stealthy enemy – and the Zulu was a master of stealth – was not to slip by unobserved or, worse still, was not to strike suddenly out of the long grass. In the later stages of the war, the successful stalking of vedettes was not unheard of, one trooper escaping with no fewer than half a dozen assegai-inflicted wounds pouring blood.

There were two other vedette posts to man, further still from the camp.

Looking straight down the Isandlwana Plain towards Isipesi, there appeared to be another Conical Hill, much smaller in height, a low ridge called Qwabe, poking up from the undulations of the plain. It was an ideal vedette post commanding an all-round view, and little under half way between the camp and the Magogo Valley where Chelmsford was soon to be chasing an ever vanishing Zulu army. Nineteen-year-old trooper William Walwyn Barker and his 'bosom friend,' (with an equally imposing name) twenty-year-old Villiers Caesar Hawkins, were ordered to establish themselves on Qwabe for the day. Though merely troopers, these two young men, one of whom would shortly die, would play a small but significant part in the outcome of the battle.

Beyond Qwabe to the north was the final vedette post to be manned, six and half miles out from the camp, on a hill called Nyezi, its highest point obscured from Conical Hill by the southern shoulder of the Nqutu Ridge. It would, however, be well within view of the troopers on Qwabe who would provide visual communication back to Scott's command post. Two carbineers, one by the name of Whitelaw, were selected to man this isolated position[◊] near the entrance to the Ngwebini Valley which, unbeknown to Whitelaw, was less than half a mile from the bivouac of the Zulu army.

There had been little chance of further sleep for the men left to guard the Isandlwana camp. Despite an attempt at stealth (the absence of bugle calls and muted orders) by Chelmsford's departing column, the rattle and clank of artillery limbers, snorting horses and stomping men ensured the whole camp was aroused.

For Lieutenant-Colonel Henry Pulleine it was an exhilarating moment. It was his first regimental command and he had the added responsibility of defending the camp, transport and equipment for the whole column. Not that Pulleine would have thought for a moment that he would be called upon to fight a defensive engagement; the likelihood of thousands of Zulus launching a full-blooded attack at Isandlwana did not warrant consideration. Despite his twenty-four years of service, Pulleine had yet to be involved in combat. Although his career had taken him to various parts of the Empire, including Ireland, Mauritius, Rangoon and Secunderabad, peace had always prevailed during his presence. At forty-one years of age he was young for his newly acquired rank. His advancement had come by dint of talent as an administrator assisted by two promotions by purchase: to captain in 1860 and to major eleven years later. Since arriving in South Africa four years earlier, much of his duty had been detached from the regiment. He had served as military commander of King Williams Town, Durban and Pietermaritzburg and had recently served as president of the remount depot. It had taken a personal plea to Lord Chelmsford to secure his recent return to the 24th. Although his personality was most amiable there was a tough side to Pulleine's character which had been much in evidence when he had raised and disciplined a new unit in the Eastern Cape. Pulleine's Rangers, as the unit was named, was recruited from British navvies and mixed-race toughs working on the Cape Railway. He also helped to raise the Frontier Light Horse (FLH) which became an elite colonial cavalry regiment. Seldom more than 200 strong, the FLH won no fewer than four Victoria Crosses during the Anglo-Zulu War.

Although Pulleine might have been new to the job of battalion commander, there can be no doubt that he would have pursued his duty with enthusiasm and vigour. That he had received specific instructions that day concerning the defence of the camp is open to doubt. He would have been well aware of standing orders, most of which were spelt out in *Field Force Regulations*. In addition he may have known of Chelmsford's addendum of 23 December 1878, which gave specific advice regarding the deployment of troops under threat of attack. And he would certainly have known that regulations required camps to be entrenched and that both Glyn and Chelmsford had ignored that particular regulation. He would have assumed that he was expected to do likewise. In fact, rather than entrench the camp – which in any event was an impossible task due to the stony nature of the ground – it was more likely that Pulleine had received orders to strike, or prepare to strike camp, that day. Pulleine's thoughts would have therefore centred more around the problem of moving the camp than of defending it. However, whatever the problems, Pulleine knew that he could rely on the unstinting support of his experienced and outspoken adjutant, Lieutenant Teignmouth Melvill.

Melvill came from a family in the service of the East India Company. He had been educated at Harrow and later attended Cambridge University where he obtained a BA. Bypassing Sandhurst, Melvill had been commissioned direct from university into the 1/24th in 1868. Although only four years younger than Pulleine, Melvill had a long way to go in order to reach similar rank. Unlike Pulleine, perhaps he had earlier lacked the advantage of being able to purchase promotion. He had also been unfortunate in that, having passed the entrance examination to Staff College, a helpful route to promotion, he had lost his place. On arriving in England the previous year to take up his position on the two-year staff course, he found that, owing to some bureaucratic error, his place had been already taken. He had no option but to about-turn and catch the next ship to Cape Town.

Pulleine and Melvill had served together previously during the Ninth Frontier War. For a short period Pulleine had held a field command (his first) at a remote outpost in the Transkei. It was a command that had proved to be uneventful and peaceful for Pulleine,◊ whilst Melvill had been able to ride off to adventure. For a few weeks, with only a handful of men, Melvill had pursued an elusive rebel chief through the hills and forests along the Transkei coast. The pursuit was unsuccessful, but an excellent experience for any soldier – an experience which would have been envied by Pulleine.

Now that Pulleine had overall command of the camp, command of the 1/24th devolved upon Captain William Degacher, Pulleine's second-in-command. Thus, by a remarkable coincidence, at that moment both battalions of the 24th were commanded by brothers: Lieutenant-Colonel Henry Degacher commanded the 2nd Battalion, presently marching with Chelmsford's column. William Degacher, a melancholy looking man of thirty-eight, had been gazetted an ensign of the 24th two decades earlier and for the following twenty years had accompanied the 24th on its various home and Mediterranean postings. Whilst on recent leave to England, William Degacher had made up his mind to quit the army but, on hearing news of the Ninth Frontier War, had embarked immediately for Cape Town.

Prior to Pulleine moving across to the column's headquarters, he stood outside his tent surveying his command and, as he gazed east in the direction of Chelmsford's departed column, no doubt he too was struck by the eerie light that illuminated the long spindrifts of cloud hanging over the Isandlwana Plain. His tent was close by the *nek* that separated Isandlwana Hill from Black's Koppie. Immediately below were the battalion tents of the 1/24th where the men were about the early activities of the day and looking for their breakfasts. To the north, on his immediate left, were the *nek* and wagon park containing the transport that Smith-Dorrien thought was destined for Rorke's Drift that day. Also on the *nek*, loaded and ready, was Chelmsford's ammunition cart. Beyond the *nek* stood the tents and horse lines of the cavalry and artillery, all but deserted except for a few horses and their minders. Next came the lines of the 2/24th, likewise deserted but for Pope's G Company which, at 6.00 a.m., had just returned from night guard. Inside the empty tents, the meagre belongings of the soldiers lay scattered, bearing testimony to a hurried departure in the dark. Further away stood the officers' and NCOs' tents of the NNC, whilst a rash of makeshift bivouacs beyond that gave rudimentary shelter to the luckless black rank and file. It had been thought necessary to push the NNC out as far as possible on the flanks of the camp due to their perceived unsanitary habits which, according to the NNC officers, were incurable. For the same reason it was always considered advisable to place the NNC on the flank that was furthest downstream.

The paraphernalia of the camp sprawled for over 1,300 yards along the eastern face of Isandlwana Hill. In front of the headquarters' tents the Union flag, without a breeze to stir it, hung limply at the top of its mast. And behind the tent lines stood the parked wagons of the individual companies. The 2,000 oxen required to draw the transport had been taken out to graze and were scattered far and wide with their herders around the perimeter of the camp, wherever the grass was greener.

Having seen Lieutenant Scott and his vedettes on their way, Pulleine's next task was to organise the relief and posting of the NNC. At that time there were six companies in camp. The two companies brought in by Captain Orlando Murray the previous evening were off duty. Since the initial placing of the picquets, as directed by Clery two days earlier, there were look-outs to the rear of Isandlwana and on top of the hill itself.◊ The rear picquet was manned by No. 9 Company 1/3rd Regiment, a detachment of fifty men or so of Captain James Lonsdale's (not to be confused with Commandant Rupert Lonsdale) iZigqoza NNC, the survivors of Mbuyazi's faction, led by Sikhota of royal Zulu blood. The remaining men of 9 Company, under James Lonsdale himself, occupied a position about half way out on the plain, between the camp and Conical Hill, and were due to be relieved by Captain Krohn's No. 6 Company

Captain Wally Erskine of No. 4 Company 2/3rd NNC, of the amaChunu tribe, had been on Magaga Knoll all the previous day and had been relieved by Captain Barry and his No. 5 Company, also of the amaChunu, led by Gabangaye and his son Mbonjana. They had spent a cold and disquieting night on the knoll. Zulus, presumably the enemy, had crept close to their position, calling to them from the darkness. Lieutenant the Honourable Standish Vereker, Barry's second-in-command, came down to report that the gist of the Zulu calls was unclear.

Twenty-five-year-old Vereker, a son of Viscount Gort, had spent two years studying agriculture at the Royal Agricultural College, Cirencester, before arriving in Africa five months earlier. He was to have pursued a farming career, but instead he joined the Frontier Light Horse, serving as a trooper for a few weeks, before recently attaining a commission in the NNC. His knowledge of the Zulu language was negligible and he was unable to offer any explanation for the nocturnal visit; perhaps it was one of the mysteries of Africa. It was disturbing nevertheless. In any event, whoever the visitors might have been, they were no longer around and the incident was shrugged off. Pulleine decided he would make no immediate changes to the NNC picquets. Instead of No. 6 Company proceeding to relieve Lonsdale out on the plain, as initially planned, Krohn was ordered to have his men fall in in front of the NNC lines and there await further orders.

At the other end of the camp, twenty-eight-year-old Australian-born Lieutenant Edgar Oliphant Anstey led out a portion of Captain Mostyn's F Company Having only arrived at Isandlwana the night before after a twelve-day march, F Company was set for a fatiguing day of road repairing. Otherwise there was not a great deal of activity around the camp. Off-loading of wagons would be about the only task. The small army of drivers and *voorloopers*, their transport staying put for the day, set about brewing coffee. Like the dozens of servants and camp followers of various ilk, they had little to do that required urgent thought. It seemed that most could look forward to an idle morning.

Troopers Barker and Hawkins, riding in company with Whitelaw and his partner, reached the Qwabe Ridge where they were to spend the day. They climbed up in the shadow of its western slope waving a cheerful farewell to Whitelaw whose post on Nyezi was two miles further to the north-east. The Zulu scouts, active since daybreak, had been pacing the carbineers for most of their ride. Now there was no option but for Ntshingwayo to show his hand. Six miles away to the south-east his remaining decoys continued to play hide-and-seek with Chelmsford on Magogo. Closer still, thousands of warriors, no longer required in the deception, jogged through the concealing undulations of the plain towards Ngwebini.

Barker and Hawkins reached the high point of Qwabe and dismounted, letting their horses crop at the sparse grass – but not for long. They suddenly became aware of a group of horsemen in the distance.[◊] It was immediately concluded that they must be Russell's mounted infantry. But there was something in the way the horsemen rode that did not look quite right – and they were miles in the wrong direction to be Russell's men. Now considerably alarmed, the carbineers waved at the oncoming strangers and circled their horses, but neither movement was acknowledged. It then became evident that not only were 500–600 men on foot coming up behind the horsemen, but also that they were fast being encircled. In an instant the carbineers realised that they were confronting a powerful Zulu *impi*. At once they set their horses plunging down the slopes of Qwabe and, at a full gallop, headed for Scott on Conical Hill, drawing rein only to negotiate several massive *dongas* en route.

Scott had seen their wild ride and rode out to meet them. Their news was hard to believe and Scott suspected their story was coloured by a large measure of exaggeration. He needed to witness the *impi* for himself before alerting the camp. Accompanied by Barker and Hawkins, he started towards Qwabe. They had not gone more than a mile when Whitelaw and his partner, riding hard, came into view. Whitelaw's news made Barker's report mundane by comparison. He spoke of a massive Zulu army, thousands strong, emerging from the Ngwebini Valley. And, almost as if to confirm his story, the carbineers became aware that the Qwabe Ridge, recently vacated by Barker and Hawkins, was now teeming with Zulus. Scott about-turned and they all hurried back to Conical Hill, from whence Scott despatched Whitelaw and his partner back to camp with orders to report direct to Colonel Pulleine. The time was approximately 7.30 a.m. The battle for Isandlwana camp had begun.

Whitelaw arrived at the camp in a flurry of haste, galloping straight to the column commander's tent. Lieutenant Coghill, Glyn's orderly officer, had put himself on duty despite his injured knee – an injury that had prevented him from accompanying Chelmsford's column that morning. Coghill hobbled to Pulleine with Whitelaw's message. The two officers conferred and Whitelaw was sent back to Scott with orders that the carbineers were to watch the Zulu and report their movements. At the time Scott was about a mile east of his command post on Conical Hill.

Hardly had Whitelaw returned when Zulus started to appear along the whole length of the Nqutu Ridge above and in the undulating ground to the carbineers' immediate front. Trooper Swift was sent galloping to camp with this alarming information. Then an aggressive Zulu detachment of 200 warriors advanced threateningly towards Scott and his men. Not to be intimidated, Scott moved forward and at 300 yards the Zulus retired. Finding undulations and *dongas* in which to shelter, they disappeared from sight.

The strength of Scott's little force at that moment is uncertain. He did receive reinforcements, but as there were only around 100 mounted men in camp, some of whom would already be on vedette duty elsewhere, it is unlikely that his horsemen amounted to more than fifty. Conversely it is also unlikely that Scott would have advanced on a 200-strong Zulu detachment with anything much less than fifty men.

The enemy having retired, Scott despatched scouts to follow up their movements. Barker and Hawkins were sent up onto the Nqutu Ridge. Well aware that the enemy were masters of concealment and ambush, they must have ridden with great trepidation. As they approached the north-eastern slopes of iThusi, they discovered a large army – but at a comfortable distance. Six hundred yards away a mass of warriors sat waiting. The time would have been about 8.30 a.m. The Zulu army had begun to deploy but Ntshingwayo was in no hurry. Many warriors were still making their way from Isipesi, having broken off their mock engagement with Chelmsford's column.

Barker and Hawkins hastened back to Scott who sent another messenger, the third so far that morning, back to camp with the news.◊ What happened next is clouded in uncertainty. Barker, one of the few to survive the day and the only person to leave an account of the early morning encounters, later wrote that the vedettes had orders not to fire the first shot. Yet, about that time, firing began. Probably other vedettes, those on iThusi being the most likely, opened fire on the advancing Zulu army.

It will be remembered that the courier who had taken Pulleine's message to Chelmsford had added orally that all the mounted men in camp had gone out on patrol in the direction of Scott's encounter; and it is significant that Chelmsford himself, when making his report to the Secretary of State for War, on 27 January, also mentions firing. It seems that, whilst writing his report, Chelmsford had wished to make reference to Pulleine's note, but having handed it to Clery immediately after reading it, he could no longer remember its exact wording. What had stuck in his mind was not the actual content of the written message, but the courier's oral account of firing beyond Conical Hill. Chelmsford wrote:

> '[I] received, about 9 a.m., a short note from Lieutenant-Colonel Pulleine, saying that firing was heard to the left front of the camp, but gave no further particulars.'

Pulleine's note, as we have seen, had actually read: 'Report just come in that Zulus are advancing in force from left front of camp (08.05).'

There were many others who had heard the firing. Mr Foley, a wagon conductor, reported that early in the morning he had heard 'firing in volleys' from the 'General's direction'. Many assumed that the firing came from an engagement between Chelmsford's column and the enemy. But the earliest that any shots had been fired by that column was when the NMP had engaged Matshana's warriors on the eastern side of Magogo, over ten miles away. Two of Drummond's men of the intelligence department also mentioned the sound of firing from the direction of 'the General'. It is not improbable that, because firing was expected from that quarter, it was immediately assumed that was where it came from. Thus, the alarm that the vedettes' shooting should have aroused in camp was ignored.

Pulleine's note had not been particularly informative. He had listened to Whitelaw's estimate of 'thousands of Zulus' heading towards the camp, but diluted this dramatic information to a tamer 'Zulus are advancing in force from left front.' No estimate of numbers, nor the distance of the enemy from the British lines, was given. It being Pulleine's first command that held the prospect of a battle, perhaps he wished to avoid any suggestion that he became an alarmist at the first hint of danger. Or, having waited so long for an opportunity to prove himself, it may be that he wished to reserve any glory for himself alone. Had his message been more explicit, the outcome of the day might well have been different.

Not long after Whitelaw had returned to Conical Hill, there were further disquieting events at Isandlwana camp. Bypassing Scott and his mounted men below, the first contingent of Zulu skirmishers appeared brazenly along the Nqutu Ridge above the camp. A wagon driver by the name of Abraham was amongst the first to spot the enemy. He later reported:

'On that day I saw about 100 of them... the Zulus looked at the camp for a little time and then disappeared.'

It may well have been the same Zulu detachment that a mule driver, Hans Boer, had seen, up on the ridge at about 7.00 a.m. by his reckoning.◊ Lieutenant Pope, in the briefest of jottings in his diary, recorded a 'great firing' at about the same time.◊ Brickhill, the interpreter, later wrote:

'On the morning of 22nd January, 1879, between six and seven o'clock the Zulus shewed in considerable force at the southeast end of Ingutu [Nqutu]. Shortly afterwards another force came into sight at about the middle of Ingutu and the intervening space was speedily filled in.'

Private John Williams of the 1/24th, Colonel Glyn's groom, had been left in camp that day to look after Glyn's spare horses. He had been hanging around outside headquarters and witnessed the arrival of one of Scott's carbineers. Melvill, on that occasion, rather than Coghill, took the horseman's message and on reading it shouted for the bugler to sound 'column alert'. Williams gives the time for this incident as about 9.00 a.m.◊ However, Private Bickley, also a witness, states the time as being approximately 7.45 a.m.

As the bugle sounded the camp scrambled to 'fall in'. Orderlies were sent to recall Lieutenant Anstey's company from its road making; outlying picquets were brought back; the Royal Artillery gunners harnessed their horses; the infantry, struggling into their equipment, doubled to their posts and the urgent bugle calls echoed back from the hills. Within minutes the whole column was fallen in and ready for action. It paraded in the space between the NNC lines and the 2/24th tents facing the Nqutu Ridge, the artillery harnessed up, the infantry formed in columns of companies while the enemy appeared and disappeared at various points along the ridge. Lieutenant Henry Curling of the Royal Artillery later gave evidence of 'the large body of Zulus' seen above the camp at 7.30 a.m. – too far away to fire upon but close enough to be intimidating.◊ Captain Edward Essex of the 75th Regiment, a special service officer and the transport director of No. 3 Column, viewed the Zulu movements from his tent. He watched a detachment of the enemy on the skyline who showed themselves briefly and then disappeared.

With the knowledge that the Zulu were in force beyond Conical Hill, and had been for some time, and were now making will-o'-the-wisp appearances above the camp, Pulleine had cause for serious concern.

At this time Barry's No. 5 Company, of the amaChunu NNC, was still on Magaga Knoll, in close proximity to the marauding bands of Zulu.◊ Magaga is an outstanding topographical feature in countryside abounding in extraordinary landmarks. From only 100 feet below it appears to be no more than a little stony ridge, but its summit, a three-acre area of land, reveals itself as a natural viewpoint, giving visibility for miles in every direction. Barry's amaChunu, within hailing distance of the enemy during the hours of darkness, were now within rifle shot of the Zulus. Nevertheless the amaChunu were not withdrawn and, alarming though their position must have been, they were able to send a runner to the camp with information that three separate columns of the enemy had been sighted.

Then, a little later, Barry reported that two of the columns were retiring whilst the third was heading north-west in the direction of Rorke's Drift or, as an alternative that did not occur to anyone in the camp, in a circular movement that would take it into the Manzimnyama Valley a mile away, and thence to the unguarded rear of Isandlwana camp. The erratic Zulu movements were confounding the onlookers in the camp in much the same manner as Chelmsford's column had been deceived.

Lieutenant Chard, the Royal Engineer officer from Rorke's Drift, having reached the camp and clarified his orders, had been watching the Zulus on the skyline with considerable fascination. An NCO of the 24th had lent him a 'very fine' telescope through which he had been able to watch the Zulu column moving west until the shoulder of Isandlwana Hill hid it from his view. It occurred to Chard that the column might be heading to Rorke's Drift so he decided to return immediately.

With the news from Barry that the Zulus were retiring, Pulleine gave the order for the column to stand down. Nevertheless, the men were ordered to keep their equipment on.

On his return ride, and less than half a mile after leaving Isandlwana, Chard met Durnford and his NNH hurrying towards the camp. The two men paused to talk. For officers in the same corps their appearance and duties could not have been more dissimilar. Chard was newly arrived and inexperienced. He was engaged in the mundane duty of keeping the *pont* working. His undress uniform and helmet were equally mundane, the apparel of a working man. Durnford had been five years in Africa, and bore his withered arm, a souvenir of an enemy spear thrust, like a decoration across his chest. His wide-brimmed hat with scarlet band, his revolver, sword and spurs were all appropriate for a leader of black horsemen.

Chard, in some awe of Durnford, pointed to the Nqutu Ridge and described the movement of the Zulus to the west. Durnford nodded and requested Chard, when meeting the convoy coming along behind, to pass on an instruction to Major Russell who commanded the rocket battery. He was to detach one company of his NNC escort to guard the wagons, and with the remaining company to hurry and catch up as fast as possible. Durnford then shouted the order 'walk march, trot!' and the horsemen moved on.

Durnford had always been fastidious in the selection of men to fill the ranks of his Native Horse and infantry, so much so that he had exasperated Governor Bulwer who had recruited on his behalf. Bulwer wrote:

> 'It appears that Colonel Durnford does not approve of these men, but wants other men, from other tribes and localities, amounting to about 3,000; and in addition to them he also wants the 2,000 named by [illegible] but of whom he does not approve!'[6]

Durnford was equally selective in choosing white men for his column, such as George Shepstone, from the most influential family in Natal.

No. 1 Troop of the NNH was generally referred to as Zikali's Horse, and included Jantee's men. Charles Raw who came from a family of farmers and transport riders led No. 1 Troop. He was a former trooper in the Karkloof Carbineers, and had stuck by Durnford after Durnford had been wounded at Bushman's Pass in 1873. No doubt Raw owed his present commission in the NNH to the loyalty he had displayed on that occasion. No. 2 Troop was commanded by Lieutenant J.A. Roberts of Durban, described as being a smart and courageous young man, well known in Durban business circles. Lieutenant Richard Wyatt Vause, whose father was a co-founder of the *Natal Mercury* and was also to be five times mayor of Durban, led No. 3 Troop. Vause, aged twenty-four, like so many other young men in South Africa at that time had sought his fortune at the Kimberley diamond fields. Nos. 2 and 3 Troops were also sometimes known as Zikali's Horse. Lieutenant Henderson, who earlier that day had galloped to find Durnford with Smith-Dorrien's message commanded No. 4 Troop, also known as Hlubi's Horse. No. 5 Troop, the Edendale Troop was under the command of twenty-nine-year-old Lieutenant Harry Davies from the Harding district who had transferred from the NNC. He had once been a junior clerk in the service of a previous governor of Natal and had worked for the *Natal Witness*.

Captain William Barton, the next senior officer to Durnford, acted as Durnford's second-in-command. Barton is somewhat of a mystery figure. *The Times Weekly Edition* was to describe him as an Irishman, who had spent seven years fighting in South America. Durnford's transport officer, thirty-two-year-old Captain Francis Dundonald Cochrane, of the 32nd Regiment, was a special service officer. He had been in South Africa for little more than seven weeks having travelled out from England with Zulu-speaking Lieutenant Henry Harford. He was reported as always being ready to sit down at a piano and sing a good song. Acting Commissary Officer J.H. Hamer completed the tally of white NNH officers. There were no white NCOs, all were black. The strength of each of the five troops was between fifty and fifty-five mounted men.

Before leaving camp Durnford had ordered Hamer to ride ahead to Isandlwana with a message for Chelmsford. It most likely advised the general that No. 2 Column was on the way and asked for further orders. Hamer arrived at Isandlwana an hour before the rest of the column, but Chelmsford had, of course, long since ridden off to 'rescue' Dartnell.

Meanwhile, there had been more activity in and around Isandlwana camp. Some of Gamdana's people – if not Gamdana himself – had come in under a white flag to surrender eleven firearms. They requested the return of their hostage cattle. Permission was granted and Brickhill, who had been acting as interpreter, escorted the visitors out of camp, ensuring that they saw nothing that would be of intelligence value to the enemy.[◊] On his way back, Brickhill paused to chat with Captain Bradstreet of the NMR, Quartermaster William London and Quartermaster-Sergeant John Bullock, both of the carbineers. The four men listened to the sound of distant firing. It was difficult to place as it echoed and re-echoed around the hills. At first they thought it came from Chelmsford's column but, despite the echoing, they could discern that the firing came from the north. Not knowing that their own mounted men were engaged below iThusi, they speculated that Colonel Wood must be nearby, but Wood and his column, at that moment, were fifty miles away.

Brickhill, having returned to the column commander's tent, was instructed to assemble the wagoners and order the hundreds of oxen and cattle to be rounded up and brought closer to the camp. A number of draft oxen were yoked to their wagons, but for what purpose has never been determined, though it could perhaps have been preparatory to forming a *laager*, or to striking camp. It had already been established that the wagons would not be sent to Rorke's Drift to ferry supplies.

There had been further Zulu movement on the Nqutu Ridge, exasperating Pulleine and his officers. One of the weaknesses of Isandlwana as a defensive position became blatantly apparent; the enemy commanded the high ground enabling him to appear and disappear at will beyond the skyline. The summits of Isandlwana and Conical Hill were both lower by at least sixty feet than the top of the ridge. Closer to the camp, just beyond the NNC lines, the Tahelane Ridge was lower than the summit of Isandlwana but the land on the reverse side of the ridge dropped away, providing concealment for an enemy.

Shortly after a Zulu spy bought news that there were over 6,000 warriors beyond the Tahelane Ridge and Captain Krohn was ordered to send an officer up to Barry's picquet on Magaga Knoll and to report back with all haste. Lieutenant Adendorff, formerly an officer in the Kaffrarian Rifles, who had transferred to the NNC six weeks earlier, was despatched to the knoll.◊ Adendorff did not stay long, and the report that he brought down does not seem to have been understood or satisfactory. Lieutenant Walter Higginson, Krohn's second-in-command, was immediately sent up to Magaga to report afresh. Perhaps what Adendorff had seen up there beyond the rim, had been enough to convince him that the camp must be overwhelmed, for Adendorff was amongst the first to leave Isandlwana. Higginson enlisted the support of Williams, a sergeant-major of the 3rd NNC, and together they made the steep climb on horseback. There for the first time they were able to see over the rim of the Nqutu Ridge into the plateau beyond.

Durnford's arrival, with his 250 horsemen clattering over the stony *nek* of the wagon park, must have caused a stir among the imperial infantry who would be seeing black cavalry in force for the first time. (The infantry and artillery were again drawn up in front of the camp in the same position as they had paraded three hours earlier). The five troops wheeled left around the centre of the camp where Durnford gave the order 'front, form troop' and the cavalcade halted. It says much for the clandestine instruction that the native horsemen must have received, that they could execute such a disciplined cavalry manoeuvre with only a couple of weeks' official training. The troopers were ordered to dismount but not off-saddle. There is dispute as to the precise time of Durnford's arrival, but it was most probably close to 10.30 a.m.

As Durnford strolled off he met up with Brickhill and they walked together to Pulleine's headquarters' tent.

Durnford had not been gone for long when he returned to his troops and ordered them to move from the centre of the camp, to below the NNC lines, closer to the Nqutu Ridge. There they dismounted again, removed the bits and gave their horses a light feed. On his return to Pulleine, it was established that Durnford was senior in service and thus the command of the camp automatically devolved on him. It must have been a blow to Pulleine, to have the opportunity of command in battle suddenly taken from him. Lieutenant Cochrane, who was present, later reported Pulleine as having expressed his regret at Durnford's sudden appearance, to which Durnford, apparently replied, 'I'm not going to interfere with you, I'm not going to remain in camp.' However, there were no orders from Chelmsford, though Durnford had expected to find orders at the camp. It almost seemed as though he had a choice: either stay and take command of the camp or follow up Chelmsford's column in compliance with Chelmsford's vague instructions of the 19th: 'I shall want you to operate against the Matyana's but will send you fresh instructions on the subject.' Clearly those were his last orders and must be followed.

Nevertheless, Pulleine acquainted Durnford with his oral orders 'To defend the camp', and with the disposition and number of troops. He then informed Durnford of enemy activity which, according to Cochrane, included the various reports that:

> 'The enemy are in force behind the hills on the left.'

> 'The enemy are in three columns.'

> 'The column's are separating, one moving to the left rear and one towards the General.'

> 'The enemy are retiring in every direction.'

All this was most confusing, but strangely, there seems to have been no mention of the three messages sent in by Scott from Conical Hill.

On hearing Pulleine's news Durnford gave thought to his vulnerable wagon train still three miles from the camp. He returned to his men and ordered Lieutenant Vause to take No. 3 Troop, Zikali's Horse, and to hasten back and escort the wagons in. At that moment, Lieutenant Wally Stafford with 120 of Durnford's Zikali infantry arrived in camp having hurried ahead of the rocket battery that he and his men had been detailed to support. Stafford was immediately instructed to about-turn and accompany Vause back to the wagon train.◊ It was a necessary precaution, but Durnford felt Pulleine's reports were no cause for alarm. With over five years in Africa he had a saying, 'One believes half of what one sees, and less than what one hears.' He strode back to Pulleine's tent to eat a hurried breakfast whilst he stood and talked with his and Pulleine's officers. Ten miles away, Lord Chelmsford and his staff were also eating breakfast.

Chelmsford, still located at the head of the Magogo Valley, at the spot where Pulleine's message had been received, had decisions to make. His column, and that of Durnford's which now came under his immediate command, were scattered, willy-nilly, over a vast area in which there was clearly a strong enemy presence. It was time to gather his forces together. On the morrow he would continue to pursue his plan of clearing an enemy-free corridor before advancing further into Zululand. He instructed an orderly to find Commandant Hamilton-Browne, and to order him to report immediately.

However, there was still an opportunity for local punitive action. Russell and his IMI were nearby awaiting orders. At about 9.40 a.m. Chelmsford gave instructions that the IMI were to proceed north towards the open Isandlwana plain, then find a way around the Phindo Hills to the east, and, if possible, join up with the NMP and carbineers coming from the opposite direction *(see Map 2, pages 88–9)*.◊

Then, having pondered further on Pulleine's message, Chelmsford decided to send his naval ADC, Lieutenant Berkeley Milne, to the top of Silutshana Hill. There, with his powerful naval telescope, Milne was to observe the camp for any sign of enemy activity.◊ Accompanied by Captain W. Penn Symonds and, presumably a small escort, Milne started his climb.

Just as he departed, Hamilton-Browne arrived with his weary, disgruntled and hungry 1/3rd Battalion NNC. They had been engaged with some of Matshana's men when summoned by Chelmsford's orderly. Hamilton-Browne was offered breakfast but declined, making the point that he could not eat in front of his ravenous troops. Years later he described the scene:

> 'I shall never forget the sight of that peaceful picnic. Here were the staff quietly breakfasting and the whole column scattered over the country! Over there the guns unlimbered, over the hills parties of mounted infantry and volunteers looting the scattered kraals for grain for their horses, a company of the 24th one place and another far away.'◊

Hamilton-Browne was given orders to return to Isandlwana, reconnoitring any *dongas* en route that might conceal the enemy. On arrival at Isandlwana he was to assist Pulleine in striking the camp which was to move either partly, or in its entirety, to Mangeni Falls. There is confusion on this important point.

Hamilton-Browne and his NNC moved off west down the Magogo Valley, following the footsteps of Harness, the guns, and the two companies of the 2/24th that had left a little earlier. On reaching the plain Harness and his troops, led by Inspector Mansel, had turned south-east towards Mangeni. Hamilton-Browne's route was in the opposite direction, north-west towards Isandlwana. The Qudeni–Isandlwana track back to camp was about two miles away to the south. Hamilton-Browne chose to strike across country, cutting some distance off the ten-mile slog to Isandlwana. His foot-weary white NCOs were suffering the most as the day had turned hot and sultry.

The battalion had not gone far across the plain when Hamilton-Browne and his adjutant, Lieutenant W.D. Campbell, riding ahead, flushed two Zulu scouts. They had been resting in the shade of a large boulder and had not heard the enemy approaching. Campbell shot and killed one while Hamilton-Browne captured the other. The Zulu was little more than a boy and very frightened. Under questioning he admitted to having come from the king's army of twelve full regiments and that these were in position above Isandlwana camp. Hamilton-Browne immediately sent Lieutenant B. Pohl galloping back to Chelmsford with the alarming news.

Russell and his IMI had ridden north from Chelmsford's picnic spot, onto the open plain. Their way had been criss-crossed with what seemed to be an endless succession of enormous *dongas*, obstacles that broke up any attempt at orderly formation, causing the riders continually to have to reform. As they emerged from the valley the frequency of *dongas* diminished and they were able to pursue a few of the enemy who had suddenly appeared. But the chase did not last long. The Zulu were moving fast, too fast over the broken ground and after two miles Russell abandoned the pursuit. Instead he led the IMI east towards Isipesi Hill where the Zulu army had encamped two nights earlier. A large number of them were still much in evidence. Russell later reported:

> 'This hill was covered with the enemy in very large numbers and we saw
> the spoor [tracks] in the valley where their masses had come down from
> the hills where they had been in front of the General in the morning.'

It did not occur to Russell that the 'masses' of warriors, their spoor heading directly towards Isandlwana, might be on their way to attack the camp.

When Russell broke off the chase after the fast moving Zulus, he paused to send a pencilled report back to Chelmsford which read:

> 'A considerable number, 50/100 Zulus, were seen retreating in a NE
> direction. I followed them about two miles but they went too fast for me.
>   I fired a few shots at their rear and one man is supposed to be hit. I am
> now going to carry out the General's instructions which I could not do if
> I followed the Zulus any further. 10.15 a.m.
>   J.C. Russell.'

He made no mention of the spoor heading west. This note was initialled by Clery as 'Received 10.40 a.m. Jan. 22nd'. It was just about the time that Durnford and his NNH had ridden into Isandlwana camp.

Milne and his companion finally made it to the top of Silutshana, a steep climb of over 600 feet. The view was breathtaking: Isandlwana camp lay ten miles away with the purple blue haze of the Biggarsberg Mountains twenty miles beyond. To the north, down on the plain, they could see Russell and the IMI approaching Isipesi. Milne was to later write:

> 'The main body of the enemy who had been in our front all the morning
> were now assembled at the foot of Isipesi Hill, watching the movements
> of the mounted infantry, who were scouring the plain some short distance

off, but on their near approach they [the Zulus] all retreated to the table land on the top of Isipesi Mount.'

Milne also wrote with justified apprehension:

'I also saw small clusters of the enemy on every hilltop all around us, observing our movements.'

Training his telescope to the west Milne studied the camp, which was in bright sunlight, for about an hour. Detail was impossible but he could discern that herds of oxen and cattle had been brought in close to the tents. Apart from that there appeared to be no cause for alarm. It was particularly reassuring to see that all the tents were still erect. Standing orders required tents to be struck, by the simple method of pulling out the centre pole, at the first sign of an enemy.

Milne observed the camp for almost an hour and then, having decided that there was nothing untoward happening, made his way down to the picnic spot where Chelmsford and his staff, alone and unprotected except for the escort of twelve mounted infantry, reclined. That they had not been overwhelmed by a sudden rush of warriors must be attributed to Zulu priorities being elsewhere at that moment.

Lieutenant Pohl, riding with Hamilton-Browne's warning, was still making his way back across the plain. His message, like other messages that day, supposedly never reached its destination.

Milne reported his observations to Chelmsford who, reassured by the news that the tents were still standing, decided to send Captain Allan Gardner, 14th Hussars, back to the camp. His orders were to hurry the despatch of the tents and equipment of all troops now engaged locally. A new camp would be established adjacent to Mangeni Falls. The remainder of No. 3 Column, and Durnford's column wherever it might be, were to stay put it seems until the morrow. Despite the enemy being evident in almost every direction, Chelmsford had decided to keep his forces split for the next twenty-four hours.

With a small escort of IMI, and accompanied by three officers, Lieutenant McDougall of the Royal Engineers and Lieutenants Dyer and Griffiths, both of the 2/24th, who would assist in the move, Gardner set off for Isandlwana. Along the way they would be joined by Major Smith of N Battery, RA, also making his way back to camp. Before the day was out, Gardner's four companions would all be dead.

Chelmsford then decided to ride back to Mangeni himself, but not by the route taken by Harness. Without informing Russell, or any other of his officers, he and his staff made their way over the top of Magogo and thus, for the next crucial hour or more, Chelmsford's whereabouts were completely unknown.

Lieutenant Higginson and Sergeant-Major Williams, their horses heaving and slipping as they made the final ascent, dislodging a small avalanche of rocks that tumbled back behind them, reached Magaga Knoll. Dismounting, they walked out onto the flat grassy summit and found Barry and Vereker, surrounded by the amaChunu NNC, watching in rapt consternation the movements of the enemy.◊ Some 900 yards away – across the Magaga plateau, and just out of effective rifle range – a body of warriors had assembled. To the east, all along the Nyoni Heights and the Nqutu Ridge, as far as iThusi two miles distant, warriors abounded.

On the plain below Lonsdale's iZigqoza NNC could be seen still occupying the low-lying ground between the camp and Conical Hill. Hidden by the rim of the Nqutu Ridge, the carbineers and NMP still held the *donga* beyond Conical Hill from where they had been exchanging fire with the enemy for the last two hours. Apprehensive, Higginson and Williams watched the manoeuvring for upwards of half an hour, then, having remounted, they scrambled back down to the camp. Higginson reported direct to Pulleine but by that time Durnford had arrived and it was he who took Higginson's report.

Probably rather irritated by so much conflicting information, Durnford brusquely questioned Higginson, the second colonial courier to return from the Magaga lookout. Adendorff's earlier report, most likely delivered in an excited German accent, had perhaps not been incomplete but, rather, incomprehensible. Higginson was easier to understand and Durnford was impressed. He ordered Higginson to send some NNC scouts to the top of Isandlwana Hill and from there report back on Zulu movements. However, Durnford was deceived by the height of Isandlwana and was not aware that even from that elevated lookout, the whole of the Zulu army could assemble beyond the rim of the Nqutu Ridge without being seen.

Higginson collected half a dozen men from the NNC as ordered and rode to the base of Isandlwana hill. He directed the men to climb to the summit and to report back on the enemy as soon as possible. He watched them climb until they reached the sloping plateau and then, having scaled the rocky face leading to the summit, they vanished, never to appear again as far as Higginson was concerned. He waited for half an hour but, as it takes forty minutes for a fit man to climb to the summit and back, he did not wait long enough. So Higginson commandeered another scout from the NNC and sent him scurrying up the eastern slope of the hill with orders to, 'come down with news at once.' In Higginson's own words, 'he returned very soon'.

In the time that the man accomplished his mission, it would not have been possible for him to have climbed very far; perhaps high enough to see over the rows and rows of tents that might well have obscured a clear view of the plain. Then, being unable to see any Zulus, and being under pressure to return, he probably hurried back reporting the enemy as having gone. This was then translated into military terminology by Higginson who informed Durnford that, 'the Natives were retiring'. Durnford replied, 'Ah! Is that so; well then we will have to follow them up.' He is also reported to have remarked to Pulleine, 'Well, my idea is that wherever Zulus appear, we ought to attack.'

Although Durnford had already made it clear that he did not intend to take over command of the camp, he nevertheless let it be understood that whilst he was in camp, he was the senior officer and it would be he who would give the orders. It was Durnford who had authorised the release of Gamdana's people and their cattle, not Pulleine.◊

During Higginson's absence, Durnford, in response to a report that 6,000 Zulus had been sighted on the Nqutu Ridge,◊ had sent two NNH troops to investigate. Led by Captain Barton, and accompanied by George Shepstone and Hamer, the commissariat officer, two troops of Zikali's Horse, those of Raw and Roberts, had climbed the Tahelane spur, just beyond the NNC lines, up onto the ridge *(see Map 3, pages 152–3).*◊ There they turned east towards Magaga Knoll a mile away. Durnford had again usurped Pulleine's authority by ordering Roberts to commandeer Barry's company of amaChunu NNC and to take them with him as additional support.◊

Durnford decided to follow up the 'retiring enemy', whom he believed might well be on their way to attack Chelmsford. He asked Pulleine for two companies of the 24th to support him.◊ He did not want them to accompany his horsemen – the infantry would be far too slow for that – but most likely to form a protective line out from the camp, that his horsemen could fall back behind if pursued by overwhelming odds. Pulleine strongly demurred, pointing out that his orders were to defend the camp. Durnford was persuasive but not sufficiently so to overcome Pulleine's objections. No doubt there was resentment that this engineer officer, with his native troops, although senior in service, had the gall to start ordering around a regiment of imperial infantry. Lieutenant Melvill was sufficiently incensed to confront Durnford remarking, 'Colonel, I really do not think Colonel Pulleine would be doing right to send any men out of the camp when his orders are "to defend the camp".' Having been refused, Durnford turned towards his troops and their saddled horses, 'Very well,' he said; 'it does not matter much, perhaps I had better not take them, I will go with my own men', and added, 'If you see us in difficulties you must send and support us.'

By this time the hard pressed rocket battery had arrived, its mounted officer and gunners having been hampered by the pace of the NNC infantry escort. Major Francis Broadfoot Russell, RA, who commanded the outfit, was an experienced artilleryman with over fourteen years service, much of it having been spent in Malta, Canada, Aden and the Upper Sind district of India. He had been in South Africa for over two years and was to have accompanied No. 1 Column as district-adjutant when ordered to organise a rocket battery. Russell must have found his new job rather demeaning. A rocket trough was little more than a tin-pot contraption in comparison to a proper artillery gun. A battery of 7-pounders would have been a command more befitting Russell's rank.

A rocket trough, no more than a launching pad, was a flimsy affair resting on metal legs. It fired a twelve-inch long six-pound shell that was discharged by a hand-lit fuse. In flight the passage of air over its fins produced a frightening shriek that was designed to terrorise a primitive foe. However, it was a missile that was likely to miss any target smaller than a massed formation. Only one of Russell's complement of 'gunners' was even an artilleryman; the rest were men seconded from the 24th. The final indignity was the calibre of his plodding escort, men armed with spear and shield.

The 120-man escort of D Company 1/1st NNC, commanded by Captain Cracroft Nourse, were all exhausted by having been forced to jog much of the way in order to keep up with the mounted gunners. However, they were of Zikali's tribe, and amongst the best of the NNC troops. But, having finally arrived at Isandlwana, there would be no respite.

Durnford was ready to go. It had not occurred to him that the camp itself could be in peril. He asked Pulleine if Higginson could be seconded to him for the day – a request that was readily granted. Higginson was ordered to ride to where Scott and the carbineers still held their ground. He was to tell them that Durnford would be following up the Zulus further east from their position, and that he, Durnford, expected their co-operation.

Durnford had already split his mounted force by sending one troop back to the convoy and two to the plateau, leaving two remaining under his direct command. (Besides this, a bewildered Major Bengough and his battalion were isolated eighteen miles away in the Buffalo Valley, at Kwa Mahamba Drift – but Bengough's predicament was of Chelmsford's making, not Durnford's). Durnford now fragmented his force once more and spurred off at a canter from Isandlwana. On their own the rocket battery and its puny escort of fatigued NNC, an ill-conceived marriage of modern and primitive weaponry, were highly vulnerable. Impatient to get to grips with the enemy and with discreditable disregard for the safety of the battery, Durnford left it to follow on at the best speed it could muster.

Chapter 7

Descent of the Whirlwind

'We spared no lives and asked for no mercy for ourselves. We killed every white man left in camp, and their horses and their cattle too.'

Zibhebhu kaMaphitha, hereditary chief of the Mandalakazi, 1879

'So ended the four days during which No. 3 Column advanced into Zululand... four days which will be memorable so long as the colony exists, and so long as England takes interest in the deeds of her little armies in foreign lands...'

Charles Norris-Newman, January 1879

———————

At about 11.30 a.m. Durnford rode east across the Isandlwana plain. It was his intention to attack a Zulu *impi* that appeared to be retiring from Isandlwana in order to intercept Chelmsford's column.

Ntshingwayo, Mavumengwana and the Zulu army were also about to attack. Ntshingwayo had with satisfaction learnt of the disarray of Chelmsford's expedition as, responding to Zulu decoys, it manoeuvred this way and that amongst the distant hills. His warriors, having completed their deception and slipped past Russell and his IMI, had taken little more than an hour to jog the nine miles from Isipesi and most had already arrived to join the rest of the army. Ntshingwayo had also sensed the uncertainty of the soldiers in the British camp as his decoys had appeared and then vanished only to reappear again. Although his army had been sighted early in the day by the enemy vedettes, he had turned the sightings to his advantage. By deploying his warriors to and fro, he had drawn other horsemen into joining the vedettes in their isolated *donga*, far from their camp. The desultory fire of his skirmishers had kept the horsemen occupied while his army had assembled and deployed without threat or interference. Even the enemy reinforcement of black horsemen, which had earlier caused him concern, was also reacting to his deceptions. Some had gone into the hills and the rest were moving out of the camp directly into the intended path of his waiting left horn. Ntshingwayo gave the order and his warriors rose up. The younger regiments, that had the furthest to go in the attack, the Nkobamakosi, uVe and uMbonambi, would form the left horn.

All were eager in their anticipation of the fight to come and in their rivalry to be the first regiment into the British camp. The commanders watched and as Ntshingwayo gave the signal the army let out a great pent-up cry of *'uSuthu'*. It was followed by an ominous silence that was maintained as the warriors jogged forward, spreading out into skirmishing order, creating the illusion of doubling and trebling their numbers, making their thousands appear as tens of thousands. With those who would have disciplined them now departed, the older *izindibi* boys began to discard their sleeping mats and pots, giving them over to younger boys for safekeeping. Then, egging each other on with excited boasts and gestures, they followed the warriors to Isandlwana.[◊]

The uDududu, uNokhenke and uNodwengu regiments that formed the right horn had also emerged from the Ngwebini Valley. They had crossed the *donga*-riddled plain beyond and had climbed the concealing eastern slopes of iThusi. There the main body had paused while the skirmishers and decoys had performed their deceptions above the British camp. The

---

Note

The Zulu accounts of the battle have all come down to us having first been translated, and then recorded in writing by white men – often officers of Chelmsford's army such as Drummond and Longcast. The Zulu witnesses, more often than not, are described as either deserters, prisoners or spies. In the opinion of the authors, some of these testimonies are not to be wholly trusted. Most 'official' Zulu reports seem to reflect what the interrogator wished to hear and that which the witness thought wise to say.

As part of the cover-up, which will be described in later chapters, it was essential that Chelmsford and his staff should not be seen as having fallen for the Zulu decoys of 21 and 22 January. It was also vital that a good excuse be found for failing to have discovered the Zulu army on the 21st, or early on the morning of the battle itself. Part of an excuse was, in fact, provided by the Zulus themselves. That it was originally the Zulu intention not to attack until the 23rd was true enough. (But all that changed as has already been described). Chelmsford and his staff elaborated on this part-truth by inventing the myth that the whole Zulu army was hidden far away in the north-west end of Ngwebini Valley, and that it would not have attacked at all on the 22nd had it not been for Durnford's horsemen stumbling upon it by chance. The Ngwebini Valley extends approximately three miles in an east-west direction before swinging south for a further mile. It was at this south-east end of the valley that the Zulu army bivouacked *(see Map 2, pages 88–9)*. It is interesting to note that the only contemporary map that indicates the bivouac position of the Zulu army on the night

regiments that would form the chest of the attack, the mCijo and Khandempemvu were also there as were the uThulwana regiment and the Undi corps of the reserve. The uNokhenke also formed part of the reserve.

The excitement was intense. The regimental commanders strolled back and forth letting their authority be felt, keeping discipline by the force of their personalities. The lookouts on iThusi Heights, watching the plain below, indicated that the left horn was on the move, and then, to the jubilation of the host, the enemy horsemen were seen fast approaching along the ridge in their direction.

⟫•⟪

The two Zikali troops of the NNH that Durnford had despatched to the Nqutu Ridge soon after their arrival in camp, had made their way east towards iThusi. One troop under Roberts rode parallel to the edge of the ridge, about half a mile out onto the plateau, while Raw's troop, within sight and hailing distance, kept close to the edge of the ridge itself. Both troops were under the command of Captains Barton and Shepstone. In places the going was atrocious. This was the terrain that Trooper Clarke, after being on vedette duty two days previously, had described as 'such vile country.' It was broken ground, strewn with rocks and boulders. As the troops rode east, Roberts had given Barry and Vereker what could only have been unwelcome

---

of 21 January 1879 is that drawn by Captain Anstey and Lieutenant Penrose, RE, dated 13 November 1879 *(see Map 4, pages 156–7).*

Lieutenant Charlie Raw is the person usually credited with the discovery of the Zulu army; in chasing after some herded cattle, he all but canters over the edge of a deep ravine. Reining back just in time, there below him, stretching as far as the eye can see, are the packed ranks of the Zulu army, sitting in silence on their great war shields. Dramatic stuff, but as will be seen, far different from the description of events as contained in Raw's official report written shortly after the battle. In any event the heights above the Ngwebini Valley are two miles further to the north-east of Raw's position, and there would not have been time for the NNH – and especially not for the NNC on foot, to have travelled that additional distance. Raw's report was not submitted as evidence at the Court of Inquiry, but it was later sent to the War Office as supplementary evidence.

Likewise, many accounts of the battle fail to mention that the carbineers and the NMP, under Scott, had been in action since early morning on the 22nd, and fail to credit that the Zulu movements taking place at that time were preparatory to its planned deployment and attack. From a Zulu perspective the battle had already started by 7.00 a.m. It is also significant that Ntshingwayo, who commanded the Zulu army at Isandlwana, was never questioned. Although after the war Sir Garnet Wolseley gave Ntshingwayo one of the thirteen chiefdoms of the former kingdom, it seems no one recorded Ntshingwayo's views on the conduct of the battle.

The Authors

news.◊ Far from being relieved after a full night on Magaga Knoll, they and their NNC now had to leave the knoll and accompany the NNH – and, worse still, in the direction from whence the enemy had appeared. The amaChunu rank and file were particularly unhappy. Psychologically they were drained. It had been a frightening night with the Zulus calling to them from the darkness and an equally frightening morning. Now, instead of retiring on the perceived safety of the camp, they were being marched straight towards a Zulu army. They did not have the comfort of hefting a Martini-Henry rifle with a pouchful of shining cartridges that could kill at long range. They would only be able to fight at close quarters where they knew they would be vastly outnumbered. Barry, Vereker and their white NCOs, all on foot, felt as apprehensive as their men did.

There were Zulus ahead of the NNH. Small groups of warriors appeared here and there, loping away in retreat, drawing on the horsemen who trotted where the ground permitted, trying to get to grips with the Zulu skirmishers.◊ The NNH followed them east for four miles, until they were almost level with the carbineers and NMP in their *donga* 100 feet below. Then, at last, the deception complete, the Zulu army began to move. As the NNH and NNC approached the hump of iThusi with its serrated crest of rocks, the Zulu right horn and chest emerged from behind the iThusi Ridge (*see Map 3, pages 152–3*). Raw later described the encounter:

> 'We left the camp, proceeding over the hills, Captain George Shepstone going with us. The enemy in small groups retiring before us for some time, drawing us on for four or five miles [it was nearer to four miles] from the camp where they turned and fell upon us, the whole army showing itself from behind a hill in front where they had evidently been waiting.'

Sergeant-Major Nyanda, brother of Zikali, son of Matiwane and chief of the amaNgwane, rode alongside Shepstone. He described the scene three days later:

> 'We saw a handful (not many) of Zulus who kept running from us, all of a sudden, just as Mr Shepstone joined me on the crest of a ridge, the army of Zulus sprung up, 15,000 men.'

Hamer, who would survive, described the incident in a letter to his father:

> 'I went along with him [George Shepstone] and after going some little way, we tried to capture some cattle. They disappeared over a ridge, and on coming up we saw the Zulus, like ants in front of us, in perfect order as quiet as mice and stretched across in an even line. We estimated those we saw at 12,000.'

The Zulus, 800 yards away, immediately began to deploy and open fire while the two troops of NNH drew together. They then dismounted, fired a volley, remounted and retired preparatory to dismounting again. George Shepstone, now aware of the danger to the camp, ordered the NNH to make a fighting retreat, delaying the enemy as long as possible. Leaving Barton in command, Shepstone and Hamer spurred off over the broken ground to take warning to the camp four miles away. The time was about 11.45 a.m. It was too much for the amaChunu NNC. Armed with only spear and shield they turned and fled towards the camp, leaving Barry and Vereker behind.◊

On the plain below Barker and Hawkins had again reported to the camp. They had taken advantage of their visit to persuade Quartermaster London to replenish their ammunition supply. Each now had a full bandolier of fifty rounds. They were returning to their outpost when they encountered the rocket battery.   ·

In an effort to keep up with Durnford, who had disappeared to the right of Conical Hill, Major Russell had decided to try a short cut to the left. It was then that the rocket battery met up with Barker and Hawkins who advised Russell that the NNH were heavily engaged on the ridge above. The carbineers volunteered to show Russell a shortcut to the action, a re-entrant (a feature later to be known as 'the Notch') leading to the top of the ridge. Having pointed out the way, Barker and Hawkins continued on to their outpost amongst the *dongas* below iThusi.

Russell halted his command at the bottom of the ridge. Gauging that the steep ascent would be too much for his tired rocket-laden mules, he ordered the NNC escort to unload and to carry the rockets up themselves. In the confusion of unloading and hefting the rockets, Russell decided to see what was happening above as the sound of firing was fast drawing nearer and gaining in intensity.◊ He took the re-entrant at a gallop and on reaching the top almost rode full tilt into a mass of Zulus. The going had been so steep that there was hardly need to rein back. Russell swung his horse round on the shaly rim and, with the Zulus hard behind, descended in a shower of loose stones shouting 'Action front!' to his astounded men below.

The rocket battery had been caught unprepared. Some of the amaNgwane NNC were still milling about, holding comrades' weapons, while others began to unload and shoulder the rockets up the ridge. Captain Nourse was dismounted, as were the eight gunners of the 1/24th. And when Russell shouted the artillery order, 'Action front', it meant nothing except to Nourse and the men of the 1/24th. Despite the confusion they reacted immediately, managing to unload one trough and prop it up in the direction of the enemy. Then, snatching rockets from the unnerved amaNgwane, the gunners loaded the trough. Whether on Russell's orders, or by a gunner's initiative, a rocket was ignited. With a banshee shriek it took off. It was frightening but ineffective. The Zulus chasing Russell halted at 100 yards and fired a volley that was as devastating and accurate as that expected of trained imperial infantry. Three of the eight gunners were killed instantly, Russell fell mortally wounded, most of the amaNgwane fled, discarding their rockets, and the mules stampeded in every direction. It all happened in a matter of seconds. With the exception of five men, the amaNgwane flight continued past Isandlwana camp and on in the direction of their homes amongst the distant Drakensberg mountains. They were never seen again.◊ Nourse, whose mount had bolted with the mules – as had all but six of the artillery horses – found himself on foot with two of the five surviving gunners, Privates Johnson and Trainer. Flight was their only hope. Taking to the labyrinth of *dongas*, and hopefully heading towards the carbineers' outpost, they fled. Fortunately the *dongas* gave concealment and the warriors did not pursue.

Just before the first volley, Private Grant and another of the gunners had been detailed to hold the horses and despite the chaos, they had hung onto the terrified animals. Still holding the jumble of reins, they managed to mount and with great resolve and commendable horsemanship they galloped away, Grant leading two spare horses and the other gunner leading one.◊ Bombardier Gough, with a spare horse, also escaped. These additional horses would be the means of survival for several men in the hours ahead.

Durnford, completely unaware of the rocket battery's destruction, and still yet to comprehend the peril to the camp, was still cantering east at the head of his Edendale and Hlubi Troops, just over 100 mounted men in all. It was not long before they heard the sound of firing to the rear. Scott and his men had watched Durnford's progress with great consternation. Higginson was yet to arrive with Durnford's orders and Scott was well aware that Durnford was riding directly in the path of a vast Zulu army. Scott decided to send warning. Two carbineers were despatched at a gallop to intercept. They reached Durnford just before he rounded the eastern shoulder of iThusi that concealed the advancing regiments of the Zulu left horn. To Durnford's indignation he was told that he had better return to the camp as he was about to be surrounded.◊ The identity of the two carbineers who brought the message is uncertain, but their outspoken confidence in addressing Durnford marks them as a product of an elite colonial community. Perhaps it was Barker and Hawkins, each twenty years old, one the son of the dean of Pietermaritzburg and the other the grandson of Sir John Hawkins, High Sheriff of Somerset. Or perhaps it was Whitelaw and his partner who knew the terrain. Whoever they were, they were not to be intimidated by Durnford. Clearly flustered Durnford turned to Davies, the commander of the Edendale Troop, and testily asked for the whereabouts of the rocket battery. Davies told him pointedly that it was 'a very long way behind'. Durnford then called angrily to Sergeant-Major Jabez Molife of the Hlubi Troop, demanding to know what had happened to the scouts who had been sent ahead. Their whereabouts were also unknown.

Durnford then turned to the two carbineers and told them to return to Scott with the order that Scott was to give his best support. He further remarked, 'The enemy can't surround us, and if they do, we will cut our way through them.' To his surprise one of the carbineers replied, 'Lieutenant Scott would not leave his post on any account whatsoever, as he had strict instructions from Colonel Pulleine not to leave his post on any pretence whatever.'

Durnford glared at the carbineers and with commendable self-control replied, 'I am Colonel Pulleine's senior; you will please tell Lieutenant Scott to do as I tell him' – and at that moment the vanguard of the Zulu left horn appeared in its thousands, the warriors loping forward in utter silence. They were about 1,500 yards away and as they drew near, the front rank paused to fire and then advance steadily again.

It is possible that at this moment, Durnford thought not only of the peril to the camp, but also of the vulnerability of Chelmsford's column. It is likely that he detailed six men of the Hlubi troop to gallop away and warn the general.◊

To stop the tide of warriors with 100 horsemen was impossible, but they could be delayed. Durnford gave the order and the horsemen extended their ranks, spreading out ten yards apart in a line half a mile wide. There they waited looking north towards the Ngwebini Valley, the Christian Edendale Troop on the left closest to the camp, the amaNgwane Hlubis to the right with Durnford in the centre. The order was given to dismount. With left arm through the reins the troopers loaded, took aim and, on Durnford's command, at 400 yards, fired a volley. The lines of warriors, one behind the other twelve deep, were not difficult to hit. Many warriors fell only to be passed over without a pause by those coming behind.

As the volley crashed out, the troop horses shied, trying to pull away, but most were gun-trained and their fright was but fleeting. With pats and reassuring words, the troopers remounted, trotted back 100 yards, dismounted and fired again. The continual mounting and dismounting was not difficult to accomplish as the sturdy Basuto ponies of the NNH were little more than fourteen hands in height.

⋙◊⋘

Higginson and Williams, carrying Durnford's earlier orders to Scott, still had a short distance to ride when they saw a portion of the Zulu army on the ridge in hot pursuit of the two troops of Zikali NNH. The warriors were also coming down the Notch not far behind the amaChunu NNC and gaining fast on Barry and Vereker. Higginson abandoned all thought of delivering Durnford's orders. Instead he made his way back to the camp leaving Williams to assist Barry and Vereker as best he could. In Higginson's words:

> 'I left Sgt Major Williams with Captain Barry as he [Barry] was without his horse, and as I knew he [Williams] would assist him back to the camp if overpowered, he being a good shot, a good rider, and a very cool man under fire, I rode back to camp.'

Williams, in fact, helped not only Barry but Vereker as well. With about a mile and a half to go back to the camp, Williams dismounted and let Barry and Vereker ride turn and turn about while he, with whoever was not riding, ran alongside hanging on to the stirrup leathers. They eventually got into camp as the battle raged, with the enemy hard behind them.◊

Durnford, now fully aware that he was confronting something more than a Zulu demonstration, moved back towards the camp as rapidly as a fighting retreat would permit. The two troops were firing alternately. As one troop dismounted and fired, the other rode back through its ranks to some distance behind, where it in turn dismounted and fired. The NNH volleys were taking a toll on the Zulu left horn, keeping the young warriors at bay. Much of the terrain was cut by gullies, covered in loose stones and with pockets of marsh here and there. As the Zulus jogged further to the south, parallel to the line of horsemen in an endeavour to outflank them, so the NNH were forced to extend their right front further and further towards the Qudeni Track. At the opposite end of the NNH line, Davies and his troop drew near to Scott's outpost below iThusi. As they passed Qwabe, the ridge that Barker and Hawkins had been forced to vacate earlier in the day, hidden Zulu marksmen, still occupying Qwabe, opened fire but failed to score a hit.

It was time for the carbineers and NMP also to retire on the camp. A short while ago they had witnessed the destruction of the rocket battery and now, as the two troops of Durnford's horsemen retreated on Isandlwana, it was high time to depart. They did so, firing from the cover of numerous gullies and *dongas* that criss-crossed the landscape, never allowing the enemy to get closer than 300 yards.[◊]

Davies, heading towards the British lines, rode close to the remains of the rocket battery and, as he got nearer to the camp, he discovered Nourse who was still accompanied by the five of the amaNgwane NNC who had not bolted with their comrades.[◊] Nourse and his men were close to being surrounded by advancing Zulus. Nearby a number of mules grazed unconcernedly, some still laden with rockets and seemingly oblivious to the clamour that a short time previously had caused them to stampede. Davies, a conscientious officer, ordered a trooper to catch one of the rocket-laden mules but hardly had this been accomplished when, being suddenly hard-pressed by the Zulus, the trooper had to release it. Nourse and his men, now protected by Davies, fled towards the camp.

Durnford, retreating to the south of Conical Hill, came upon Private Johnson of the rocket battery who was still trying to make his way to the shelter of the carbineers' *donga*. Johnson had possibly run out of some hiding place, no doubt expecting to be rescued. If so, he was to be disappointed. Durnford, full of anxiety and self-recrimination at that moment, was in no mood to be magnanimous or gallant to a private of the 24th. He peremptorily demanded to know the whereabouts of the rocket battery. Johnson blurted out that the battery had been cut up and Russell shot. Durnford retorted icily, 'You better go back and fetch him.'[◊] An astonished Johnson replied that they were all but surrounded, whereupon Durnford, with his escort of troopers and with an orderly leading a spare horse, turned towards the camp and left the stranded soldier to his fate.

The retreating Edendale and Hlubi Troops were less than a mile from the camp when they arrived at the Nyokana *donga*, a great furrow that cut deeply across the plain parallel to the British lines. Durnford dismounted both troops. The horses drank greedily from a little stream that ran along the *donga* bottom. Here the two troops would make a stand. Strung out many yards apart, but completely protected from enemy rifle fire, at 400 yards the black horsemen began to wreak destruction on the fast approaching regiments of the Nkobamakosi, the uVe and uMbonambi *(see Map 6, pages 200–01)*.

⋙•◦•≪

Pulleine had watched the departure of Durnford and his black horsemen with some satisfaction. The camp was his again and there had seemed to be at least some prospect of an encounter with the enemy. In the unlikely event of the Zulus advancing on the camp itself, the firepower of the Martini-Henry and the two 7-pounder cannons, would halt them in their tracks in the same way as the Gcaleka tribesmen had been dispersed at Centane the previous year.

Durnford had hardly disappeared beyond Conical Hill when the first sounds of Shepstone's encounter with the Zulu right horn came reverberating across the plain. Looking towards iThusi, Pulleine beheld an astounding sight. With his telescope he could clearly see a line of retreating horsemen pursued by what appeared to be the whole of Zululand. The warriors moved with incredible speed, as fast as cavalry, faster indeed than the troopers of the NNH who, pausing to fire, were being overtaken and outflanked. One wing of the enemy raced ahead to cut off the NNH from descending by the Notch, an easy way to the plain below and a much shorter route back to the camp. Some of the NNH also managed to descend by the Notch, but most were forced back along the ridge to the Tahelane spur.

In camp the alarm had already sounded and the troops having fallen in once again stood ready, watching in fascination the approaching waves of warriors 'swarming like bees', as one witness was to recall. Trooper Richard Stevens of the NMP also saw a similarity to an angry hive of bees, writing to his father, '[The] hill was black with them coming like swarms.' Even at that moment most in the camp felt there was no cause for anxiety but rather a sense of satisfaction that they were going to have a fight after all, despite being left merely to guard the camp.

Lieutenant Henry Curling of the Royal Artillery would later recall in a letter to his mother that, earlier in the morning, while having breakfast with twenty other officers (none of whom survived the day), all present were congratulating themselves on the chance of their being attacked. Curling wrote, 'Not one of us dreamt that there was the least danger and all we hoped for was that the fight might come off before the General returned.'

But how quickly the scene had changed; no one had expected the enemy in such numbers – a veritable avalanche of warriors was pouring down from the hills. Now there was a hint of alarm and urgency about the camp. The number of defenders was not large while the perimeter of the camp was vast. Excluding the horsemen who had left the camp led by Durnford, Pulleine had been left approximately 1,450 men of all ranks to defend it. Of these, two Zikali troops of the NNH, totalling 100 men, were already engaged and 400 NNC either engaged or deployed as already described. Of the remaining 950 men about thirty were either staff or men of support units, leaving seventy gunners of the Royal Artillery and only 580 imperial infantry. The latter were divided into six companies: five of the 1/24th, each of approximately eighty men, and one of the 2/24th, much larger in number, with a complement of 180, a number of whom would have been sick or left behind to perform camp chores. The companies were commanded as follows:

A Company 1/24th: Lieutenant Francis Porteous

Thirty-one-year-old Porteous, who had been with the regiment for thirteen years, was temporarily in command of A Company. He had served in Ireland and the Mediterranean and had spent four years in South Africa.

C Company 1/24th: Captain Reginald Younghusband

Younghusband had celebrated his thirty-fifth birthday a week before. A tall, good-looking man whose Northumbrian family traced its ancestry back to AD 559. He had been in action before and had served with the 24th in Mauritius, Burma and India before being posted to the Cape in 1876.

E Company 1/24th: Lieutenant Charles Cavaye

The twenty-nine-year-old son of an Indian Army general, Cavaye had spent most of his service with the 24th at Gibraltar and on St Helena before his transfer to the Cape in 1877. Thereafter he had served throughout the Ninth Frontier War.

F Company 1/24th: Captain William Mostyn

Thirty-seven years old, Mostyn had been with the regiment for sixteen years serving in Ireland, Malta, Burma, India and throughout the Ninth Frontier War. He had been aide-de-camp to General Cunynghame, Lord Chelmsford's predecessor. He and his company had reached Isandlwana the previous day.

H Company 1/24th: Captain George Wardell

At thirty-nine years of age the heavily bearded Wardell was the oldest of the six company commanders. He had been born and educated in Canada and had passed an examination for direct entry into the infantry. Wardell had been with the 24th for over twenty years, serving in the Mediterranean and commanding a detachment on St Helena. During the Ninth Frontier War, he had seen more action than most. He had constructed a fort on the Great Kei River in which he and his men had been besieged for several weeks.

G Company 2/24th: Lieutenant Charles Pope

At twenty-nine years of age, Pope commanded the only company of the 2nd Battalion at Isandlwana. Had his company not been on picquet duty the previous night, it would have accompanied Chelmsford's column. Pope's service included three years in India and a year in the Cape, plus a course at the School of Musketry in Kent where he obtained a first-class certificate.

The two 7-pounder cannon were commanded by Curling who believed he had been blessed with a wonderful stroke of good fortune in that it would be he, rather than his seniors, Lieutenant-Colonel Harness and Major Smith, who would bring the guns into action.

Of the many imperial officers who were to fight in the firing line that day, Curling would be the only one to survive. Four other imperial officers would escape, but during the battle they would be elsewhere in the camp: Captain Essex, in charge of the column transport, would carry ammunition to the firing line, but spend little time there; Lieutenant Smith-Dorrien, Essex's transport assistant, would also be involved with the ammunition supply, opening boxes in the camp area; Lieutenant Cochrane, Durnford's transport officer, would fight out the battle with the NNH, and Captain Gardner, who was yet to arrive at Isandlwana bringing Chelmsford's order to pack up half of the camp, would spend most of his time with Pulleine.

It is from the testimonies of these officers and those of three private soldiers, Bickley, Williams and Wilson, that much of the official War Office account of the battle is compiled. As Curling's is the one and only firing-line account, much of what occurred there remains obscure. Curling's attention throughout the battle would naturally have been focused on his guns, but in a letter to his mother, undated but clearly written about three weeks after his escape, he mentions the composition of the infantry companies, adding fuel to the controversy that still surrounds the battle. He wrote, 'The companies of the [1/24th] were very weak, no more than fifty [men] in each.' If that was correct it would mean there were only 300 infantry in the firing line out of the 580 known to have been in the camp that day.

Curling had made no statement to this effect in his evidence at the Court of Inquiry that had been held two weeks previous to his letter on 27th January. Nor was it only Curling who alluded to the lack of infantry. Mr Foley, a conductor of government wagons, reported, 'There only remained in the camp two companies of the 24th Regiment, numbering with staff and others about 200 regulars.' On 29 January a Durban newspaper interviewed an NNC officer who was on his way to the Cape:

'His most important statement, however, has to do with our own numbers. He believed at the time that only three companies of the 24th were engaged; if there were more, then he thinks they must have been short-handed as he is convinced that not more than 350 infantry were at the camp.'◊

A newspaper report of an interview on 24 January with Sergeant Walsh of the Newcastle Mounted Rifles, informed readers that the camp:

> 'was protected only by such volunteers who had weak horses and could not go forward with the main body, and some 250 of the 1/24th.'

Concluding an interview on 25 January with Lieutenant Vause of the NNH and several other officers, a Durban newspaper added, 'Some of them say that, taken as an average, there were not more than fifty [1/24th] in each company.' However, the most extraordinary reference to the lack of imperial infantry was contained in a letter written from Osborne, 6,000 miles away on the Isle of Wight, only twenty days after the battle. General Sir Henry Ponsonby, Queen Victoria's private secretary, wrote to Colonel Fred Stanley, the Secretary of State for War:

> 'With but few details it is difficult to offer any explanation [of the Isandlwana defeat] but apparently the main column proceeded northwards leaving 500 men to guard the camp.'

If the men were not in the firing line where else would they have been employed? It is possible that Pulleine was confronted with a considerable dilemma that might explain the mystery.

With the camp under imminent attack there were a number of actions that Pulleine could have put into effect, or was duty bound by standing orders to carry out. It was not too late to form a small *laager*/redoubt or draw in the troops ready to take up a defensive formation. He could have ordered the ammunition boxes to be opened, with mules and transport standing by ready to be loaded. But more than any other consideration, Pulleine omitted to carry out standing orders stipulating that on the sounding of the alarm the tents were to be struck. His failure to do so was the prime reason for Chelmsford's later assumption that the camp was not under serious attack. The logic behind the order was that standing tents obstructed vision, restricted the defenders' field of fire and offered concealment to an enemy.

There would seem to be three possible reasons for Pulleine's failure to strike the tents: that he was not convinced that the Zulu would press home their attack; that the attack was so sudden and executed with such speed that there was neither the time nor manpower to strike the tents; that the whole camp was in the process of being packed in order to move that day to another destination. (The rigmarole involved in erecting and dismantling a camp has been mentioned in a previous chapter). If the last were the reason, a portion of each infantry company would have been employed in packing the camp. There is evidence supporting this possibility. Brickhill maintained that Pulleine was ordered by Chelmsford:

> 'to strike the camps and come [to Mangeni] with all speed leaving sufficient guard behind to protect such as could not be moved without delay.'

Norris-Newman recorded:

> 'The General... then left us with instructions to return... to the head of
> the Amange [Mangeni] gorge, and there remain, his intention being that
> the camp at Isandlwana should be struck that afternoon (Wednesday) [22
> January] and the entire force moved forward to the spot selected as our
> halting-ground.'

Perhaps the order given to Gardner, that only the tents of Chelmsford's
force were to be brought on to Mangeni, was another of Chelmsford's
vacillations. Could it be that he had changed his mind from bringing the
whole camp to Mangeni that day to moving only half of it?

Many years later Hamilton-Browne wrote that he was ordered to assist
Pulleine, 'to strike the camp and come on here [Mangeni].'

If Pulleine had been given orders to move the camp, he would have
indeed been in a quandary when the Zulu army came in sight. If he had left
the tents standing and the Zulus got close to the camp, he would have
disobeyed orders. On the other hand, if he struck the tents and the Zulus
kept their distance, he would likely be branded as an alarmist – especially
as it would have been his first time in action – and be ridiculed throughout
the column. He would also have earned Chelmsford's displeasure as, by
striking the tents unnecessarily, they would have had to be re-erected
before they could be packed, delaying any move to Mangeni. This could
have resulted in moving the camp after nightfall thus endangering the
column. If, in fact, Pulleine was faced with such a dilemma, he could have
chosen to leave the tents standing and by doing so unintentionally given the
impression that all was well at Isandlwana camp.

As Pulleine watched the fighting retreat of Barton, Raw, Roberts and the
two Zikali Troops rapidly drawing closer to the camp along the Nqutu Ridge,
he had cause to remember Durnford's recent words that were part
instruction and part request: 'If you see us in difficulties you must send and
support us.'

Pulleine, now aware that a Zulu army, vaster than anyone had imagined,
was about to attack the camp, gave orders to Melvill. The two Royal Artillery
7-pounders commanded by Curling, were to go forward supported by
Captain Wardell's H Company; the three companies commanded by
Porteous, Mostyn and Pope were to be deployed parallel to, and about 300
yards back, from the base of the Tahelane Ridge; Younghusband's company
was to be held in reserve; and finally, to fulfil his obligation to Durnford,
Cavaye's company was to climb Tahelane, down which it was obvious the
NNH intended to complete their retreat onto the camp, and there give the
horsemen covering fire.

Melvill cantered down to where Captain William Degacher, for the
moment commanding the 1/24th, waited. Pulleine's orders were put swiftly
into effect. The guns, already harnessed, trotted out to take up a position
just above the slight depression where James Lonsdale's *iZigqoza* NNC, now

exposed to the enemy, still remained on picquet. At a range of 3,200 yards the guns opened fire. Seconds later two shells exploded in the thick of the oncoming Zulu army. The soldiers, elated by the results of their gunnery skill, let out a cheer and hurriedly reloaded.

Lieutenant Cavaye at the head of E Company, with twenty-year-old 2nd Lieutenant Dyson second-in-command, did not exactly double his men to the top of the Tahelane Ridge, it was too steep for that. He followed a well-trodden native path that wound its way for 140 feet up to the crest line. Nevertheless, E Company arrived sweating and short of breath. Apart from the pathway, the slopes of the ridge were a nightmare of jumbled rock and spiky aloe plants. The crest, a natural fortification of boulders and rocks, was also interspersed with aloes, many ten feet in height, providing good cover and concealment for riflemen. One hundred yards or so from the crest, out onto the plateau beyond, the rocks and aloes petered out, denying any form of cover to an approaching enemy, except for the slight undulations of the plateau itself.

As Cavaye waited, the retreating horsemen were yet to come into sight around Magaga Knoll, a mile away to the north-east. But the uNokhenke and uNodwengu regiments of the Zulu right horn, ignoring and by-passing the horsemen, suddenly arrived and were soon parallel to the crest line, jogging past at a distance of 800 yards. Cavaye immediately deployed his men about five yards apart amongst the rocks and gave the order to load. There could be no doubt that they had been seen, yet the warriors, coming on at an easy gait, did not detour from their intended path. E Company, now in a ragged line some 400 yards long, opened fire on Cavaye's command. With sights set at 800 yards, supposedly medium range for the Martini-Henry, a volley was fired.

Undeterred the warriors jogged on without pause. If the volley had scored any hits, the falling casualties were concealed by the moving mass of their comrades. Another volley was fired to be followed immediately by further volleys, one after the other. But soon the leading ranks began to disappear behind a low ridge that rose from the plain, so insignificant that it was hardly discernible from the crest line.

Using his glass, Cavaye could see that the ridge was less than half a mile in length and that inevitably the enemy would reappear, but beyond the effective range of E Company's volleys. Sprinting down the line amongst the rocks, Cavaye found Dyson whom he ordered to take some men about 500 yards to the left, until he was in a position to fire on the enemy as they reappeared beyond the little ridge. Dyson shouted an order and at the double, with rifles carried at the trail, he and his section eventually took up a position a mile and quarter distant from the camp. As the warriors emerged, Dyson and his men fired, reloaded and fired, as fast as discipline allowed.

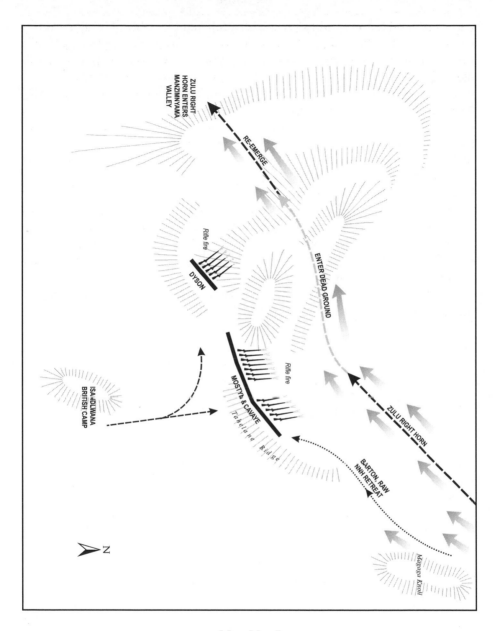

Map No. 5

Deployment of Cavaye's and Mostyn's companies of the 1/24th on the Tahelane Ridge. Cavaye arrived at approximately 11.45 a.m., followed by Mostyn some twenty minutes later.

Out on the Isandlwana plain, still about four and a half miles short of the camp, Hamilton-Browne and his weary battalion of NNC were suddenly halted by the sight of a great mass of warriors, just over a mile away heading directly towards the camp. At that moment Hamilton-Browne would have been able to see Durnford and his NNH, had the advancing warriors and the hump of Qwabe Hill not obscured them. Captain Alan Gardner and his companions, carrying Lord Chelmsford's order to move camp, were also somewhere out on the plain. Unbeknown to Hamilton-Browne, who had probably seen them cantering past earlier, they had had the great good fortune to have already safely passed the position from which the Zulu left horn was now emerging only minutes behind them.

Hamilton-Browne paused just long enough to comprehend the situation. As he watched, any doubts as to the Zulu intent were quickly dispelled. He could see the puffs of white smoke as Curling's guns fired on the advancing army. The camp was clearly under a massive attack. Lieutenant Pohl had already been sent with an earlier warning and now Hamilton-Browne dispatched Sergeant Turner to ride and find the general. Hamilton-Browne then tentatively moved forward again in a more westerly direction, with the forlorn thought that he and his battalion might enter the camp from the south.

It was not long before it became apparent that far from there being any possibility that he might assist the defenders, he was more likely to be cut off and overwhelmed himself. In addition to the regiments advancing on the camp he could see huge numbers of warriors being held back in reserve.◊ Seeking a defensive position, Hamilton-Browne moved to a red coloured ridge that rose about fifty feet above the plain. Its elevated position provided a lofty and uninterrupted view of Isandlwana camp. Having scaled the ridge by at about 12.30 p.m., Hamilton-Browne sent a third messenger, a mounted orderly, to seek out the general.

At roughly the same time, six miles away to the east, Lieutenant-Colonel Russell and his mounted infantry, having had a frustrating morning, had off-saddled and were taking a rest. It was there that Russell was found by the first of Hamilton-Browne's messengers, no doubt guided by the bright red tunics of the IMI. Russell later reported:

> 'I believe about one o'clock a mounted European of the native contingent came up and said that he was sent to tell the General that the camp was attacked. We could not tell him where the General was, but he was told whereabouts he had been in the morning.'◊

Russell then ordered the IMI to, 'move quietly along the outside of the hills' back towards the Mangeni track, while he with an escort – and presumably Hamilton-Browne's messenger, rode down the Magogo Valley to Chelmsford's breakfast spot but, of course, Chelmsford and his staff had long since gone. (It is interesting to note that Crealock, on reading Russell's report when it was written two months later, disputed what Russell had written. He scrawled in the margin of Russell's report, in thick black ink, words to the effect that on 22 January Russell had told him that far from going back down the dangerous Magogo Valley to seek Chelmsford personally, he had merely pointed out to the messenger the direction that Chelmsford had taken, whereupon the messenger had offered the opinion that it was too dangerous a place to go alone. It seems that Russell agreed with the messenger, caring little whether Chelmsford was found or not.) Whatever the case, it was not long before Hamilton-Browne's second messenger, Turner, arrived and reported to Russell that the camp was under full attack with guns firing on the enemy. Turner also failed to locate the general.

Ntshingwayo's deployment of his army was spectacularly efficient if completely conventional in the Zulu tradition of attack. When Shaka had first devolved the tactic of 'eating up' an enemy army by encircling it with two fast moving wings, or horns, of warriors, he had been dealing with comparatively small forces, all armed similarly with spear and shield. Now Ntshingwayo faced an enemy who could kill at over twenty times the distance of a thrown spear. And instead of a few thousand warriors with whom to fight the red soldiers, he had 20,000 with whom to overwhelm the defenders of Isandlwana camp. He was aware that he had more warriors than the work required. Many, to their chagrin, would be held in reserve and denied the opportunity to wash their spears. Nevertheless Ntshingwayo had accepted that the weapons of the red soldiers would cut down many of his warriors as they drew within killing distance of the camp. For that reason the horns of his army must be far flung, deceiving and confusing, until all were ready to be committed. Then, when the moment came, the whole army must move swiftly, close with the enemy and overwhelm all resistance in hand-to-hand combat.

The likely Zulu tactics were known to their opponents. All the officers in Chelmsford's army had been issued with a diagram of the Zulu method of attack and encirclement. Yet it is doubtful if Pulleine or any of his staff were aware of what was taking place. As the horns flared out, the left down on the plain outflanking Durnford, and the right bypassing Barton and Raw above the camp, their points were over four miles apart.

With Curling's guns firing over their heads, James Lonsdale's iZigqoza NNC picquet had a front row view of abandoned huts, situated just below the Notch, being demolished. A crowd of warriors had congregated there, either to seek shelter or had perhaps pursued some fugitive NNH who, having been cut off, were likewise seeking protection. In any event Curling's guns were destroying the huts in a spectacular fashion causing those who could to bolt in every direction.

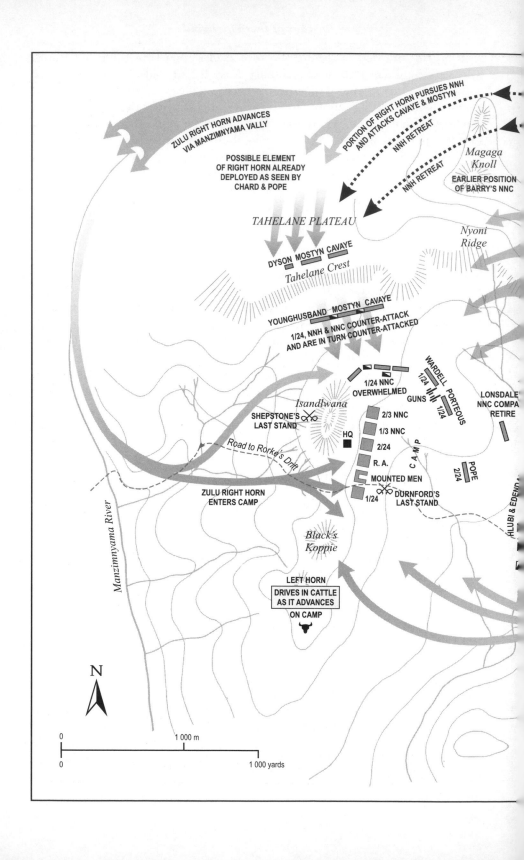

ZULU RIGHT HORN ADVANCES
VIA MANZIMNYAMA VALLY

PORTION OF RIGHT HORN PURSUES NNH
AND ATTACKS CAVAYE & MOSTYN

NNH RETREAT

POSSIBLE ELEMENT
OF RIGHT HORN ALREADY
DEPLOYED AS SEEN BY
CHARD & POPE

NNH RETREAT

*Magaga
Knoll*

EARLIER POSITION
OF BARRY'S NNC

TAHELANE PLATEAU

*Nyoni
Ridge*

DYSON MOSTYN CAVAYE

Tahelane Crest

YOUNGHUSBAND MOSTYN CAVAYE

1/24, NNH & NNC COUNTER-ATTACK
AND ARE IN TURN COUNTER-ATTACKED

WARDELL
1/24

PORTEOUS

1/24 NNC
OVERWHELMED

GUNS

LONSDALE
NNC COMPA
RETIRE

Isandlwana

SHEPSTONE'S
LAST STAND

2/3 NNC

HQ

1/3 NNC

2/24

Road to Rorke's Drift

R. A.

C A M P

POPE
2/24

ZULU RIGHT HORN
ENTERS CAMP

MOUNTED MEN

1/24

DURNFORD'S
LAST STAND

Manzimnyama River

HLUBI & EDEND..

*Black's
Koppie*

LEFT HORN

DRIVES IN CATTLE
AS IT ADVANCES

ON CAMP

N

0   1 000 m

0   1 000 yards

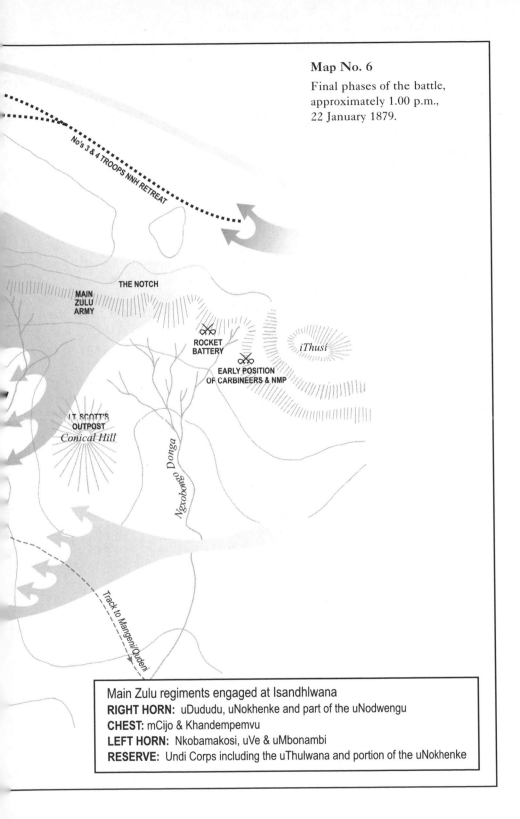

Map No. 6

Final phases of the battle, approximately 1.00 p.m., 22 January 1879.

No's 3 & 4 TROOPS NNH RETREAT

THE NOTCH

MAIN ZULU ARMY

ROCKET BATTERY

iThusi

EARLY POSITION OF CARBINEERS & NMP

LT SCOTT'S OUTPOST
Conical Hill

Ngxobongo Donga

Track to Mangeni/Quderi

Main Zulu regiments engaged at Isandhlwana
RIGHT HORN: uDududu, uNokhenke and part of the uNodwengu
CHEST: mCijo & Khandempemvu
LEFT HORN: Nkobamakosi, uVe & uMbonambi
RESERVE: Undi Corps including the uThulwana and portion of the uNokhenke

To the iZigqoza it appeared as though a replay of the battle of nDondakusuka was about to take place, but on this occasion the odds in favour of their enemy would be far greater than when Cetshwayo's *Usuthu* had massacred their forebears on the banks of the Tugela twenty-three years earlier. The iZigqoza seemed to have been somewhat overlooked and forgotten by Pulleine. Consequently, with Lonsdale and his officers, they arose from their perilous picquet post and retired in good order towards the camp.

Up on the Tahelane crest, the Zulu right horn was still streaming past Cavaye's company, at about 800 yards, like so many moving targets on a shooting range, when the retreating NNH burst into sight. They came around and over the Magaga Knoll a mile away, closely followed by the packed regiments, the uNokhenke and mCijo of the Zulu chest. At that moment Cavaye must have realised he would no longer be dealing with a passing parade of distant Zulu warriors and he sent an orderly leaping down the pathway to Degacher with a request for reinforcements. Yet the rank and file were full of cheer and enjoying themselves as they blazed away at the far-off foe.

Degacher was dealing with the biggest challenge of his life. A hazardous situation had evolved in what must have seemed to have been a matter of minutes. Above the Tahelane crest, he could hear Cavaye heavily engaged but could see nothing. To his right and front the juggernaut-like Zulu army was drawing closer. Still keeping Younghusband's company in reserve, Pulleine ordered Degacher to send Mostyn's F Company scurrying up the ridge to reinforce Cavaye, and a mounted orderly to the camp for extra ammunition.

Despite all this activity, incredibly the mood in the actual camp, a mile or so from Degacher, was still one of relative complacency. Transport officer, Captain Essex, with wagons at a standstill, was enjoying an idle day. He was writing letters in his tent when a passing NCO advised him that firing was to be heard, 'behind the hill [the Tahelane Ridge] where the company of the 1st Battalion 24th had been sent.'[0]

It is extraordinary that earlier in the day many in the camp believed that they could hear firing from Chelmsford's column twelve miles away and yet, closer at hand, Essex seems to have heard nothing of Curling's guns, Cavaye's engagement, nor the destruction of the rocket battery. Four days after the battle Essex wrote home in the most casual manner:

> 'I had my glasses [binoculars] over my shoulder and thought I might as well take my revolver; but did not trouble to take my sword, as I thought nothing of the matter and expected to be back in half an hour to complete my letters.'

Apart from the sounds of battle, Essex should have been able to see, albeit still at some distance, the mass of warriors moving west along the Nqutu Ridge – except for one possible reason. Depending where his tent was situated, the unstruck tents, each ten feet in height, might well have blocked out his view.

Essex, having mounted his horse, set off at a gallop and on reaching the base of Tahelane Ridge – and presumably having conferred with Degacher, set out for the crest. On the way up he overtook Captain Mostyn and his F Company hurrying to reinforce Cavaye. As Essex passed, Mostyn shouted out a request that Essex should warn Cavaye that he (Mostyn) was on his way and would be taking up a position on Cavaye's left, and that Cavaye and his men should take special care not to shoot them by mistake.

Essex arrived just as the NNH began to reach the crest hotly pursued by warriors of the uNokhenke regiment. Immediately the Zulus began to fan out in an encircling movement, a miniature version of Ntshingwayo's encirclement of the camp. Both horns of the Zulu movement were soon amongst the rocks and aloes, beyond the extremities of the British line, from where they began to open fire. Many of the NNH dismounted and joined in with Cavaye's men who were being hard pressed by the Zulus who, in some places, had closed in to within 200 yards.

Pulleine, appalled by the mass of Zulus descending on the camp, and with only four companies of infantry at hand with which to face them, now sent Melvill galloping to bring back Cavaye and Mostyn. As Melvill arrived at the Tahelane crest, Essex was close at hand. Melvill shouted to him that both companies were ordered back, and that they should retire keeping up a steady fire, as a fresh body of the enemy had appeared behind the camp. At the moment the line of riflemen was extended along the crest for over half a mile with Dyson's section still on the extreme left and furthest from the camp. Mostyn's men had just filled the gap between Dyson and Cavaye.◊ However, the two companies could not retire down the pathway by which they had ascended. They would have to make their descent through the rocks and aloes, keeping line as best they could before tackling the steep slope beyond. Along the crest there were two re-entrants, which could have provided a fairly gentle descent, allowing the men to spread out again once beyond the crest. Essex first rode to bring in Dyson's section then found when he returned that the centre of the line had already retired. Essex followed close on their heels but discovered that even the re-entrant descent was extremely difficult for a mounted man.

Younghusband's company, which had been held in reserve, was waiting in support at the bottom of the slope, drawn up in echelon formation about 400 yards away. Cavaye's and Mostyn's companies, sorting themselves out as they got into line, fell in on Younghusband's right. The NNH, having also successfully descended to the plain, dismounted and lined up beside the infantry.◊

The enemy could now be seen to have taken possession of the crest. It was only moments before a wave of warriors, more agile than their red coated enemies, began to descend all the way along the slope, almost skipping it seemed from rock to rock.

—————

Gardner's arrival at the camp had coincided with that of George Shepstone, who was breathless from his pell-mell descent from the ridge and full of apprehension. They met up and, guided by Brickhill, the interpreter, made their way to Pulleine's tent. Gardner, a staff officer and bearing an order from the general, was the first to get Pulleine's attention whilst an agitated George Shepstone waited his turn to speak. Pulleine took Chelmsford's note ordering that the camp (in entirety or only in part?) should be struck immediately and moved to Mangeni Falls. Pulleine paused and, according to Brickhill, looked perplexed. Shepstone could wait no longer and still breathless with excitement blurted out:

> 'I'm not an alarmist, Sir, but the Zulus are in such black masses over there [on Nqutu and Tahelane] such long lines that you'll have to give us all the assistance you can. They are fast driving our men this way.'◊

In fact at that moment the NNH could be plainly seen from the camp retreating along the ridge closely followed by the enemy.

Gardner then offered Pulleine some advice suggesting that, as Chelmsford knew nothing of the present circumstances, Chelmsford's orders should be disobeyed for the moment. Shepstone received no further attention while Pulleine and Gardner walked off together. Gardner at Pulleine's request, gathered all the mounted men he could find about the camp, and under the command of Captain Bradstreet of the Newcastle Mounted Rifles, took them to a small *donga* about a quarter of a mile in front of the camp, ordering them to hold the position until further orders. Pulleine and Gardner then decided to write brief notes advising Chelmsford of the situation:

> 'Heavy firing to left of our camp. Cannot move camp at present.
>   HB Pulleine, Lieut-Colonel.'

> 'Heavy firing near left of camp. Shepstone has come in for reinforcements, and reports that the Basuto's [NNH] are falling back. Whole camp turned out and fighting about one mile to left flank.
>   Alan Gardner, Captain, S.O.'

The messages were then given to some brave orderly with instructions to find the general. History has failed to record the orderly's name but this resolute and courageous horseman somehow made his way past the oncoming Zulus, delivering his messages to Chelmsford and his staff officers about two hours later.

Brickhill, who had been privy to the whole discussion, wisely went off to find and saddle his horse. That done he went about the camp trying to borrow a rifle so that he could join in the fight. Being unsuccessful he took himself and his horse to a commanding position in front of the camp office from where he watched the battle unfold.

Shepstone, having been dismissed (probably in the minds of Pulleine and Gardner as an alarmist), was about to ride back with Hamer to join the fighting line of soldiers at the bottom of the Tahelane Ridge, when the last of the reinforcements that would reach the camp that day arrived. Durnford's wagon train, escorted by Lieutenant Vause's No. 3 Troop Zikali NNH and Captain Stafford's company of Zikali NNC came clattering into the wagon park. Rallied by Shepstone they all made haste towards the Tahelane Ridge where some of Scott's retreating carbineers and NMP had also joined the firing line while others made their way back to camp to replenish their ammunition. Barker was one of them and he made his way to the carbineer tents where he found Quartermaster London and Sergeant Bullock, the former already wounded, 'handing out rounds to all who asked'.◊

—➤•◄—

Out on the plain to the south-east, Durnford's two troops of NNH had retreated to the Nyokana *donga*. Having reached the *donga*, the horsemen dismounted, securing their ponies in the deep, natural shelter, while Durnford rode on to the camp to confer with Pulleine. Here at the *donga* the Edendale and Hlubi Troops would make a stand spread out right across the Zulu left horn's line of advance. Shortly they were joined by some of the NMP and carbineers, Barker and Hawkins were amongst them. They had ridden into the camp, and had procured additional ammunition, when they encountered Durnford. He ordered them to ride at once to the Nyokana *donga* where they were to assist Hlubi's Troop.

Apprehensive of leaving their horses unattended while they were engaged in the firing line, the carbineers gave their horses to the care of a black trooper promising to tip him when the fight was over. Davies with the Edendale Troop was on the left of Durnford's line and closest to the Nqutu Ridge. He was joined there by Cochrane,◊ and they took turn and turn about with Davies' carbine shooting at the enemy and watching the shrapnel from the guns bursting amongst the Zulus. The fire of the Edendale Troop became so brisk that it halted and sent the enemy to ground for a while. Having done so the Troop directed its aim at the regiments making their way down from the Nqutu Ridge.

—➤•◄—

For the moment the left of the British line was still held by the three companies of Younghusband, Mostyn and Cavaye supported by 150 dismounted troopers of the NNH and Stafford's newly arrived company of NNC. It is likely that the remnants of Barry's NNC were also there. Out in front of the camp, Durnford's Edendale and Hlubi Troops, now desperately short of ammunition, held the Nyokana *donga* while behind them, the two 7-pounder guns continued to fire over their heads. Supporting the guns, the

205

three other companies of the 24th, those of Wardell, Porteous and Pope stood firm. There was also Krohn's NNC, still drawn up but seemingly forgotten. The whereabouts of the two companies, commanded by Murray, that had brought in the captured cattle the previous afternoon, remain unknown.

Opposing the British centre was the weight of the Zulu army, the head of the buffalo. Curling's satisfaction at being left in charge of the two 7-pounders had been short-lived as Major Stuart Smith, who had returned to the camp with Gardner, immediately rode to the guns and took over command. The 7-pounders, which had caused severe casualties, had now become less effective, not because of any inefficiency on the part of the gunners, but due to astute observation and evasive action by the enemy. The Zulus had observed that as the cannon were about to be fired the gunners would stand away from the guns to avoid the recoil. In the instant that the gunners moved, the advancing warriors would throw themselves to the ground thus avoiding the worst effects of the exploding shells that followed. One British soldier recalled:

> 'There was no confusion or hurry in these movements of theirs, but all was done as though they had been drilled to do it.'

With the line of concealed black horsemen in the Nyokama *donga* in front of them, the fire of the three companies of infantry and the guns had been restricted. But as the mass of Zulu army surged towards the centre of the camp, the Edendale Troop, on the left of the line and near to being out of ammunition, could do no more. They mounted their ponies and rode for the camp, providing the guns and the three companies of infantry with an unencumbered field of fire.

Durnford, having conferred with Pulleine, returned to the Nyokana *donga* and there, believing he would inspire the Hlubi Troop with his bravado, he exposed himself to the Zulu marksmen in a manner that was not uncommon amongst Victorian officers. Sergeant-Major Jabez Molife later remembered:

> 'Here we made a long stand firing incessantly. The Colonel [Durnford] rode up and down the line continually encouraging us all, he was very calm and cheerful, talking and even laughing with us, "Fire, my boys! Well done, my boys!" he cried, some of us did not like his exposing himself so much to the enemy, and wanted him to keep back behind us, but he laughed at us and said, "Alright, nonsense!" ...one of the men brought his gun with the old cartridge sticking so he dismounted, and taking the gun between his knees, because of only having one hand with strength in it, he pulled the cartridge out and gave back the gun.'

Apart from Durnford, exposed on top of the *donga*, all that the advancing left horn could see of their enemy were the tops of their hats. Up until now, despite their long fighting retreat, the Hlubi Troop had hardly sustained a

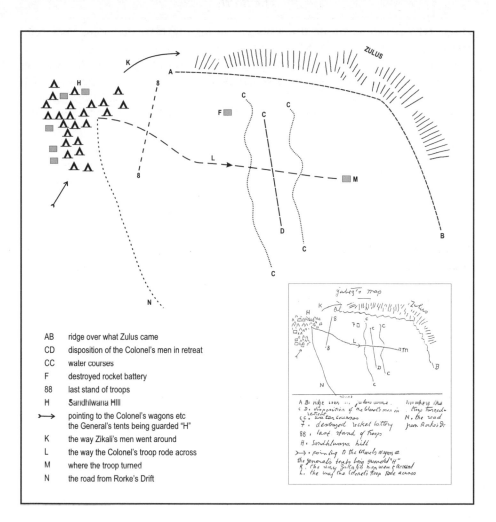

AB	ridge over what Zulus came
CD	disposition of the Colonel's men in retreat
CC	water courses
F	destroyed rocket battery
88	last stand of troops
H	Sandhlwana Hill
——>	pointing to the Colonel's wagons etc the General's tents being guarded "H"
K	the way Zikali's men went around
L	the way the Colonel's troop rode across
M	where the troop turned
N	the road from Rorke's Drift

Map No. 7

Reproduction of Sergeant-Major Jabez Molife's map which is one of the few maps to survive that was actually drawn by a participant in the battle (inset a copy of his map). Molife's captions are reproduced as spelt on the original.

casualty. With their ammunition also running low, they nevertheless forced the young warriors of the Nkobamakosi, uVe and uMbonambi regiments to veer away to the south. But it was merely a matter of the warriors going on a little further until they could outflank the Hlubi and enter the British camp unopposed. Desperate for ammunition Durnford had sent several troopers to the camp but all returned empty-handed.◊ The imperial quartermaster had told them that all the ammunition (400,000 rounds) was required for the infantry. It seemed that nothing less than the presence of a white officer was needed in order to acquire more rounds.◊ Henderson was despatched to the camp to bring back supplies at all costs. But, before he could successfully return, the Hlubi Troop, ammunition exhausted, was also forced to retreat on to the tent lines. It is ironic that Vause, with No. 2 Column's own ammunition supply, had just arrived at Isandlwana when the Hlubi started their retreat. But it was too late for the Hlubi to go back; the Zulus had already taken occupation of the Nyokana *donga*.

Under the Tahelane Ridge, E Company, having been the first of the imperial troops to open fire, was also desperate for ammunition, as were the three troops of NNH. With a profusion of warriors coming down the slope, the British line prepared to retire, only to stand firm again as Shepstone, leading Vause and Stafford's reinforcements, arrived in support. All the horsemen dismounted and joined in line with the infantry.◊ Then for no tactical reason of any worth, but driven by the heat of battle, they counter-attacked, charging up the slope and pushing the warriors back to the very crest line. There they were met by overwhelming odds and driven down again to the plain below where Younghusband's company remained in support, giving covering fire.

Yet there was more danger. One of Younghusband's flank men, glancing west, perhaps hoping to see reinforcements coming from Rorke's Drift, saw instead a fresh wave of warriors. The uDududu, uNokhenke and uNodwengu regiments of the right horn had emerged from the concealment of the Manzimnyana stream and were fanning out. Most were advancing along the western side of Isandlwana towards the Rorke's Drift road and the wagon park, but others, still about 1,500 yards away, were coming straight for Younghusband's left flank. To meet this threat, Younghusband ordered his company to move up on to the northern slopes of Isandlwana where, as the warriors came on, his field of fire would be enhanced. It is likely that Shepstone, collaborating with Younghusband, rode out to meet the uNokhenke and uNodwengu and was forced south. His body, amongst those of a number of troopers, was found four months later on the western slopes of Isandlwana.

In the meantime, Essex, like Davies and Henderson, had returned to camp seeking ammunition. He found no organised supply and so set about procuring ammunition from the 2nd Battalion, grabbing any handy personnel around the camp to carry the rounds out to Cavaye and Mostyn. He also found a mule cart that he sent off loaded with ammunition. Yet the oncoming warriors were closing fast and there was nowhere in the British camp that was safe any longer. Quartermaster London of the carbineers had already been wounded and now, as Essex spoke to Edward Bloomfield, the quartermaster of the 2/24th, Bloomfield was shot dead. Undeterred Essex mounted his horse with the intention of advising Cavaye and Mostyn that ammunition was on its way, but before going far, found that they were already in retreat.[◊]

It is unlikely that many of Cavaye and Mostyn's men survived to reach the camp.[◊] Raw described the end:

> 'The company of the 24th then retired towards the tents, and the enemy following close after, cut them up before they could rally, killing them close in to the tents.'

The troopers of the NNH and their four surviving officers, Barton, Raw, Vause and Hamer, scrambled to retrieve their ponies which had been held at the rear. Followed by Stafford and his Zikali NNC, all of whom were virtually out of ammunition, they fled through the tent lines. The less nimble were overtaken and put to death. Vause, having been in the fight for little more than minutes, lost thirty killed out of his fifty Zikali NNH and another ten wounded.[◊]

Younghusband's company did not suffer the same fate as that of Mostyn and Cavaye. Keeping some way up the lower slopes of Isandlwana, Younghusband made a fighting retreat above the tent lines towards the wagon park.

The gunners and the other three infantry companies, those of Wardell, Porteous and Pope, were probably oblivious to the annihilation of their comrades that had taken place behind them. The excitement was intense as they faced the fast approaching chest of the Zulu army, the warriors quite silent as they came except for the emission of an eerie bee-like humming sound *(see Map 6, pages 200–01)*.

At about 1,000 yards, as the leading warriors of the chest reached the lower slopes of the Nqutu Ridge the first volley was discharged. This was exactly the work the Martini-Henry had been designed for: controlled volley fire, delivered by disciplined infantry over open ground against a massed advancing foe. It was the perfect scenario to prove the efficacy of the weapon. Hardly had the reverberating crash of the first volley sounded, when the next rang out, to be followed almost without pause by another and another. Firing at a steady rate of one round per ten seconds, 250 trained infantrymen could pump 1,500 rounds a minute into an oncoming enemy. It was not work that required marksmen. It was just a question of the officer in command judging the distance correctly and yelling out the appropriate setting for the sights.

That done, the infantrymen had merely to take a steady aim at the mass ahead and, on the command, squeeze the trigger, then instantly eject the spent cartridge case, slide a new round into the empty breech, raise the locking lever and stand ready to fire again. It was a process that would have stopped or scattered many armies. But these were Zulus and they came on, just as the British hoped they would, without faltering.

They would later be described by Mary Frere as 'reckless of death', as indeed they were. Even at that moment, and in the days to follow when British enmity towards the Zulu was at its height, survivors would recall with grudging admiration the skirmishing skill and courage of the Zulu warriors. Norris-Newman was shortly to tell his readers:

> 'No soldier can I think, fail to admire and respect the soldier-like qualities then displayed by the enemy... and in the future the Zulu army will command that amount of precaution and respect which is necessary before it can be conquered.'

The great commanders of the Zulu army, led by Ntshingwayo, had moved to a vantage point on a rocky platform called Nyoni just below the Magaga Knoll. Several of Cetshwayo's royal brothers were among them. They included Prince Ndabuko of the uMbonambi regiment and his half brother Shingana, both of whom had fought at nDondakusuka, Prince Sitheku and Prince Dabulamanzi, the king's half brother who was well known to white traders, Zibhebhu, hereditary chief of the Mandalakazi, and amongst the regimental commanders, Sigcwelegecwele of the Nkobamakosi whom Cetshwayo had threatened to execute two years previously and had later forgiven. They now watched their charging army.

In the words of a British soldier, the Zulu army was 'taking an awful hammering'. The velocity and weight of the volleys were inflicting death and appalling wounds.

Directly in the Zulu line of advance, and only 200 yards in front of British infantry and guns, there is a depression in the Isandlwana plain, about fifteen acres of dead ground. It had been occupied until only minutes before by James Lonsdale's iZigqoza NNC and, as the Zulu regiments came on, encountering the crushing fire, despite Zulu courage the front ranks took to the depression. There, milling and uncertain, they were loath to re-enter the rain of lead that lay beyond. Brickhill later described the scene:

> 'A general forward movement was now made by the enemy... right away up to the northern nek. This was opposed by the two guns and the infantry alone... I could see nothing of the details of the infantry fighting because of the low lying land, but if the increasing [fire?] they kept up was any indication at all then the enemy's losses must have been terrible indeed.'

The Zulu charge had lost its impetus. Many warriors lay in the grass refusing to move and those who did encountered the British volleys at close quarters. The attack had stalled and the outcome of the battle lay in the balance. But not for long. Seventy rounds in the heat of battle are quickly fired away. The volleys were losing their intensity. In those crucial moments the ammunition supply to the British firing line was found wanting (*see Appendix C, page 322*), while the Zulu army found inspiration.

As the Zulu commanders watched the slaughter of their warriors, a sub-chief of the Biyela, Mkhosana kaMvundlana, came leaping and striding down into the dead ground, castigating the reluctant warriors, telling them they would have the whole Zulu army defeated. He strode back and forth, displaying his own courage and inspiring the men. Then, just as the warriors began to respond, the brave Mkhosana was shot dead. It was all that was needed to re-fire Zulu valour. In their shame and anger the warriors burst out of the dead ground, waving their shields, shouting *uSuthu!* and 'charged the soldiers with great fury'. Yet their dead 'lay just like peppercorns upon the plain'.◊

Back in the camp, those not engaged in the firing line watched the last of the battle develop. Private Williams, Colonel Glyn's groom, and Private Hough, the colonel's cook, accompanied by three servants, got themselves to an elevated position at the back of the camp, alongside Chelmsford's tent.◊ There they fired forty to fifty rounds apiece. Out in front of the camp they had seen the Zulus being cut down by the guns and the infantry as they had emerged from the dead ground. Williams and his comrades had also seen bandsmen leading mules laden with ammunition boxes attempting to get to the firing line. But whether sufficient ammunition ever got there – and whether it would have made any difference to the outcome of the battle had it done so – is extremely doubtful.

With Mostyn and Cavaye's companies overrun, with what was left of the NNH about to make their escape, and with Younghusband's company at bay on the slopes of Isandlwana, all that was left to oppose the charging Zulu chest, numbering upwards of 8,000 warriors, were the two guns and about 250 infantry. Once the warriors were out of the dead ground the outcome of the battle was inevitable. And as they came 'like the Tugela in flood', stampeding before them, prodded with their spears, were fear and pain-maddened oxen that had earlier been grazing nearby. It was so sudden that Smith and Curling commanding the guns had but moments to change their loads from shrapnel to case shot. And before they were able to fire more than two rounds of case, they were overrun. Curling was to write, 'we limbered up at once but were hardly in time as the Zulus were on us at once.'

Smith was wounded but the guns, having been quickly harnessed, made for the camp, Curling assuming that they would make a stand somewhere to the rear. But as they went the gunners were dragged from the gun limbers and stabbed to death.◊

Somewhere a bugle sounded 'retreat' and all along the British line men tried desperately to rally together in small fighting bodies, many as small as three or four men together, bayonets fixed and fighting for dear life. Major Francis White, the paymaster of the 1/24th, who had served with the battalion continuously for twenty-nine years – and who undoubtedly had the opportunity to attempt escape on horseback – chose to join the remnants of the retreat and died there. Surgeon-Major Peter Shepherd, attached to the 1/24th, was killed when he paused in his escape to tend a wounded man.

The Battle of Isandlwana had been all but won, yet the fighting around the unstruck tents, and up on the slopes of Isandlwana, and around the wagon park and for several miles over the broken ground towards the Buffalo River, would continue for some time to come.

One warrior recalled:

> 'There was so much smoke we could not see... the tumult and firing was wonderful; every warrior shouted "Usuthu!"... and the sun got very dark like night with the smoke. [Shortly after the battle there was a partial eclipse of the sun, but few noticed it.◊] The English fought long and hard. There were so many people in front of me I did not get into the thick of it until the end.'

James Pullen, the quartermaster of the 1/24th, now abandoned his ammunition supply and ordered his horse to be saddled; then seeing what could only have been a forlorn chance to turn the enemy flank, he gathered several fleeing men and with them went off never to be seen again.◊

Smith-Dorrien, who had got into the camp shortly after Durnford and had been all the while involved in opening ammunition boxes, now mounted his weary nag and with many others made towards the Rorke's Drift road. Lieutenant Adendorff, who had been amongst the first to see the Zulu army, was also amongst the first to leave. Before the Rorke's Drift road was cut by the Zulu right horn, he galloped straight to the Drift bearing news of the defeat to the little British garrison and later he helped with its defence.

Essex had also abandoned any further thoughts of getting ammunition to the line, and having got into camp before Mostyn and Cavaye were overwhelmed, came upon Colonel Durnford, both men becoming suddenly aware that the Zulus were also entering the camp from the rear. Durnford hurried off to rally some men while Essex, following a rabble of camp followers, made for the Rorke's Drift road.◊ Private Williams and his mates, without orders and uncertain what to do, had just returned to the officers' mess area when Coghill galloped up and issued Williams with instructions to strike Glyn's tents and place them in a wagon, an extraordinary order in the circumstances. This done, Williams and the other grooms were told to take all the horses to the rear of the camp.◊

Wisely, Williams kept one back for his own account and then collected forty more rounds of ammunition that he immediately put to use.

Moments later, Lieutenant Melvill, carrying the Queen's Colour of the 1/24th, enclosed in its heavy leather cylinder, galloped past. Whether Melvill had been ordered to save the colour by Pulleine or Degacher, or whether as adjutant he had decided to save it on his own initiative, will never be known. Melvill was shortly followed by Coghill who, going at a gallop, had abandoned the idea of saving Glyn's belongings. Instead he yelled to Williams 'to come on' or get himself killed and, just at that moment, the guns thundered by. Williams waited no longer and mounting his horse followed the artillery; even as he did so Zulus were coming into the camp from the rear, through the wagon park, herding men on foot back amongst the tents.◊

By a stroke of good fortune Private Johnson from the rocket battery, having been earlier abandoned by Durnford, had managed to reach the camp, as had Trainer, Grant and Bombardier Gough, the latter two still leading spare horses. Johnson and Trainer, their chances of escape having suddenly and miraculously improved, mounted up and the four survivors of the rocket battery galloped off towards the wagon park and eventual safety.

The Hlubi Troop paused to replenish ammunition from their own column's supply and, still a formidable body of mounted fighting men, made their way across the *nek*, pushing through the encircling warriors who let them by with little opposition, there being easier pickings.◊

Sergeant-Major Kambule of the Edendale Troop, when crossing the *nek*, came upon Chelmsford's cart still loaded with the Mangeni column's reserve ammunition supply. It was guarded by a young drummer boy who, awed by the frightening responsibility of guarding the general's cart, refused to give Kambule any rounds. Then, when offered the chance of escape on the back of Kambule's horse, the boy refused to leave his post despite the slaughter that had begun close by, a nightmare preview of the appalling fate that would shortly befall him.◊

Gardner, the only imperial cavalry officer present, had recently, on Colonel Pulleine's orders, placed a number of dismounted colonials and IMI, under the command of Captain Bradstreet, in a *donga* close to the camp. He now saw them retreating in the direction of the tents. Durnford had ordered them to do so and as he passed by he told Gardner that the line had been too extended. Gardner, suddenly finding himself surrounded by a mêlée of fighting men, also decided to stay no longer.

Barker and Hawkins had been amongst those who had held Bradstreet's *donga*. They had been completely unaware that they were all but surrounded until they 'heard a rush from behind' and, looking around, 'saw the soldiers who were left in camp literally surrounded by Zulus'. The colonials made a run for the tent lines where their horses were tethered, Barker finding one of his shot and kicking on the ground – luckily the unsaddled one. He recalled, 'I mounted my horse, the Zulus being busy now all over the camp stabbing the soldiers.' Barker and Hawkins mounted up but at the *nek* found their way blocked and were forced back into camp, 'which was now a mass of Zulus'. Skirting further left under Black's Koppie, they eventually broke through.◊

Brickhill, who had been watching the progress of the battle, prudently holding the reins of his saddled horse, seemed to have been rooted to the spot. He had seen his tent companion, Quartermaster Pullen, rally a few soldiers before he went to his death. Then, seeing troops of all description 'streaming through the various camps' and the only soldiers visible rise from firing their last shot to join the general flight, Brickhill spurred his horse towards the Buffalo River.

Barton and Raw with the survivors of the Zikali troops also sped through the tent lines heading south. Sergeant-Major Nyanda later described the scene:

> 'We were then chased into the centre of the camp – and also saw a large number of soldiers being assagaied... and on their right were the mounted men [carbineers, police and IMI] then the Zulus drove in the right wing and the whole of the force, white and black – foot and horse, were mixed together and being assegaied – a rush was then made for the Nek and we were met by Zulus on the other side and everyone who could save himself tried to do so.'◊

There comes a time in a battle when it is believed honourable for the individual soldier to save himself. The French have a term for it, *sauve qui peut*, and there is a fine line between the departing soldier being seen as a courageous survivor instead of a fleeing coward. At Isandlwana, when the Zulus were swarming into the camp from all directions in overwhelming numbers, it would seem to have been a moment for *sauve qui peut* – every man for himself. Yet Sir Garnet Wolseley who was to replace Lord Chelmsford, had other ideas. When, four months later, he looked upon the graves of Melvill and Coghill, he mused in his diary:

> 'I am sorry that both of these officers were not killed with their men at Isandlwana instead of where they were: I don't like the idea of officers escaping on horseback when their men on foot are killed.'

And at Isandlwana any man without a horse was virtually doomed.

⇒◈⇐

Out on the plain Hamilton-Browne, aghast at what he was witnessing and enraged that there had been no response to his calls for help, wrote a final desperate message, 'For God's sake come back, the camp is surrounded, and things I fear are going badly.' He gave the note to Captain Develin with orders to hand it to the general or to any staff officer he could find.

If Hamilton-Browne's previous messages had not reached Chelmsford those carrying them had undoubtedly told everyone they had encountered along the way that the camp was under attack. This startling news, confirmed by the sound of the guns, spawned rumours throughout the column.

Lieutenant Mainwaring, whose company formed part of the escort to Colonel Harness' four 7-pounders, was on his way to Mangeni when he heard the distant gunfire from the camp. A little further on he caught up with Harness and the rest of the infantry whose attention was focused on a large body of men some distance away that appeared to be a Zulu *impi*.◊ However, it was not long before Captain Develin appeared, looking 'very white and exhausted', who confirmed that the *impi* was in fact Hamilton-Browne's battalion of NNC. Develin then handed over Hamilton-Browne's message.

Major Wilsone Black of the 2/24th, a no-nonsense Scot and the senior infantry officer accompanying the guns, immediately ordered an about-turn. He informed the men that the camp was under attack, received three rousing cheers and started immediately for Isandlwana. With the guns in the lead and the horses kept at a steady pace, the infantry were hard pressed to keep up. They had gone little more than half a mile, making good time despite the fatigues of the day, when they were brought to an abrupt halt by Major Gosset, Chelmsford's aide, demanding to know why they were proceeding in the opposite direction to Mangeni. Gosset ordered Black to turn about at once. Despite being told that the camp was under attack, Gosset insisted that they go back to Mangeni, remarking that the rumour of the camp being taken was all nonsense and that, if Black continued marching his men towards Isandlwana, he would have to take the responsibility for disobeying orders. Black, most probably fuming with anger and frustration, decided to halt where he was but sent Lieutenant Parsons galloping to find Chelmsford to obtain his direct orders.

Chelmsford at this time, about 12.45 p.m., having ridden the four miles over the Magogo Hills from the spot in the valley where he had taken breakfast, was approaching the new campsite at Mangeni. Some of the troops were already there. The carbineers were taking a rest, some forcing themselves to eat their rations of repulsive tinned fish; a short distance away most of the NMP, including Inspector Mansel, had stripped off and were enjoying a cooling dip in the Mangeni stream just short of the waterfall; two companies of the 2/24th were marching up the track; and the men of the NNC were scattered about collecting some firewood in hopeful anticipation of rations arriving. Glyn and Clery were also there awaiting Chelmsford's arrival. All at once everyone became aware of the sound of distant gunfire.

The correspondent of the *Natal Witness* reported:

> 'It was at this time of day, viz., about 12.30 p.m. that a suspicion that something was going on first struck us. Mr Longcast, interpreter to the Lieut. General, learnt from one of the prisoners that an immense army was expected that day... He was employed in examining some of the other prisoners, when suddenly he and those standing around heard the distant report of big guns in the direction of the camp.'

Trooper Symons and some fellow carbineers were bringing in nine prisoners to the new campsite, when they met up with 'some of Colonel Durnford's mounted natives' (this would seem to confirm that Durnford did in fact send a warning to Chelmsford) who told them that, 'fighting was

215

going on' but it was not clear to Symons exactly where. They, too, heard the sound of gunfire.

Lieutenant Milne, riding down the southern slopes of Magogo with Chelmsford, could see in the distance the various bodies of troops scattered around the new camp area. All of Chelmsford's entourage had heard the firing but assumed it was the result of local skirmishing. They rode past the lounging troops and just as they were approaching Glyn, they saw a black horseman (most likely from Durnford) galloping and shouting wildly. Fynn hurried forward to meet the man and heard his astounding tidings that:

> 'The Zulus have taken and demolished the camp at Sandlwana completely.'◊

There is another conical hill close by Mangeni Falls that affords a clear view, ten miles across the plain, towards Isandlwana. With Chelmsford leading the way, he and his staff took the hill at a gallop. Once at the summit Milne trained his naval telescope upon the camp and once again the tents could be seen still standing and again it was assumed that all was well.◊ Chelmsford and his staff then returned and just as they reached the bottom of the hill Lieutenant Parsons arrived requesting permission for Black and Harness to proceed forthwith to Isandlwana. Chelmsford did not approve of Harness' unilateral action in halting when he had been ordered to Mangeni and informed Parsons – who must have pressed the point that the camp was under attack – that the guns and infantry 'were to return immediately and rejoin Glyn.'◊

The time taken by Chelmsford to react to the reports and rumours that the camp was in trouble varies considerably depending on who is describing the event. Milne indicates that it was more or less immediate on having given orders to Parsons: 'The General now made up his mind to return to camp [this would have been about 1.15 p.m.] and leave Glyn with the troops.' Crealock infers that it took somewhat longer. He later scribbled a note on Lieutenant-Colonel Russell's report: '2.30 [the] General had now been aware for some twenty minutes that there had been firing near the camp, not that the camp had been in any danger.' Clery however later stated that Chelmsford did not leave for Isandlwana until around 3.30 p.m.

It seems likely that Milne and Crealock, as members of Chelmsford's staff, attempted to protect their chief by reducing the time that he spent dallying about the new campsite, refusing to believe that Isandlwana could be in any peril. Norris-Newman told his readers that, having observed the camp from the little conical hill at about 1.45 p.m., 'We believed an attack had been made on the camp and had been repulsed.' He then went on to say that some time was spent at Mangeni and that it was not until 2.45 p.m. that Chelmsford decided to return to Isandlwana, giving the reason as, 'anxiety to hear what attack on the camp there had really been.'

There can be little doubt that after emphatically refusing to believe for upwards of two hours that the camp was in any danger, the reason why

Chelmsford eventually rode to Isandlwana in such haste was the receipt of the two messages sent by Pulleine and Gardner. It is significant that these scribbled messages were noted as having been received, one by Chelmsford and the other by Major Gosset at 3.00 p.m,[◊] but the fact that they were received was not mentioned by either Chelmsford, Crealock, Gosset or Milne, nor were the messages recorded in the War Office *Narrative of Field Operations*.

As the last of the horsemen fought their way out of the doomed British camp, it is told that Lieutenant Daly, who had returned to Isandlwana with Gardner, waved the horsemen a carefree farewell as he stood with his infantry. Months later his body, with that of Wardell, was found amongst a group of sixty men who had rallied and died together.

Lieutenant Godwin-Austen was particularly remembered by the warrior who killed him, because of the 'glass in his eye' (a monocle). Godwin-Austen, armed with a revolver, had inflicted a wound in the warrior's neck and another in his leg. A thrown spear took Godwin-Austen in the chest; he tried to heave it out but his opponent had another and with it delivered a mortal blow.

Another warrior recalled killing a British officer:

'He was firing a revolver right to left, I came alongside him, stuck my assegai under his right arm, pushing it through until it came out of his body on the left side. As soon as he fell I split his stomach so that I knew he would not kill any more of my people.'

Months later, on a rocky mound some way in front of the camp, the body of Colour-Sergeant Wolfe of the 1/24th was recognised amongst a pile of redcoat corpses. The mound was strewn with empty cartridge cases that told their own tale of a prolonged fight.

The colour of the 1/24th that had been taken by Melvill was not the only regimental colour in the camp; both colours of the 2nd Battalion had been left behind when Chelmsford's column had marched out that morning. Almost a year later, a trail of two broken colour poles and an empty colour case were found, providing mute clues to another 'fight for the Colours', that led through the camp, over Black's Koppie and down into the Manzimnyama stream.[◊] It was rumoured that the hero was Lieutenant Henry Dyer, adjutant of the 2/24th, riding a chestnut horse.

Fynn tells of a single-handed fight that was related to him by warriors who had encountered the wrath of Lord Chelmsford's orderly, a giant of an Irishman of the 24th. It had been the man's duty to guard the general's tent and for long he kept the warriors at bay by the reach of his bayonet. Finally, he too was assegaied and at about 1.30 p.m. the Union flag that flew outside the tent was torn from its mast by those who slew him.

There are no clues as to the fate of Captain Degacher, nor of his participation in the battle. Of Lieutenant-Colonel Pulleine, there were rumours that he was last seen fighting with a group of soldiers who had rallied beyond the *nek*. However, it is more probable that he died earlier as when Coghill had galloped through the camp, he was overheard to shout that Pulleine had already been shot.

Conversely the fate of Colonel Durnford (who was to be blamed for the British defeat) became legendary. After Durnford had briefly conferred with Gardner he was seen accompanied by his mounted orderly who carried a drawn sword. Durnford, for whatever reason best known to himself, had decided to die but it would be a glorious soldier's death – which for some Victorian officers could be a fate to be desired in certain circumstances. As one Boer was later to observe, 'British officers find glory in death',◊ a concept perhaps impossible to understand today but a reality in 1879. Even the wives and mothers of the officer class had an understanding of it. One wife was to write of her husband's death in Zululand, 'the thought of his glorious soldier's death is such a grand thought that I shall ever love to dwell upon it.'◊

That Durnford had the opportunity to escape is evident. Molife later wrote that he should have had Durnford bound and carried from the battlefield in order to save his life. Simeon Kambule recalled:

> 'Before I left the saddle [the *nek*] I looked back and there I could see my chief [Durnford] in the centre of his square with his long moustaches, and one good arm in the air. He was shouting and laughing, "Come round me, come round me. There is no point in running from these people, I know them too well."'

A trooper of the NMP who escaped reported that Durnford had shouted to the troopers 'Now, my men, let me see what you can do!'

In 1881 Colonel Evelyn Wood eulogised the death of Durnford and those he had gathered around him:

> 'Imagine a gentle slope up which is storming a resistless, surging wave of encircling black bodies, which, though constantly smitten by leaden hail, braced but to sweep on again with renewed force... then there comes on the scene a one-armed man, who, having slowly fallen back before the ever-increasing foe, is now determined to die. "Save yourself, as for me I shall remain." Thus dismissing the staff officer, and Hlubi's black soldiers who vainly urged the great chief to retreat with them. Recognising his commanding courage, around him gathered some twenty similar spirits, who, nobly disdaining death, resolved to cover the retreat of the guns, or die with them.'◊

It is highly improbable that anyone had nobly disdained death and had gathered around Durnford in order to save the guns, as the guns had already gone. Those Durnford had gathered about him were colonials, carbineers and NMP who knew him well – if not personally then by reputation. In the past he had been intimately involved with both units. At one time he had acted as commandant of the NMP and in 1873 he had commanded the carbineers at Bushman's Pass. There the carbineers had wavered with Durnford shouting, 'Will no-one stand with me?' Several carbineers did so and paid the price. More would do so now. They gathered to him because he had ordered them to do so, to perform a futile last stand when the camp had already been overrun and while there was still the possibility of escape for a mounted man.

Mehlokazulu, son of Chief Sihayo and a captain of the Nkobamakosi regiment, was an eye witness to the scene; he later reported that he had watched the colonials ride back from the Nyokana *donga* after the Edendale and Hlubi Troops had vacated the position, and that when the colonials reached the camp, 'they jumped off their horses and never succeeded in getting on them again.'[◊] A few months later the corpses of nineteen carbineers 'all in a heap' and over twenty NMP were found lying around Durnford's body while nearby 'a line of horses' that would have given them the chance of escape 'lay killed on the picquet rope.'

Inspector Mansel believed that Durnford had acted correctly and courageously in rallying the troopers. He later wrote to Durnford's brother Edward:

> 'Your brother had rallied my own Corps, falling and fighting amongst them. He acted as our Commandant for a short time and the men naturally followed him.'

Mansel also believed that Durnford had been deserted not only by his own black horsemen, but also by the imperial infantry:

> 'All the volunteer officers too were killed around your brother and nearly all their men... the despatches too have always said that the Imperial Troops died fighting back to back, thus pointing that the Colonial Troops did not do so though quite untrue. Nearly two thirds of the Imperial Troops were killed between the Nek and Fugitives' Drift. Killed scattered all over the country, cowardly in flight whilst every Colonial Soldier was killed fighting in the Camp thus setting the Regulars an example they might have done well to follow.'[◊]

Those who had succeeded in escaping from the camp – and at that stage there were still many footmen amongst them – were being forced by the right horn to turn south, towards the Buffalo River about six miles distant. Their route lay downhill through scattered thorn trees to the Manzimnyama stream which, having gathered momentum in its descent from the Nqutu Plateau, had, over the millenia, cut a ravine-like passage through the rock and shale, a shallow ravine but too wide for a horse to jump and in most places too steep to descend. The way then led uphill, through scrub and boulders, where a horse could trip or break a leg. Ahead, at the top of the hill, was a green pasture – or so it seemed – but was in fact a bog into which a galloping horse would sink up to its hocks. Beyond the bog was a precipice with a drop of 200 feet into the gorge of the Buffalo where the river churned and boiled white in flood.

The exodus from the camp was now a nightmare of stampeding animals, frantic with the smell of so much blood, fleeing soldiers and colonials pursued by 4,000 fleet-footed warriors, all intent to kill a man and return home with honour. Brickhill's description of the awful scene is as fresh and compelling as it was when written over 120 years ago:

> 'Our flight I shall never forget. No path, no track, boulders everywhere – on we went, borne now into some dry torrent bed, now weaving our way amongst trees of stunted growth… our way was already strewn with shields, assegais, hats, clothing of all description, guns, ammunition belts, and I don't know what not. Whilst our stampede was composed of mules, with and without pack saddles, oxen, horses in all stages of equipment, and fleeing men all strangely intermingled – man and beast apparently all infected with the danger which surrounded us. How one's bosom steels itself to pity at such a time. I came up with poor Band-Sergeant Gamble tottering and tumbling about amongst the stones. He said, "For God's sake give me a lift." I said, "My dear fellow it's a case of life and death with me", and closing my eyes I put spurs to my horse and bounded ahead.'

Poor Gamble, he was also passed by Private Williams who, safely aboard Colonel Glyn's horse, 'could give him no assistance'.

James Hamer, who had earlier galloped down from the Nqutu Ridge with Shepstone, had escaped the camp but found that his horse, 'Dick', was utterly exhausted. With warriors all around him, and with Dick refusing to 'move a step further' it looked all up with Hamer when the last of the rocket battery survivors, whose name is unknown, galloped up with a lead horse. Knowing Hamer, the gunner gallantly gave him the spare horse. But the gunner's luck, unlike that of his other mates from the battery, did not hold. He had hardly handed the spare mount to Hamer when he was shot dead. Hamer found the artillery horse a splendid beast, one that finally took him down and across the Buffalo River.

Curling also praised the quality of his own artillery charger. The guns, an obvious prize of distinction, had been pursued through the camp by an excited mob of warriors and did not get very far. After careering madly over the broken stony ground one gun overturned while the other stuck fast above a small ravine, the horses suspended in their harness. The gunners who had rode on the limbers stood no chance. They were pounced upon and killed, but the few on horseback, including Smith, Curling and the battery's sixteen-year-old trumpeter, rode on following the dwindling band of survivors.

Most who escaped by the Fugitives' Trail, as the route of the fleeing men was soon to become known, praised the horses that saved them. Essex wrote:

> 'I had thank God, a very good horse, and a sure footed one, but I saw many
> poor fellows roll over, their horses stumbling over the rocky ground. It
> was now a race for dear life. The Zulus kept up with us on both sides,
> being able to run down the steep rocky ground quite as fast as a horse
> could travel.'

Trooper Barker remembered the scream of a frenzied horse as, riderless, it galloped past him:

> 'I heard for the first and only time the awful scream of a terrified horse...
> he was a black horse with the saddle turned round, and as he passed and
> went crash against a mounted man in front of us, rolling over the krantz
> [ravine], this awful scream was heard.'

Captain Stafford, who had arrived at Isandlwana with Durnford's wagons so shortly before, passed many maimed and wounded horses as he made his way to the river and thought with sadness that, 'these noble animals are called upon to suffer in their masters' wars.' Finding a wounded comrade called Erskine along the way, Stafford was fortunate that at the same moment a riderless white horse, instinctively seeking the protection of company, came alongside and stopped. Although it was saddleless, a rein was tied around its lower jaw as a makeshift bit and Erskine was heaved aboard – both men made it safely to the river. There was also one man who, against all odds, escaped on foot. Stafford later mentioned those who escaped with him and concluded that there was also, 'one of the mounted infantrymen who ran all the way and kept up with us. He was gifted with marvellous staying power.' Alas his name was not mentioned.

Smith-Dorrien's borrowed horse left much to be desired:

> 'I was riding a broken-kneed old crock which did not belong to me and I
> expected it to go down on its head every minute... the enemy were going
> at a kind of very fast half-walk half-run... and kept killing all the way.'

When Smith-Dorrien finally got close to the river he stopped for a moment to help a wounded soldier and so temporarily blocked the way, causing Major Smith to shout, 'For God's sake get on, man, the Zulus are on top of us.' Indeed they were, for moments later Smith-Dorrien's horse was assegaied, while Smith and the wounded man were speared to death. With Zulus all around him Smith-Dorrien, 'with the strong hope that everybody clings to that some accident will turn up', rushed off on foot and plunged into the river. He survived the day, as he would many other adventures, to become one of Britain's leading generals by the start of the First World War.

Richard Vause reached the river and finally the Natal bank utterly exhausted and without a horse. There he sat, too done in to move, and would undoubtedly have been slain had not a little black boy, perhaps a kitchen hand, who had likewise escaped, offered him a seat behind on his horse. Together they rode away from immediate danger and later Vause dismounted as the horse had difficulty in carrying two riders.

There were many acts of selfishness as the survivors made their way to the river, but only Brickhill had the courage to admit his own cowardice, how his bosom had steeled itself – as he quaintly put it – against Band-Sergeant Gamble's plea for help. Yet, as already seen, there were also many brave acts that would go unrecognised – except for one. Only one man was granted an immediate award of the Victoria Cross during the battle. Private Sam Wassall of the 80th Regiment, attached to the IMI, saved the life of a comrade. Wassall, seeing the man in difficulties in the river, dismounted and brought the man to safety then, taking him up behind, successfully crossed with him to the Natal bank, while all the time under Zulu fire.

At the time there was no provision for the posthumous award of the Victoria Cross and although the saving of the Queen's Colour by Melvill and Coghill epitomised the Victorian idea of heroism, it was not until 1907 that the posthumous award was made to both officers. Yet Melvill and Coghill did not leave the camp together as legend, supported by numerous heroic-style paintings, would have it. As we have seen, Coghill was the later of the two to leave the camp but was first to arrive at the river. He had crossed in safety when, glancing back, he saw Melvill, who had been joined by Higginson, clinging to a large rock a short distance out in the river.

Melvill's ride, with the colour encumbered by its heavy case and pole, must have been a nightmare as the flag snagged and stuck amongst the scrub along the way. On one occasion, Brickhill saw Melvill almost unseated as his horse carried him under a tree dragging the colour behind him. A less courageous man would have discarded the burden and increased his chances of survival. In the river, with his red jacket attracting a gathering of warriors on the bank, he was utterly exhausted but still clung to the colour. Coghill, seeing his plight, with great bravery set his horse back across the river, intent to rescue both Melvill and the flag. He had hardly got into the water when his horse was shot. All three were now horseless and Coghill, with his injured knee, almost unable to walk. As they pushed off for the Natal bank the force of the current swept the colour away.

They all survived the crossing but, once on dry land, both Melvill and Coghill pleaded exhaustion. There Higginson left them and ran on to escape. According to Higginson both men were still armed with revolvers at the time and had, in fact, just shot two Zulus who had attacked them. They struggled on together, with Coghill only hobbling at best. They got about half a mile above the river before they were overtaken and speared to death. But they were not alone as has been shown in so many illustrations of their celebrated end. Lieutenant Hillier, NNC, who was amongst those who found their bodies some days later, wrote that Melvill and Coghill, 'lay behind the bodies of two soldiers', most likely IMI, 'where they had made a stand.' But as the soldiers were merely rank and file, nobody bothered to record their regiment or made any attempt to discover their names, despite the fact that the men had died in the same heroic circumstances as Melvill and Coghill. Who killed them will never be known; most likely it was men of Gamdana's clan who had crossed the river higher up.

When the Edendale Troop, unscathed except for two casualties and replenished with ammunition, had led the way to Fugitives' Drift riding through a rabble of camp followers and certain elements of the NNC, they too had found the Natal bank already lined with warriors ready to attack anyone who successfully crossed the river. Dismounting, the troop quickly dispersed the enemy with several volleys. Had it not been for the early arrival of the Edendale men, there would have been little chance of survival for the hundreds of fleeing men who followed.

Finally the drift was empty of survivors, the banks and shallows strewn with bodies and debris of discarded equipment. Many days later, with the river no longer in spate, a wagonload of arms and equipment was retrieved from the shallows by Fynn, who maintained that the British lost more lives between the camp and the drift than at the battlefield itself.

Many of the warriors who had unsuccessfully pursued the survivors and had failed to kill, went on to Rorke's Drift, while the rest returned to the camp in the hopes that there would still be plunder to be had.

—»•«—

During the hour-long chase to the drift, scattered fighting had continued amongst the tents and wagons and high up on the slopes of Isandlwana hill. Here and there a single man or group with ammunition had kept fighting, knowing that mercy or rescue were out of the question. Durnford and the colonials had fought on and when their ammunition dwindled to the last few rounds, they continued to fight with clubbed carbines and hunting knives. Captain Younghusband's C Company was probably the last to be overwhelmed. Having fought their way along the upper slopes of Isandlwana, C Company came to bay on a rocky ledge high above the wagon park. A warrior remembered how some of the soldiers had got up on to a steep slope where they were difficult to get at, and how the Zulus were 'shot or bayoneted as fast as they came up,' and how finally the soldiers gave a cheer and, led by an *induna* (officer) with a long flashing sword, they charged the Zulus and were finally put to death.

Among the last to die were the portly Gabangaye, chief of No 3 Column amaChunu NNC, and his son Mbonjana. The oral history told by the present-day Isandlwana community has it that Gabangaye, who had been shooting at the Nkobamakosi regiment of the left horn, was recognised and finally captured. When all the redcoats had been dealt with, Gabangaye was paraded before the Nkobamakosi commanders, Lukhwazi, Mtombela, Sigcwelegecwele and Mehlokazulu.

By that time the *udibi* boys who had followed close on the heels of the warriors, had entered the camp. They had been instructed to commence *inseme*, that is to kill the wounded by throwing spears. Gabangaye, seeing so many of his followers put to death, asked for mercy and then threw down his rifle. But Lukhwazi mocked Gabangaye saying his young lions would eat him up and so the *izindibi* killed Gabangaye. The Zulu generals then gave orders that every body be checked for death and in doing so each body was to be ripped open to free the spirit of the corpse. Mbonjana, son of Gabangaye was not dead. He was feigning death amongst the wounded and when he heard the footsteps of the *udibi* boys coming closer he jumped to his feet, pointing his empty rifle at them. But he too was killed by thrown spears and his rifle taken. The NNC men were regarded as traitors and were decapitated. Gabangaye's body was cut to pieces, some body parts being used by the *iziNyanga*.

The amaChunu NNC lost 240 killed at Isandlwana fighting for the British and Zikali's men lost 103. To this day the descendants of the amaChunu visit the battlefield each year and commune with the spirits of their ancestors.

Legend has it that the last man to die was a soldier of the 24th, most likely a redcoat of Younghusband's company, who had reached a little cave, barely big enough to shelter one person, high up on the side of Isandlwana. Looking over the plain towards Mangeni and amply supplied with ammunition, the soldier held out for many hours, long enough to witness Chelmsford's relief column approaching but not long enough to be saved. Ten months later Mainwaring found his skeleton with a rope still around its neck.

When Chelmsford eventually rode for Isandlwana, he took with him an escort of weary carbineers. Trooper Symons noted that by the time they were in the saddle the booming of the guns had ceased. A little way along the track Chelmsford, in silence, passed Black and Harness, the guns and infantry all marching in the opposite direction towards Mangeni.

Hamilton-Browne had spent the long vigil of the afternoon watching the destruction of the camp, he and his battalion helpless in their inadequacy. Captain Develin had returned, reporting that Hamilton-Browne's final message had sent the guns and the infantry marching to Isandlwana only, inexplicably, for them later to about-turn and march the other way. At about 3.15 p.m. Russell and the IMI came into view some distance away and Hamilton-Browne sent yet a fifth note, carried by Captain Hay, offering to advance on the camp if the IMI would support.

According to Hamilton-Browne's memoirs,◊ written many years later, Russell acknowledged the message but made no comment. Russell's version,◊ written within two months of the battle, was that he recalled receiving a note from Hamilton-Browne informing him that there was a large force of enemy before him and the camp. However, as far as he could remember, he believed that he later communicated this information to Chelmsford, as for the note itself, regrettably it had been lost in the subsequent confusion.

Close to 3.30 p.m. Chelmsford came upon Hamilton-Browne and the NNC. There he halted, straining his gaze to the north-west, whilst struggling to conceal the dread that had suddenly come upon him, the awful realisation that the camp, containing all the equipment and transport for the entire column of 5,000 men, was now in the hands of the enemy. Hamilton-Browne, a colonial and thus, in Chelmsford's estimation, less reliable than an imperial officer, had been almost belligerent a few minutes earlier when he had imparted the shattering news.

Moments passed in silence, neither Chelmsford's staff nor escort wishing to make comment,◊ then, not far distant, a lone figure came into view, a tired slouching figure, leading an equally tired pony, frequently glancing behind, clearly apprehensive of pursuit. Chelmsford rode forward to meet the man, familiar to them all, another colonial but previously an imperial officer, Commandant Rupert Lonsdale, who earlier in the day had ridden to Isandlwana to organise rations. However, as Lonsdale spoke, whatever fragments of optimism there may have remained were brutally dispelled. Lonsdale had, by a miracle, survived his visit to the camp; there was nothing left there but chaos, death and destruction. In the stunned silence that followed Lonsdale's brief testimony, Chelmsford finally spoke, perhaps more to himself than anyone else; in a whisper of disbelief he said, 'But I left over 1,000 men to guard the camp!'◊

Other than that there was no emotion. That an awesome defeat had taken place was clear and that there was but one course of action to follow. The camp must be retaken or they must fight their way through it, back to the Rorke's Drift road and Natal. There was no other way to go. The predicament of Chelmsford's column was extreme. It had no reserve ammunition or rations. Nobody dared to mention Rorke's Drift, its likely fate too awful to contemplate.

Major Gosset was instructed to ride at once to Mangeni and hasten the rest of the column to Chelmsford's position. It was with some surprise that many witnessed Gosset's headlong arrival, only to be more astounded at his news – the very news that he had dismissed as nonsense a few hours earlier he now declared to be the truth. Hallam Parr's reaction was that the whole thing, 'seemed so improbable, so impossible, there must have been exaggeration somewhere.'◊ Yet as Hallam Parr marched he was quite cheerful, feeling convinced that the column would take the Zulu in the rear whilst they were still attacking.

Glyn and his staff were at Mangeni when they received the shattering news but within fifteen minutes, accompanied by Harness and his guns, the mounted men and the infantry were on their way back to Isandlwana. The men of the 24th, who had been awake and on the go for twelve hours, marching and counter-marching over tough terrain in the peak of the South African summer, stepped out well despite their weariness, all anxious to know the worst and to save their mates in camp if that were still at all possible.

Trooper Symons watched them march and in admiration wrote:

'Hurrah for the 24th! I never saw men march so well. They kept the Native Contingent at a trot.'

Meanwhile, Chelmsford and those about him watched the plunder of the camp three and a half miles away. Sergeant-Major Scott of the carbineers, with three men, was ordered forward to a low ridge. He soon returned to report that masses of Zulus were moving around in the camp. Then, from Chelmsford's position, large groups could be seen moving away onto the Nqutu Ridge and towards the Ngwebini Valley. Many were seen to be pushing wagons, these most likely laden with their wounded and captured ammunition.

As Chelmsford and those about him watched, one by one, the tents began to disappear, cut into sheets of canvas to be taken back to some Zulu homestead. The impatience was intense. Where were the infantry and the guns?

Then Chelmsford ordered Russell and the IMI forward to take a closer look. It was not long before they returned to report that:

'The camp was in complete possession of the enemy... who were like bees in the camp, and all along the plain to the foothills, and on the hills, they were swarming.'[0]

At last Glyn and the rest of the column arrived, Clery later wrote to a friend at the War Office in London:

'The General's countenance is always an expressive one, and the look of gloom and pain that met one as we arrived told only too plainly what was going on within. But he was all there – never apparently flinched – he had quite made up his mind. He formed up the 2/24th and said to them a few pithy words – "Men, the enemy have taken our camp – many of our friends must have lost their lives in defending it. There is nothing left for us now but to fight our way through, and mind we must fight hard for we will have to fight for our lives. I know you and I know I can depend on you."'

It was a good speech, a soldier's speech. The men cheered and as dusk began to fall Chelmsford formed the column for attack. Guns in the centre, one half of the infantry on either side, the NNC deployed to the rear and the various horsemen, marching in half sections, to the front and the flanks. Half the horsemen, every other man, dismounted, his horse being led by his half section. Trooper Clarke recalled his concern that in the event of a scare, his companion, Trooper Day, might clear off with his horse. As Clarke stumbled along in the gloom he frequently called to Day, warning him against bunking with his mount.

As the column got to within 1,000 yards of the camp it began to encounter Zulu dead. Trooper Clarke remembered:

> 'The dead were lying in such numbers that we constantly fell over corpses, but whether European or Zulu it was too dark to see. The gunners of the RA had to pull bodies out of the way because the horses would not pass them.'

At 600 yards the column stopped. The guns were unlimbered and brought to bear on the *nek* where it seemed – or had seemed while it was still light, a barricade of wagons had been built. Some twenty rounds were fired, the exploding shells illuminating for an eerie instant, the dishevelled camp and black mass of Isandlwana beyond.

With the guns still firing, four companies of the 2/24th led by Wilsone Black, with bayonets fixed and cheering as they went, stumbled through the darkness and stormed Black's Koppie. The guns then ceased to fire and minutes later a great shout from the koppie broke the silence. The enemy had gone. The column then reformed with the NNC, who had become fractious and difficult to handle, placed to the front. According to Fynn they were distraught with fear that their great chief, Gabangaye, had been killed in the camp – as indeed he had. Dartnell then approached Chelmsford and strongly suggested that all 1,600 of the NNC should be positioned to the rear to prevent any possibility of them stampeding in panic back through the horsemen, guns and infantry.◊ This done, the column moved forward and without opposition retook the camp.

Before reaching the tent lines, Lieutenant John Maxwell and his company of NNC fell straight into the *donga* directly in front of the camp. Maxwell found himself lying on his back with his horse standing over him. Most of his men had likewise fallen and it took them some time to find their way out. When they finally made the camp, they discovered half a dozen Zulu warriors who had found the column's rum supply and had drunk deeply of it. The Zulus were more or less unconscious but, by the light of a lantern, some men of the 24th bayoneted them to death.◊

Lord Chelmsford bore up well, though surrounded by defeat; he personally saw to the placing of the picquets. On one occasion, after he had mistakenly accused a junior officer of the NNC of not knowing where his own sentries were placed, good mannered as ever, he apologised saying, 'I beg your pardon, and I am sorry you were disturbed.'◊

The night that followed would, for every man present, remain the most terrifying and memorable night of his life. There was no moon and the sky was more often than not covered by scattered cloud. On one occasion it rained for a while. It was rather like walking blindfold into some horror of a haunted house, to be surrounded by unspeakable things that could be touched but not seen.

There were many individual descriptions of the night's ordeal:

> 'It was a mercy that the surrounding darkness shut off from our view many
> ghastly sights... '

> 'We lay down in a square for the night, literally amongst our slaughtered
> comrades... '

> 'No pen could adequately express the feelings of those who spent the
> night at that ghastly halting place amidst the debris of the plundered and
> mutilated bodies of men, horses and cattle... '

> 'In the morning we found that we had literally been lying in blood, for we
> were peeling cakes of it and mud from our mackintoshes. And the stench!
> It was awful, I can still smell it at times. Some things remind me of it, for
> instance a sweet potato that has been cooked when it just beginning to go
> bad... The child-like crying of the mules and the groans of a wounded
> man who appeared to be close under Isandlwana, would have unnerved
> many men, and there was a cold, unearthly smell about the place which
> must have arisen from the numerous dead bodies.'

Those were not the only smells. The veterinary surgeon's wagon had
been ransacked and warriors, mistaking the various medicines and
chemicals for alcohol, had drunk deep. Fynn found the stench of the spilt
chemicals quite sickening. Many warriors who had drunk these substances
died of poisoning. Fynn found one elderly Zulu of the uThulwana regiment
still conscious but he died an hour later.

Darkness concealed the worst, but born out of sensationalism, even the
worst would be exaggerated with lurid stories of torture and many hinted
horrors too awful to disclose. Maxwell wrote on the subject:

> 'I mention this because on the way I heard some terrible stories about
> mutilated bodies. These were invented for the occasion, as it was
> impossible for those who told these yarns to have distinguished anything
> in the night, it being extremely dark.'

That most corpses were disembowelled and that there were
decapitations is a fact. There would also have been an *iziNyanga* element
amongst the Zulu regiments, eager for body parts and, as in any army,
ancient or modern, an element delighting in cruelty. But generally the Zulu
did not torture for torture's sake. It was not the Zulu way. It is also well to
remember that less than 300 years earlier any traitor to the English crown
would likely be hung, drawn and quartered.

The worst accusation of atrocity levelled at the Zulus concerned the fate
of the drummer boys of the 2nd Battalion. They had been left behind in
camp with Band-Sergeant Gamble and the rest of the musicians. The
drummer boys are often referred to as eleven-year-olds, but it is most
unlikely that any of those with the 24th were any younger than fourteen or
fifteen. Most drummers were mature men who performed an important

function during battle. There are numerous 'eye witness' accounts of the drummer boys' fate which describe them as being hung from a wagon by a meat hook inserted under the chin and disembowelled. Several accounts by responsible people ring true. One actually names a boy. A soldier of the 2/24th, W. Sweeney, himself a drummer, wrote home to his parents after the battle, his letter being subsequently published in a local paper, recounting the number of dead and mentioning by name band members who had died:

> 'Two drummers, Anderson and Holmes, and five little boys of the band about fourteen years of age. They butchered most awfully indeed. One little chap named M'Every, they hung up by the chin to a hook.'◊

Between Sweeney and the newspaper, the boy's name seems to have been misspelt; undoubtedly Sweeney was referring to fifteen-year old Boy Joseph McEwan who had enlisted at Dover, age fourteen, and died at Isandlwana.

———◊◊◊———

The Zulus had carried many of their dead from the battlefield and the true number of their casualties has never been established. Many of the wounded were carried to the Ngwebini Valley where the very worst, in mercy, were put to death. That their victory was bought at a high price, perhaps between 1,500 and 2,000 dead, is well known. The dead were buried mostly in mealie pits and *dongas*. King Cetshwayo on hearing the death toll is reputed to have remarked that an assegai had been thrust into the belly of the Zulu nation.

There was a young white man, a Boer trader, Cornelius Vijn, travelling in Zululand at the time, who was given the protection of Cetshwayo. Vijn later described the agony of the local community when news of the Zulu death toll was brought to the homestead in which he sheltered:

> 'Our attention was drawn to a troop of people, who came back from their gardens crying and wailing. As they approached, I recognised them as persons belonging to the kraal in which I was staying. When they came into or close to the kraal, they kept on wailing in front of the kraal, rolling themselves on the ground and never quietening down; nay, in the night they wailed so as to cut through the heart of anyone. And this wailing went on, night and day, for a fortnight; the effect of it was very depressing; I wished I could not hear it.'◊

The number of British dead has been more accurately recorded: approximately 850 whites and about 500 blacks including non-combatants.

———◊◊◊———

With Zulu campfires burning in the hills close by, with the incessant drumming and the fear of attack by overwhelming numbers, the night passed slowly for the column. Chelmsford had given orders that the men – those lucky enough to find sleep – should be roused long before first light.

Believing that the sight of so many mutilated comrades would affect morale, Chelmsford was determined to leave before dawn disclosed the worst.

During the night the western skyline had been lit by several fires, the largest silhouetting the outline of the Oskarberg at Rorke's Drift. It could only mean one thing, that the depot at Rorke's Drift, defended by B Company of the 2/24th and 100 men of the NNC had been attacked. It had likely fallen to the enemy. It was no doubt felt that the column should, if possible, depart Isandlwana without a battle, as all its ammunition would be required to fight its way across the Buffalo. No attempt was made to recover ammunition from the camp, even though it would seem that there was plenty amongst the wagons at the time; within days an entrepreneurial local Zulu was retailing rounds to warriors lucky enough to have captured a British rifle.

As the column moved off towards Rorke's Drift, the nearby Zulu population watched in curiosity. A few hundred yards along the road a homestead that had not been seen occupied before was now full of men and women. Milne mused that they must all have blood on their hands and regretted there was no time to kill them. Trooper Clarke was amongst the rearguard who would have fifteen minutes of daylight in the camp before taking up position. Clarke had gone off the previous morning without his spurs and had earlier tried to sneak to the tent lines in hope of finding them, but had been caught by Dartnell and sent back. As he waited for the order to move off, Clarke contemplated the dead body of his mate Trooper Stimson that was still booted and spurred. Assuming that Stimson would not mind Clarke dismounted to remove Stimson's spurs, but was caught again, and severely reprimanded, much to his indignation, by Inspector Mansel for 'robbing the dead'.

As the column got on the move, it began to occur to some that they had been outmanoeuvred by the Zulu generals and had fallen for their decoys. Three days later Milne was to write to Commodore Sullivan, RN:

> 'No doubt the force we were after on Wednesday [22 January] was a blind as we never could get near them, they kept edging away, drawing us further from the camp.'

And the *Natal Witness* was shortly to tell its readers that:

> 'It was the opinion of all who understand the natives and their method of fighting that this small body of Zulus [the decoys on Magogo] who paraded themselves so openly had certainly an army behind them which was only awaiting the proper moment to come into action.'

The column had not marched far when groups of warriors began to appear, though most merely stood and gazed as the soldiers passed. One warrior, braver than the rest, or perhaps still fired by plundered British rum, did his utmost to incite his disinterested comrades to attack. Finally disdaining their lack of interest, the warrior charged the column alone, only to be brought down by a ragged volley from the infantry who were only too eager to shoot a Zulu. His death was treated with indifference by his comrades and the column continued on uninterrupted. Everyone was now under orders not to fire unless attacked.

Mansel, bringing up the rearguard, was ordered to remain with one troop of the NMP until the column was well away. He had the opportunity to look around the tent lines and counted 'eighty men lying all together' in the camp of the 1/24th and about 40 in the area of the 2nd Battalion 'who had evidently died fighting' – perhaps the remnants of Cavaye's and Mostyn's men?

Before Mansel and his troop had caught up with the column, a force of Zulus, over 2,000 strong, suddenly emerged from a valley to the left of the road. So sudden was their appearance that they were only 300 yards away when first seen.⁰ Although at one time the more daring warriors got within 200 yards, and were seen to cut off some NNC stragglers who had stayed behind to loot, neither side fired a shot.

Eventually the column came within sight of Rorke's Drift and, full of apprehension, those with field glasses trained them on the distant buildings. Men could be seen on top of a roof, one of whom appeared to be waving a flag. It was too much to hope that the little garrison had survived. But against all odds, B Company of the 2/24th with a few men from other corps and patients from the hospital – approximately 130 men in total – had held out for eleven hours against the sustained attacks of 3,000 Zulu warriors. The battle that had been fought at Rorke's Drift would become as famous a victory for the British as the Battle of Isandlwana would become a triumph for the Zulu nation, but any hope that a significant number of survivors from Isandlwana would be found was quickly dispelled. Many had passed by but only one had stayed: Lieutenant Adendorff, who was amongst the first to leave the battlefield of Isandlwana, had fought all night at Rorke's Drift.

But it was not a time for complacency. There was little ammunition to be had at Rorke's Drift, and it would be several days before more could be expected. The men owned nothing except what they stood up in and, with fear of a renewed Zulu attack, the fortifications needed to be repaired and extended. The first task, however, was to bury the hundreds of Zulu dead that lay in heaps. The shocked and exhausted men who had fought all night, were left to lie and sleep as best they could, while the weary soldiers of the column set to extend the defences and collect the corpses. Officers and men worked side by side in the gruesome task of digging a mass grave or in dragging bodies to nearby *dongas*.

There would be no compassion or mercy for the Zulu wounded; most likely they were bayoneted or, worse still, buried with the dead. Trooper Clarke recorded:

> 'Altogether we buried 375 dead Zulus and some wounded were thrown
> into the grave. Seeing the manner in which our wounded had been

mutilated after being dragged from the hospital (men who were wounded in the skirmish on the 12th January) we were very bitter and did not spare wounded Zulus.'[◊]

Lieutenant-Colonel Crealock mentioned in his private journal that '351 dead Zulus were found, and 500 wounded'.[◊] As there is no record of attending to Zulu wounded – and in any event it would not have been feasible for so many to have received medical attention – it is possible that all the Zulu wounded were put to death.[◊] Twenty-eight years later, Smith-Dorrien was to comment on the harness-drying contraption that he had constructed earlier, that the first use he saw it put to, 'was for hanging Zulus who were supposed to have behaved treacherously the day after the Rorke's Drift fight.'[◊] And in 1914, Samuel Pitts, who had been a private in B Company at Rorke's Drift, said, 'We reckon we had accounted for 875 [Zulus killed] but the books will tell you 400 or 500.'[◊]

Lord Chelmsford and his staff spent the night amongst the shambles of Rorke's Drift but the following morning departed for Pietermaritzburg. There he would meet with Sir Bartle Frere and together they would ponder anew on the conquest of Zululand.

PART THREE

The Cover-Up

'There are three kinds of lies: lies, damned lies and statistics.'

Benjamin Disraeli

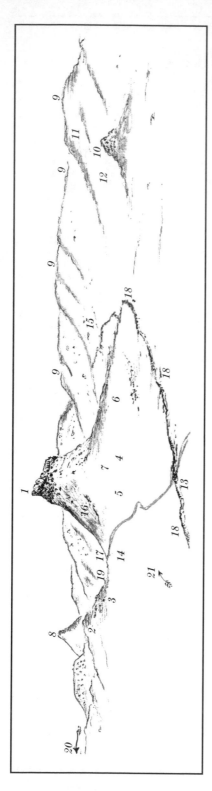

Map No. 8

A copy of Inspector George Mansel's map of the battlefield. Mansel sent the original to Colonel Edward Durnford, the brother of Anthony. The map is captioned:

1. The Hill
2. Black's Koppie
3. Camp of 1/24th Regt
4. Camp of 2/24th
5. Camp of R.A. and Mtd Corps
6. Camp of Native Contingent
7. Headquarter's Tents
8. Signal Hill. Rorke's Drift.
9. Nqutu Range. The figures are put in the places I placed my videttes on the day we pitched camp. I also had videttes on the right front about 2 miles away.
10. Stony Koppie [Conical Hill]
11. Where the Zulus came down & attacked Colonel Durnford's Basutos.
12. Where the Rocket Battery was destroyed, distant from camp 3½ miles.
13. Donga held by Police & Volunteers, and where Col. Durnford joined them when the Basutos left him, and where they checked the left horn of the Zulus.
14. Where Col. Durnford fell, surrounded by the Police & Volunteers.
15. Where the 2 companies 1/24th went up and were driven in by the right horn of the Zulus.
16. Where about 50 of the 1/24th were killed.
17. Where the right horn of the Zulus came round the Hill, and came into the rear of the camp.
18. Donga and small stream in front of camp, from which it was supplied with water, about 600 yards from Neck.
19. Neck.
20. Position of Fugitives' Drift.
21. Where the left horn of the Zulus came into camp.

(Spellings as in original document.)

Chapter 8
Web of Deception

'Lord Chelmsford and staff, especially Colonel Crealock tried in every way to shift the responsibility of the disaster from their own shoulders onto those of your brother.'

Inspector George Mansel, NMP, to Colonel Edward Durnford, 23 November 1879

⇒►◄⇐

Standing at Rorke's Drift on Thursday morning, 23 January 1879, Lord Chelmsford looked back across the Buffalo River into Zululand. He could clearly discern, at a distance of ten miles as the crow flies, the outline of Isandlwana. At the foot and surrounds of the sphinx-like mountain lay the bodies of his ruined camp, destined to become carrion for wild animals or skin and bone bleached by the hot African sun.

Chelmsford was both exhausted and demoralised. It was beyond his immediate comprehension as to how his camp could have been overrun. Sufficient infantry in a compact formation should surely have defeated the oncoming rush of Zulu. On reflection, he probably realised that he had failed when he left Isandlwana to leave any instructions with Colonel Glyn regarding the defence of the camp. He had reconnoitred the Malakatha hills to the south, the Mangeni Falls to the east, and traversed part of the Nqutu Range to the north and north-east and it had seemed clear to him that there had been no Zulu in strength within a ten mile radius of the camp.

As a result of the intelligence reports of Zulu movements supplied by Fynn, he had felt entirely justified in assuming that any action which might be forthcoming would take place in the Mangeni Falls area, the area to which he had marched with half of Glyn's command. The possibility of the camp being attacked was unthinkable, and consequently he had neither considered nor issued specific orders for its defence.

This omission now magnified itself a thousand fold to become an error of judgement on his part, from which he could see no escape. Yet, within a few hours, statements and comments made by Crealock and Clery would provide Chelmsford with an opportunity to extricate himself from a seemingly impossible situation, allowing the finger of blame to be pointed directly at Colonel Anthony Durnford, Royal Engineers. Had Lieutenant Melvill had the strength to continue his climb to the plateau some yards from where he was killed on the Natal bank of the Buffalo River, a very different story might have emerged. Melvill was at Colonel Pulleine's side for much of the battle and would have been privy to Pulleine's tactical thinking and to orders received and given. Fate had regrettably decreed otherwise.

———◆———

At approximately 1.30 a.m. on Wednesday 22 January, Dartnell's messenger had made his way slowly through the night picquets of the 24th Regiment. As he neared the neck of Isandlwana, he dismounted close to the pioneer wagons and threaded his way to Major Clery's tent. The message he was to deliver was addressed to 'staff officer', and was destined for Glyn. Clery lit his candle and read the pencilled note in which Dartnell requested reinforcements. Having put on his boots he hurried to Glyn's tent, and awakened him. As expected Glyn's response was, 'Take it to the general.'◊ Clery now made his way some fifty paces to where the general's tent was located. He should have delivered the note to Crealock but chose to ignore protocol and entered the general's tent. Later Clery was to write:

> 'Lying on my face and hands, close by his camp bed, I can still remember how I read out from the crumpled piece of notebook paper written across in pencil, word after word.'◊

Immediately Clery had finished, the general without hesitation responded:

> 'Order the 2nd Battalion 24th Regiment, four guns and all the mounted troops to get ready at daybreak. Order up Colonel Durnford with the troops to reinforce the camp.'

Crealock, sleeping lightly in an adjacent tent and awakened by the ongoing conversation, hastened to join Chelmsford. He had overheard the instruction given to Clery regarding Durnford and interjected, asking, 'Is Major Clery to issue orders to Colonel Durnford?' Chelmsford, instantly acknowledging that Durnford's was an independent command, responded to Crealock, 'No, you do it', whereupon Crealock returned to his tent to execute the order.

Crealock had served four years in India, had passed through staff college, and had held a number of staff appointments which included the post of Deputy Assistant Quarter-Master General at the Army headquarters, Horse Guards, from January 1876 to January 1878. As well as describing the location of their offices, 'Horse Guards' was the name given to that august body of military officers based in Whitehall, London, under the Commander-in-Chief of the Army, George, Duke of Cambridge, cousin of Queen Victoria. Chelmsford enjoyed the unequivocal support of Horse Guards having served there himself and, like Crealock, had been an officer in the 95th (Derbyshire) Regiment.

Crealock, on hearing that Chelmsford was to replace General

Cunyngehame as military commander in Southern Africa, had asked to be appointed as his military secretary. Chelmsford, who had not previously considered Crealock, approved, and officially appointed him 'Assistant Military Secretary'. In effect, Crealock was both Chelmsford's military secretary and chief-of-staff. It was a poor choice, for Crealock was not a popular officer. He had a reputation for sarcasm, sharp retorts and for being a snob. In Victorian times the word 'snob' had the connotation of being a cad or a bounder. With some justification the word could be applied to Crealock for later he proved to have a propensity for adjusting the truth to fit the circumstances.

Unpopular with the troops and his brother officers, Crealock had one saving grace, his ability to paint. Some 310 of his sketches and watercolours depicting events and locations of the Anglo-Zulu War and the Indian Mutiny are held in the museum of the Sherwood Foresters, Nottingham Castle, the descendant regiment of the 95th, a legacy for which history can be grateful.

Hunched over his field-desk by the light of a candle Crealock wrote in his order book the following instruction to Durnford:

> 'You are to march to the camp at once with all the force you have with you of No 2 column. Major Bengough's Battalion is to move to Rorke's Drift as ordered yesterday, 2/24th, artillery, and mounted men with the General and Colonel Glyn move off at once to attack a Zulu force about ten miles distant.'◊

Colonel Durnford acted upon this letter. The instruction written that night was of great importance. Crealock, in a deliberate attempt to discredit Durnford and protect Chelmsford, was to alter, with a single sentence, the whole meaning of the order.

On 9 February 1879 Crealock made a statement which formed a supplement to the evidence given to the Court of Inquiry held afterwards, in which he said:

> 'Soon after 2 a.m. on the 22nd January I received instructions from the Lieutenant General to send a written order to Lieutenant Colonel Durnford to the following effect (I copied it in my note-book which was afterwards lost). Move up to Sandhlawana camp at once with all your mounted men and Rocket Battery – take command of it [author's emphasis].'◊

It was neither Lord Chelmsford's intention nor instruction that Colonel Durnford should take command of the camp, but by inserting the phrase 'take command of it', Crealock had deliberately placed the blame on Durnford for failing to carry out his purported orders. Crealock continued in his statement:

> 'He, [Lord Chelmsford] would also consider that the presence of an officer of Colonel Durnford's rank and corps would prove of value in the defence of the camp – if it should be attacked.'

This statement carries little credence as at the time nobody, least of all Chelmsford, believed that there was the remotest danger of an attack. It was yet another nail in Durnford's coffin, as was Crealock's further comment:

> 'It was evident to me that the Zulu forces were in our neighbourhood and the General had decided on the evening of the 21st to make a reconnaissance to our left front.'

If it had been Crealock's opinion that the Zulu were in force near the camp, he was the only one with such a view. Certainly Chelmsford was not of that opinion, for he believed the Zulu to be in strength ten miles to the south-east. In a separate document, part of which was an extract written from 'The Private Journal of Colonel Crealock', he wrote:

> 'Major Clery, (Col Glyn's staff officer), said later in the day [22 January], in Col. Crealock's hearing, that Col. Pulleine had been distinctly ordered to draw his circle of picquet closer in, and to <u>defend</u> [Crealock's emphasis] the camp.'

This statement is questionable, for it was only on the morning of 23 January, at Rorke's Drift, that Clery, for the first time mentioned to Chelmsford that he had given orders to Pulleine (these are discussed below). The burial party sent to the battlefield in May located numerous documents and papers, all of which were recovered and taken back to Rorke's Drift. Included in these papers, most of which belonged to Chelmsford, was Crealock's missing notebook in which he had written Chelmsford's order to Durnford. A number of staff officers probably saw the document and read the contents but, if they did, all maintained a conspiracy of silence.

This order book, which was relevant to the Court of Inquiry, was forwarded to Crealock in England late in 1879 by military headquarters South Africa, as if it were his personal property. However Crealock, now in possession of the vital evidence, chose to remain silent, and in doing so continued to shield Lord Chelmsford. Throughout the debate in parliament in 1880, the accepted facts showed that Durnford was instructed to take command of the camp. Still Crealock remained silent. It is possible that Chelmsford might have had an inkling of the truth but he never questioned Crealock as to why his original order was at variance with Crealock's supplementary statement.

On 27 January, days after the battle, Lord Chelmsford wrote to Colonel Fred Stanley, Secretary of State for War, giving his official version of events leading to the battle:

> 'An express was sent off to Lieutenant-Colonel Durnford, Royal Engineers, who was at Rorke's Drift with 500 natives, half of whom were mounted men and armed with breech-loaders to move up to strengthen the force left to guard the camp.'

Chelmsford clearly intended Durnford to move up to the camp and await further orders. Yet on 25 August 1880 Chelmsford accepted Crealock's incorrect version of events and wrote to *The Times* in response to an article relating to Isandlwana written by General Sir Linton Simmons (Member of Parliament) stating:

'In my speech I distinctly stated that written orders were sent to Colonel Durnford to move up to Sandlana camp and take command of it. That order was, I maintain as binding upon Colonel Durnford as those which a soldier takes over from a sentry he relieves on a post.'

Thus one year after Crealock was in possession of the correct version of his order to Durnford, Chelmsford perpetuated the error in order to defend his actions, and still Crealock remained silent. The saga of the order book does not end here. Edward Durnford (brother of the slain colonel) in 1882, on hearing rumours that the original order not only existed, but was in Colonel Crealock's possession, challenged Crealock. Edward Durnford was to write:

'It has been officially stated that Colonel Durnford was ordered to take command of the camp at Isandlwana. Various facts convinced me that this was untrue, and at last I have obtained a copy of the original order as it appears in Colonel Crealock's note book, which he says "was recovered from the field of Sandlhana and sent me in England in 1879." This copy was received by me from Lieutenant-Colonel Crealock on 18 May 1882.'◊

Edward Durnford then came to a damning conclusion, for he was to write on 24 July 1882:

'But the main spring of my action has been that the closing scene of my dear brother's life, during which he in all things upheld the honour and fame of his country, has been misrepresented, I grieve to say, wilfully and deliberately, and my endeavour has therefore been plainly to set forth the truth, and thus to vindicate the military reputation of a soldier who deserves well of his country.'◊

Well deserved was Crealock's reputation of being a 'Victorian' snob. Still the matter did not rest for, in January 1886, Major Jekyl, writing on behalf of General Nicholson the Inspector General of the Army, asked Crealock for a copy of the order. Crealock was to reply:

'I imagine you refer to the copy of the orders which I made at 2 am which was found on the field six or seven months later and forwarded me and which, stained with mud of the field lies before me, and is I believe almost verbatim with what I officially stated to be my memory.'◊

Clearly Crealock either did not understand the issue involved or did not wish to understand, the latter being more probable. General Nicholson did not pursue the matter.

The satirical magazine *Punch* saw matters in a different light. On 5 April 1879 it was to lampoon both Chelmsford and Crealock:

'After this, he [Chelmsford] shall lose no time in instituting a strict official inquiry how the mischief has come about. Should it be proved by "supplementary testimony" (furnished by officers of his personal staff) that the commander-in-chief is not responsible and that somebody else has been to blame, all the better for the commander-in-chief, and all the worse for somebody else!'

Sitting at Rorke's Drift on the morning of 23 January, it is probable that Chelmsford heard for the first time, much to his relief, Crealock's incorrect version of the controversial order, and it was to provide Chelmsford with a partial lifeline. (Major Clery would be the provider of a second lifeline). Chelmsford, on the morning of the 23rd, sent a telegram to Colonel Pearson, his coastal column commander, informing him of the Isandlwana defeat. Pearson was to respond:

'Telegram of 23rd detailing poor Durnford's defeat, and the losses sustained.'◊

Subsequently, on Chelmsford's arrival in Pietermaritzburg on 27 January, Sir Bartle Frere, with whom Chelmsford stayed, wrote to the Duke of Cambridge. Sir Bartle's letter indicated the reason for the defeat, and could only have been based on discussions with Chelmsford:

'He [Chelmsford] feels the calamity the more because he is naturally averse, pending the result of the inquiry he has ordered, to express any opinion as to who, of the poor fellows who are gone, was to be blamed <u>for the undoubted neglect of orders which led to the disaster</u> [author's emphasis].'◊

Sir Bartle was merely echoing Chelmsford's statement that Durnford had taken command and that defence orders for the camp had been neglected. Both statements were void of truth. Already, days after the battle, Durnford was being blamed, helped by Crealock's devious version of events.

So what happened to the original order received by Colonel Durnford in the early hours of 22 January? It is logical to assume that he would either have placed it in his portmanteau, together with other papers in his wagon, or, more likely, not having the time to file it, have retained it on his person.

There were four significant visits to the battlefield in the months following the disaster. On 14 March Major Wilsone Black, 2/24th, with twenty-seven volunteers, visited the site. They found approximately one hundred wagons in good order, and brought back papers located in the area of the Chelmsford tent. No body identification or burials took place. On 15 May, Black again led a party composed of officers of the 24th Regiment and volunteers, totalling approximately twenty. The *Natal Witness* reported:

'Advancing to the camp without opposition they found things much as they had left them on their former visit. The number of wagons seemed to have seriously diminished; but the bodies of the dead lay quietly though, and presented a ghastly sight. They are rapidly approaching dissolution, being now little more than skeletons, the skin retaining its position over the face, gives an appearance of greater preservation than is actually possessed.'

No burials were conducted and it was on this occasion that Lieutenant Charlie Pope's diary, mentioned in Chapter 6, was found.

The third visit to the camp, made with the express purpose of burying the dead, was undertaken on 21 May, when a force under Major-General Frederick Marshall and Colonel Drury Lowe, 17th Lancers, set out from Rorke's Drift before daylight. The special war correspondent for the *London Standard*, Charles Norris-Newman accompanied the expedition and was vividly to describe the event in the *Times of Natal*:

'The force under the immediate command of General Marshall, consisting of the first regiment of the King's Dragoon Guards, second of the Lancers, Natal Carbineers under Captain Shepstone, part of the mounted police under Major Dartnell, Carbett's Rangers, mounted scouts and two guns under Colonel Harness, accompanied by a detachment of the Army Service Corps with seventy five pairs of led horses. While the four companies of the 2/24th under Colonel Black which at the last moment remained on the rising ground after leaving the Bashee [Batshe] valley so as to protect our rear.'

Norris-Newman depicted the scene they met on reaching the campsite:

'The grass had grown up over the whole site of what had been our camp and was thickly intermixed with mealie stalks and oat hay, green and growing yet. Among these lay the bodies of our poor soldiers scattered about in all postures, and in all stages of decay; while the positions of our tents were indicated by the broken remains of boxes, trunks, tins of preserved meats, remnants of the tents themselves, and masses of disordered papers, books and letters etc.

I had the melancholy satisfaction of seeing my own tent, or rather the remains of it, with all my papers, letters and books lying about torn up, but nothing of value was left. The skeleton of my servants and horses lay just behind my tent, as I was in the habit of having them picqueted in that way. Many interesting relics were found and brought away by others... 40 wagons we brought away included two water carts in good preservation, one gun limber, a rocket battery cart, and three Scotch carts. All that we left behind in number not more than twenty were in a partially or entirely disabled condition. Counting all there, therefore, there are still sixty or seventy wagons missing which have been taken away at different times.'

If this report is correct it would indicate that at the time of the battle there were between 120 and 130 wagons at Isandlwana. On express orders from Major-General Edward Newdigate, the 24th's bodies were to be left untouched as the regiment wished to perform burial duties themselves, which they duly did on 20 June, the fourth visit, under command of the newly promoted Lieutenant-Colonel Wilsone Black. This task, a full five months after the battle, took Black and his men four days.

What of the body of Colonel Anthony Durnford? Captain Theophilus 'Offy' Shepstone accompanied Marshall's party. Durnford's body was found and easily identified, his features being relatively well preserved. He was then wrapped in the remnants of a tent and a pile of stones was placed over the body. Six days later, on 27 May 1879, the *Natal Witness* wrote:

> 'After the papers and maps found on Durnford's person had been removed, a pile of stones was heaped over the body.'

It was Shepstone who supervised the burial and on being questioned about the *Natal Witness* report, responded that this was a mistake, and that no papers were recovered for the simple reason that there were none. The matter was then dropped.

However, on 22 May 1879, the day after Marshall's visit to Isandlwana, the King's Dragoon Guards' veterinary officer, Surgeon S. Longhurst, wrote a letter to friends in England describing the burial of Durnford, at which he had been present. Longhurst was uncooperative when subsequently questioned regarding these events and, in due course, the King's Dragoon Guards were posted to India. Edward Durnford wrote twice to Longhurst, but both letters were ignored. In frustration Durnford wrote to Colonel Master, the commanding officer of the King's Dragoon Guards who, in turn, applied pressure on Longhurst to respond. This he did from Meerut, India, in a letter dated 20 February 1882 addressed to Edward Durnford:

> 'Dear Colonel Durnford,
>   I must apologise for not having answered your letter. I beg to state on the morning of 21 May 1879 I marched with the King's Dragoon Guards from our camp at Rorke's Drift to Isandlwana, and when on the hill between the two koppies we dismounted our horses and commenced to inspect the scene of the disaster which occurred about four months before. After having walked some considerable distance in the tambooki grass (leading my horse) among the dead, the first officer's body I saw was that of your brother, wearing his scarlet vest under his coat... Whilst we were conversing the native servant picked up the remnant of an old tent to lay your brother's body in, and before it was rolled round it, Captain Shepstone searched the body, and I saw him distinctly take from it two finger rings, a pocket knife with your brother's name engraved on the metallic handle, also a packet of letters from his coat pocket, but as I did not touch anything belonging to the Colonel I am unable to say whether the letters in question were of an official nature or otherwise, but judging by the contour of the packet I am of the opinion that there were official papers in it.'[6]

Subsequently, months later, Colonel C.E. Luard, commanding officer of the Royal Engineers stationed in Pietermaritzburg, took up the cudgels on Colonel Anthony Durnford's behalf, demanding that Shepstone be brought to trial in order to establish the truth. Shepstone then produced affidavits from three people who had been present when Colonel Anthony Durnford's body was found, all stating that there was no coat, therefore no papers. In due course, Shepstone agreed to attend a Court of Inquiry on the matter. This in turn might well have implicated others, and the acting High Commissioner in South Africa, Lieutenant-General H. Torrens, was to write to Luard, telling him that the proceedings would be limited in order to prevent distinguished names from being dragged into the affair.

'Offy' Shepstone was the son of Sir Theophilus Shepstone, and in this respect Luard was to note:

> 'Offy is a prominent member of the most powerful and influential family
> in the colony. He himself is one of the most astute lawyers in the colony
> and is what is termed a general favourite.'◊

The inquiry was then limited to whether or not papers had been removed from Durnford's body. Longhurst, still in India, was unable to attend and the case collapsed, with Luard being humbled and ordered to apologise to Shepstone. Yet Longhurst had been unbiased, and had nothing to gain from his statement. He had given precise and very detailed information and had no reason to lie. The only conclusion that one can reach is that, on the balance of probability, Colonel Crealock's orders might well have been removed from Durnford's body, returned to headquarters, perused and quietly suppressed. The secrets of the dead remain just that, and it unlikely that the truth will ever be known.

———⋙⋘———

During all this time Clery was also mulling over the events of 22 January. Cornelius Francis Clery was an Irishman of considerable charm and intellect. Educated at Sandhurst, he later published a book entitled: *C.F. Clery, Minor Tactics – 1875*, without having seen active service or having heard a shot fired in anger. He arrived in South Africa in 1878. His original appointment during the first invasion of Zululand was that of principal staff officer to Colonel Evelyn Wood, commanding No. 4 Column. Lord Chelmsford, despite protestations from Wood, transferred Clery to No. 3 Column to act as Glyn's principal staff officer.

Thus Crealock and Clery, of opposing personalities, were soon to clash in the aftermath of Isandlwana as Crealock, bent on protecting the general's reputation, attempted to shift blame not only to Durnford, but also to Glyn, the column commander. One suspects that Chelmsford harboured doubts about Glyn's ability, for Clery was to write:

> 'Glyn's extreme stickiness was so well known that he (Clery) had been
> sent as principal Staff Officer to act as a "blister".'◊

Yet Clery's part in the post Isandlwana cover-up, hitherto unsuspected, may indeed have been significant.

When Clery left the general's tent in the early hours of 22 January to inform Glyn of the orders received to reinforce Dartnell, Glyn, no doubt surprised, did not question events. Under normal circumstances, bugle calls would have aroused the camp but Clery, not wishing to disturb the remainder of the camp, or possibly to alert any enemy, personally visited all the 2/24th company commanders, and Harness of the artillery, to relay Chelmsford's orders. Clery was to explain:

'I went direct to each of the commanders and gave the General's orders – this took some time and the General was soon dressed and impatient to be starting. The troops too turned out well. The General had given no orders about the camp, except that Colonel Durnford was to move troops up there; but in trying to gather my wits together after giving out the different orders for the march personally myself, as to what further should be cared for before marching off, it occurred to me that some instructions should be left to the officer left in command of the camp – it was too late to refer to Colonel Glyn who of course would only have referred me to the general, so I ventured on the responsibility of issuing them myself.

So I wrote to poor Colonel Pulleine who commanded the 1st Battalion 24th Regiment officially as follows: "You will be in command of the camp in the absence of Colonel Glyn. Draw in your line of defence while the force with the general is out of camp. Draw in your infantry outpost line in conformity. Keep your cavalry videttes still well to the front. Act strictly on the defensive. Keep a wagon loaded with ammunition ready to start at once, should the general's force be in need of it. Colonel Durnford has been ordered up from Rorke's Drift to reinforce the camp." I sent this to Colonel Pulleine by my own servant, I went myself to his tent to ensure that he had got it. I saw him and again verbally repeated what he had already received in writing, laying stress on the point that his mission was simply to hold and keep camp. I must add that at that moment nobody from the General downward had the least suspicion that there was a chance of the camp being attacked.'◊

This verbatim statement, expressed in a private letter dated 17 February 1879, written from Rorke's Drift to his friend Colonel George Harman, 34th Regiment, Deputy Adjutant-General Ireland, has been accepted as historically accurate, yet anomalies arise. No matter how Clery explains his actions, it is not for a junior officer to issue orders on his own initiative to an officer senior in rank. To say that 'it was too late to refer to Colonel Glyn' defies logic. Glyn's tent was adjacent to Clery's and in order to write his note to Pulleine, Clery would probably have used the field desk in his tent. It would have taken him a few minutes to put pen to paper – but just a few seconds to appraise Glyn orally of the situation. The excuse offered by Clery that Glyn would merely have told him to refer the question to the general was both weak and illogical. Regrettably Clery's servant was killed on the battlefield and therefore was unable to corroborate Clery's statement.

The entire circumstances of the purported written orders require careful analysis. In the first instance they were given without authority. In the second instance, that authority could easily have been obtained, notwithstanding Clery's claim that there was insufficient time. In the third instance it seems strange that Clery, who was in close proximity to Glyn throughout the day of the 22nd, failed to inform Glyn that he had issued specific orders to Pulleine. No doubt Clery would have ensured that Pulleine was made aware of the pending departure of Glyn and the general. The logical sequence of events was that Pulleine, being the senior officer left in camp, would be duty bound to defend the camp. There was certainly no urgency in the circumstances that warranted written instructions.

Finally, there is no record of Durnford being handed Pulleine's purported written instructions, which would have been normal military procedure. The most conclusive and critical evidence of this is provided by Cochrane, Durnford's transport officer, who was privy to the conversation held between the two colonels. In Cochrane's official statement dated 8 February 1879 he wrote that Pulleine gave Durnford a state of the troops, which would be correct military protocol. He went on to add, 'and the verbal orders which were to defend the camp.'[◊]

Had written instructions been in Pulleine's possession he would surely have handed them to Durnford. Pulleine would also have referred to his written instructions, not verbal instructions, thus evidencing that in all probability, written instructions were never issued. Finally, the manner in which Chelmsford was informed was both casual and opportunistic. Clery explained the circumstances to General Archibald Alison, Deputy Quartermaster-General for Intelligence, in a private letter dated 23 April, three months after the event.

'But I think you will have to understand from some of my previous letters that the General had not the very smallest apprehension about the camp being attacked, and danger of that kind never dawned – nor did he feel after the first shock of the thing that anyone was to blame for not thinking of such a thing, though he was perfectly alive to the heavy consequences that might arise to himself, for neither he nor Colonel Glyn knew that I had issued the orders and when on the morning after Isandlwana, after our return to Rorke's Drift, he had gathered the facts that the troops were taken out of camp to attack the Zulus, he only remarked: "How unfortunate!" but when I pointed out to him that this was directly contrary to the written orders I had left for the defence of the camp, he scarcely seemed able for an instant to realize that I had left these orders, and then said: "I cannot tell you what a relief it is to me to hear this."'[◊]

This was to be the critical second lifeline that was thrown to Chelmsford, the first being Crealock's alleged order to Durnford. On the evidence available, the balance of probability is that Clery did not issue written instructions to Pulleine. It was obvious that Pulleine's duty, as senior officer left in charge of the camp, was to defend it. In all probability, assuming that neither Chelmsford nor Glyn gave any direct instructions as is evidenced, Clery more likely informed Pulleine orally that he was to be left in charge and was to defend the camp until Glyn's force arrived back that evening. It would be unlikely that specific tactical instructions were given by Clery, but Clery's evidence later would make Durnford culpable, as not only would it seem that he was ordered to take command of the camp, as stated by Crealock, but that he thereafter wilfully disobeyed the written orders inherited from Pulleine.

In due course, the general would infer that it was he who left the instruction for Pulleine, whilst Clery, in *Parliamentary Papers* of 1879, failed to disclose that no instruction had been left by Chelmsford for Pulleine. Durnford's supporters were left with little ammunition with which to mount a meaningful defence, and the cover-up was to gain momentum.

Although Durnford commanded an independent column which fell under the direct control of Chelmsford, he was an Engineer, and therefore did not represent such a prestigious body as a 'Regiment', nor in the broader context, the 'Imperial Infantry'. He did not even follow his mustering as a Royal Engineer. Effectively, he had become a cavalryman commanding native mounted infantry, therefore any tactical errors he might make would affect his personal reputation and not that of 'the Regiment' or 'the Establishment.' Durnford could therefore be blamed with impunity. He was expendable – the honour of the regiment was not! Thus ranks were closed with alacrity, and the living dishonoured the dead.

In the attempts to clear Durnford's reputation, it is worth considering the extensive role played by Frances Colenso, daughter of the controversial Bishop Colenso, formerly Bishop of Natal. Born in 1849 she was the second eldest of five children. She preferred to be known as Nell and, for her, the death of Durnford was 'sorrow beyond earthly help.' She had met him in 1873. He was nineteen years her senior, and one can but surmise that they loved each other deeply.

Durnford had previously ignored conventional Victorian military wisdom that decreed that lieutenants must not marry, captains may marry, majors should marry, and colonels must marry. He had married as a lieutenant and this marriage had collapsed. Whilst he was in South Africa, his wife and daughter were both living in England. Durnford became a friend of the Colensos in 1873 and frequently visited the family home at Bishopstowe near Pietermaritzburg.

Nell Colenso wrote a book titled *My Chief and I* under the pseudonym Atherton Wylde. It was written before Durnford was killed but only published after his death. The book eulogised Durnford and provided a platform upon which Nell mounted a spirited and relentless defence of Durnford's actions. She subsequently published *The History of the Zulu War and its Origins* in conjunction with Edward Durnford, who scripted the military portions. Edward Durnford in turn wrote *Memoir of Colonel A.W. Durnford* and here Nell assisted him.

She was convinced, as was Edward Durnford, that papers had been removed from Anthony Durnford's body, and that such papers had deliberately been destroyed in order to protect the case made against Durnford. She subsequently described 'Offy' Shepstone's enquiry as 'A Court of Iniquity', since evidence was only admitted from witnesses who could actually be present, thus discounting the written evidence she had accumulated.

She never ceased waging her personal crusade. She consulted a prominent Cape Town attorney, Charles Fairbridge who, on examining her evidence, pronounced that it was 'irresistible'. In 1886 she continued her vendetta by visiting Horse Guards to no avail. The matter of Durnford, his purported orders and vindication of his actions was not a Horse Guards priority. Nell Colenso died of tuberculosis in 1887.

Nevertheless, the following year, Sir Andrew Clarke pursued the issue with the Secretary of State for War, Edward Stanhope, and Brackenbury, one of the original members of Wolseley's 'Ashanti ring', who was now serving with military intelligence. In spite of written evidence that Durnford was not ordered to take command of the camp, the War Office made a final decision not to review the case. Clearly neither the Army's political chiefs nor the Horse Guards had the will to reopen a potential can of worms.

With the possibility of a further Zulu attack, Chelmsford spent an uncomfortable night at Rorke's Drift. The next day, 24 January, he set off with his staff to the supply base at Helpmekaar some twelve miles south-west of Rorke's Drift. He had already decided to hold a Court of Inquiry into the circumstances relating to the defeat. Having spent the night at Helpmekaar, Chelmsford departed for Pietermaritzburg on 25 January, via Ladysmith, reaching the capital city of Natal on the morning of 26th, where he immediately conferred with Sir Bartle Frere. What was odd about his journey from Ladysmith was his mode of travel. Lieutenant Milne, his naval ADC, was to write a letter from Ladysmith dated 25 January:

> 'General and Crealock are starting now in a trap hoping to reach Pietermaritzburg tomorrow, we follow slowly on with horses.'[◊]

Riding in a trap over rough Natal tracks would have been as physically demanding as riding a horse, thus fatigue would not be sufficient cause to use a trap, but a trap did enable Chelmsford and his military secretary to travel in privacy for twenty-four hours. No record exists of their conversation, but the battle must have been the major topic. Whilst no evidence of collusion exists, it would be reasonable to assume that Crealock would have drawn Chelmsford's attention both to the controversial order he had issued to Durnford (taking comfort that the original and the copy were almost certainly lost on the battlefield) and to Clery's purported written orders to Pulleine. The twin pillars of Chelmsford's defence were now placed firmly in position.

———≫•◦•≪———

What of the subsequent actions of the NNC? Much maligned, the NNC was despised by the imperial infantry who viewed them at best as unreliable and heaped upon them, at worst, the ultimate indignity of branding them as cowards. Lonsdale's two remaining battalions disbanded themselves from Rorke's Drift on the night of the 23rd and the morning of the 24th. They had been privy to the full fury of the battle resulting in the death of some 500 of their comrades, and to cap it all they had witnessed their commander-in-chief, together with his staff and escort, leaving the field of battle from Rorke's Drift to return to Pietermaritzburg. This, from their viewpoint, was difficult to comprehend. Milne was to report:

> 'During the night the native contingent had bivouacked on the ledge of rock on the hillside close by, but in the morning numbers had bolted.'◊

Glyn, left in command at Rorke's Drift, penned a pathetic note to Chelmsford dated 24 January.

> 'My Dear General,
>   The whole of the Native Contingent walked off this morning. Their rifles were taken from them; all the hospital bearers then went, and now the native pioneers are going. I am now left without any natives.'◊

None of these reports reflected Lonsdale's efforts to retain the NNC as a fighting force. Not being a fluent Zulu speaker, he, through an interpreter, attempted to persuade the men to air their grievances and remain at their posts. Hamilton-Browne (who commanded the two indigenous Zulu companies) conferred with his *induna* Mvubi, of No. 8 Company. Lonsdale spoke to his *induna* Sikhota. The consensus was that it was of great tribal importance for the men to pay homage to those who had perished, and in order to achieve this, they must first return home. It was at this stage that the general was seen departing for Helpmekaar, which considerably exacerbated the situation. Lonsdale lost control, became irritated and promptly dismissed what remained of his force. The loyal Mvubi, however, suggested to Hamilton-Browne that he be allowed to kill those who wished to leave. The request was denied and all arms and blankets were handed over and the men dispersed.

Hamilton-Browne described graphically the final moments of Mvubi's companies:

> 'They formed up, called me their father, which was not true, gave me the royal salute, to which I was not entitled, and moved off to their camp.'◊

As we have also seen, Major Bengough's battalion was, on 21 January

248

deployed at Kwa Mahamba Drift. He had received intelligence that a large Zulu *impi* was in the area. On the morning of the 21st, expecting to be attacked by a force of 'between six and seven thousand men', Bengough decided to withdraw to Rorke's Drift. The *Natal Witness* special correspondent who accompanied the battalion wrote:

> 'We thought that at last we were going to have a brush with the enemy. Orders were given to load, and our gun-men not only stripped but came readily to the command "Gun-men to the front!" We found however, that a strong impi was mustered on a high hill about two miles distance.'◊

It was here that Bengough heard the news of Isandlwana. He immediately marched to Helpmekaar where the men of the battalion wavered, the perception being that, if Lonsdale's NNC had discharged themselves, they too had a right to leave. Bengough made little effort to reason with them and proposed following the lead of Lonsdale. Chelmsford also arrived at Helpmekaar on the 24th and took instant action. Milne was to record:

> 'They were paraded forming three sides of a square, the 4th side formed of 3 companies of infantry, the garrison of Helpmekaar. The General told them that if they were all cowards, he would shoot them on the spot, and therefore gave orders that should any man attempt to leave the regiment, he was to be shot. The regiment then marched to Umsinga [M'singa].'◊

Chelmsford's words had a salutary effect, for this regiment remained intact, the only one to do so, and at M'singa the men built a fort named after their commander, Bengough.

It was a far cry from the heady days of the successful assault on Sihayo's stronghold on 12 January, which Lieutenant Vause of Durnford's Natal Native Horse, although not present at the attack, was to describe in a letter to his lady friend Miss Katie, dated 18 January 1879:

> 'If only they would come out into the open to fight there would not be so much to fear, but I think they are too cowardly and will only fight from behind a rock or a bush.'◊

This reflected the gross underestimation of the Zulu, which had evidently filtered down from Glyn's command to Durnford's column.

As described in a previous chapter it was incumbent on Sir Henry Bulwer, the Governor of Natal, to meet the requests of Bartle Frere and Chelmsford in providing the manpower requirements of the NNC. Bulwer was adamant that for the NNC to be successful, what he described as the 'tribal system' should be adopted. Chelmsford alternatively believed that the NNC should be placed into a military system. More dramatically Chelmsford, as already shown, had little faith in the loyalty of the Natal Zulu.

On 29 January, following the defeat, Bulwer wrote to Bartle Frere expressing the seriousness of the disbanding of Londale's contingent, and suggesting that not only had the departure of the general and his staff on the 24th had a depressing effect on the contingent, but that the previous night, on an alarm being given, the European officers and non-commissioned officers had left their men and taken refuge within the Rorke's Drift entrenchment leaving their men not only on the outside, but leaderless. Bulwer went on to add:

> 'My opinion, as your Excellency is aware, has from the first been that the attempt to do away with the native system and organisation such as they are, and to substitute a regimental system and regimental organisation was one of very doubtful advisableness.'◊

Bulwer, when he originally consented to provide the men who would form the NNC, did so on the basis of only having Zulu-speaking officers and no white non-commissioned officers, as he knew well that few would be qualified in either military or linguistic skills. Chelmsford overruled this and Bulwer was to record, referring to non-commissioned officers:

> 'This had not entered the programme of the system at the time I consented out of deference to the Lt. General's views, to give the 6000 men he asked for, but was introduced afterwards without reference to me.'◊

On 2 February 1879, Bulwer wrote a forty-three page memorandum to Chelmsford in which he reiterated that, in his view, the NNC had been incorrectly organised and led in a loose military type organisation instead of on tribal lines. Bulwer had received a report by Major-General Lloyd, a retired officer living in Escourt, Natal, who had, together with Pieter Paterson the resident magistrate in Weenen County, interviewed three chiefs and their entourage. They were Chiefs Umkungo, Domba and Mgana. The first named had escaped from Isandlwana. The points raised reiterated that:

> 'Their people did not like being under strange officers unacquainted with their language and customs. They wish to be under their own native leaders, headed by Europeans who know and understand them and to be allowed to fight in their own way. They do not like our systems of drill: but they are quite prepared to submit to the enforcement of discipline, or even a hasty word or blow, if from an officer whom they know and have confidence in… all concurred that they would resist any invasion to the utmost, but they begged to be allowed to fight in their own way, aided by a few white leaders who would understand them. They also entreated to be supplied with arms and ammunition.'◊

Bulwer wrote that Paterson, a fluent Zulu speaker and known to all Zulu in the Weenen area:

> 'hopes the system so far as the men of his division were concerned may be abandoned; and that if they are again to go to the front, they may be

reorganised upon a better footing. This, the view of the chiefs and indunas themselves. If used in their own way the native forces will prove most valuable. If again called out under the late military system, they will be worse than useless; they will be discontented and may become dangerous.'

This was the saga of the NNC. Clearly Chelmsford envisaged a paramilitary force, and indeed entrusted the task of raising such a force to Colonel Anthony Durnford who expected overall command. This force, poorly armed, poorly led and ill-trained was not equipped to fight a conventional battle. Its correct role should have been one of reconnaissance, scouting and intelligence gathering. If the men broke and ran at Isandlwana, as has been alleged, the fault lay in the very foundation of their recruitment and the military system imposed upon them, magnified by poor leadership which resulted in lack both of communication and confidence which would normally exist between officers and their men. History should not place undue blame on the military performance of the NNC at Isandlwana.

<hr>

The official instruction to hold a Court of Inquiry was issued by Lord Chelmsford at Helpmekaar on 24 January. In all probability Chelmsford had made the decision the day before at Rorke's Drift. His military secretary, Crealock, would have been instrumental in appointing the various members of the court, and would have executed the order but it is reasonable to assume that Chelmsford concurred with Crealock's choices. The officer chosen as President was Colonel Fairfax Hassard, Royal Engineers. Hassard was nearly sixty years old, and was considered to be non-controversial, innocuous, and 'rather feeble.' Clery was contemptuous of Hassard, and in a letter to Sir Archibald Alison, dated 25 May 1879, wrote highly disparagingly:

'Colonel Hassard, R.E., had only just arrived up and knew nothing of anything that had taken place except that the general's camp had been taken and his column practically knocked into a cocked hat, so, Royal Engineer like, he built a fort at Helpmekaar and shut himself in it, and strongly recommended everybody else do the same! Colonel Hassard remained in command about three weeks after Isandlwana and during that time not a mounted man went I believe a mile beyond the post. To be just to Colonel Hassard, however, it is only fair to say that he always complained of having been left in command at Helpmekaar saying that the work was quite out of his line, etc.'[◊]

This, then, was the officer tasked by Chelmsford and Crealock to conduct the Court of Inquiry. Two other members were appointed. The first was Lieutenant-Colonel Francis Adeane Law, Royal Artillery. Law certainly was not considered by Chelmsford to be gifted with an appetite for hard work for, prior to the invasion of Zululand, Chelmsford wrote to Wood, the commander of No. 4 Column:

> 'I could send you up Lt. Col. Law to do the work well enough if he chose, but he is not over-fond of work and his present idle life style suits him down to the ground.'◊

The third officer was none other than Lieutenant-Colonel Arthur Harness, Royal Artillery, the same Harness who commanded N Battery at Isandlwana, and who, with four of the six guns, accompanied Chelmsford out of the camp on 22 January. Harness, born in 1838 at Woolwich, was commissioned into the Royal Artillery and gained his majority in 1877, simultaneously being given command of N Battery, 5th Brigade. His service in the Ninth Frontier War was recognised by being mentioned-in-dispatches twice and was accompanied by further promotion to lieutenant-colonel.

The choice of Harness was to cause great controversy, for he was a witness to many of Chelmsford's actions on 22 January and, by being appointed to the Court of Inquiry, was precluded from giving evidence. His appointment was made deliberately by Chelmsford and Crealock and justifiably received criticism from both press and parliament.

To summarise events already recorded in a previous chapter, after various movements Harness had been ordered to make his way to the proposed new camp site near Mangeni Falls. En route to the new site and escorted by two companies of the 2/24th commanded by Captains Church and Harvey, Harness, having received Hamilton-Browne's message that the camp was under attack, set off immediately towards Isandlwana at approximately 1.30 p.m. Having progressed some two miles towards the camp he was ordered to return. Thus his attempt on his own initiative to save the camp was thwarted. Had he continued his march he would have been too late to alter the course of the battle as it would have taken him at least two hours to arrive, in a fatigued condition, within close proximity to the camp. He might, however, have caused the Zulu army to withdraw prematurely from the field, thus possibly limiting the carnage and sacking of the camp. The officers and men present with Harness were aware that the camp was being attacked, for they could hear the sound of battle yet, inexplicably, they were ordered to return.

This incident was never revealed and was excluded from subsequent dispatches. It was undoubtedly the reason that Harness was made a member of the Court of Inquiry, for he would thus be unable to give evidence on this or any other matter. The *Natal Witness* on 29 May 1879 published a description of the occurrence, and in doing so noted Chelmsford's culpability. It concluded by saying:

> 'The field of Isandlwana is beginning to give up its secrets; the mists of fiction are being dispersed by the dry light of facts.'

Trooper Fred Symons of the carbineers later recalled:

> 'I cannot describe my feelings at this time. There was a mixture of anger at the delay in returning to camp when the guns had warned us in the morning that the camp was being attacked; foreboding as to the fate of the garrison, for I knew that the Zulu would give no quarter, that's not their way; and grief at the thought that we could do nothing to help. Shortly afterwards the mounted infantry, general and staff overtook us; but the artillery and ambulance still moved in the opposite direction. Heavens I thought, what madness is this?'◊

Three days after the battle, Harness wrote to his brother from Helpmekaar:

> 'While I was going to the new camping ground I received a message from the camp saying that the camp was surrounded by Zulu and, unless it had assistance must be taken. Upon this I went about and meeting Cecil Russell who commands the cavalry with a force of mounted infantry, I proposed with his escort to take the guns back to the camp. We had no sooner agreed upon this than the general came up: he had received a report of the state of the camp but nothing like so strong as the message I received. He thought the camp with six companies of infantry quite strong enough to defend itself against any number of blacks, so we marched back to our proposed new camping ground. We had heard the Zulus firing in the camp before.'◊

Harness indicated that it was Chelmsford himself who gave him the order to return whereas it is generally accepted that Gosset relayed the situation to Chelmsford, indicating to his general that no urgency existed, indeed that the report of a Zulu attack had been exaggerated. The recall of Harness was a tactical error of some magnitude, and the appointment of Harness as a member of the Court of Inquiry effectively silenced him.

The mandate given to the court was to inquire into the 'loss of the camp on the 22nd January'. The court was not asked to give an opinion. As such it merely took statements and declined to question or interrogate witnesses. Harness wrote in *Fraser's Magazine*, April 1880:

> 'The duties of the Court were, I hold to be, to ascertain what orders were given for the defence of the camp, and how these orders were carried out. It was assembled solely for the purpose of assisting the General Commanding in forming an opinion.'

Thus the mandate was restricted to the narrow events of the battle within the camp, instead of the wider implications of Chelmsford's actions. In any event, if the inquiry was intended to assist Chelmsford in forming an opinion, such opinion was not forthcoming. Chelmsford, in forwarding the results to the Secretary of State for War on 8 February 1879, wrote:

'The Court has very properly abstained from giving an opinion, and I myself refrain also from making any observations, or from drawing any conclusions from the evidence recorded.'◊

What then was the purpose of the exercise if Chelmsford, who had convened the Court of Inquiry, was not prepared to make any observations or draw any conclusions? The silent implication was that the result of the inquiry clearly blamed Durnford, and as such required no further expansion or explanation.

There seems little doubt that Harness controlled the running of the inquiry notwithstanding Hassard's seniority. In a letter to his brother dated 27 April 1879, Harness wrote:

'A great deal more evidence was <u>heard</u> [emphasis in original] but was either only corroboratory evidence already recorded or so unreliable that it was worthless. I wrote it all myself and indeed I think managed the thing entirely, and might have recorded or rejected nearly what I liked... The duty of the court was to sift the evidence and record what was of value; if it was simply to take a mass of statements the court might well have been composed of three subalterns or three clerks.'◊

The proceedings duly commenced on 27 January at Helpmekaar, and concluded two days later on 29 January. Eight statements formed the basis of the inquiry and were provided by Glyn, Clery, Gardner, Essex, Cochrane, Smith-Dorrien, Nourse and Curling. Although supplementary statements from Crealock and others followed in due course, vital evidence which might have been provided by Harness himself, Gosset, Black, Buller, Lonsdale, Dartnell, Russell, Raw and Barton was all missing.

To this day there is no evidence of Dartnell having made a statement, or recorded events in either a diary or letters which would have thrown light on certain aspects of the battle leading to Chelmsford's decision to split his command. Yet, astonishingly, he did write a brief summary of the battle of Rorke's Drift in which he was not involved. It is inconceivable that Dartnell did not record events, yet any and all evidence remains untraced.

Similarly Captain Barton, Durnford's second-in-command who accompanied Robert's No. 2 Troop over the Nqutu ridge and survived the battle, mysteriously left no report. Gosset, too, was by the side of the general for most of the time and would have been able to report at least the number of messages received by Chelmsford, and may have been privy to their contents and the general's thoughts.

Numerous questions that should have been asked of all witnesses remained unasked, for the very reason that proper examination and interrogation would have revealed Chelmsford's culpability. Certainly Mansel of the NMP was of that view, for he was to write to Edward Durnford on 23 November 1879:

'Of course I know that a dead set was made against your brother. Lord

Chelmsford and staff, especially Colonel Crealock tried in every way to shift the responsibility of the disaster from their own shoulders onto those of your brother.'◊

Glyn, as column commander, had a story to tell. The various messages from the beleaguered camp addressed to 'Staff Officer' were all meant for him. How many did he receive and how many were handed on to Chelmsford? Did he hear the sounds of battle? What were his views on the day's activity? In due course he responded to the question as to the messages he received, but not at the Court of Inquiry. His statement was the epitome of brevity, yet it made crystal clear that the command and control of the column together with all tactical decisions lay entirely in the hands of Chelmsford:

'From the time the column under my command crossed the border I was in the habit of receiving instructions from the Lieutenant-General Commanding as to the movements of the column, and I accompanied him on most of the patrols and reconnaissance carried out by him. I corroborate Major Clery's statement.'◊

Clery's evidence concentrated on the purported written instructions given to Pulleine the existence of which, as has been shown, seems to be in grave doubt. Archibald Forbes, a war correspondent and arch-critic of Chelmsford, was to describe the Court of Inquiry as 'a solemn mockery'. Whatever bias Forbes may have had, few would disagree with this phrase.

The official telegram conveying the news of the defeat left Cape Town aboard the steamer *Asiatic* in the early hours of 28 January. At that time there was no direct telegraphic communication between South Africa and London and so messages were conveyed by ship to Cape Verde, from whence they were telegraphed to England via Madeira and Lisbon. At Cape Verde, the Reuters correspondent aboard the steamer bribed the telegraph operator to send his message before Sir Bartle Frere's official despatch, hence Reuters in London was slightly ahead of officialdom in breaking the news.

The Secretary of State for War, Colonel Stanley, met immediately with Sir Charles Ellice the Adjutant-General and Sir Daniel Lysons, Quartermaster-General. A short time later a meeting was held with the Commander-in-Chief of the Army, the Duke of Cambridge. Shock and disbelief greeted the news. The nation was aghast.

Queen Victoria had taken exceptional interest in the war and, on hearing the news of the tragedy, penned a note to her private secretary, fifty-four-year-old General Henry Frederick Ponsonby.

'These news are fearful. How could this happen. Pray find out from Captain Edwards who the E officers were.'◊

Fleetwood Isham Edwards, RE, held the official title of Extra Groom-in-Waiting from October 1878 to March 1880, and also acted as assistant military secretary. The letter E referred to English, and the queen's concern was considerable as the families of many serving officers were known to her. In due course the casualty list would shock her. The queen's continued interest and questions provoked Colonel Stanley to add a postscript to a letter written on 12 February 1879 to General Ponsonby, 'Does the Queen want a good map?'◊

No doubt Ponsonby replied in the affirmative, and it was probably left to Lieutenant Walter James, RE, serving in the intelligence branch of the Quartermaster-General's department to provide Ponsonby with maps. These were drawn from sketches received, appended to the Court of Inquiry statements, and from deductions made from such statements. Errors in topography (*see Map 9, pages 258–9*) reflected for example, Conical Hill being omitted. Bearing in mind that in March 1879 James had never visited Isandlwana, it must nevertheless be accepted that a fair degree of accuracy obtained from first hand reports was reflected in the positioning of the skirmishing line and Zulu advance at 1.00 p.m. What is extraordinary is that Major French in his 1939 book, *Lord Chelmsford and the Zulu War*, a biography written in defence of Lord Chelmsford, used the same map but altered the configuration to show, falsely, the NNC positioned between the artillery and infantry (*see Map 10, pages 260–1*). James' original map (*Map 9*) showed Zulu between the infantry and artillery. French also added a footnote to his map which was not on the original. This concocted evidence was to reinforce the theory that the NNC withdrawal was the primary cause of the imperial line collapsing.

Whilst Sir Bartle Frere was in Pietermaritzburg, one thousand miles to the south at Government House, Cape Town, Lady Catherine Frere and her daughter Mary were enjoying the warm summer sunshine. They were privy to Sir Bartle's official correspondence together with private correspondence in which he expressed his personal views. Sir Bartle was popular in royal circles and enjoyed the confidence of both Queen Victoria and the Duke of Cambridge. This gave Lady Frere and her daughter an entrée to correspond directly with the Royal Household. It was a connection which would be used to the full, as both mother and daughter sought to ensure that Sir Bartle's reputation remained intact. No doubt their views were sincere and reflected those of Sir Bartle. However, factual inaccuracies in their correspondence were frequent and could only have resulted from incorrect information or gossip provided from Pietermaritzburg. On 2 February, for example, Mary Frere wrote to General Ponsonby:

> 'It appears to be too sadly true that the body of poor Colonel Durnford was decapitated & the head taken, it is presumed to Cetewayo.◊

In some instances 'colonial' versus 'imperial' was central to the issue. On 18 March Lady Frere responded to adverse British and South African press reports on Chelmsford's conduct of the war. She wrote a memorandum to Ponsonby:

'It should be noted that poor Colonel Durnford having been long in the Colony & being in command of the Natal Native Contingent was regarded by the Colonists of his opinions... as a representative "Colonial" man. He was on very intimate terms with Bishop Colenso & I have been told much shared his views – The tendency of this was naturally on the part of his friends to resent any blame being attached to him for the disaster of 22nd & to endeavour to exculpate him by throwing it on the Generals or other officers of the "Imperial" troops. Her Majesty by telegraphing Her sympathy with the loss sustained by the regular and Colonial [emphasis in original] forces put an effectual check on any such party or personal feeling & by intimating Her refusal to listen to adverse comments on "officers or men" where the principal actors were killed, puts a term to the effort to exonerate the dead at the expense of the living.'◊

This version of events clearly manifested itself into royal thinking and was in all probability the reason that Chelmsford continued to enjoy the patronage of the queen.

The Freres were also well acquainted with the Prince of Wales. Sir Bartle had acted in an advisory capacity to the prince during his visit to India in 1875. It was on 27 March that the most direct attack by royalty was targeted at Durnford. The prince, in a letter to Catherine Frere, wrote:

'I cannot tell you how my thoughts have been constantly with you and good Sir Bartle during the last six weeks, and how I felt for his anxiety and the sorrow he has naturally felt at the disasters which befell Durnford's gallant band. I have however never ceased exonerating Lord Chelmsford from the blame which many here attach to him. Alas! He who fell and led the attack was in my mind the only culprit.'◊

This remark was clearly directed at Durnford. No doubt the opinion of the prince was influenced by the publication of the Court of Inquiry findings, together with the views held by Sir Bartle.

In London the queen and Horse Guards continued their support of Chelmsford in the short term. The press and parliament were more critical with Sir Robert Peel, Member of Parliament for Tamworth, expressing the opinion that Chelmsford was worthy of the fate of Admiral Byng (executed for neglect of duty in 1757). Mr E. Jenkins, Member of Parliament for Dundee, supported by Peel, launched vitriolic attacks on Chelmsford's conduct and prosecution of the war during parliamentary debates in March 1879. However, by then the results of the Court of Inquiry were known and support and sympathy for Chelmsford were extensive. Jenkins' efforts to speak were subjected to continued interruption. On 14 March in the House of Commons, Jenkins stated:

'Now, Sir, I wish to say in the first place in regard to this question, that when any General suffers such a defeat as was suffered by General Lord Chelmsford at Isandula there is a prima facie case of incompetence

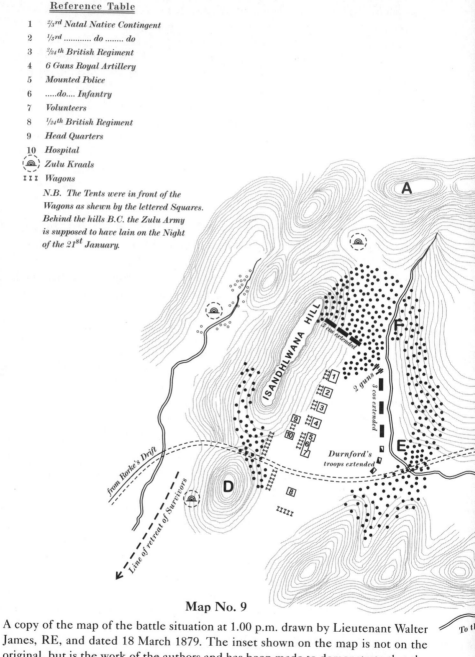

Reference Table

1 ⅔rd *Natal Native Contingent*
2 ⅓rd .... *do* .... *do*
3 ²/₂₄th *British Regiment*
4 *6 Guns Royal Artillery*
5 *Mounted Police*
6 .....*do*.... *Infantry*
7 *Volunteers*
8 ¹/₂₄th *British Regiment*
9 *Head Quarters*
10 *Hospital*
   Zulu Kraals
ꟼꟼꟼ *Wagons*

N.B. *The Tents were in front of the*
Wagons as shewn by the lettered Squares.
Behind the hills B.C. the Zulu Army
is supposed to have lain on the Night
of the 21ˢᵗ January.

ISANDHLWANA HILL

from Rorke's Drift

Line of retreat of Survivors

Durnford's troops extended

A

F

E

D

Map No. 9

A copy of the map of the battle situation at 1.00 p.m. drawn by Lieutenant Walter
James, RE, and dated 18 March 1879. The inset shown on the map is not on the
original, but is the work of the authors and has been made to demonstrate that the
original clearly shows Zulus breaking the infantry line. The original map was
uncaptioned save for the words 'Third Position at 1 PM.' The map is held in the
Royal Archives, Windsor, and the copy is reproduced here by gracious permission
of Her Majesty Queen Elizabeth II.

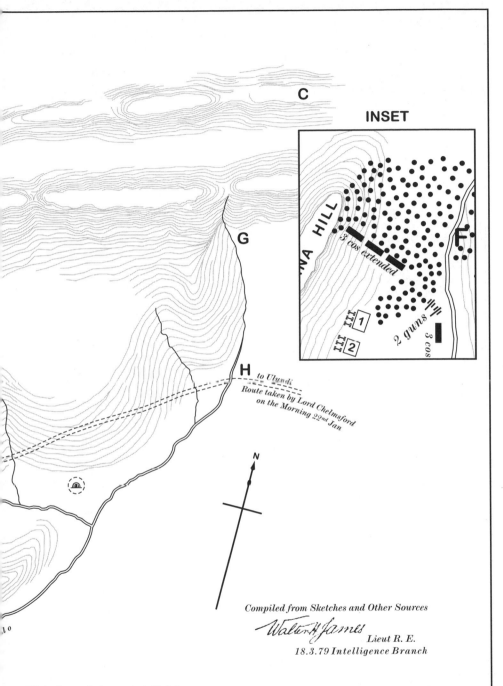

C

INSET

G

3 cos extended

NA HILL

F

III 1

III 2

2 guns

3 cos

H to Ulundi
Route taken by Lord Chelmsford
on the Morning 22ⁿᵈ Jan

N

Compiled from Sketches and Other Sources

Walter H James
            Lieut R. E.
18.3.79 Intelligence Branch

Third position at 1 P M

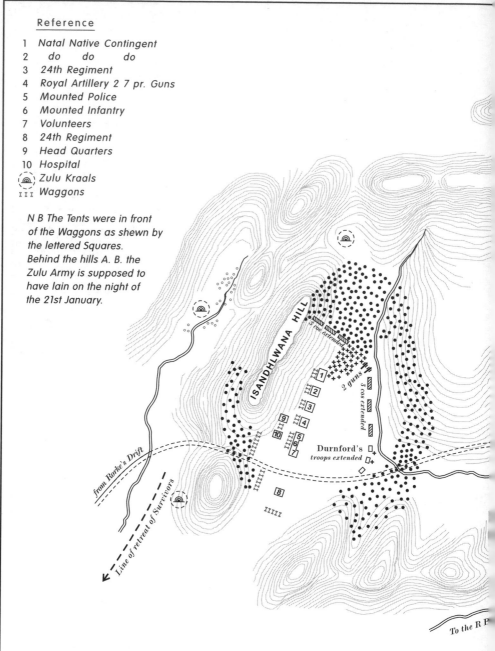

Reference

1. Natal Native Contingent
2.   do   do   do
3. 24th Regiment
4. Royal Artillery 2 7 pr. Guns
5. Mounted Police
6. Mounted Infantry
7. Volunteers
8. 24th Regiment
9. Head Quarters
10. Hospital
- Zulu Kraals
- Waggons

N B The Tents were in front
of the Waggons as shewn by
the lettered Squares.
Behind the hills A. B. the
Zulu Army is supposed to
have lain on the night of
the 21st January.

ISANDHLWANA HILL

from Rorke's Drift

Line of retreat of Survivors

Durnford's
troops extended

To the R P

Map No. 10

A reproduction of Gerald French's map from his biography *Lord Chelmsford and the Zulu War* published in 1939, which was copied from James' original map. French added the captions (right) which were not on the original map and substituted the NNC (native troops) for Zulus as shown in the inset (added by the authors).

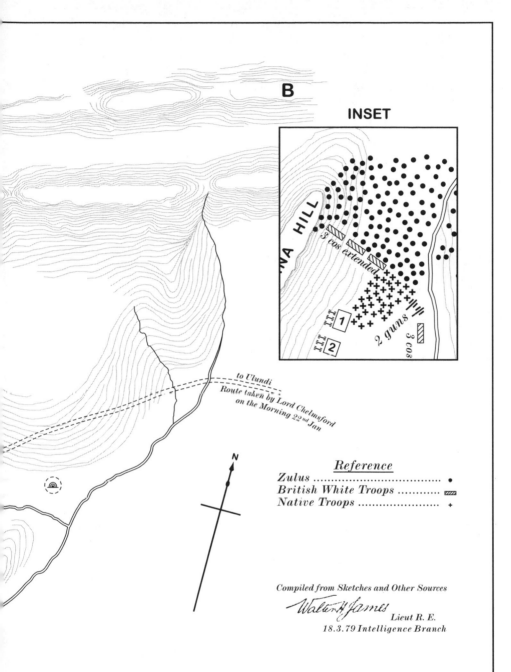

B

INSET

NA HILL

3 cos extended.

III 1

III 2

2 guns

3 cos

to Ulundi

Route taken by Lord Chelmsford
on the Morning 22ⁿᵈ Jan

N

Reference

Zulus .... •
British White Troops .... ▨
Native Troops .... +

Compiled from Sketches and Other Sources

Lieut R. E.
18.3.79 Intelligence Branch

Position at 1 P. M. 22ⁿᵈ January

*Native Contingent retreating from centre and Zulus pouring in and forcing troops back.
Durnford's men and Volunteers on the right*

against him; and it lies with him to demonstrate to the country and military authorities that the defeat in question was not owing to any want either of ability or care on his behalf...

Some explanation is required from the Government to justify their continuing in command a man who seems to have exhibited a great deal of want of discretion, if not of military misconduct and incapacity.'◊

The government benches rose with cries of 'order' and 'withdraw,' and an appeal not to attack 'an absent man without notice'. Jenkins was not to be deterred and switched his attack to the Duke of Cambridge and Queen Victoria herself by saying:

'It is time someone should rise in his place in the House to point out that the Horse Guards is a centre of intrigue, where incompetence is shielded by court influence or by favour with the Royal Person at the head of it.'

His words were drowned by cries from the government benches and luckily for Jenkins failed to reach the ear of the Speaker.

Sir Charles Dilke, Member of Parliament for Chelsea, stood up in the Commons on 28 March and made a lengthy statement. Quoting General Havelock of Indian Mutiny fame, he began, 'Soldiers, your sufferings, your privations, your valour, will never be forgotten by a grateful country.'◊ He went on to add:

'We might say the same for the gallant fellows who fell in that miserable affair at Isandula – 53 officers and nearly 1,400 men – through the gross incompetence of a General upon whose head rests the blood of these men until he has been tried by Court Martial and acquitted,'

This statement was greeted by howls of protest, but Dilke continued:

'Lord Chelmsford blames Colonel Durnford for not having fortified the camp. Why, he was there 48 hours himself with the whole of his ammunition for the campaign, and during all those 48 hours he never made the slightest attempt to do what he says Colonel Durnford should have done in 4 hours. The other day I asked a distinguished General his opinion about Lord Chelmsford's conduct, and his answer was – "It is to me perfectly incomprehensible. He seems to have left the camp with all his ammunition and to have gone fiddling about looking for a parade ground, with a hostile army of 30 thousand men on his flank." After the disaster we find him riding and flying for his life.

And here is one of the most painful circumstances of the whole affair – Lord Chelmsford arrives at the desolated camp at nightfall and leaves before daybreak. So far as the Papers go, he does not seem to have made the slightest search to see whether any of those poor brave, gallant fellows might not be lying in the field dying, if not, perhaps, quite dead.'

This was indeed a point on which to ponder.

The Secretary of State for War, Colonel Stanley, responded by vigorously defending Chelmsford:

'Though the court of inquiry pronounced no opinion, and that he himself [Chelmsford] did not think it necessary to pronounce any opinion, nevertheless the circumstances were pretty clear that it was, to use the mildest term, owing to the neglect of his orders that the unfortunate disaster occurred.'◊

Jenkins, Peel and Dilke all retained the common belief that defeated military commanders should be held accountable, no matter the circumstances. Stanley's viewpoint was guided by the incorrect and hitherto accepted version of Crealock's and Clery's statements.

Whilst controversy raged in Parliament and press there was unease at Horse Guards as the Duke of Cambridge, dissatisfied and disturbed by the controversy, initiated his own inquiry, thus placing both Chelmsford and Crealock under additional pressure.

Chapter 9

Horse Guards' Interrogation and Verdict

'Speak to me on the whole question of questions and answers put and answered.'

The Duke of Cambridge, Commander-in-Chief, British Army

———◆———

The stunning Zulu victory at Isandlwana left Chelmsford's invasion plan in tatters. Wood, commanding No. 4 Column to the north, was left to his own devices, whilst Pearson, commanding No. 1 Column and providing modest leadership, was under siege. Chelmsford's letters to Wood prior to 22 January were peremptory, but softened markedly in tone thereafter. On 27 January he wrote to Wood:

> 'I am afraid the misfortune which has happened to No. 3 column will increase your own difficulties very much and I shall be very glad when I hear that you have found a good place for a permanent camp where you can calmly await a Zulu attack without anxiety. Unless the Swazi's come down and help us I do not see how we are to make any impression in Zululand.'◊

Moreover, on trivial matters he wrote:

> 'I am thinking of doing away with tents and making the men sleep under the wagons and sail-clothes. What do you think of the idea?◊

Finally, in the gloom of depression and inactivity, a despairing postscript:

> 'I wish I saw my way with honour out of this beastly country, and you as my travelling companion. Best love to Buller – you two will have to pull me out of this mire.'

Whilst stalemate and despondency had settled over Natal, Horse Guards was busy pouring reinforcements into the colony. The Zulu War was now taking precedence over the requirements of the concurrent Afghanistan campaign. Five infantry regiments, two cavalry regiments, artillery and ancillary units were embarked for Africa. The Cabinet was serious about reaching a swift conclusion to a war that was not of its making, but were the politicians confident that they had the right general? The reports resulting from the Court of Inquiry and subsequent dispatches indicated that perhaps Durnford was the prime cause of the defeat. Although the Court of Inquiry abstained from giving an opinion, this was not the view of Colonel William Bellairs, Deputy Assistant Adjutant- and Quartermaster-General on Chelmsford's staff. He was of the firm opinion that the blame lay on the shoulders of Durnford alone and as such this view should be published. Bellairs accordingly, in his report to Chelmsford, wrote:

'From the statements made before the court of inquiry it may be clearly gathered that the cause of the reversal sustained at Isandlwana was that Lt. Colonel Durnford, as senior officer, overruled the orders which Lt. Colonel Pulleine had received to defend the camp, and directed that the troops should be moved into the open... had Lt. Colonel Pulleine not been interfered with and had been allowed to carry out the distinct order given him to defend the camp, it cannot be doubted that a different result would have been obtained. I would advocate that the proceedings of the court of inquiry should be published at once as calculated to remove many erroneous impressions now entertained.'◊

The Duke of Cambridge might well have been influenced by similar views expressed, for he was to write:

'HRH has perfect confidence in Lord Chelmsford's ability. He has now acquired from experience a perfect knowledge of the country in which he will have to operate and of the enemy with whom he would have to contend. It was a keen saying of President Lincoln's "that it was a bad thing to change horses in the middle of a ford" but this is exactly what we would do if we changed commanders.'◊

This view would alter in the months ahead. The Cabinet, and particularly the Secretary of State for War, Colonel Stanley, were in favour of relieving Chelmsford of his command and appointing Sir Garnet Wolseley, widely considered to be Britain's ablest general. Wolseley had served in the Crimea, the Indian Mutiny, the Chinese expedition of 1859 and the Ashanti War in West Africa. It was here that he established the so-called 'Ashanti Ring' consisting of handpicked officers who shared his views on Army reforms.

Horse Guards disagreed with Wolseley's views and the duke's dislike of him was the probable reason Chelmsford retained his command. Wolseley's quick, incisive mind and strategic abilities left him with little room to suffer fools; but perhaps most exceptional military commanders enjoy that degree of confidence bordering on arrogance. Prime Minister Disraeli was to admit:

'It is quite true that Wolseley is an egotist and a braggart, so was Nelson. Men of action when eminently successful in early life are generally full of themselves.'◊

However, for the time being the views of Horse Guards prevailed and Wolseley would have to wait until May 1879 before Disraeli, backed by the War Office, finally made the decision that Wolseley would supersede Chelmsford.

Meanwhile, the Court of Inquiry results were anxiously awaited in London, in the hope that they would counter the mounting furore created by a vociferous and critical press. The first dispatch sent by Chelmsford to the Secretary of State for War on 27 January threw little light on what had occurred, causing the duke to write to Sir Bartle Frere:

> 'I must honestly tell you that Chelmsford's account of the whole proceedings of 22 January have left us in much perplexity as to what actually happened.'◊

The duke, anxious to understand the real cause of the defeat, commenced his own inquiry by ruthlessly questioning Chelmsford. The latter, aided by Crealock, attempted to deflect the blame not only on to Durnford but also on to the shoulders of Glyn. The issue weighed heavily on Chelmsford's mind, to the extent that in due course he wrote to the duke, in a clear attempt to clarify his position:

> 'It would be hardly fair to saddle me with the responsibility of any neglect of details connected with the command of No. 3 Column for the performance of which the officer commanding the column was held accountable to me... as from what I can gather an attempt is being made to saddle me with responsibilities which did not properly belong to me. I have no desire to cast any blame upon Col. Glyn... all I ask for is that, should it be considered that important column details were neglected either before or after 22 Jany, the fact that I was not in actual command of No. 3 column may not be lost sight of.'◊

Chelmsford was correct in that day-to-day mundane matters and camp routine were Glyn's responsibility, but the all-important tactical and strategic decisions were made by Chelmsford alone and to all intents and purposes the *de facto* command of the column was vested in Chelmsford. The duke's opening salvo, in a letter marked private and dated 6 March, said:

> 'The Secretary of State & myself have agreed to call for further information on what has occurred to us as open to criticism in Parliament & by the general public.'◊

On the same day as the duke penned his letter, the Adjutant-General, Major-General Sir Charles Ellice, wrote to Chelmsford, under confidential cover, requesting detailed information about Isandlwana and answers to specific questions:

> 'HRH is well aware that your Lordship's dispatch was written when many and grave affairs requiring your instant attention were pressing upon you,

and that it was impossible that a complete narrative could at the time be framed.'◊

The Court of Inquiry findings were awaited in London but Ellice's letter pre-empted the possibility that the answers required might not be forthcoming in those, for Ellice continued:

'But in case it [the court] does not cover the whole of the ground in regard to which information is sought by the government and public opinion in this country, H.R.H thinks it right to draw your attention to the following points on which he would like full details to enable the Secretary of State to answer any questions which may be put or brought forward in Parliament.

1. How did it happen that the post at Rorke's Drift, covering as it did the passage into Zululand and the ford on the Buffalo river was not put into a state of defence previous to your Lordship's advance to Isandlwana Hill?

2. How was it that the camp pitched under Isandlwana Hill on the 22nd January was not put into some state of defence by "laagering" or otherwise, either on that or the succeeding day?

3. When your Lordship left that camp at daybreak on the 22nd with the bulk of your forces to reinforce your advance guard ten or eleven miles off on the Ulundi road when the circumstances were serious enough to induce you to order up Colonel Durnford with 450 men of the Native Contingent from Rorke's Drift to reinforce the camp, and when orders were left with the senior officer in camp to defend it, were orders also given to that officer to place the camp itself in a state of defence?

4. As your Lordship had a considerable number of mounted men in Colonel Glyn's column it should be stated what steps were taken on the 21st to reconnoitre and thoroughly search the country on your flanks – it seems difficult to understand how a large Zulu army could have massed itself to the North and within attacking distance of your camp without some evidence of its proximity having been afforded. Were no native reports regarding the movements of the Zulus received by you at this time?

5. When you heard at 9am on the 22nd from Lt.-Colonel Pulleine that firing was going on to the left front of the camp, did you make any endeavour to communicate with the camp by sending a detachment of Cavalry into it?

6. Did you at any period after this and before Commandant Lonsdale reported to you that the camp was in the hands of the enemy, receive any reports native or otherwise which led you to suppose that an action was going on near the camp, and, if so, what steps did you take?

7. When you directed Colonel Glyn to move out on the morning of the 22nd, did that officer make any arrangements for reserve ammunition and a day's supply of rations accompanying his force?

HRH has no doubt that upon all these points, your Lordship will be able to give most satisfactory replies, but the means of doing so completely are not to be found in your dispatch now under consideration nor in that of 3rd February which has just been received.'

The receipt of Ellice's letter brought Crealock and Clery into conflict as Crealock attempted to make Glyn culpable by indicating that Glyn had effectively commanded the column, whilst Clery fought to ensure that his chief was not used as a scapegoat. On 11 March Clery wrote a most revealing confidential letter to Major-General Alison, exposing his inner feelings, his opinion of Crealock, and the conflict that existed within Chelmsford's and Glyn's command:

'The General and his staff joined our camp just before we advanced and of course the general took command of the whole column for we only had all told, about 1500 whites and 2000 savages. It was not much of a command, was it? Colonel Glyn and his staff however were allowed to work the details – posting the guards, etc… In this state of affairs Colonel Glyn, who nominally commanded the column, was scarcely ever seen or heard of – the more so as he got anything but encouragement to interest himself much in what was going on – so that as far as commanding the column in anything outside the details of the camp, Colonel Glyn had not so much even to do as a Brigadier at Aldershot has to do with working the division at a field day on the Chatham Ridges…

After a lapse of several weeks after the Isandlwana affair it dawned upon some honest mind of the headquarter staff [clearly implying Crealock], that as Colonel Glyn was in orders to "command the 3rd Column", perhaps some part of the odium of that business could be transferred from the general's shoulders to his.

The idea was a sycophantic one certainly, but under all the circumstances so well known to those who witnessed them, it was not wanting in daring, to say nothing of audacity. The attempt too was entered on with a certain amount of skill, for it was insidiously cloaked under the form of apparently ordinary inquiries as to how certain regulations had been carried out. Colonel Glyn is a guileless, unsuspicious man, very upright and scrupulously truthful, yet of a slow lethargic temperament; so when this document arrived he regarded it in the way an easy-going man would solve a problem that he did not quite see his way to solving. So he chucked the paper over to me with the remark, "Odd the general asking me to tell him about what he knows more about than I do."'

All correspondence was channelled through Colonel Bellairs, and Crealock, having seen Ellice's letter to Chelmsford, responded to Bellairs on the first question:

'The L. General was under the impression until a few days ago that the orders given by him to Col. Glyn commanding 3rd Column, to have a work made to defend the ponts at Rorke's Drift had been partially carried out by the 22nd January. As such would appear not to be the case he desires you will call upon Col. Glyn to state what orders he gave on the subject, and the reason the work has not been commenced.'◊

On receipt of Crealock's note, Bellairs immediately drafted a note to Glyn, which was brief and curt:

'Col. Glyn and Major Spalding [left in command of Rorke's Drift] will have the goodness to furnish the statements and reports required.'◊

Crealock had clearly dealt with the defence of the *ponts* and chose to ignore the broader question of Rorke's Drift itself, where no instructions had been issued. Glyn responded on 7 May:

'It is now so long ago since the occurrences under investigation that although I have a very distinct recollection of the <u>facts</u>, I regret I cannot be precise as to <u>dates</u> [both emphases in original].'◊

Glyn went on to explain that, over a period of time, he had sent three messages to Captain Rainforth commanding a company of the 24th Regiment stationed at Helpmekaar, to move to Rorke's Drift and commence work on building a defence for the *ponts* on the river. For some inexplicable reason either the order failed to reach Rainforth or was not complied with. Glyn then added:

'Regarding the defence of the ponts I submitted a proposal to H.E. the L. General Commanding to construct a Field work or entrenchment for their work, and of this he approved. This was put in order for the guidance of the officers concerned, and Lt. Bromhead's company was left at, and Capt. Rainforth's company ordered to Rorke's Drift for the purpose of executing the work and organising it, Major Spalding being placed in command of the Post and under my orders as commanding 3rd Column.'

Major Henry Spalding, 104th Regiment, also responded to Bellairs:

'Captain Rainforth's company 1/24th Regt. was ordered from Helpmekaar to Rorke's Drift by the O.C no.3 Column for the purpose of taking up and entrenching a position commanding and defending the ponts on the Buffalo River – I know of no other order touching the erection of a work for such a purpose.'◊

Spalding went on to express concern at the non-arrival of Rainforth's company which should have reached the drift on 22 January. Spalding then told how, at about 2.00 p.m. on the afternoon of 22 January, he decided to ride to Helpmekaar to see what was delaying Rainforth:

'I rode over to Helpmekaar with a written order in my pocket directing Captain Rainforth positively to reach the ponts by sundown on that day.'◊

Spalding was subsequently the subject of much gossip and rumour for having left his post at Rorke's Drift at a time when it must have been apparent that the camp at Isandlwana was threatened, for not only had Chard seen the Zulu in force moving westwards behind Isandlwana when he was present at the camp at approximately 9.30 a.m. on the 22nd, but his sighting resulted in his riding back immediately to Rorke's Drift and reporting to Spalding. Chard's fear was that the Zulu were outflanking Isandlwana to make a direct attack on the *ponts* at Rorke's Drift.

Thus Spalding had been aware of a possible threat and his decision to leave his post, although later defended by Chelmsford, was questionable. With all the signs of pending action he could just as easily have remained at his post and sent a mounted officer with an urgent dispatch. Had Rorke's Drift fallen, one suspects that Spalding might well have faced censure. Chelmsford, having read the response from Glyn and Spalding, wrote again to Ellice on 19 May:

> 'I was under the impression until very lately that the orders I had personally given to Col. Glyn to have a work made at Rorke's Drift previous to our leaving it, had been partially carried out. It will be seen now that this is not the case... It does not appear, however, why the company already at Rorke's Drift [Bromhead's] did not commence the work.'◊

It is clear from the correspondence that Glyn initiated the proposal to erect the field works overlooking the ponts. If Glyn was in effective command of the column, the approval of Chelmsford would not have been necessary. From a strategic viewpoint, the base camp and supply point at Rorke's Drift should have been placed in a state of defence. Doubtless this was not considered necessary by Chelmsford as it would be he who would be doing the invading, not the Zulu. The duke's query remained unanswered with the peripheral issue of ponts deflecting the real question of the post at Rorke's Drift itself being placed in a state of defence. Chelmsford responded to London on 11 April in vague and evasive fashion, skillfully avoiding the question:

> 'The labour of getting troops and supplies across the Buffalo river, and of making the roads passable for wheeled transport, absorbed nearly the entire strength of No. 3 Column from its arrival on the banks of the river, to its advance to Sandhlwana. I know, however, that Colonel Glyn had given orders to Lieutenant Chard, Royal Engineers, to construct an entrenched post on the Natal side, and that it had been commenced by the detachments left behind before the column moved off. So long as the force was in occupation of the position at Sandhlwana it covered directly the ford on the Buffalo river.'◊

Horse Guards and the War Office may well have expressed astonishment at Chelmsford's final sentence. The ford was approachable by outflanking

Isandlwana from the north-west or south-east, a manoeuvre, which, if executed at night, would have passed unnoticed by those at the camp, effectively severing the line of communication from Isandlwana to Rorke's Drift. Clearly on the duke's first question, Chelmsford was culpable.

—➤◦◄—

The second question asked was why the camp was not *laagered* or 'otherwise' prepared for defence.

A general order for local regulations and instructions for troops in the field, known as *Field Force Regulations* was promulgated in Pietermaritzburg in November in 1878, signed by Bellairs on behalf of Chelmsford. It was issued down to company level. As mentioned in an earlier chapter, Paragraph 19 read, 'The camp should be partially entrenched on all sides.'◊

Clery, on behalf of Glyn, responded to Chelmsford's request calling for a full report of the movements of No. 3 Column from the time of leaving Rorke's Drift to its return, with special reference to *Field Force Regulations*. Clery stated:

> 'The Isandlwana hill had been the point selected by the Lieutenant-General commanding as the halting place for that night.'◊

Crealock made an immediate note against this sentence, which read:

> '"The neighbourhood of the" would have been more correct, had the General fixed the site. I know from his own lips on the 22nd that it would not have been on the same spot.'

This comment was both mischievous and misleading, as Chelmsford had previously not only selected the campsite but also described it as follows:

> 'There was no ground that commanded it to the left within a distance of 1,200 yards and there was no ground that commanded it on the right at a less distance than 600 yards. Taking therefore into consideration the nature of weapons with which the Zulus were armed, it might practically be said that the camp was not commanded from any position near it.'◊

Later, in a memorandum, Chelmsford expressed a firmer opinion:

> 'I consider that there never was a position where a small force could have made a better defensive stand.'◊

Clery also seemed to think the site was suitable:

> 'I would call this position a good defensible one for the amount of the force to be camped there...
>
> With reference to paragraph 19, Field Force Regulations, – The camp was not entrenched. On the night of the 20th it would have been hard on the men, unless the thing was essential, to ask them to do this, as the part of the force that reached the camp had had a very fatiguing day's work. I

doubt even from the lateness of the hour it would have been possible, but I might state that the impression I was under myself with regard to this matter was that the camp at Isandlwana was meant to be entirely a temporary one – simply a halting place – and that our first entrenched camp would be further on, where the first advance depot was to be established. An entrenchment to be of use would entail considerable labour, and I did not understand this was to be undertaken every time the force halted. Being under the impression therefore that the force might be ordered to move out at any moment, I was not surprised that no order had been issued for entrenching the camp, and in the correctness of this opinion I appear to have borne out by the order for movement of part of the camp the following morning.'◊

Glyn had earlier suggested that a *laager* be formed but this was brushed aside by Chelmsford who responded, 'It would take a week to make.' Chelmsford's decision not to entrench must be regarded with sympathy. The camp was temporary, the ground rocky, the troops tired and to entrench would have extended his stay at Isandlwana, which in turn would disrupt his programme to advance to his next halting ground, the Mangeni Falls area. However, had the camp been put into a state of defence, the defeat might have been avoided and Horse Guards was entitled to an answer. Chelmsford duly responded:

'The wagons which accompanied the troops at Sandhlawana were under orders to return to Rorke's Drift on the 22nd January, in order to bring up more supplies, and were therefore not available for use as a laager owing to the bad state of the roads; a good number of them did not reach camp till the 21st January.'◊

However, Chelmsford omitted to say that he had specifically ordered all wagons earmarked for Rorke's Drift to remain in camp, and no mention was made of the majority of wagons not earmarked for return and which could have been used to form a *laager*. Paragraph 19 instructing the partial entrenchment of the camp was completely ignored. The inescapable conclusion was that on the duke's second question, Chelmsford was also culpable.

The third question related to whether Pulleine had been given additional orders to entrench the camp. Chelmsford misunderstood the question and assumed it was directed as to whether Durnford had been given additional instructions and not Pulleine. In a nebulous response he wrote:

'Distinct orders were left by Colonel Glyn with Lieutenant-Colonel Pulleine regarding the defence of the camp, and, therefore, when I ordered Lieutenant-Colonel Durnford to come to it from Rorke's Drift I refrained from sending fresh instructions to that officer which might only have caused confusion.'◊

He then went on to add:

> 'With reference to the wording of the paragraph in which No. 3 question
> is put, I would venture to remark that the force under Major Dartnell was
> not an advance guard. My orders to that officer were distinct, that he was
> to return to camp after completing his reconnaissance, and I was much
> vexed at my orders not being attended to. I went out to extricate Major
> Dartnell's force from what I considered a false position, as I felt that any
> repulse of the Native Contingent would seriously affect the moral [*sic*] of
> that force, without whose assistance the column could hardly advance.'

Chelmsford implicitly blamed Dartnell for disobedience of orders, yet as
described previously, Dartnell specifically requested permission to spend
the night of the 21st in the Hlazakazi hills area overlooking the Mangeni
Falls, which permission Chelmsford granted. Dartnell also asked permission
to attack the Zulu the following morning, such permission also being
granted. Chelmsford had no justification whatever in stating that he was
'much vexed' with Dartnell.

The sub-division of the column lies central to any analysis of the cause
of the defeat. Clearly the reasons advanced by Chelmsford were weak. He
had ample time to recall Dartnell both during the afternoon of the 21st and
later that evening. Escorted by Russell's mounted infantry, both Dartnell
and the NNC could have made it safely back to camp. Apart from the
reasons advanced in an earlier chapter, namely unshakeable over-
confidence and unwarranted disdain for the Zulu army, Chelmsford's very
character and past activities may help us understand why he made that vital
error of judgement in splitting the force.

It would seem that Chelmsford enjoyed a reputation for vacillation and
changed his mind frequently at a whim. Edward Durnford gave three
examples of this. Although cognisance must be taken of the fact that
Durnford was vigorously defending his slain brother's reputation, the claim
would appear to be of substance. Edward Durnford wrote, referring to the
NNC:

> 'The contingent was to consist of three regiments, to be commanded by
> three officers of suitable rank, and the whole placed under the control of
> Colonel Durnford. This arrangement however, did not quite meet the
> views of some members of his staff [presumably Bellairs and Crealock];
> and, when it appeared in orders, it did so with the difference that Colonel
> Durnford was placed in command of the one regiment only, the other two
> being placed under two other officers independently of him.'[◊]

When Anthony Durnford queried this directly with Chelmsford:

> 'The latter informed him that he still adhered to his original arrangement,
> and that the written order was a mistake on the part of the Military
> Secretary [Crealock]. At a later hour, however, the General sent for
> Colonel Durnford again, and now informed him that the written order

was to be carried out, and the spoken one was the mistake. This, however, is only one of the many instances of extreme vacillation shown in the orders issued by the general, whose own staff, although personally attached to him, complained freely that he "never knew his own mind for an hour together."'

A friend of Colonel Anthony Durnford, commenting at the time on the changes in the plan for the Native Contingent, spoke of having been in conversation with two or three of the staff, when one was complaining of an alteration just made in orders which affected himself, and another replied:

'Oh never mind. The General will have had time to change his mind half-a-dozen times before tomorrow afternoon.'◊

Archibald Forbes, war correspondent and both hostile to and critical of Chelmsford, wrote in the paper *Nineteenth Century*:

'It may be, however, that I am in error in using this latter word [vacillation]. I once ventured on it in conversation with a leading member of Lord Chelmsford's staff, under the invitation to speak, given by the question how I thought affairs were proceeding. He triumphantly corrected me, and explained that the rapid and perplexing changes of intention on his lordship's part, which rendered nothing certain within his command for a quarter of an hour at a time, sprang, not from vacillation and inability to make up his mind, but from very exceptional promptitude in doing so.'

Finally an extract from Crealock's private journal confirms Chelmsford's indecisiveness:

'Col. Glyn with the 2/24th was to move out with 4 guns to attack Zulus. Thus Lord Chelmsford on news received during the night had changed his mind [author's emphasis].'◊

This is exactly what occurred in the early hours of the 22nd: a hasty reversal of previous decisions, instead of a measured tactical plan to bring Dartnell back, keep the force together, and reconnoitre, as planned, the Nqutu Plateau to the north and north-east. The upshot was an attempt to place the blame on the blameless Dartnell.

The fourth question pointedly asked Chelmsford why the area to the north and north-east of the camp had not been reconnoitred prior to 22 January. Here one must examine Chelmsford's perception that any major threat to the camp would be from a southerly or south-easterly direction, from behind the Malakatha hills. This conclusion was influenced by intelligence reports received by Chelmsford from Fynn. The whole layout of the camp was based on this premise, with the 1/24th occupying an area to the south of the track that cut through the *nek*, and beneath Black's Koppie. The NNC would normally have occupied that position, since it was on the downstream side of the water supply. In addition, the 24th's company picquets were located to the east and south-east of the camp, clearly on the basis that the threat, if any, would emanate from that direction. The NNC company picquets on the other hand, were located to the north on Magaga Knoll, and east near Conical Hill, with a small contingent located to the west and behind Isandlwana, as described in a previous chapter.

Chelmsford's reconnaissance was targeted primarily to the east, south-east and south, substantially ignoring the north and north-east, where the Zulu army eventually camped on the 21st. Had Chelmsford carried out his intended reconnaissance on the morning of the 22nd, he himself would in all probability have located the Zulu army. The ensuing battle would have been fought with even greater ferocity, though with a British victory by no means certain.

With adequate mounted men at his disposal Chelmsford could and should have paid close attention to an extensive reconnaissance, prior to the 22nd, of the vast expanse of hills, valleys and plateau land to the north and north-east in which the Zulu so skilfully remained undetected until the morning of the battle. Chelmsford's response to the duke's question was again evasive:

> 'Major Dartnell took with him on the 21st all the colonial mounted men, and the mounted infantry who had been doing hard work previously were allowed a rest. A small party of them, under Lieutenant Edward Browne, 1st battalion 24th Regiment, however, did make a long patrol in the direction from which the enemy eventually advanced but failed to discover more than a few Zulus who were evidently Scouts.'◊

Dartnell took the colonial mounted men on a reconnaissance to the south-east because he was ordered to do so. If Chelmsford had wished a reconnaissance to the north on the 21st Dartnell would have been instructed accordingly. It was Chelmsford who gave his attention to the south-east with priority being given to the submission of the two Matshana chiefs. Browne may well have considered himself unfortunate in not locating the *impi*, but his patrol was targeted east across the open plain and thence to the Isipesi Hill area and not north over the Nyoni ridge and towards the Nqutu hills and thence to Isipesi.

The section of the question regarding native reports received on the 21st was again skilfully evaded by Chelmsford, who maintained that:

> 'The only native report was received at 4.30 p.m. on the 21st January from Gamdana, brother to Usirayo [Sihayo], who had surrendered to us, to the effect that he had heard the Umcityu [mCijo] Regiment was assembled not far from the Isipesi hill; this confirmed the report which had just come in from Major Dartnell that a large force was in front of him.'◊

This response implied that it was the mCijo regiment that was confronting Dartnell, whereas in reality from Dartnell's bivouacked position on Hlazakazi Hill to Isipesi Mountain, as the crow flies, was nearly seven miles. Clearly Gamdana meant the immediate area of Isipesi.

Chelmsford chose to ignore, in his response, additional reports that had been received on the 21st, over and above Gamdana's. George Mansel, for example, had reported on the 21st that he had seen a Zulu near the camp running away:

> 'I took a couple of mounted men and gave chase. We soon came up to him and found he was a very old Zulu – as I could not talk Zulu very well, I brought him back to Phillips who talks it well. The old Zulu said to Phillips "why are you looking for the Zulu this way, the Big Impi is coming from that direction," pointing to the Inqutu [Nqutu] range. I sent Phillips in to camp at once to Cleary [Clery] and he reported what the Zulu had said, but Phillips said Clery made no remark.'◊

Clery's duty was to inform Glyn, who would then have instructed that the information be passed to the general. It is possible that this valuable snippet of intelligence remained with Clery, who chose to ignore it. Had all intelligence reports been properly collated and in due course disseminated they would have led Chelmsford to a different conclusion as to the whereabouts of the Zulu, and here Hamilton-Browne provided additional reports previously recorded.

Captain Murray was sent back to inform the camp of these reports, both identifying the possible whereabouts of the main Zulu army. No acknowledgement of receipt of this information has been recorded but it is inconceivable that Murray failed to deliver the message, as he not only reached the camp, but remained there and was killed in the ensuing action. Clearly information obtained from colonial sources was considered suspect. It is also possible that Chelmsford was not informed, or alternatively chose to ignore the information. Either way, there was more than just the one Zulu report that was admitted by Chelmsford.

The duke's fifth question asked whether Chelmsford had communicated with the camp, via a cavalry detachment after receipt of Pulleine's note at 9.30 a.m. Yet again, the answer was evasive, and in one respect, incorrect. Chelmsford replied:

> 'I have already reported, my aide-de-camp [Milne] was on a high hill from which the camp at Sandhlwana could be clearly seen with a telescope for 1½ hours after the only message received from Lieutenant-Colonel Pulleine during the day arrived; the mounted men were all away at the time searching the country around… I had, however, sent back to camp at 9.30 a.m. one of the Natal Native Contingent battalions, and as all the officers belonging to it were mounted, I felt that one or more of these would be available to bring me any intelligence of importance.'◊

It was incorrect of Chelmsford to state that all the mounted men were occupied in a search operation. Dartnell certainly was, but Russell's mounted infantry, some 120 strong, were resting on the *nek* between Silutshana and Magogo at 9.30 a.m. on the 22nd. Chelmsford even contradicted himself when he wrote to the Secretary of State for War:

> 'Whilst the operations were going on Colonel Glyn received, about 9 a.m. a short note from Lieutenant-Colonel Pulleine saying that firing was heard to the left front of the camp, but giving no further particulars. I sent Lieutenant Milne, R.N., my ADC at once to the top of a high hill from which the camp could be seen, and he remained there for an hour with a very powerful telescope, but could detect nothing unusual in that direction. Having no cause, therefore, to feel any anxiety about the safety of the camp, I ordered Lieutenant-Colonel Russell to make a sweep to the main track.'[◊]

It was therefore only after receipt of Pulleine's note that Chelmsford sent Russell on reconnaissance. Milne in his report confirms this by stating:

> 'A slip of paper was received by the General from Colonel Pulleine, saying that the enemy was collecting in large numbers on the high ground to the left of the camp... Colonel Russell with the mounted men was sent to the plain on our left to reconnoitre.'[◊]

Had Chelmsford wished, he could have dispatched cavalry from Russell's command in response to Pulleine's note but chose not to do so, and inaccurately reported that cavalry were not available to him. On the fifth question Chelmsford was yet again culpable.

The sixth question was whether Chelmsford had received any indication that an action was taking place near the camp after the receipt of Pulleine's note. Irrespective of the numerous messages sent, including four by Hamilton-Browne, the sound of artillery fire, and the Harness debacle, all described in previous chapters, Chelmsford steadfastly reiterated his stance which, in the months to come, never altered:

> 'I received no report whatever previous to Commandant Lonsdale's report that the camp was in the hands of the enemy, or that led me to suppose that an action was going on near the camp, or that it was in any danger.'[◊]

The gods must have frowned, for nowhere was there *mea culpa*, a plain admission of gross error of judgement; rather a stubborn denial with a propensity for self-justification.

The seventh and last question regarding rations and ammunition was probably a direct result of Sir Bartle Frere's letter to Queen Victoria, in which Sir Bartle wrote:

'When morning broke on their miserable bivouac Lord Chelmsford found his men had nothing but the ammunition in their pouches, much reduced by the previous days firing, no food & and had not they found the Rorke's Drift post safe, it might have gone hard with them.'◊

This was coupled with Chelmsford's letter to the duke dated 1 February in which Chelmsford, pre-empted the query by writing:

'The question will no doubt be asked as to why I made no effort to bury the bodies and why having obtained possession of the camp again I did not retain it. The answer is clear. I had no supplies and no spare ammunition nearer than ten miles, at a post which was very open to attack, and I could not afford to delay as the troops wanted food and rest.'◊

Paragraph 37 of *Field Force Regulations* made the issue plain.

'Seventy rounds are carried by each soldier, but these are quickly expended, if he is carried away by excitement, and does not fire with coolness and precision. There is an obvious danger should men run short of ammunition when any distance from the reserves. Whenever, therefore, there appears any likely-hood of troops becoming hotly engaged, thirty rounds extra had better be carried by the soldier [author's emphasis].'

The total issue of ammunition per soldier was 270 rounds per man, with 200 rounds per man being held in the company ammunition wagons. Glyn, correctly, was asked to respond. It will be remembered that the 2/24th companies which left camp on the 22nd only carried seventy rounds per man instead of the 100 required under Paragraph 37 of *Field Force Regulations* and that Clery had had Chelmsford's personal cart loaded and ready to move out if called upon. Should an emergency have arisen it would have been doubtful if the cart could have reached Glyn in under three hours at best. However, Clery was merely obeying Chelmsford's instruction that the ammunition cart was not to accompany Glyn.

On 16 April Glyn responded to Bellairs:

'With regard to reserve ammunition I acted in compliance with Lord Chelmsford's orders that no reserve ammunition should be taken out with the force, but that a wagon be kept loaded in camp with ammunition and ready to follow the force that was going out, at a moments notice; all this was done.'◊

A ping-pong of correspondence now started with Chelmsford asking Glyn:

'I should be obliged by your asking Major Clery to state the circumstances which I issued the order regarding reserve ammunition to which you allude…

I am anxious to have placed on record the reason why such a question was asked instead of, as is customary, the regimental reserve ammunition being taken as a matter of course, and why I decided the question in the negative.'◊

Clery responded that the terrain from the camp to the Mangeni Falls area was difficult to traverse and intersected by *dongas* and river beds. In those circumstances:

'The wagons would not be able to follow beyond a certain point and a strong detachment would then have to be left behind to protect them.'

Clery then concluded by saying:

'I might add that the L. General although authorising the force to proceed without reserve ammunition ordered that a wagon should be kept loaded with ammunition in camp ready to start at short notice.'

The ammunition question created a red herring. Was the reserve ammunition defined as the extra thirty rounds per man that should have been carried in the event of a pending engagement? In this event the fault lay with Colonel Degacher, commanding the 2/24th. If it referred to the 200 rounds of reserve ammunition per man laid down in Table II of the *Regulations*, this would amount to some 100,000 rounds to accompany the 2/24th. Certainly Chelmsford's cart was incapable of carrying anything like that quantity.

In any event the skirmishes which took place in the Mangeni Falls area were carried out almost exclusively by Dartnell's force. The six companies of the 2/24th scarcely fired a round and certainly retained the bulk of the seventy rounds carried out that morning. The duke remained perplexed by this unsatisfactory answer, as he would with the question on rations. Here again the purpose of the question was to ascertain the reason for the undue haste in which Chelmsford departed back to Rorke's Drift on the 23rd, Chelmsford's reason being that the lack of food and ammunition forced an early retreat, apart from the aspect of morale which would effect the troops when daylight revealed the full extent of the death, destruction and mutilation of their comrades.

Glyn's force had taken one day's cooked rations with it on the 22nd, expecting to return that day, and this seemed an adequate arrangement. Dartnell and the NNC, however, had been without rations throughout the previous night and all of the 22nd as, according to Glyn, 'The wagon having stuck fast in a river bed.' When the order to return to the camp was received there was no time for either Dartnell's force or the NNC to be served their rations, which were only issued that evening.

In any event sufficient evidence exists that there were certainly enough rations left behind in the camp by the Zulu on their withdrawal. Plunder they might have, but hundreds of tins of preserved meats, milk and jam, some punctured by assegais but mostly intact, were found by Black's reconnaissance of the camp in June. Had a thorough search been made there would, in all probability, have been sufficient food for several days.

All this mundane correspondence both irritated and perplexed the duke. The last question required specific answers, which answers were, at best, unsatisfactory, at worst evasive and unacceptable. In a private internal memorandum to an aide dated 14 June 1879, the duke vented his frustration and vexation:

> 'I think with you that this explanation is anything but satisfactory. No troops should move in an enemy's country without reserve ammunition always <u>at hand</u> and as far as the rations they are a <u>necessity</u> [both emphases in original] without which troops cannot exist. The want of arrangements in this force seems to me to have been deplorable. Speak to me on the whole question of questions and answers put and answered.'◊

The duke's support and patronage of Chelmsford was fast weakening in the face of mounting evidence that perhaps Durnford was by no means the sole cause of the defeat.

The duke was to hold his peace until after Chelmsford's victory at Ulundi on 4 July. Ellice, the Adjutant-General, then drafted a memorandum for the duke outlining the major causes of the defeat. The duke made a few additions which included reference to Rorke's Drift defences, and the alteration of phrases such as 'the scattering of the one regular battalion which remained in camp on its being actually attacked' to 'the dissemination in two directions of the one regular battalion which remained in camp on the attack being actually delivered'.◊

Ellice then, on 11 August 1879, wrote a confidential letter on behalf of the duke to Chelmsford. This letter stands the test of time. It clearly indicates the lack of satisfaction on Horse Guards' part with Chelmsford's response to the duke's original questions. The letter is of vital historical importance in attempting to unravel and substantiate the underlying causes of the defeat, and the subsequent blame.

> 'My Lord,
>
> The Field Marshal Commanding in Chief, having very carefully considered the evidence taken before the Court of Inquiry on the Isandlana disaster; the supplementary evidence afterwards sent home, and the answers transmitted by your Lordship to certain questions I had the honour to address to you on the subject, I have it in Command to acquaint your Lordship that His Royal Highness has come to the conclusion that the primary cause of the misfortune, and that which led to all the others, was the under estimate formed of the offensive fighting power of the Zulu army.
>
> This was not unnatural. Nowhere, either in Southern or Central Africa, did such a powerfully organised, well disciplined and thoroughly trained force of courageous men exist as lay at the disposal of Ketchwayo.
>
> It would appear that your Lordship, and those with you, expected to

encounter foes and a mode of warfare differing in degree indeed, but not in kind, from that of the Caffres [*sic*] with whom they had lately been contending in the Cape Colony.

The idea of a well disciplined native Force advancing firmly on, and closing rapidly in the open with British battalions armed with the breechloader and supported by Rifled guns was not duly realised.

In fact such confidence in the superiority of the breechloader in British hands was felt that your Lordship did not hesitate to base your plan of campaign upon the power of three isolated columns, none of which contained a real fighting force of more than a couple of English battalions, a battery, and a small body of mounted infantry or Irregular Cavalry, to penetrate, unsupported, into the heart of Zululand. Such a division of force was justifiable only on the belief that each of these columns was able to support alone, the impact of the whole Zulu power.

To this belief in the crushing effect of our weapons, and the small probability of the enemy venturing upon a flank attack in the open, is evidently due the immediate causes of the defeat at Isandlana, viz:-

1. The advance from Rorke's Drift without any persistent effort being made to put this, the immediate base of our operations in Zululand, in a proper state of defence before it commenced.

2. The non-preparation on the 21st January, either by the formation of a laager formed out of the wagons not told off to return to Rorke's Drift for supplies on the following day, or by the construction of a small redoubt of any means of defence for the Troops in Camp in case of attack.

3. Your Lordship moving out of Camp on the morning of the 22nd with a battalion of Infantry, four guns, and the mounted Infantry to attack the enemy some ten miles off, whilst it was in this defenceless state, even though you had ordered up Colonel Durnford's Native Contingent to reinforce it.

4. The not thoroughly searching, with horsemen, the country to the North-East of the Camp, when the enemy was known to be in force ten miles to the East on the Ulundi Road.

5. The evident discredit attached from the first, by those at Head Quarters, to the idea of a really serious attack being made upon the Camp when thus left.

6. The dissemination, in two directions, of the one regular battalion which remained in Camp on the attack being actually delivered, when the only chance of safety consisted in the immediate construction of a small laager, or in massing the troops in square, with a supply of ammunition in the centre, ready to break through one or other of the Zulu encircling wings.'[0]

Horse Guards' verdict was clearly spelt out. Chelmsford had underestimated his foe and in doing so, had based his plan of campaign on the three separate columns, instead of concentrating the six imperial infantry battalions available to him in a single or double thrust, though it might be argued that No. 3 Column, in its entirety, could have withstood an assault by the Zulu army as Wood had successfully done at Kambula. Whatever the circumstances, the fact remained that the reverse suffered at Isandlwana was sufficient reason to question Chelmsford's invasion plan and to point out its weaknesses. Concentration of force was a principle of war and Chelmsford had disregarded it.

Points 1–5 in the memorandum clearly implied that the fault lay with Chelmsford. It is interesting to note that point 3 indicated that Durnford had been ordered up to reinforce the camp, and not to take command, thus ignoring Crealock's false evidence.

Point 6 indicated that the tactical error in advancing the 24th's companies away from the camp in skirmishing order was not of Chelmsford's making but rather Pulleine's. Evidence exists that Durnford had requested assistance from Pulleine should the former run into trouble and this may have influenced Pulleine's tactical thinking. It does not however account for 50 per cent of the infantry being deployed to the north (Cavaye, Mostyn and Younghusband) and the guns well forward to the north-east.

An interesting War Office memorandum throws light on the official viewpoint on this aspect. The document is neither signed nor dated but bears the authentic seal of the War Office and reads:

> 'The facts were as follows. Col. Durnford was commanding an independent column and received his orders from the general. The column commanded by Col. Glyn was at Isandlwana and on the force marching out Col. Pulleine recd orders to take command during Col. Glyn's absence. It could never have been intended and doubtless was never intended to put an officer in command of another column over Col. Pulleine's head for a portion of a day. Col. Durnford's move up to join the general, "cooperate" in the general's own words was entirely in accord with his previous orders. Doubtless finding himself senior officer on the spot when the action had already commenced he, according to the custom of the service, took command, but this was now at too late a period to remedy the fatal errors of position selected before his arrival.'◊

Two issues arise from this memorandum. First, Crealock's assertion that he had ordered Durnford to take command of the camp is discredited. The War Office had now accepted that Crealock's supplementary statement to the Court of Inquiry was incorrect. Second, the writer indicates that Pulleine made fatal errors prior to Durnford's arrival, which errors were too late to rectify. This could only refer to the tents not being struck, and efforts to create a *laager* not being implemented prior to Durnford's arrival, thus inferring that the responsibility lay with Pulleine.

The tactical deployment of the imperial infantry was Pulleine's decision alone. He was undoubtedly influenced by the gross over-confidence that permeated throughout the column. This is shown in a letter written by Lieutenant George Banister, H Company 2/24th. Banister was with Chelmsford's force, escorting Harness' guns. Five days after the battle, Banister wrote to his father from Rorke's Drift:

'Colonel Pulleine sent out to strengthen his outlying picquets and the guns opened fire. The Zulus appeared not to like it and were seen making their way over the hills to the left of the camp. Pulleine thinking it was over, said: "What a fool a fellow is, he only thinks of these things too late, now if we had only kept quiet in camp we should have coaxed these fellows on and given them a right good thrashing."'[1]

As Banister was not present during the attack, his evidence is hearsay. The possible source of information available to Banister would be from one of the five surviving imperial officers. Curling was with the guns. Gardner can be discounted as he had left to inform Wood of the defeat. That left Essex, Cochrane or Smith-Dorrien, all of whom might well have been in close proximity to Pulleine at that stage of the attack, as was Brickhill, the civilian interpreter. The time would probably have been noon or thereabouts.

Banister's statement was not verified at the Court of Inquiry, nor was it likely to have been, as the implication would have been detrimental to Pulleine. One can only speculate that it was gossip overheard or related to Banister, who saw fit to record it in a personal and private letter, and it was equally unlikely that he would invent the quote.

Sir Garnet Wolseley superseded Chelmsford in May 1879. The unjust war would continue until July of that year when the Battle of Ulundi finally broke Zulu resistance. Logistical problems prevented Sir Garnet from taking physical command at Ulundi, and it was left to Chelmsford to enjoy the fruits of victory, thus partially salvaging his reputation. In due course Cetshwayo was captured and exiled to Cape Town, thus ending an unsavoury chapter in British colonial history.

Epilogue

The question must be posed, what would have happened if Lord Chelmsford had reacted immediately to Lieutenant-Colonel Pulleine's first message, received by Chelmsford at 9.30 a.m., that Zulus were advancing on the camp? Or, perhaps more to the point, what would have happened if Pulleine had sent a more imperative and detailed message on which Chelmsford would have been compelled to act?

At 9.30 a.m. various elements of Chelmsford's column were scattered over a wide area from Mangeni Falls to the Magogo and Phindo Hills. It would have taken at least an hour to regroup and commence the return march to camp. The men had taken three and a half hours to cover the outward journey and it would have taken no less to return, suggesting an arrival time at the camp of 2.00 p.m. – too late to render assistance. Furthermore, Hamilton-Browne subsequently reported that during the morning large bodies of the enemy were between him and the camp, and that many had been held in reserve, never taking part in the battle. In all probability Ntshingwayo had placed reserves in that position in order to oppose Chelmsford's column should it attempt to relieve the camp. Had Chelmsford marched back immediately, he would not only have been too late to save the camp but, without reserve ammunition and in the open, would most probably have been annihilated, compounding the defeat of Isandlwana.

During the next few weeks, further defeats were to dog Chelmsford and his army. The coastal column under Colonel Pearson was attacked at the Nyezane River on the same day as Isandlwana was fought and, although Pearson won the engagement, he and most of his column were surrounded at Eshowe and besieged for almost two months. Then, several weeks after Isandlwana, a convoy escorted by a company of the 80th Regiment and carrying 90,000 rounds of Martini-Henry ammunition, rifles and stores, was ambushed close to the town of Luneberg, about seventy miles north of Isandlwana. The escort was virtually wiped out and all the stores and equipment captured. Two weeks later, Colonel Wood of No. 4 Column who, until then, had been the most successful of the column commanders, made the decision to attack an enemy mountain stronghold called Hlobane. Wood had been requested to create a diversion whilst Chelmsford attempted to relieve Pearson at Eshowe. Again British intelligence was sadly at fault. It had been assumed that the Zulu army would oppose Chelmsford at Eshowe, instead it was on its way to attack Wood's camp at Kambula on the very day that Wood decided to attack Hlobane. As Wood's mounted force, supported by black auxiliaries, gained the flat summit of Hlobane mountain and was busy rounding up enemy cattle, it was surprised by the appearance of the rapidly deploying Zulu army, 20,000 strong, on the plain below. Greatly encouraged by the sight, the local abaQulusi clan who occupied Hlobane, came out of hiding and fell upon Wood's horsemen and auxiliaries, trapping them against a boulder-strewn descent later to be named 'Devil's Pass'. Suffering severe casualties, the force fled back to Wood's fortified camp at Kambula twenty miles away.

The following morning the Zulu army, at the zenith of its power and morale, advanced on Kambula shouting taunts at the defenders, 'we are the boys from Isandlwana, come here Johnnie and talk to us'. But Wood's camp was a far different affair from that at Isandlwana. It had been established for many weeks and its *laagered* wagons had been converted into protected two-tier firing platforms. On all sides, as far as a mile from the camp, range markers had been placed every 100 yards to assist in infantry marksmanship. At 5.00 p.m., after a battle that had lasted almost five hours and one that had been touch and go for the British on at least one occasion, the magnificent Zulu regiments, decimated at short range by volley fire and canister shot, began to retire. Immediately the British and colonial horsemen, led by Lieutenant-Colonel Redvers Buller who was described during the chase as being 'like a tiger drunk with blood', set out in pursuit. Out for revenge, they shouted as they galloped after their retreating foe, 'Remember Hlobane! Remember Isandlwana!' The pursuit did not end until darkness fell, leaving close on 1,000 Zulu dead in its wake and a further 1,000 bodies littered around the camp.

Kambula was not the final battle of the war but the decisive one. However, Chelmsford was still on a run of bad luck. The young Prince Napoleon of France, exiled with his family to England after the Franco-Prussian War of 1870, managed to persuade the British government to allow him to join Lord Chelmsford's staff in Zululand. He was a brave but reckless young man who inveigled himself, against orders and restraint, into a front-line patrol during which he was ambushed and killed. The subsequent furore in Britain and France caused a greater sensation than the British defeat at Isandlwana.

Chelmsford, desperately seeking a victory before the arrival of Sir Garnet Wolseley, finally confronted the Zulu army at Ulundi on 4 July 1879. There, taking no chances, with over 4,000 white troops and 1,000 blacks, twelve cannon and two Gatling guns, Chelmsford inflicted 1,500 Zulu casualties in less than an hour at the expense of thirteen British killed. Zulu morale and the will to continue the fight were shattered.

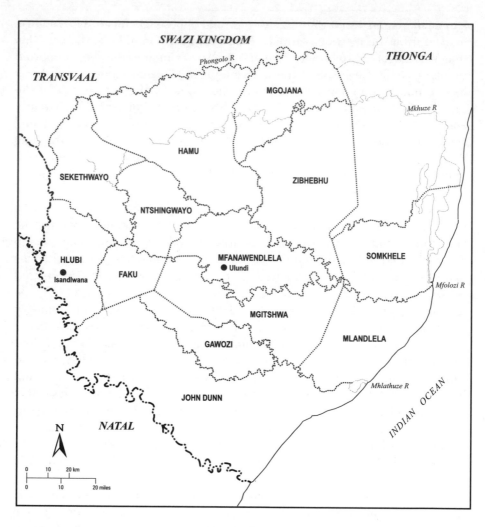

Map No. 11

Wolseley's division of Zululand into thirteen 'chiefdoms', which effectively destroyed the Zulu kingdom.

King Cetshwayo escaped and, with a price on his head, was pursued by British patrols throughout much of Zululand for weeks. Although the Zulu people never betrayed their monarch, Cetshwayo was eventually captured, taken by sea to the Cape and imprisoned 1,200 miles from his homeland, in the bleak confines of Cape Town Castle.

Once Cetshwayo had been incarcerated as a prisoner-of-war, he came under the custody of Captain Ruscombe Poole and interpreter Henry Longcast. In 1881 his status was changed to that of being under civil custody and he was relocated from the Castle to the farm *Oude Molen*. A Cape official, J. Storr-Lister and interpreter Robert Charles Samuelson replaced Poole and Longcast. Cetshwayo was now to enjoy a greater degree of freedom, and spent much of his time anguishing over the injustice of the loss of his kingdom. Helped by Samuelson, he wrote numerous letters, including one to the Governor of the Cape, Sir Hercules Robinson, which concluded by saying:

> 'My father, Mpande, belonged to the English, and when anything happened to him he used to report it to the English, and he made a move when he heard from the English. I have been doing the same and why am I now here? I never for a moment thought that the English would invade my country. I wish the English nation to tell me when they see this my letter, if they find anything in it for which I deserved to be treated as I have been treated, taken away captive from my country.'◊

In due course his wish to visit England was granted. He arrived in London on 5 August 1882, accompanied by a retinue of Zulu attendants. He enjoyed an audience with Queen Victoria who presented him with a large, ornate, three-handled silver beer tankard. Cetshwayo aroused considerable public interest and became a much sought-after social figure, always conducting himself with natural grace and dignity.

Gladstone's government told him that his return to Zululand was conditional, and he soon found that one of the conditions that he would have to bear would be the fragmentation of Zululand into thirteen chiefdoms. Clause 6 of the document that Cetshwayo was obliged to sign read:

> 'I will not make any treaty or agreement without the consent of the British government. I will not make war upon any chief, or chiefs, or people without the sanction of the British government; and in any unsettled dispute with any chief, people or Government, I will appeal to the arbitration of the British government, through the British Resident.'◊

Stripped of effective power, his kingdom splintered, Cetshwayo returned to a central portion of Zululand in January 1883. Internal bickering and fighting left him in a much weakened position. He died at Eshowe on 8 February 1884. His death was certified, rather strangely, as being due to syncope, the result of disease of the heart. Important sections of Zulu society to this day believe that he was poisoned by the Resident Commissioner of Zululand, Sir Melmoth Osborne. An alternative suspicion was that rival factions had poisoned him.

Cetshwayo's body was placed in the custody of the fiercely loyal Shezi clan. He was buried on 23 April 1884, seventy-four days after his death, permission having been granted by Osborne. A cube-shaped coffin-cum-box, measuring three feet on each side, was constructed in which the body was placed in a sitting position. His ceremonial assegai, sleeping mats, utensils and other personal belongings were placed in the coffin. Escorted by a Zulu regiment, he was moved from Eshowe to his final burial place twelve miles south-west of Nkandla and close to Mome Gorge. Here, on high ground commanding the surrounding countryside, the coffin, covered in a black cloth, was buried in a grave marked by a twelve foot mound. The metal parts of the cart used to convey the body were dismantled and left on the grave.

On the centenary of the Anglo-Zulu War in 1979, the remains of the cart were removed and a tombstone flanked by granite posts linked by chains, was erected to commemorate the final resting place of a revered monarch.

Ntshingwayo kaMahole Khoza, the outstanding Zulu commander at Isandlwana, was caught up in the civil war of 1883 which effectively destroyed the old Zulu order. He met his death in July of that year in a battle fought against the anti-royal faction led by Zibhebhu kaMaphitha.

As mentioned earlier the British never saw fit to debrief and interrogate Ntshingwayo in 1879, which would have been a logical process if they had wished to gain an insight into Zulu movements and actions at Isandlwana. Lack of interest in the immediate post-war period might have been the reason; alternatively the truth may have been all too painful to digest.

Mnyamana Buthelezi, Prince Mangosuthu Buthelezi's paternal great-grandfather, not only held the position of commander-in-chief of the Zulu army in 1879, but was also present at pivotal events in Zulu history, such as the Battle of Ndondakusuka in 1856, supporting the then Prince Cetshwayo against the forces of Mbuyazi. He was also witness to King Cetshwayo pronouncing Prince Dinuzulu to be his heir.

Wolseley, the chief architect of the disintegration of the Zulu empire, took over command not only from Chelmsford, but also from Frere. He decided to divide Zululand into thirteen chiefdoms of which John Dunn would receive one of the largest slices. Former enemies such as Ntshingwayo and Zibhebhu were given chiefdoms along with Hamu, who had defected to the British early in the war. The post-war irony concerning the Nqutu district centred around Isandlwana was that Jabez Molife, the sergeant-major of Durnford's Hlubi Troop, was appointed to rule the area – to the victor the spoils of war. All this added up to an odd mixture of rulers to say the least. However, if Wolseley's policy was designed to divide and rule it turned out to be one of divide and destroy. It resulted in civil war throughout Zululand causing far more deaths and privation than the Anglo-Zulu War ever did. The effects of Wolseley's policy, manifesting in strife and faction fighting, are still to be found in kwaZulu-Natal to the present day.

Zululand was finally annexed by Britain in 1888 and, although the colonial soldiers never got their free farms promised by Chelmsford, large chunks of the former Zulu kingdom passed into white ownership. The descendants of those warriors who in 1879 had aspired only to be warriors, now had no prospects other than to be labourers on the land and in the mines.

Although the *amabutho* regimental system of the Zulu army continued for a number of years, the regiments were now under the control of different factions and fought each other rather than a foreign foe. In 1906, there was a brief resurgence of Zulu nationalism when, after a series of catastrophes both natural and man-made, the young men rose up against colonial rule. In 1905 the colonial Natal government, which had already taken close on 70 per cent of what was left of the old Zulu kingdom for white settlement, imposed a tax of £1 per annum on every adult male with the exception of those who already paid hut tax. Offenders were arrested, scuffles took place, four policemen were killed and open rebellion soon challenged the government, putting the white colony into a state of the utmost alarm.

Led by a chief named Bambata kaMancinza, who was supported by none other than the aging Mehlokazulu, thousands of warriors began to assemble north of the Tugela. But the rebellion, as it was called, did not last long. The warriors were pursued relentlessly by Natal colonial forces armed with the latest weaponry including artillery and machine guns. It was estimated that 3,000 Zulus were killed at the cost of thirty colonial troops.

Of the many colonial units and regiments that existed in 1879, most were disbanded shortly after the Battle of Ulundi. Of those that accompanied Lord Chelmsford's column to Isandlwana, only the Natal Carbineers is still an active regiment today. Its colours now carry twenty-six battle honours earned in many theatres of war since the regiment's formation in 1855.◊ The Natal Mounted Police survived until after the Anglo-Boer War, eventually being amalgamated into the South African Police.

The Natal Native Horse was likewise disbanded after Ulundi, but had the distinction of being awarded a regimental colour by Queen Victoria – and, as one would expect, all ranks were awarded the silver South African General Service Medal with the bar 1879.◊ With the advent of the Anglo-Boer War, the NNH was raised again and was led once more by Sergeant-Majors Kambule and Molife. The unit, scouting for the British Army, faced many dangers and rendered valuable service.

However, when it came to awarding the British campaign medal that had been specially struck, the Governor of Natal and the GOC South Africa, despicably decided that the black men of the NNH should only rate a bronze medal thus causing bitter resentment.◊ Nevertheless, the descendants of the black troopers who had fought with Chelmsford volunteered for service in 1914, but by then there was little call for black horsemen.

There was, however, a continuous demand for manual labourers in the South African Native Labour Contingent (SANLC)◊ which was a far cry from a warrior's role of mounted scout. Yet hundreds of young men joined the SANLC, Simeon Kambule's son, Job, being amongst the first volunteers. Over 900 of them were killed in Europe, 616 perishing in the icy English Channel when their transport ship was involved in a collision and sank within minutes, the Zulus singing a warriors' chant of defiance as the vessel went down.◊ At the end of the war, the South African authorities denied the men of the SANLC any recognition for their service. Despite the issue of seven million British War Medals 1914–20 throughout the empire, not one was awarded to the men of the SANLC.

Some years after the Anglo-Zulu War the Intelligence Division of the War Office published a report stating:

> 'There can be no doubt that the Zulu is a born soldier. No one who knows the Zulu nation can doubt their high military qualities, and it may be taken as admitted that better rough military material could scarcely be found. A Zulu by birth, by tradition and from earliest training is a soldier. He is brave, hardy and enduring.'◊

Yet, while the black tribesmen of East and West Africa were recruited into such regiments as the King's African Rifles, the Zulu were refused a warrior's role as fighting soldiers, their service being confined to work merely as labourers in the SANLC.

The descendant regiment of the old 24th Foot is the Royal Regiment of Wales. In 1997, at an historic and heart-warming ceremony in Zululand, the regiment affiliated with No. 121 Infantry Battalion of the South African Defence Force, then known as "Zulu Battalion".◊ It was the closest the RRW could get to a descendant regiment of the old Zulu order.

Of the imperial officers, John North Crealock, the deceiver and master purveyor of misinformation, astonishingly rose to the rank of major-general. Certainly General Ponsonby saw through his façade, for he was to confide to his wife:

> 'I don't feel satisfied. There is always someone who has not served him [Chelmsford] properly. He [Chelmsford] does not abuse Crealock just for his mistakes about the dispatches, but these should not have occurred.'◊

Wolseley took an instant dislike to Crealock and, on 23 June 1879, recorded in his diary:

> 'That offensive snob [Crealock] is his [Chelmsford's] ruin, and I hear generally detested by everyone in Natal. Report says Chelmsford had lost all his influence and is care-worn and will be very glad to be relieved. If he wishes to go home when I arrive, I shall gladly let him do so, and hope he will take his Crealock with him.'

Crealock's appointment was a major error of judgement on Chelmsford's part, for Crealock undoubtedly held considerable influence over his general which he turned to his own advantage. This was confirmed by Wolseley, who commented in a conversation between himself and Sir Henry Bulwer:

> 'That his [Bulwer's] opinions and views were pooh-poohed and that in the end he was barely treated with even ordinary civility. He attributed this more to Crealock, who he very justly described as a snob, than to the General, who was only weak in allowing his military secretary to assume and obtain such an undue influence.'[◊]

Bulwer concluded with a damning condemnation of Crealock by stating that he saw 'young Crealock as the origin of all poor Chelmsford's mistakes'. Crealock, the master fabricator and architect of the cover-up, died in 1895 of ptomaine poisoning while commanding the Rawalpindi district in India (now Pakistan).

Francis Cornelius Clery, another conspirator in the cover-up, rose to the rank of lieutenant-general in 1899 and commanded the 2nd Division during the Anglo-Boer War, but was not considered a success. He retired from the army in 1901 and died, aged 88, in 1926.

Henry Pulleine's remains still lie somewhere on the field of Isandlwana. His body was not easily identifiable in the aftermath and a hearsay Zulu report indicated that he had shot himself in his tent during the later stages of the battle. This is highly unlikely and does little justice to Pulleine. There are two primary source reports on the circumstances of his death. The first was Lieutenant Curling, who recorded in his statement at the Court of Inquiry:

> 'I then left the guns. Shortly after this I again saw Lieutenant Coghill, who told me Colonel Pulleine had been killed.'[◊]

The second report was that of Private J. Bickley, 1/24th Regiment, who also escaped. He stated:

> 'About quarter of a mile on I found a pony standing in the path which I mounted, and shortly after caught up to Lieut. Melville [*sic*] who was carrying the Queen's colour; Lieut. Coghill afterwards joined us, and reported to the Adjutant that Colonel Pulleine had been shot.'[◊]

Both reports are clear. It is possible that Coghill had witnessed Pulleine's death. He would have certainly have been at Pulleine's side for much of the battle. The first report indicated that Pulleine 'had been killed', the second that he 'had been shot'. Nowhere is there any indication that he committed suicide. If Pulleine is to be faulted, it is because he failed to realise, in spite of early warnings, that a major attack was pending. The overwhelming speed of that attack restricted his ability to respond tactically. His belief that the Martini-Henry would ultimately decide the fate of the battle was entirely misplaced.

The number of surviving imperial officers in No. 3 Column who rose to high rank was remarkable. Apart from Crealock and Clery, Wilsone Black rose to the rank of major-general, and was duly knighted. He retired in 1899 after command in Jamaica, Ireland, China and Hong Kong. He died in 1909.

The 'dull' Richard Glyn surprised everyone. Ever loyal to Chelmsford he was made a KCB and rose to the rank of lieutenant-general in 1887. He was appointed colonel of the South Wales Borderers in 1898 and died in 1900 aged sixty-eight.

William Bellairs took part in the First Anglo-Boer War, and in 1885 wrote about his experiences in *The Transvaal War*. He was knighted and rose to the rank of lieutenant-general in 1887. He died in 1913 aged 85.

Mathew Gosset went on to command the Dorsetshire Regiment and rose to the rank of major-general in 1896. In 1903 he was appointed colonel of his regiment. He retired in 1901 after commanding the Dublin District in Ireland and died in 1909.

William Francis Dundonald Cochrane, Durnford's imperial transport officer, was able to confirm that the Zulu army's deployment on the morning of 22 January 1879 commenced from beyond iThusi. He further confirmed that its right horn simultaneously engaged Raw's and Roberts' troops of the NNH. After Isandlwana, Cochrane went on to join Wood's column and fought with the Edendale Troop at Kambula. Cochrane was also present in the party which discovered the body of the Prince Imperial. He went on to command a brigade of the Egyptian Army and was awarded a CB in 1896 and later was appointed the first Governor of Nubia province, Sudan.

Perhaps most surprising of all, John Cecil Russell rose to become a major-general in 1895. He commanded the cavalry depot at Canterbury until 1892, and finished his career as an extra equerry to King Edward VII. He died in 1909.

Horace Smith-Dorrien fought in many subsequent campaigns, experiencing a similar battle situation to that of Isandlwana when he and his Sudanese troops, armed with Martini-Henry rifles, faced the charging Dervishes at Omdurman in 1898. He later rose to the rank of general and was duly knighted. Smith-Dorrien commanded the II Corps of the British Expeditionary Force during the retreat from Mons in 1914 and later commanded British forces in German East Africa. He died in 1930 in a motor car accident, aged seventy-two.

Captain Alan Gardner's actions after escaping from Isandlwana became subject to controversy. Having reached Helpmekaar he then decided to ride north to Utrecht in order to warn Wood, commanding No. 4 Column. Clery obliquely hinted that Gardner's ride was prompted by cowardice. It was an unjust accusation probably inspired by jealousy as it was rumoured Gardner had been recommended for a VC. He duly served with No. 4 Column as Redvers Buller's chief staff officer. He was present on Hlobane and was badly wounded at Kambula thus being one of a handful of men who participated in the three hardest-fought battles of the Anglo-Zulu War.

Gardner attempted to join Lord Roberts' staff in Afghanistan in late 1879 but failed. He resigned from the army in 1881 with the honorary rank of lieutenant-colonel. In 1906 he entered politics and became a Member of Parliament, but died the following year aged sixty-four.

Lieutenant Henry Mainwaring was to rise to the rank of brigadier and wrote an account of Isandlwana whilst in Cairo with the 1/24th on the anniversary of the battle on 22 January 1895. He added further evidence of the Zulu deception plan by writing:

> 'The Mounted Infantry reported the Zulus to be retiring from hill-top to hill-top, and it must have been their plan to draw us away from the camp.'◊

He died in 1922 at Hastings aged seventy and was buried in Kensal Green cemetery in London.

Archibald Berkeley Milne, RN, was the only naval officer to accompany No. 3 Column. His subsequent reports to Commodore F.W. Sullivan, RN, were both detailed and descriptive. He was knighted and rose to the rank of admiral. He died in 1938 aged eighty-three.

Captain Henry Hallam Parr, the recipient of Pulleine's note received at 9.30 a.m. on 22 January, rose to become Major-General Sir Henry Hallam Parr. His letters from Rorke's Drift, written to Sir Bartle Frere, dated 23 and 24 January 1879, made no mention that he was the initial recipient of the note, possibly because he would have heard Chelmsford respond to Clery that, 'there is nothing to be done on that,' such remark being construed as detrimental to Chelmsford. He did add evidence of Pulleine's death by stating:

> 'In the evening we heard more of the matter. Pulleine, who was shot early, had been left with instructions, if attacked, to strike camp, contract his lines & act steadily on the defensive.'◊

After the Battle of Ulundi, most of Chelmsford's imperial battalions were soon scattered to other parts of the Empire, but the rank and file were not forgotten by the Great White Queen. She instructed her Secretary of State for War to write:

> 'Her Most Gracious Majesty acknowledges the services rendered by the troops, and expresses her regret at the losses which have occurred.'◊

It was reported that her message produced a 'feeling of great satisfaction' in the ranks and that those sick in hospital were 'most appreciative.'

A number of the colonials also rose to high rank. John Dartnell of the Natal Mounted Police, whose early morning message to Chelmsford on 22 January started the chain of events that lead to the defeat, rose to the rank of brigadier. He fought with success in the Second Anglo-Boer War. Although by then in his sixties, he cut an imposing figure with thick, long white hair, side whiskers, moustache and a pointed beard rather in the style of the

Boers whom he was opposing. He was duly knighted in 1902 and served as the Imperial Commissioner for the Zululand Lands Delimitation Commission. He died in 1904.

Inspector George Mansel, Dartnell's second-in-command at Isandlwana, subsequently had charge of a short-lived unit named the Zululand Reserve Territory Carbineers that policed portions of the former kingdom prior to the British annexation. Later, after returning to Natal, Mansel commanded the NMP.

A number of the colonials who survived Isandlwana subsequently fought in later battles of the war. Raw for instance was also one of the few present at both Hlobane and Kambula, having already fought at Isandlwana. He died several years later at the early age of thirty-four. His family, like many descendants of Vause, Henderson and Shepstone, all of the NNH, and Symons of the carbineers, still farm or follow other careers in kwaZulu-Natal today. Captain 'Offy' Shepstone detached himself from the Natal Carbineers and raised Shepstone's Horse which, together with the NNH, pursued the defeated Zulu army from Ulundi alongside the 17th Lancers and the 1st Dragoon Guards.

The young NMP trooper, William James Clarke, whom Mansel had accused of robbing the dead at Isandlwana, also rose, years later, to command the NMP with the rank of colonel. But before doing so he led an adventurous life. He was actively engaged in the Gun War (in Basutoland) of 1880. During the First Anglo-Boer War of 1880–81 he fought at the Battle of Laing's Nek and during the Anglo-Boer War of 1899–1902 he served as an intelligence officer with the Imperial Light Horse. During WWI he saw action in both German South-West Africa and German East Africa. Finally, in 1918 Clarke was sent to Russia and took part in the fighting against the Bolsheviks. As a sportsman he was a renowned shot and accomplished amateur jockey.

The escape of Trooper Barker, Natal Carbineers, from Isandlwana and across Fugitives' Drift, becomes entwined with that of Lieutenant Walter Higginson whose conduct in his encounter with Barker casts doubts on the often quoted story of his gallantry in returning to assist Melvill and Coghill. Donald Morris in *Washing of the Spears* relates, 'Higginson reached the bank with them [Melvill and Coghill]. The three men rested for a few moments and Higginson wandered off to find some horses.'

The story continues with Melvill and Coghill managing to stagger up the Natal bank, pursued by the enemy, and about to be put to death when Higginson returns:

> 'Higginson found a horse on the ridge, gathered two or three men, and raced down the slope to the rescue. While still fifty yards away, with the scene hidden by the jutting rock, he heard the end. There were a few shots and the sound of a scuffle, and when thirty Zulus dropped down to the trail he was forced to turn away.'

That is the last we hear of Higginson in Morris' book. However, Trooper Barker left an account that differs markedly from Morris' narrative. He tells how, having successfully crossed Fugitives' Drift in company with Lieutenant Raw, he reached the high ground in the vicinity of where Melvill and Coghill had met their deaths, or were about to do so. There he and a trooper named Tarboton paused, looking back to see if any of their comrades were following. Barker spied a lone figure on foot and, thinking it might be his 'bosom pal' Hawkins (who unbeknown to Barker had already perished at Isandlwana), therefore bravely rode back:

> 'but [it] turned out to be Lieutenant Higginson, so he informed me, of the Natal native contingent, and got hurt in the river where his horse was washed away. As my horse was too tired to carry two, I assisted him to mount, and he rode away leaving me to follow on foot. Tarboton, Henderson and Raw, recognising him on my horse, took the horse from him and came back to meet me with it, of which I was right glad, as I had to run for about three miles. Higginson told them he could not have walked any further, and he knew I was fresh, and that he was sending the horse back for me.'

Barker, who lived to become a respected figure of the colony and a magistrate in later life, was recommended for the Victoria Cross by Sir Evelyn Wood, but only several years later, by which time the war had already reaped a fair number of VCs, and no further awards were forthcoming.

Despite the severe criticism of his peers, Higginson found an unlikely ally in none other than Coghill's father who, in April 1879, wrote to the *Daily Telegraph* in London from his home in Ireland:

> 'Sir,
>
> In thanking you very gratefully for the warm terms of phrase you have bestowed upon my dear son's conduct at Isandula in your leading article yesterday, I wish to remove a sort of possible reproach which seems to have been conveyed on a very gallant young officer, Lieutenant Higginson of stating that he was "either unable or unwilling" to help Melvill when his horse was shot under him in the river. I enclose you a cutting from a Dublin paper containing the account of the affair, in which you will perceive that Lieutenant Higginson did everything that an unarmed and dismounted man could do to succour poor Melvill and my son, and that he only left them when any risk to himself could not possibly benefit them. I owe so much to Lieutenant Higginson as the sole survivor who has been able to give me details of my dear son's last moments, and for the testimony he has borne to the gallantry and devotion of both the young heroes, that it would add much to my sorrow to think that his own character should be tarnished by any misconception!
>
> J.J. Coghill.'

History records that Coghill was incapacitated as a result of a knee injury and that Melvill sacrificed his life to stay by his side. This story has been perpetuated probably as a result of Glyn's report, stating that Melvill could have saved himself, had it not been for Coghill's injury. The knee injury was caused on 20 January by chasing chickens whilst on reconnaissance. Coghill confirmed this in one of his last diary entries, dated 21 January and recovered from the battlefield:

> 'On the way home we found some fowls at a deserted kraal and in capturing them I put my knee out wh. [*sic*] kept me in my tent for some days.'◊

Both officers were totally exhausted and it was Melvill who first stated that he could not move any further. This was recorded by Higginson, who in his report stated, 'Melvill said he could go no further and Coghill said the same.'◊ This is the only primary source evidence available on the subject.

Both bodies were interred in February 1879, but only temporarily. Sir Bartle Frere in due course erected a headstone and sandstone cross and had both bodies placed in pine coffins prior to reburial. Sadly neither Melvill nor Coghill was to rest in peace. In 1973, Arthur Konigkramer, at the time a reporter for the Durban *Daily News* and now Chairman of AMAFA (Heritage Council) told the authors:

> 'On January 10th, 1973 I visited the grave sites of Lieutenants Teignmouth Melvill and Nevill Coghill in the company of the late George Bunting on whose farm the graves and monument were situated. On arrival we found that the graves had been desecrated and the monument erected by Sir Bartle Frere in 1879 vandalized the sandstone cross had been pushed from its pedestal and lay on the graves. There was evidence that the cross had been struck by a light caliber rifle, since small slivers of stone had sheared off, and traces of lead clearly visible. The desecration bore all signs of grave robbers bent on collecting memorabilia relating to the Anglo-Zulu war, and organised mainly from overseas, using local people. The cairns had been moved aside and numerous bone fragments lay on the surface. I removed the cross and left it at the house of Mr. Bunting having reported the occurrence to Mr. George Chadwick of the National Monuments Council. The cross was taken to the Natal Provincial Administration offices in Ladysmith, and subsequently wrongly reported to have been lost. The custodians of the Monuments Council in due course re-erected the cross back to the historical site where it now stands.
>
> I again visited the site later that year, this time to find further extensive digging had taken place, and items such as clothing, boots, and the outline of the original coffins, were clearly visible. The remains of the two officers were then placed in small coffins, I would estimate about three feet long, and reburied. I understand that concrete was poured over the coffins for additional protection.'

It is to be hoped that there will be no further postscripts to this sad saga.

However, the desecration of war graves and monuments situated in hundreds of different locations – some extremely remote – throughout kwaZulu-Natal continues. The mistaken belief that there are treasures, or powerful *muti* (medicine) buried below, has taken a hold on the imagination of many local communities, the whole unfortunate business having been instigated and abetted by overseas and local relic dealers.

Sir Garnet Wolseley continued to reiterate his views on the conduct of Melvill and Coghill when, on 19 March 1880, he recorded in his diary:

> 'Heroes have been made of men like Melvill and Coghill who taking advantage of their having horses bolted from the scene of action to save their lives.'[◊]

This was not the view of Horse Guards. As described in Chapter 7, Melvill and Coghill were posthumously awarded the Victoria Cross in January 1907. This award was no doubt influenced by a previously published memorandum in the *London Gazette* dated 2 May 1879 which read:

> 'Lieutenant Melvill of the 1st Bn 24th Foot on account of the gallant efforts made by him to save the Queen's Colour of his regiment after the disaster at Isandhlwana [*sic*] and also Lieutenant Coghill 1st Bn 24th Foot on account of his heroic conduct in endeavoring to save his brother officer's life, would have been recommended to Her Majesty for the Victoria Cross had they survived.'

Melvill's watch, recovered from his body, had stopped at 2.10 p.m. It is reasonable to assume this occurred on his entering the waters of the Buffalo River. Careful analysis indicates that at best, it would have taken Melvill, mounted and encumbered by the Colour, one and a quarter hours to reach the river. This would place his time of departure from the camp at about 12.55 p.m. at the latest. There can be little doubt as to Melvill's determination to save the Colour, nor of Coghill's bravery in returning from relative safety to sacrifice his life for Melvill.

On 15 January 1907, King Edward VII presented the VCs to Coghill's family and Melvill's widow, Sarah. Melvill's eldest son, Teignmouth Philip, went on to command the 17th Lancers. He also became an international polo player. His younger son, Charles William, rose to the rank of brigadier and went on to command the 1st New Zealand Infantry Brigade in the First World War.

Amongst the many dead, the body of Anthony William Durnford lay in a shallow grave on the field of Isandlwana until October 1879. A hearsay report on the circumstances of his death appeared in the local press on 26 January 1879:

> 'One of the Carbineers, who arrived in Maritzburg from Rorke's Drift yesterday, stated that he saw Colonel Durnford stabbed through the heart with an assegai. He made this statement to two gentlemen who arrived in Durban from Maritzburg last night.'[◊]

Durnford's family specifically requested that he be buried in the military cemetery at Fort Napier, Pietermaritzburg. His remains were brought in an ambulance from Isandlwana by his faithful follower Jabez Molife. They were then handed to Lieutenant-Colonel Harding Stewart, RE, who was in charge of the funeral arrangements. The burial took place at 4.00 p.m. on Sunday, 13 October 1879. The *Times of Natal* recorded the event:

> 'The whole of the garrison, consisting of detachments of the 2/24th and 99th Regiments, 60th Rifles, Artillery, Army Service Corps etc., numbering about 1,500 men turned out in addition to the Maritzburg Rifles, the Natal Carbineers, the Mounted Police, Native Contingent officers and about 60 Edendale men who were with the late Colonel at Isandlwana. Preceded by the firing party consisting of 300 men under Captain Harvey, 2/24th Regiment and the band of the 99th Regiment playing the "Death March," the body, in a coffin on a gun carriage was taken to the camp chapel, where the Rev. Mr. Richie read the first portion of the burial service... It is seldom that the solemn yet withal hopeful strains of this immortal marche funebre fall upon ones ear with such impressiveness. It was the association more than the actual music – the calm cloudy weather, the Sabbath stillness, and the occasion. Arriving at the grave, the Rev. Mr. Richie performed the concluding rites, and the body was consigned to its last resting place.'◊

Durnford may have had many faults: impetuosity; a burning inner desire to redeem his reputation following the Langalibalele rebellion; and his failure to take effective command when it became apparent that the camp was facing the entire Zulu army. He could have escaped with his horsemen, but chose to die a hero's death. However, he was not ordered to take command of the camp and did not inherit written instructions from Pulleine regarding its defence. He acted in accordance with his orders as he perceived them and died bravely enhancing the reputation of the colonials at Isandlwana. His contemporary, the historian J.A. Froude, wrote:

> 'I have rarely met a man who, at first sight, made a more pleasing impression upon me. He was more than I expected... He has done the State good service. He alone did his duty when others forgot theirs.'◊

'Faithful unto Death', was the inscription on his headstone.

At least seventy-eight white officers and NCOs of the NNC met their deaths at Isandlwana including James Lonsdale, Standish Vereker and Captains Barry, Murray and Krohn.

Prince Dabulamazi kaMpande later told Colonel Adolf Schiel, a Transvaal border agent, that at the height of the battle when it was obvious the camp would be overrun, a number of the NNC rank and file tore off their distinguishing red head bands and set about the British soldiers in the hope that they would be mistaken for Zulus themselves.◊

Lord Chelmsford, flushed with victory, embarked for England, arriving on 26 August 1879. Wood, Buller and Crealock accompanied him. Prior to embarking, he addressed a gathering in Cape Town where, aware of criticism levelled at him, he defended himself in these terms:

> 'Gentlemen,
>
> I have been publicly accused of hesitation and vacillation, and it has been stated that I had completely lost the confidence of all but my personal staff. As regards this last charge, I am proud to feel justified in meeting it with a distinct denial and I am confident it never had the slightest foundation. With regard to the charge of hesitation and vacillation, I can only assure you that I made up my mind at a very early date that I would endeavour to reach Ulundi by the route which I eventually took, and that I never swerved from the determination.'◊

On his arrival home, Queen Victoria immediately summoned Chelmsford to Balmoral where, on 2 September, she conferred upon him the insignia of the Grand Cross of the Bath. That evening he was seated in the place of honour next to her at dinner. In a letter to Wood dated 12 September 1879, Chelmsford, with a rare flash of humour recorded, 'Her Majesty was so gracious to me that I began to be afraid lest Mr. Brown should become jealous!'◊

Controversy however, continued to shadow Chelmsford and he never commanded troops in the field again. In April 1882 he was promoted to the substantive rank of lieutenant-general and subsequently, under the Queen's patronage, appointed Lieutenant of the Tower and Gold Stick at Court.

Before Isandlwana, Chelmsford enjoyed great popularity within the army. He was a teetotaler and was regarded as a strict disciplinarian. He might today be considered a workaholic. Unable to delegate responsibility, he insisted on attending to every minor detail personally. In mitigation it should be noted that his commissariat problems were huge and were a major hindrance to his invasion plans.

However, in order to reach a balanced perspective, the views of his peers are significant. Prior to the invasion, Clery, for example, was greatly concerned about the quality of the headquarters staff. On 6 November 1878 he wrote:

> 'The headquarters staff is very weak. This I think is the general's own fault as he not only does too much himself but thinks he can do without immediate staff.'◊

Prime Minister Disraeli lost confidence in Chelmsford prior to Wolseley's appointment. On 8 May 1879, he wrote to Lady Chesterfield that:

> 'The news from the Cape very unsatisfactory. Chelmsford wanting more forces, tho' he does nothing with the 15,000 men he has. He seems cowed and confused. I wish Lord Lytton and Gen. Roberts were at the Cape of Good Hope.'◊

Sir Garnet Wolseley was undoubtedly Chelmsford's severest critic. Chelmsford's conduct of the war destroyed whatever respect Wolseley may have had for Chelmsford. On 20 July 1879 Wolseley wrote:

> 'My line is to get Chelmsford out of the country as soon as possible: he has now no power and although I have the poorest opinion of his ability as a general or a public servant, I have a feeling for the position in which he finds himself at present and don't want to rake up old complaints against him. Why kill a dead horse? In war he can never be employed again although I have no doubt the Horse Guards will cover him with Honours and give him Aldershot or some equally good place.'◊

By the time the advance to Ulundi was underway, the general feeling was that the only commander who had enhanced his reputation was Wood. Many expressed the view that they would have preferred to serve directly under him. This led to a riddle current at headquarters which Wolseley cruelly took delight in relating:

> '"Why is it that the men with Lord Chelmsford's column cannot be regarded as Christians?" Answer: "Because they make an idol of Wood (Evelyn) and did [not] believe in the Lord."'◊

When the Prince Imperial was killed, Wolseley compared the blame given for the defeat at Isandlwana to that of the Prince's death. On 30 September 1879 he wrote:

> 'I think this is very unfair, and is merely a repetition of what was done regarding the Isandlwana disaster where the blame was thrown upon Durnford, the real object in both instances being apparently to screen Chelmsford.'◊

This statement was not made public at the time, but represents the most conclusive vindication of Durnford's actions.

Chelmsford would have been distressed at the comments made to Sir Garnet by both Wood and Buller. Chelmsford considered both not only to be able field commanders but loyal friends. On 15 July 1879 Sir Garnet wrote:

> 'I put up with dear old Wood: both he and Buller say Chelmsford is not fit to be a Corporal.'◊

Wood's and Buller's apparent disloyalty would undoubtedly have caused Chelmsford much anguish had he known of these remarks; fortunately he would never know.

If one person alone is to be singled out as responsible for the British defeat at Isandlwana, then it is Chelmsford who must be found guilty. A questionable invasion strategy; inadequate staff; poor field decisions exacerbated by vacillation; all coupled with gross over-confidence and complete under-estimation of the Zulu were the direct causes of the defeat, resulting in a totally unacceptable casualty list.

On 9 April 1905 Chelmsford died at the age of seventy-eight of a heart attack whilst playing billiards at the United Services Club in London. He was buried in the Brompton Cemetery in London.

In the final analysis, the Battle of Isandlwana should deservedly be remembered not as a British defeat, but rather as a great Zulu victory in which Chelmsford was out-thought, out-manouevred and out-generalled by Ntshingwayo.

——————

And what of the battlefield today? If it changed little in the first hundred years after the battle, the reverse is the case since the early 1980s. At that time there were very few visitors and, apart from the vandalised St Vincent's church and abandoned mission buildings, the only sign of habitation was a scattering of traditional thatched homes. A night spent camping on the battlefield was an eerie experience. It was especially eerie just before nightfall when the black, brooding shape of Isandlwana became silhouetted against the last light in the western sky. Aware that one was about to sleep amidst cairns covering the bones of many dead men and within the confines of a field that had hosted one of the most brutal and terrifying pitched battles in history, the appearance of a spectre seemed inevitable. It was prudent to ensure that there was no need to venture from one's tent during the hours of darkness lest with the night wind and the jackals calling, the shadows of the field be mistaken for things that were not there.

——————

We shall never really know the complete truth of what happened at Isandlwana in 1879. The dead and the battlefield keep their secrets. A preliminary archeological expedition has recently sought to unravel some of the battlefield's remaining mysteries and in doing so unearthed from their shallow hiding places, a small and insignificant haul of relics which were viewed by the authors at Pietermaritzburg. It was hoped that a trove of spent Martini-Henry cartridge cases would be discovered, thus demarcating the exact position of the British firing line. But the dig was perhaps forty years too late to reveal secrets from a battlefield that has been scoured by relic hunters, both amateur and professional, for over a century. Having seen some of the relic collections accumulated by enthusiastic battlefield scavengers, the authors doubt if more than one per cent of the debris that littered the battlefield 120 years ago still remains. Thus present-day finds of, say, a handful of cartridge cases or fragments of an ammunition box, are likely to be misleading rather than being indicative of past troop positions. There can be no substitute for primary source material in establishing facts relating to the battle. Three years after the battle, Bertram Mitford found ammunition boxes over a mile from the camp along the Fugitives' Trail[◊] but, of course, they were no indication of the firing line's position.

The future of the battlefield is secure, it having been declared a Provincial Landmark under the terms of the kwaZulu-Natal Heritage Act and in all likelihood it will be declared a national heritage site. Less than a decade ago only a small piece of land around the monuments was formally protected. The Provincial Landmark of Isandlwana now covers an area of almost 800 hectares (2,000 acres) and includes much of the land on which the battle took place and all the land traversed by the fugitives fleeing the scene of battle towards the Buffalo River.

The school and shop which had been erected on the battlefield itself have been demolished and rebuilt in the village to the north. The road that traversed the battlefield was closed and a new road skirting the battlefield has been built. Although Rorke's Drift has also been declared a Provincial Landmark, no protection has to date been accorded to the Mangeni Valley. Although it is still possible to experience an eerie feeling of loneliness and desolation at Isandlwana, it cannot be gainsaid that the influx of people and the concomitant development have, to a degree, detracted from its sense of remoteness.

Given the fascination people from all corners of the globe have for the Zulu people, and the fact that the African way of life is a major factor in attracting tourists to South Africa, a wise government might well consider declaring all the land that encompasses Isandlwana, Rorke's Drift, Sihayo's stronghold and the Mangeni Falls a Cultural Conservancy, for the area of Isandlwana is unique in the historical tapestry of Africa.

Notes

Page 21   '*Mthonga, still an exile...*' Mthonga led a small group of mounted scouts attached to No. 4 Column. In this capacity he accompanied Colonel Evelyn Wood at the Battle of Hlobane, 28 March 1879.

Page 26   '"*the sacred iNkatha," thus revitalising the nation...*' These events were witnessed by Paulina Dlamini, then a young girl serving at Cetshwayo's court, and were later recorded. Paulina Dlamini, *A Servant of Two Kings*.

Page 32   '*Furthermore, he had a reputation...*' The reason why Shepstone was regarded by the Zulu as untrustworthy is detailed in Chapter 5, p. 131.

Page 34   '*Nowhere in southern Africa...*' Draft of a letter for the consideration of HRH The Duke of Cambridge, Commander-in-Chief of the British Army, prepared by General Sir Charles Ellice, Adjutant-General 1876–84. PRO WO 30/129 56316.

Page 35   '*We have certainly been...*' The Royal Archives Windsor, RA RAVIC/Add E1/8513.

Page 37   '*Strangely, there was little or no fraternising...*' M/S diary of Tpr William James Clarke NMP. Killie Campbell Africana Library (KCAL), Durban.

Page 38   '*Dear Father, I can't find out the reason...*' Pte Goatham, 1/24th, letter to his father, KCAL, Durban.

Page 38   '*There would be over 500 instances...*' Brian Best, 'Campaign Life in the British Army during the Zulu War', *Journal of the Anglo-Zulu War Historical Society*, December 1997.

Page 44   '*At the Inanda location...*' Location: land set aside and reserved for 'colonial Zulus'.

Page 45   '*A motley crowd...*' Hamilton-Browne, *A Lost Legionary in South Africa*.

Page 53   '*Dingane received the Voortrekker emissaries...*' Manfred Nathan, *The Voortrekkers of South Africa*.

Page 55   '*Then, into the potential battleground...*' By an odd coincidence, the British military force hoisted the Union flag over Port Natal on the same day as the Boers were fighting the Battle of Blood River.

Page 59   '*many word in the Zulu tongue...*' An example of the similarity between certain Zulu and Swahili words:

English	Zulu	Swahili
food	*ugula*	*chakula*
firewood	*inkune*	*kune*
cow	*inkomo*	*ngombe*
people	*abantu*	*watu*
European	*umlungu*	*wazungu*
turn over	*phendula*	*penduka*
dog	*inja*	*umbwa*

Page 62   '*There had been a most serious incident...*' G.A. Chadwick and E.G. Hobson, *The Zulu War and the Colony of Natal*.

Page 62–3   '*Early in the war...*' Field Marshal Sir Evelyn Wood, *From Midshipman to Field Marshal*, Vol. II.

Page 67 *'We commenced the...'* M/S Tpr W.J. Clarke, KCAL, Durban.

Page 68 *'The NMP had been...'* M/S Tpr W.J. Clarke, KCAL, Durban.

Page 69 *'Lord Chelmsford (who reiterated...'* M/S diary of Tpr Fred Symons: 'Lord Chelmsford promised each of the Carbineers a farm in Zululand when the war was over.' 'Experiences of a Natal Carbineer', M/S KCAL, Durban.

Page 70 *'The arrival of Lord Chelmsford...'* Ron Lock & Peter Quantrill, *The Red Book.*, p. 6.

Page 71 *'Glyn and his staff...'* Sir Archibald Alison, Autograph Letters, MS 165, The Brenthurst Library, Johannesburg. Quoted in Sonia Clarke, *Zululand at War, 1879.*

Page 71–2 *'Both Clery, Glyn's principal staff officer...'* Alison letters, MS 165, The Brenthurst Library, Johannesburg.

Page 73 *'Can you wonder...'* *The Red Book*, p. 9.

Page 73 *'Helpmekaar would become a haven...'* Helpmekaar, like so many little embryo villages in South Africa at the turn of the 19th century, seemed to have the prospect of growing into a town. It did eventually boast a hotel, police station, trading store and several houses. Today, it is near to being a ghost town. The stone-walled hotel and trading store still stand but are abandoned and derelict. A couple of houses remain occupied. Only the police station seems to have flourished. With its modern radio masts and with flags flying, it is quite a gay sight, but it completely blocks from view the little overgrown graveyard at the rear with its scattering of weather-beaten headstones, where those who died at Helpmekaar in 1879 lie buried.

Page 75 *'Nevertheless, it was not a bad deal...'* Land Grant Number 2251, Colony of Natal, 1 October 1860.

Page 75–6 *'Francis Fynn, who now accompanied...'* 'My Recollections of a Famous Campaign', Henry F. Fynn, M/S KCAL, Durban, ref. KMC 98/69/135.

Page 76 *'Captain Mainwaring of the 2/24th...'* M/S account written 1895, Royal Regiment of Wales Museum, Brecon.

Page 77 *'The men of the 24th...'* M/S diary of Tpr William James Clarke NMP, KCAL, Durban.

Page 78 *'Back in Durban...'* *The Red Book*, p. 18.

Page 80 *'Suddenly the chanting...'* Hamilton-Browne, *Lost Legionary.*

Page 81 *'This was the first time...'* Tpr Fred Symons, 'Experiences of a Natal Carbineer', M/S KCAL, Durban.

Page 82 *'There were those...'* When Oham [Hamu kaMpande, half brother to Cetshwayo] was at the King's [Cetshwayo] homestead, he, in full council, asked Usirayo [Sihayo] who he was that Zululand should be embroiled by him? What family did he belong to? Was he not only a dog?' John P.C. Laband, ed., *Lord Chelmsford's Zululand Campaign.* (In March 1879, Hamu, with many members of his clan, including a number of warriors who had fought at the Battle of Isandlwana, defected to the British joining Wood's No. 4 Column, many being killed at the Battle of Hlobane on 28 March 1879. Ron Lock, *Blood on the Painted Mountain.*)

Page 82 *'Dunn states...'* *The Red Book*, p. 92.

Page 83–4 *'Ritual preparations...'* Dlamini, *Servant of Two Kings.*

Page 84 *'Only the ritual...'* L.H. Samuelson, *Zululand its Tradition, Legends, Customs and Folklore.*

Page 84 *'Yet many warriors...'* E.J. Krige, *The Social System of the Zulus.*

Page 84 *'It had been the warriors' task...'* Krige, *The Social System of the Zulus.*

Page 84 *'During the early morning...'* Krige, *The Social System of the Zulus.*

Page 87 *'absolutely impossible...'* *The Red Book*, p. 169.

Page 90 *'Nor did he consider...'* Letter from Chelmsford to Wood, dated 16 January 1879. Natal Archives, Pietermaritzburg.

Page 91   *'Despite most...'* Capt. Stafford, NNC, recalled: 'When we arrived at Kranskop, the oxen from the Free State which were unacclimatised, commenced to die like flies from red-water and by the time the Natal Native Contingent had its full compliment of men there was very little left of the oxen.' Capt. W. Stafford, private M/S, KCAL, Durban.

Page 91   *'Little has been mentioned...'* In October 1878, the Lt-Governor of Natal sent a minute to the Colonial Secretary headed 'Confidential/Pressing.' It contained instructions that various magistrates throughout the colony should provide from their districts, native horsemen. They were to be put at the disposal of Colonel Durnford. Minute 161, C133/78 Natal Archives, Pietermaritzburg.

Page 93   *'Their home had once been...'* N.J. van Warmelo, ed, *History of Matiwane and the amaNgwane Tribe.*

Page 94   *'In compliance with ...'* *Regulations Field Forces, South Africa, 1878.*

Page 94   *'It was known locally as Isandlwana...'* Isandlwana is not unique as a Zulu place name. There is another hill so named in the Mahabatini Magisterial District of kwaZulu-Natal and a rural police station near Bergville is also named Isandlwana. It is likely that some of Durnford's amaNgwane troopers of Zikali's Troop were incorporated into the government police at the conclusion of the Anglo-Zulu War. Perhaps they named the police post in commemoration of the famous battle in which they had fought. The post is situated in amaNqwane territory in the foothills of the Drakensberg Mountains.

Page 95   *'However, it is unlikely...'* Tpr Symons commented: 'They [the NNC] had not our scruples and pulled down the kraals for fuel... for the destruction of one native hut means the destruction of about 500 saplings... the man who burns a hut down, even in warfare ought to be condemned.' Lock, *Blood on the Painted Mountain.*

Page 129   *'With bellows of adulation...'* Details of Zulu Army's direction of march, *The Red Book*, p. 98.

Page 131   *'Matshana was not to be trusted...'* John P.C. Laband, *Rope of Sand.*

Page 131   *'Twenty years earlier...'* E.F. Colenso assisted by Lt Col E. Durnford, *History of the Zulu War and its Origins.*

Page 132   *'The day had been saved...'* The Red Book, p. 42.

Page 132   *'Mansel had been approached by Major Clery...'* Mansel Papers contained in the Wood Papers, KCAL, Durban.

Page 133   *'By about 2.00 p.m....'* Mansel Papers.

Page 133   *'Reluctantly, Mansel...'* Mansel Papers.

Page 135   *'Tents...'* Notes on Transport (Revised 1897). Pamphlet published by 2nd Battalion, Oxford Light Infantry.

Page 137   *'Hamilton-Browne, commanding...'* Hamilton-Browne, *Lost Legionary.*

Page 138   *'Trooper Parsons...'* M/S Tpr W.J. Clarke, KCAL, Durban.

Page 140   *'An argument ensued...'* Lt Milne, RN. PRO 16486 S 6333.

Page 140   *'They informed the General...'* PRO WO 33/34 S 6333.

Page 141   *'On reaching the summit...'* PRO 16486 S 6333.

Page 141   *'Lieutenant Browne, IMI...'* Natal Witness 30 January 1879: 'Capt. Browne, of the Mounted Infantry, had been reconnoitring towards the Isipezi Hill on our front and had not only seen several bodies [Zulu] moving in an easterly direction... '

Page 142   *'By rights...'* M/S document Royal Regiment of Wales Museum, Brecon.

Page 142   *'During the hours of darkness...'* Report by Lt Walter R. Higginson 1st Bn, 3rd Regt., NNC. WO 33/34 S6333. Enclosure 3 in No. 96, p. 68. 'Lt. Hon. S. Vereker of No. 5 Company came into camp [from the picquet on Magaga Knoll] and reported Zulus... who had come close enough to speak to his men.'

Page 145   *'Since the departure of Gosset...'* WO 33/34 S6333.

Page 145   *'The enemy was now…'* Tpr Joseph Carter, NMP. Letter to his sister dated 11 February 1879: 'Twenty of us were sent forward to reconnoitre, but finding they were several thousand strong we did not attack… ' Carter's letter was published in the Barclay's Bank (South Africa) in-house magazine, probably at some time in the 1970s. It was submitted by Miss Joan Noble of 33 Old Broad Street, Durban, a great-niece of Tpr Carter.

Page 145   *'Consequently, at about 6.30 p.m…'* Clarke, *A Record of the Services of the Natal Mounted Police.*

Page 145–6   *'As the temperature fell and darkness…'* Daphne Child, *The Zulu War Diary of Col. Henry Harford.*

Page 146   *'The night held many fears…'* Charles Norris-Newman, *In Zululand with the British Throughout the War of 1879.*

Page 146   *'Clearly they were not just a local…'* Elaine Unterhalter, *Confronting Imperialism: The People of Nquthu and the 1879 Invasion of Zululand.*

Page 147   *'Major Gosset came…'* WO 33/34 S6333.

Page 148   *'Clery, now wide awake…'* WO 33/34 S6333.

Page 148   *'Milne later recorded…'* Lt Milne, RN. PRO ADM 16486 S6333.

Page 149   *'Chelmsford would contrive…'* *Archives of Zululand: The Anglo-Zulu War 1879*, p. 75. Chelmsford to Secretary of State for War, 27 January 1879: 'Feeling that the position was rather critical I ordered Colonel Glyn to move to his [Dartnell's] assistance with all available men.'

Page 151   *'We rode on quickly…'* Lt Milne, RN. PRO ADM 16486 S6333.

Page 151   *'The thousands of Zulus of the night before had been a decoy…'* Such was also the opinion of the War Office. A memorandum from the Intelligence Department, dated 11 February 1879 states, 'He [Lord Chelmsford] was led away by the Zulus who decoyed him from the camp.' The Royal Archives, Windsor, RA VIC/033/92.

Page 155   *'Chelmsford decided to lead this force…'* Lt Milne, RN. PRO ADM 16486 S6333.

Page 155   *'The morning was spent…'* Capt Henry Hallam Parr, *A Sketch of the Kafir and Zulu Wars.*

Page 158   *'Shortly a dispatch arrived…'* Incident recorded by Lt Banister in a letter to his father, 27 January 1879, Royal Regiment of Wales Museum, Brecon.

Page 158   *'This news seemed to trigger…'* Capt Henry Hallam Parr, *A Sketch of the Kafir and Zulu Wars.*

Page 158   *'The NMP had pursued…'* Mansel Papers, contained in the Wood Papers, KCAL, Durban.

Page 160   *'At about this time a carbineer arrived…'* *Natal Witness* 30 January 1879.

Page 160   *'Chelmsford glanced at the note…'* PRO WO 33/34 S6333. Chelmsford later denied that he had said, 'There is nothing to be done on that', but Clery would not be shaken and stoutly maintained that those had been Chelmsford's words. Glyn supported Clery, stating that he had stood nearby and had overheard the conversation. Clery eventually handed Pulleine's message to Glyn who carefully put it into his pocket; it still exists and is one of the most prized relics of the Royal Regiment of Wales Museum at Brecon.

Page 160   *'The special war correspondent…'* In mid-February 1879 Drummond resigned as the 'Special War Correspondent' of the *Natal Witness*, giving the following reason for his resignation: 'I am sorry on reading your article… that you spoke of Lord Chelmsford in a manner which will prevent me, as a member of his staff, continuing to act as your correspondent.' Drummond's letter was published in the *Natal Witness* of 27 February 1879.

Page 160   *'The carbineer then added…'* *Natal Witness* 30 January 1879.

Page 161   *'At the same time…'* PRO WO 33/34.

Page 162   *'He had been joined...'* John P.C. Laband, P.S. Thompson and Sheila Henderson. *The Buffalo Border Guard 1879.*

Page 162   *'Some time on the 21st...'* *Natal Witness*, 30 January 1879.

Page 164   *'There Lieutenant Frederick Scott...'* PRO WO 33/34.

Page 164   *'Scott gathered his carbineers...'* John Stalker, *The Natal Carbineers.*

Page 165   *'Two carbineers, one by the name...'* Stalker, *The Natal Carbineers.*

Page 166   *'It was a command...'* Philip Gon, *The Road to Isandlwana.*

Page 168   *'Since the initial placing of the picquets...'* P.S. Thompson, *The Natal Native Contingent.*

Page 169   *'They suddenly became aware of...'* Stalker, *The Natal Carbineers.*

Page 170   *'Barker and Hawkins hastened back to Scott...'* Scott sent three separate messages by Whitelaw, Swift and Barker respectively.

Page 171   *'It may well have been...'* Statement by mule driver, Hans Boer. WO 33/34 S6333.

Page 171   *'Lieutenant Pope...'* J.P. Mackinnon and S.H. Shadbolt, *The South African Campaign.*

Page 171–2   *'Private John Williams of the 1/24th...'* WO 33/34 S6333.

Page 172   *'Lieutenant Henry Curling...'* Private letter written by Curling to his mother. By courtesy of Mr T. Lucking.

Page 172   *'At this time Barry's No. 5 Company...'* Statement by Lt W.R. Higginson. WO 33/34 S6333.

Page 173   *'It appears that...'* Bulwer Papers, Natal Archives.

Page 174   *'Permission was granted...'* Brickhill's report. KCAL, Durban.

Page 175   *'Lieutenant Adendorff, formerly...'* Higginson's report. WO 33/34 S6333.

Page 176   *'Stafford was immediately...'* Lt H.D. Davies' report. WO 33/34 S6333.

Page 177   *'At about 9.40 a.m...'* Lt Col J.C. Russell's report. WO 32/7731 S6333.

Page 177   *'Then, having pondered further...'* Lt Milne, RN. ADM 16486 S6333.

Page 177   *'I shall never forget...'* Hamilton-Browne, *Lost Legionary.*

Page 180   *'Lieutenant Higginson and...'* WO 33/34 S6333.

Page 181   *'It was Durnford who...'* Brickhill's report, KCAL, Durban.

Page 181   *'Durnford, in response...'* WO 33/34 S6333.

Page 181   *'Led by Captain Barton...'* Report by Lt C. Raw. WO 33/34 S6333.

Page 181   *'Durnford had again usurped...'* WO 33/34 S6333.

Page 181   *'He asked Pulleine...'* Lt W.F.D. Cochrane. WO 33/34 S6333.

Page 184   *'Then, egging each other on...'* Recorded oral history local community, Isandlwana, 1999. In January 2002 the authors were privileged to discuss Zulu tactics with Lt Col S.B. Bourquin, the eminent Zulu linguist and Anglo-Zulu War historian who supplied the following additional information: 'One of the basic tactics of any Zulu military, or hunting attack on a herd of animals, is outflanking and encirclement. The Zulu commanders were astute enough to observe or know that the effect of volleys diminished towards the flanks and that volleys from two units spaced about twenty yards apart would be least effective in the intervening gap. Some fifty years ago, in the company of a well informed colleague, Charles Hignett [the grandson of Sir Melmoth Osborne] I had a conversation with an old Zulu at the Gqikazi site at Ulundi. Charles and I were passing by an inhabited homestead and according to Zulu custom picked up a polite conversation with an old man (perhaps eighty-five years old) who was busy outside one of the huts. He remembered that he had been at the battle of Isandlwana as an 'udibi' boy (fourteen/fifteen year old baggage carriers, boys who accompany the warrors). The 'izindibi' were ordered by some commanders ('izinduna') to leave all their impediments and any shields that might draw attention to them, and to run as fast as possible into the gap between the volley firing units. In the meantime the warriors would keep the soldiers busy. If the izindibi managed to get close enough they should then attack the soldiers on the flanks, or even get behind them, and attack with assegais which they were ordered to keep, and to cause confusion.'

Page 185–6   '*As the troops rode east…*' Lt H.D. Davies. WO 33/34 S6333.

Page 186   '*There were Zulus ahead…*' Lt C. Raw. WO 33/34 S6333.

Page 187   '*It was too much for the amaChunu…*' Lt C. Raw., WO 33/34 S6333.

Page 187   '*In the confusion…*' Captain C. Nourse. WO 33/34 63908.

Page 188   '*They were never seen again…*' Captain C. Nourse. WO 33/34 63908.

Page 188   '*Still holding the jumble of reins…*' Pte H. Grant. WO 33/34 S6333.

Page 188   '*To Durnford's indignation …*' Lt H.W. Davies. WO 33/34 S6333.

Page 189   '*It is likely that he detailed…*' Later in the morning Tpr F. Symons met several men of Durnford's NNH at Mangeni and wondered how they came to be there. F. Symons, 'Experiences of a Natal Carbineer', KCAL, Durban.

Page 189   '*Williams, in fact, helped…*' *Port Elizabeth Telegraph and Eastern Province Standard*, 28 February 1879.

Page 190   '*They did so, firing from…*' Stalker, *Natal Carbineers*.

Page 190   '*Davies, heading towards the British lines…*' Lt H. Davies. WO 33/34 S 6333.

Page 190   '*Durnford retorted icily…*' Pte Johnson. WO 33/34 S 6333.

Page 193   '*His most important…*' *The Red Book*, p. 58.

Page 198   '*In addition to the regiments…*' Hamilton-Browne, *Lost Legionary*.

Page 198   '*I believe about one…*' WO 32/7731 S6333.

Page 202   '*He was writing letters in his tent…*' Lt Essex's letter dated 26 January 1879, published in *The Times*, 2 April 1879. By courtesy of John Young, Anglo-Zulu War Research Society

Page 203   '*At the moment the line of riflemen…*' Evidence of Capt E. Essex, *London Gazette*, 15 March 1879.

Page 203   '*The NNH, having also…*' Lt C. Raw. WO 33/34 S 6333.

Page 204   '*I'm not an alarmist…*' Brickhill's report, KCAL, Durban.

Page 205   '*Barker was one of them…*' Tpr Barker, in Stalker, *The Natal Carbineers*.

Page 205   '*He was joined there by Cochrane…*' WO 33/34 S6333.

Page 208   '*Desperate for ammunition…*' 'Jabez Molife: "A South African Jigsaw Puzzle"', Keith Reeves, *Medal News*, August 1990.

Page 208   '*It seemed that nothing less…*' Lt H. Davies. WO 33/34 S6333.

Page 208   '*All the horsemen dismounted…*' Vause family document. By courtesy of Robin Stayt, Durban.

Page 209   '*Undeterred, Essex mounted his horse…*' Evidence of Capt E. Essex, *London Gazette*, 15 March 1879.

Page 209   '*It is unlikely that…*' It is possible that portions of E or F Companies were overwhelmed on the Tahelane Ridge itself. There is evidence to support this possibility. The *Natal Witness*, in a long account of the battle, reported, 'and the company of the 24th which had been sent up to the Nek had returned but it was cut off by the Zulu centre and never rejoined the rest… ' The *Witness* followed up with the publication of a private letter on 7 February 1879, portions of which read, 'Barker [Tpr Barker, NC] who escaped, says he saw one company which was sent on to the high hills to the left of the camp, 'to keep the Zulus back; they shot hundreds of them, but in five minutes there was not a man left. Two other companies were served the same way.' (Pages 61 and 86 *The Red Book*.) Even Lord Chelmsford was under the impression that at least one company of the 24th never made it back to camp. In his report to the Secretary of State for War, dated 27 January 1879 (WO 32/7725), he wrote, 'As regards the proceedings of the six companies of British Infantry, two guns and two rockets tubes, the Garrison of the camp – I can obtain but little information. One Company went off to the extreme left and has never been heard of since.' In support there is also more recent evidence.

The late George Chadwick, whilst a member of the National Monuments Council, wrote a pamphlet – undated, but likely written in the 1970s – containing the following statement: 'At the same time a search was made for neglected cairns. Some 40 were found, carefully examined, photographed, fully documented and marked on the map. They included those on the ridge where the British regiments were stationed as well as on the trail of the fugitives. In view of the statements that very few were killed on the ridge mentioned above, it is interesting to note that buttons, boot protectors and bones were found when these cairns were dismantled, documented and rebuilt.' Alas, an extensive search by the authors has failed to locate the map and other items referred to by George Chadwick. (The authors are grateful to Adrian Greaves for drawing their attention to Mr Chadwick's pamphlet). It has been noted that Lt Edgar Anstey was an officer of Mostyn's F Company, yet his corpse was found along the Fugitives' Trail, a considerable distance from the Tahelane Ridge, thus casting doubt on the suggestion that all the personnel of E and F Companies were overwhelmed either before or on reaching the camp. This may be explained by the fact that as Anstey and a portion of F Company were out of camp effecting road repairs when the battle started, it is possible that they may not have rejoined F Company before it climbed to the ridge.

Page 209   *'Vause, having been in…'* Vause family document. By courtesy of Robin Stayt, Durban.

Page 211   *'As the Zulu commanders watched…'* Laband, *Rope of Sand*.

Page 211   *'Back in the camp, those not…'* Pte J. Williams. WO 33/34 S6333.

Page 211   *'But as they went the gunners…'* Private letter written by Lt Curling to his mother. By courtesy of Tony Lucking.

Page 212   *'Shortly after the battle…'* Technical details of the partial eclipse at Isandlwana: 22 January 1879. Location: 28°19'30"S 30°39'10"E; 2 hours ahead of GMT; 1000m above sea level; eclipse begins: 13:10:07; eclipse ends: 15:51:53; sun's altitude: 73°39'; azimuth 298°29'; eclipse maximum: 14:36:00; sun's altitude: 55°32', azimuth 276°15'; magnitude of eclipse: 0.650; moon's altitude: 55°23'; azimuth 276°26'; size ratio of moon to sun: 0.968; sun's altitude: 38°52', azimuth 266°44'.

Page 212   *'James Pullen, the quartermaster…'* Brickhill's report. KCAL, Durban.

Page 212   *'Durnford hurried off to rally…'* Account by Lt E. Essex. *Anglo-Zulu War Research Society Journal*, 'A Race for Dear Life'. Source *The Times* 2 April 1879.

Page 212   *'Private Williams and his mates…'* Pte J. Williams. WO 33/34 S6333.

Page 213   *'even as he did so Zulus…'* Tpr Barker in Stalker, *The Natal Carbineers*.

Page 213   *'The Hlubi Troop paused…'* 'Jabez Molife', Keith Reeves, *Medal News*, August 1990.

Page 213   *'Sergeant-Major Kambule of…'* Account by the Rev. Owen Watkins. Natal Archives.

Page 213   *'The colonials made a run…'* Tpr Barker in Stalker, *The Natal Carbineers*.

Page 214   *'We were then chased…'* Nyanda. WO 32/7713 S6316.

Page 214–5   *'A little further on…'* H.G. Mainwairing. Private M/S Cairo, 1895, Royal Regiment of Wales Museum, Brecon.

Page 216   *'Fynn hurried forward…'* Henry Francis Fynn, private M/S KCAL, Durban. Also *Natal Witness*, January 1913.

Page 216   *'With Chelmsford leading…'* Lt Milne, RN. WO 16486 S6333.

Page 216   *'Chelmsford did not approve…'* Lt Milne, RN. WO 16486 S6333.

Page 217   *'It is significant that these scribbled messages...'* WO 33/34 S6333, p. 79 reads:
'1. Copies (originals written in pencil)
Staff Officer,
Heavy firing to left of our camp. Cannot move camp at present.
  HB Pulleine, Lieut-Colonel
(Addressed Staff Officer, handed by General to A.M.S. following day, 23rd
  January).
2. Received by Major Gosset about 3 p.m. on 22nd January.
Heavy firing near left of camp. Shepstone has come in for reinforcements, and
  reports the Basutos [NNH] falling back. The white force at camp turned out
  and fighting about one mile to left flank.
  Alan Gardner, Captain, S.O.
(Addressed Major Clery, S.O., handed to A.M.S. [Crealock] 23rd January, by
  Major Gosset.)'

Page 217   *'Almost a year later...'* Lt Mainwairing found a broken colour pole on the top of
Black's Koppie and Major Bromhead found another some way along the Fugitives' Trail.

Page 218   *'As one Boer was later...'* Commandant P. Raaff, Raaff's Transvaal Rangers.

Page 218   *'One wife was to write...'* Mrs R. Campbell, wife of Captain the Hon. R.
Campbell. Lock, *Blood on the Painted Mountain*.

Page 218   *'Imagine a gentle slope...'* Wood, *Winnowed Memories*.

Page 219   *'Mehlokazulu, son of Chief Sihayo...'* *The Red Book*, p. 349.

Page 219   *'Inspector Mansel believed...'* Mansel's letters dated 1 November 1879 and 23
November 1880, KCAL, Durban.

Page 224   *'According to Hamilton-Browne's memoirs...'* Hamilton-Browne, *Lost Legionary*.

Page 224   *'Russell's version...'* Russell's report WO 32/7731 S6333.

Page 225   *'Moments passed in silence...'* Milne's report and Hamilton-Browne's memoirs.

Page 225   *'But I left over 1,000 men...'* French, *Lord Chelmsford and the Zulu War*.

Page 225   *'Hallam Parr's reaction...'* Recollections and Correspondence 1917. The Royal
Archives Windsor, VIC/O 33/118.

Page 226   *'The camp was...'* Col J.C. Russell's report. WO 32/7731 S6333.

Page 227   *'Dartnell then approached Chelmsford...'* Mansel's letters dated 1 November 1879
and 23 November 1880, KCAL, Durban.

Page 227   *'The Zulus were more or less...'* Maxwell, *Reminiscences of the Zulu War*.

Page 227   *'On one occasion...'* Maxwell, *Reminiscences of the Zulu War*.

Page 229   *'One actually names a boy...'* Letter of Private W. Sweeney 2/24th published in
the *Oldham Weekly Chronicle*, 26 April 1879. By courtesy of John Young, Anglo-Zulu War
Research Society.

Page 229   *'Our attention was drawn...'* Cornelius Vijn, *Cetshwayo's Dutchman*.

Page 231   *'So sudden was their appearance...'* Mansel's letters dated 1 November 1879 and
23 November 1880, KCAL, Durban.

Page 231–2   *'Altogether we buried...'* M/S diary of Tpr William James Clarke NMP, KCAL,
Durban.

Page 232   *'Lieutenant-Colonel Crealock mentioned...'* Extract from private journal, Royal
Archives, Windsor, RA VIC/O 33/34.

Page 232   *'it is possible that all the Zulu...'* Later in the war the non-treatment of Zulu
wounded was raised in the House of Commons (17 June 1879). Although in reply it was
quoted that in a couple of instances 'several' Zulus had been treated for their wounds,
there was no explanation of the fate of the hundreds of Zulu wounded who must have
fallen into British hands after the battles of Rorke's Drift, Kambula and Ulundi.
(Information regarding the questions raised in the House of Commons, kindly supplied
by Lee Stevenson.)

Page 232   *'Twenty-eight years later...'* Smith-Dorrien, M/S, Royal Regiment of Wales Museum, Brecon.

Page 232   *'And in 1914...'* Samuel Pitts, *Western Mail*, 11 May 1914.

Page 236   *'Take it to the General...'* Alison letters, Brenthurst Library, Johannesburg.

Page 236   *'Lying on my face and hands, close by his camp bed...'* Alison letters, Brenthurst Library, Johannesburg.

Page 237   *'You are to march to the camp...'* Edward Durnford, *A Soldier's Life and Work in South Africa.*

Page 237   *'Soon after 2 a.m. on the 22nd January...'* Supplement to the *London Gazette* No. 24695, 14 March 1879.

Page 238   *'Major Clery, (Col Glyn's...'* The Royal Archives, Windsor, RA/VIC/O 33/44

Page 238   *'An express was sent off to Lieutenant-Colonel Durnford...'* Laband and Knight, *Archives of Zululand: The Anglo-Zulu War*, p. 75.

Page 239   *'It has been officially stated that Colonel Durnford...'* Durnford, *A Soldier's Life.*

Page 239   *'But the main spring of my action has been...'* Durnford, *A Soldier's Life.*

Page 239   *'I imagine you refer to the copy of the orders...'* Royal Engineers Museum, Chatham, A31 4901/31/1.

Page 240   *'Telegram of 23rd detailing poor Durnford's defeat...'* PRO 32/7711-56316

Page 240   *'He [Chelmsford] feels the calamity more...'* The Royal Archives, Windsor, VIC/Add E 1/8514.

Page 242   *'Dear Colonel Durnford, I must apologise...'* Royal Engineers Museum, Chatham. A31 4901/31/2.

Page 243   *'Offy is a prominent member of the most powerful...'* Royal Engineers Museum, Chatham. A31 4901/31/1.

Page 243   *'Glyn's extreme stickiness was so well known...'* Alison letters, MS 165, The Brenthurst Library, Johannesburg.

Page 244   *'I went direct to each of the commanders...'* Alison letters, MS 165, The Brenthurst Library, Johannesburg.

Page 245   *'and the verbal orders...'* Supplement to the *London Gazette*, No. 24699, 15 March 1879.

Page 245   *'But I think you will have to understand...'* Alison letters, MS 165, The Brenthurst Library, Johannesburg.

Page 247   *'General and Crealock are starting now...'* PRO 1/6486 – 56333.

Page 248   *'During the night the native contingent...'* PRO 1/6486 – 56333

Page 248   *'My Dear General, The whole of the Native Contingent...'* Natal Archives, Pietermaritzburg, Natal. (Wood Papers)

Page 248   *'They formed up, called me their father...'* Hamilton-Browne, *Lost Legionary.*

Page 249   *We thought that at last we were going to have a brush...'* Special War Supplement to the *Natal Witness* dated 1 February 1879.

Page 249   *'They were paraded forming three sides of a square...'* PRO ADM 1/16486 – S6333.

Page 249   *'If only they would come out into the open...'* Vause family document. By courtesy of Robin Stayt, Durban.

Page 250   *'My opinion, as your Excellency is aware...'* Wood Papers, Natal Archives, Pietermaritzburg 1053/79.

Page 250   *'This had not entered the programme...'* Wood Papers, Natal Archives, Pietermaritzburg 1053/79.

Page 250   *'Their people did not like being under strange officers...'* Wood Papers, Natal Archives, Pietermaritzburg 1053/79.

Page 251   *'Colonel Hassard, R.E., had only just arrived up...'* Alison letters, MS 165, The Brenthurst Library, Johannesburg.

Page 252   '*I could send you up Lt. Col. Law…*' Wood Papers, Natal Archives, Pietermaritzburg.

Page 253   '*I cannot describe my feelings at the time…*' 'Experiences of a Natal Carbineer', Tpr F. Symons. KCAL, Durban.

Page 253   '*While I was going to the new camping ground…*' Arthur Harness. Autograph letters, MS 158, The Brenthurst Library, Johannesburg; cited in Clarke, *Zululand at War*.

Page 254   '*The Court has very properly abstained…*' *Supplement* to the *London Gazette*, No. 24695, 15 March 1879.

Page 254   '*A great deal more evidence was heard…*' Arthur Harness, Autograph letters, MS 158, The Brenthurst Library, Johannesburg.

Page 254–5   '*Of course I know that a dead set was made…*' KCAL 89/9/32/10

Page 255   '*From the time the column under my command…*' *Supplement* to the *London Gazette*, No. 24695, 14 March 1879.

Page 255   '*These news are fearful…*' The Royal Archives, Windsor. RA VIC/W9/135

Page 256   '*Does the Queen want a good map…*' The Royal Archives, Windsor. RA VIC/O 33/102

Page 256   '*It appears to be too sadly true that the body…*' The Royal Archives, Windsor, RA VIC/O 33/67

Page 257   '*It should be noted that poor Colonel Durnford…*' The Royal Archives, Windsor, RA VIC/O 34/20

Page 257   '*I cannot tell you how my thoughts…*' Alison letters, MS 165, The Brenthurst Library, Johannesburg.

Page 257–62   '*Now, Sir, I wish to say in the first place…*' Laband and Knight, *Archives of Zululand, The Anglo-Zulu War 1879*, p. 373.

Page 262   '*Soldiers, your sufferings, your privations, your valour…*' Laband and Knight, *Archives of Zululand, The Anglo-Zulu War 1879*, p. 485.

Page 263   '*Though the court of inquiry pronounced no opinion…*' Laband and Knight, *Archives of Zululand, The Anglo-Zulu War 1879*, p. 512.

Page 264   '*I am afraid the misfortune which has happened…*' Wood Papers, Natal Archives, Pietermaritzburg.

Page 264   '*I am thinking of doing away with tents…*' Wood Papers, Natal Archives, Pietermaritzburg.

Page 264   '*I wish I saw my way with honour…*' Wood Papers, Natal Archives, Pietermaritzburg.

Page 265   '*From the statements made before the court of inquiry…*' French, *Lord Chelmsford and the Zulu War*.

Page 265   '*HRH has perfect confidence in Lord Chelmsford's ability…*' PRO WO 30/129 56316

Page 265   '*It is quite true that Wolseley is an egotist…*' Joseph H. Lehmann, *All Sir Garnet*.

Page 266   '*I must honestly tell you that Chelmsford's account…*' Alison letters, MS 165, The Brenthurst Library, Johannesburg.

Page 266   '*It would be hardly fair to saddle me…*' The Royal Archives, Windsor. RA VIC/Add E 1/8629.

Page 266   '*The Secretary of State & myself…*' The Royal Archives, Windsor. RA VIC/Add E 1/8577

Page 266–7   '*HRH is well aware that your Lordship's dispatch…*' PRO WO 30/129 56316.

Page 268   '*The General and his staff joined our camp…*' Alison letters, MS 165, The Brenthurst Library, Johannesburg.

Page 268–9   '*The L. General was under the impression…*' PRO WO 33/34 56333.

Page 269   '*Col. Glyn and Major Spalding…*' PRO 30/129 56316.

Page 269   '*It is now so long ago since…*' PRO 30/129 56316.

Page 269   '*Captain Rainforth's company 1/24th Regt…*' PRO 30/129 56316.

Page 269   *'I rode over to Helmekaar with a written order…'* PRO 30/129 56316.

Page 270   *'I was under the impression until very lately…'* PRO 30/129 56316.

Page 270   *'The labour of getting troops and supplies…'* PRO WO 33 /34 56333.

Page 271   *'The camp should be partially entrenched…'* Regulations Field Forces South Africa 1878, paragraph 19.

Page 271   *'The Isandlwana hill had been the point selected…'* PRO 33/34 56333.

Page 271   *'There was no ground that commanded it to the left…'* Laband and Knight, *Archives of Zululand, The Anglo-Zulu War 1879*, page 479.

Page 271   *'I consider that there never was a position…'* French, *Lord Chelmsford and the Zulu War*.

Page 271–2   *'I would call this position a good defensible one…'* PRO 33/34 56333.

Page 272   *'The wagons which accompanied the troops…'* PRO WO 33/34 56333.

Page 272   *'Distinct orders were left by Colonel Glyn…'* PRO WO 30/129 56316.

Page 273   *'The contingent was to consist of three regiments…'* Durnford, *A Soldier's Life and Work in South Africa*.

Page 274   *'Oh never mind. The general will have had time…'* Durnford, *A Soldier's Life and Work in South Africa*.

Page 274   *'Col. Glyn with the 2/24th was to move…'* The Royal Archives, Windsor. RA VIC/O 33/44.

Page 275   *'Major Dartnell took with him on the 21st…'* PRO WO 33/34 56333.

Page 275   *'The only native report was received at 4.30 p.m…'* PRO 33/34 56333.

Page 276   *'I took a couple of mounted men and gave chase…'* KCAL, Durban, 89/9/32/1 (a).

Page 276   *'I have already reported, my aide-de-camp…'* PRO 33/34 56333.

Page 277   *'Whilst the operations were going on Colonel Glyn received…'* Supplement to the *London Gazette*, No. 24688, 1 March 1879.

Page 277   *'A slip of paper was received by the General…'* PRO ADM 1/6486 56333

Page 277   *'I received no report whatever…'* PRO WO 33/34 56333

Page 278   *'When morning broke on their miserable bivouac…'* The Royal Archives, Windsor. RA VIC/O 33/80

Page 278   *'The question will no doubt be asked…'* French, *Lord Chelmsford and the Zulu War.*

Page 278   *'With regard to reserve ammunition…'* PRO 33/34 56333

Page 278–9   *'I should be obliged by your asking Major Clery…'* PRO 33/34 56333.

Page 280   *'I think with you that this explanation…'* PRO WO 30/129 56316.

Page 280   *'The scattering of one regular battalion…'* PRO WO 30/129 56316.

Page 280–1   *'My Lord, The Field Marshal Commanding in Chief…'* PRO WO 30/129 56316.

Page 282   *'The facts were as follows…'* Royal Engineers Museum, Chatham, A31 4901–31/7.

Page 283   *'Colonel Pulleine sent out to strengthen his outlying picquets…'* Royal Regiment of Wales Museum, Brecon.

Page 287   *'My father, Mpande, belonged to the English…'* C. de B. Webb and J.B. Wright, eds., *A Zulu King Speaks*.

Page 287   *'I will not make any treaty or agreement…'* C.T. Binns, *The Last Zulu King*.

Page 289   *'Its colours now carry…'* Mark Coghlan, *Pro Patria* [History of the Natal Carbineers 1945–95].

Page 289   *'The Natal Native Horse…'* Wood, *Winnowed Memories*.

Page 289   *'However, when it came…'* Ron Lock, 'Britain's Tribesmen on Horseback', *Military Illustrated*, January 1997.

Page 290   *'There was, however…'* Ron Lock, 'Britain's Tribesmen on Horseback', *Military Illustrated*, January 1997.

Page 290   *'Over 900 of them…'* J.S. Mohlamme, 'Soldiers without Reward,' *Journal of the South African Military History Society*.

Page 290   *'There can be no doubt…'* Precis of Information Concerning Zululand.

Page 290   *'The descendant regiment...'* Ron Lock, 'The Making of the Peace', *Military Illustrated*, May 1997.

Page 290   *'I don't feel satisfied...'* Adrian Preston, ed., *Sir Garnet Wolseley's South African Journal, 1879–1880.*

Page 291   *'That his [Bulwer's] opinions and views were pooh-poohed...'* Preston, *Sir Garnet Wolseley's South African Journal.*

Page 291   *'I then left the guns...'* Supplement to the *London Gazette*, No. 24695.

Page 291   *'About quarter of a mile on I found a pony...'* WO 33/34 S6333.

Page 293   *'The Mounted Infantry reported the Zulus...'* Royal Regiment of Wales Museum, Brecon.

Page 293   *'In the evening we heard more of the matter...'* Royal Archives Windsor RA/VIC/O 33/118.

Page 293   *'Her most Gracious Majesty...'* The Red Book, p. 209.

Page 296   *'On the way home we found some fowls...'* National Army Museum, London. Copyright Patrick Coghill.

Page 296   *'Melvill said he could go no further and Coghill said the same...'* Higginson's report to Lord Chelmsford from Rorke's Drift dated 17 February 1879.

Page 297   *'Heroes have been made of men like Melvill and Coghill...'* Preston, *Sir Garnet Wolseley's South African Journal.*

Page 297   *'One of the Carbineers, who arrived in Maritzburg...'* The Red Book, p. 40.

Page 298   *'The whole of the garrison, consisting of detachments...'* Durnford, *A Soldier's Life.*

Page 298   *'I have rarely met a man who, at first sight...'* Lt-Col S.B. Bourquin Papers, KCAL, Durban, 39/42/107/13.

Page 298   *'Prince Dabulamanzi...'* Adolf Schiel, *23 Jahre Sturm und Sonneshein in Süd Afrika.*

Page 299   *'Gentlemen, I have been publicly accused...'* The Red Book, p. 324.

Page 299   *'Her Majesty was so gracious to me...'* Wood Papers, Natal Archives, Pietermaritzburg.

Page 299   *'The headquarters staff is very weak...'* Alison letters, MS 165, The Brenthurst Library, Johannesburg.

Page 299   *'The news from the Cape very unsatisfactory...'* Preston, *Sir Garnet Wolseley's South African Journal.*

Page 300   *'My line is to get Chelmsford out of the country...'* Preston, *Sir Garnet Wolseley's South African Journal.*

Page 300   *'Why is it that the men with Lord Chelmsford's Column... '* Preston, *Sir Garnet Wolseley's South African Journal.*

Page 300   *'I think it is very unfair, and is merely a repetition...'* Preston, *Sir Garnet Wolseley's South African Journal.*

Page 300   *'I put up with dear old Wood...'* Preston, *Sir Garnet Wolseley's South African Journal.*

Page 301   *'Three years after the battle...'* Bertram Mitford, *Through the Zulu Country.*

Page 324   *'A further consideration...'* Precis of Information Concerning Zululand.

Appendix A

Chronology

❖

Events Leading to the Invasion of Zululand

1816
: Shaka kaSenzangakhona succeeds his father and, as king, forges the Zulu nation.

1824 May
: The first British trader/settlers arrive at the site of present-day Durban harbour and obtain King Shaka's permission to establish a settlement.

1828 September
: Shaka is assassinated by his brother Dingane.

1837–38
: Boer settlers, led by Piet Retief and travelling by ox wagon from the Cape, arrive over the Drakensberg Mountains and enter the Zulu Kingdom. A party of Boers visits King Dingane and attempts to negotiate the purchase of land. Having been sent by Dingane to fulfil certain conditions, a party of seventy Boers subsequently returns only to be put to death by Dingane.

1838 December
: More Boers, travelling up from the Cape and intent on revenge, seek a confrontation with Dingane. Led by Andries Pretorius, the Boers engage and defeat a large Zulu army at Blood River. The British, concerned at Boer activities along the northern border of the Cape, send a detachment of British soldiers under the command of Captain Henry Jarvis to the future site of Durban harbour.

1839 December
: Jarvis negotiates a peace treaty between the Boers and the defeated Zulu king whereby the Boers acquire sovereignty over the Zulu Kingdom south of the Tugela River. Jarvis and his troops are withdrawn back to the Cape. The exultant Boers proclaim a republic which they name Natalia.

1840 February
: A combined force of Boers and Zulu warriors loyal to Dingane's brother, Mpande, attacks an army loyal to Dingane. Dingane is defeated and later put to death by his traditional enemies, the amaSwazi. Mpande, the father of the teenage Cetshwayo, becomes king. The Boers demand and get further land from Mpande in payment for their support.

1840/41
: The Boers, seeking to expand the boundaries of their Natalia Republic, make forays south towards the Cape, into the land of the amaPondo.

1842
: The British government, again alarmed at the disturbances on its northern border, decides to bring the Boers under British authority. A detachment of the 27th Regiment is sent north and, after an epic

	march, reaches Natalia. The Boers are unsuccessfully engaged and the British force besieged. Finally a British warship arrives, carrying reinforcements, and the Boers are put to flight.
1843	Britain proclaims the former Boer Republic of Natalia to be a District of the Cape and restores to the Zulu Kingdom all the land north of the Tugela River. The Zulu kingdom and its white neighbours in Natal are destined to live in peace for many years to come.
1856	Natal becomes a British colony. Cetshwayo, the future Zulu king, engages the forces of his rival brother, Mbuyazi, who is defeated with great slaughter.
1861	Mpande finally acknowledges Cetshwayo as his successor.
1873	Cetshwayo, with British approval and support, is crowned King of the Zulu Nation. Later in the year the Colony of Natal is put in a state of alarm when Langalibalele, a Hlubi chief living within the colony near Ladysmith, refuses to register the firearms owned by his tribe. Battle of Bushman's Pass. Langalibalele escapes.
1874	Langalibalele captured and exiled. Lord Carnarvon, Secretary of State for the Colonies, decides on a policy of confederation for southern Africa.
1876	To achieve his goal of confederation, Lord Carnarvon considers annexing the Transvaal.
1877	Instructed by Lord Carnarvon, Sir Theophilus Shepstone annexes the Transvaal. Sir Bartle Frere appointed British High Commissioner for South East Africa.
1878	Lord Carnarvon resigns as Secretary of State for the Colonies and is replaced by Sir Michael Hicks Beach. A boundary commission is appointed to settle a long standing territorial dispute between the Boers and the Zulus. The commission finds in favour of the Zulu. Sir Bartle Frere, pursuing the aim of confederation, temporarily suppresses the findings of the commission. Lord Chelmsford appointed General Officer Commanding H.M. Forces in southern Africa. As the final step to confederation, Sir Bartle contrives to justify the subjugation of Zululand and issues an ultimatum to King Cetshwayo.
1879, 11 January	The ultimatum expires. British troops invade the Zulu Kingdom.

The Battle of Isandlwana

(Please refer to the note at the beginning of Chapter Six with regard to time discrepancies. All times given in this Chronology are approximate).

11 January	No. 3 Column crosses Buffalo River. The invasion of Zululand commences.
12 January	Sihayo's stronghold attacked.

20 January

a.m.   Camp established on eastern slopes of Isandlwana.

1.00 p.m.   Lord Chelmsford arrives at camp and departs immediately to reconnoitre Mangeni Falls area ten miles to south-east. Returns at 6.30 p.m.

21 January

4.30 a.m.   Lord Chelmsford orders Major Dartnell with a mounted force and Commandant Lonsdale with sixteen companies of NNC to reconnoitre the area visited the previous day.

early a.m.   Lt Browne and small party of MI reconnoitre Isipesi Hill area. Browne returns midday and reports a skirmish with the Zulus.

4.00 p.m.   Lord Chelmsford and staff proceed to the iThusi Heights where they observe a party of fourteen mounted Zulus four miles north/north-east.

22 January

1.30 a.m.   Lord Chelmsford receives message from Dartnell requesting imperial infantry support in order to attack a large Zulu force confronting him.

During the night   Zulu scouts call to an NNC picquet on duty close to the camp.

4.30 a.m.   Lord Chelmsford, with Col Glyn, marches out of camp to link up with Dartnell, talking half of the imperial infantry and two-thirds of the artillery guns, leaving Lt-Col Pulleine to command the camp.

7.00 a.m.   Troopers of the Natal Carbineers, on vedette duty east of Conical Hill, and one mile north of Qwabe, report thousands of Zulu deploying from Ngwebini Valley.

7.30 a.m.   Lt Scott, commanding the vedettes, reports the Zulu advance to Lt-Col Pulleine.

7.45 a.m.   Alarm sounded and infantry under arms drawn up in front of camp.

8.05 a.m.   Pulleine despatches note to Glyn that Zulus are advancing in force from left front of camp.

8.30–9.00 a.m.   Mounted vedettes engage advancing Zulus close to Conical Hill.

9.45 a.m.   Lt Chard reports seeing large numbers of Zulu moving east to west over Nqutu Ridge.

9.45 a.m.   Lt Pope reports 7,000 additional Zulu on Nqutu Ridge, over and above those previously sighted.

10.30 a.m.   Col Durnford, commanding No. 2 Column, arrives at Isandlwana.

10.45 a.m.   Infantry 'stood down'.

11.00 a.m.   Alarm again sounded and infantry fall in for second time. Two troops of NNH are sent by Durnford to reconnoitre Nqutu Plateau and beyond.

11.25 a.m.   Durnford leaves camp with Hlubi and Edendale Troops to intercept Zulus. Rocket battery follows.

11.40 a.m.   Two troops of NNH on Nqutu Ridge encounter the main Zulu army.

11.45 a.m.   Cavaye's company on Tahelane Ridge open fire at 800 yards on Zulu right horn heading west.

11.45 a.m.	Mostyn's company ordered to reinforce Cavaye's company.
11.45 a.m.	Rocket battery destroyed near Conical Hill.
noon	Zulu left horn engages Durnford. Zulu right centre engages Mostyn and Cavaye. Zulu right horn continues outflanking movement behind Isandlwana.
noon	Gardner arrives at camp with instructions from Chelmsford ordering Pulleine to move portion of camp to Mangeni Falls. Both Pulleine and Gardner despatch messages to Chelmsford that camp is threatened.
noon	Capt Shepstone of the NNH informs Pulleine that the Zulu army is advancing on the camp.
noon	Durnford makes a fighting withdrawal to Nyokana *donga* east of the camp.
12.10 p.m.	Artillery guns continue firing at 3,400 yards on Zulu centre. Pope's company of the 2/24th deployed on British right flank.
12.15 p.m.	Cavaye and Mostyn ordered to retire to the camp. Younghusband's company advances to protect their left flank.
12.15 p.m.	Ntshingwayo, the Zulu commander, establishes his command post on Nyoni Ridge. Runners used to execute his tactical orders.
12.30 p.m.	Zulu right chest engaged by Younghusband as Mostyn and Cavaye retire onto the camp. Zulus follow.
12.30 p.m.	Durnford's Hlubi and Edendale Troops, reinforced by mounted volunteers, inflict severe casualties on Zulu left horn.
12.30 p.m.	General advance made by Zulu chest. Imperial infantry firing volleys inflict severe casualties. Left horn begins to outflank Durnford's position at Nyokana *donga*.
12.45 p.m.	Durnford, short of ammunition and being outflanked, retires on the camp.
12.55 p.m.	Zulu right horn enters camp.
12.55 p.m.	Lt Melvill leaves camp with encased 1/24th Queen's Colour.
1.00 p.m.	Zulu chest, showing great determination, closes with the infantry.
1.00 p.m.	Artillery guns attempt to leave camp.
1.00–1.15 p.m.	General hand-to-hand fighting in camp.
1.15 p.m.	Durnford's last stand.
1.20 p.m.	Younghusband's last stand.
1.30 p.m.	Zulus haul down Union flag from Chelmsford's headquarters flagpole. Scattered resistance whilst camp is plundered by victorious Zulus.

Chelmsford's Operation in Mangeni Falls Area

22 January

6.15 a.m.	Chelmsford links up with Major Dartnell. No sign of Zulus in strength.

7.00 a.m.	Chelmsford orders Dartnell to sweep beyond and to the north of Mangeni Falls. NNC ordered to clear Magogo Hills.
7.30–9.00 a.m.	Chelmsford and escort move up the Magogo Valley and halt for breakfast.
7.30–9.30 a.m.	Dartnell skirmishes with scattered parties of Zulu.
9.30 a.m.	Pulleine's note to Glyn, written at 8.05 a.m. indicating that Zulus were 'advancing on the camp,' handed to Chelmsford.
9.40 a.m.	Milne despatched to Silutshana Hill to observe camp.
9.40 a.m.	Russell with mounted infantry ordered to reconnoitre north towards Isipesi Hill.
10.00 a.m.	Harness' artillery, hampered by *dongas*, is ordered back to the Mangeni track.
10.30 a.m.	Gardner ordered back to camp with a note for Pulleine to strike portion of camp.
10.30 a.m.	Commandant Hamilton-Browne, NNC, ordered back to camp to assist in striking the tents.
11.15 a.m.	Chelmsford moves over Magogo Hill to the proposed camp site at Mangeni Falls.
11.15–3.00 p.m.	Numerous messages indicating that the camp is under attack allegedly fail to reach Chelmsford.
12.30 p.m.	Chelmsford arrives at Mangeni Falls area.
1.15 p.m.	Harness receives Hamilton-Browne's final message that the camp is under attack. Escorted by Russell's MI and two companies of 2/24th, he proceeds back towards Isandlwana.
2.00 p.m.	Harness recalled to Mangeni on Chelmsford's instructions.
3.00 p.m.	Chelmsford receives Pulleine's and Gardner's messages and decides to investigate the situation. With escort and staff heads back to Isandlwana.
3.30 p.m.	Chelmsford meets Hamilton-Browne who reports that the camp is in Zulu hands.
3.45 p.m.	Lonsdale confirms that the camp has fallen.
4.00 p.m.	Chelmsford sends orders to Glyn and Harness to return to Isandlwana.
6.15 p.m.	Entire column assembles two and a half miles east of Isandlwana.
6.30 p.m.	Column advances on camp.
7.30–8.00 p.m.	Camp re-occupied and troops bivouac on *nek*.
23 January	
4.30 a.m.	Column departs Isandlwana for Rorke's Drift.
8.30 a.m.	Column arrives at Rorke's Drift.

Appendix B

Regiments of the Zulu Army

An Abbreviation of F.B. Finney's List of 1878

(including Finney's spelling of Regiment Names)

Name of regiment	No of men	Age of warrior	Raised by	Headband leopard	Headband otter	Feathers	Shield
Usipexi	10	80	Shaka		*	Blue crane	white
Nokenke	2000	30	Mpande	*		Two of sakabuli	black & white
Mbelebele	?	78	Shaka	*		blue crane	white red spots
Umlanga	1000	28	Mpande	*		black & white ostrich	black with white spots
Umblambongwenya	?	75	Shaka		*	Blue crane	white
Umxapu	2000	35	Mpande	*		black ostrich	?
Udukuza	?	73	Shaka		*	blue crane	white
Iowa	500	35	Mpande	*		black & white ostrich	black & some red & white
Bulawayo	?	70	Shaka	*		blue crane	white
Nengamgeni	1000	35	Mpande	*		blue crane	
Udblambhlu	?	68	Dingane		*	blue crane	white with red or black spots
Ngwekwe	1000	55	Mpande		*	blue crane	white with red or black spots

Name of regiment	No of men	Age of warrior	Raised by	Headband leopard	Headband otter	Feathers	Shield
Ngulube	500	53	Mpande		*	blue crane	white with red or black spots
Inkulutyane	?	64	Dingane		*	blue crane	white
Umsikaka	?	54	Mpande		*	blue crane	white
Udududu	1500	35	Mpande		*	plumes of sakabuli	black with white spots
Undabakaombi	400	60	Dingane		*	plumes of sakabuli	black with white spots
Umkusi	600	55	Dingane		*	plumes of sakabuli	black with white spots
Isanqu	1500	54	Mpande		*		white
Tulwana	1500	45	Mpande		*	two large plumes sakabuli	white
Akonkone	500	43	Mpande		*	two large plumes sakabuli	white
Ndhlondhlo	900	43	Mpande		*	two large plumes sakabuli	white
Indluyengwe	1000	28	Mpande	*		two large plumes sakabuli	black with white spot
Nkobamakosi	6000	24	Cetshwayo	*		two large plumes sakabuli	black/red & spotted
Umbonambi	1500	32	Mpande	*		one plume sakabuli	black & black with white
Amashutli	500	32	Mpande	*		one plume sakabuli	black & black with white
Umcijo	2500	28	Mpande	*		one plume sakabuli	black
Ungakamatye	5000	30	Mpande	*		one plume sakabuli	black
Umtulisazwi	1500	29	Mpande	*		one plume sakabuli	black
Umzinyati	500	43	Mpande		*	blue crane	white with black spots
Uve	3500	23	Cetshwayo	*		plumes of sakabuli	black/red with spots

Appendix C
The Ammunition Controversy

<hr>

Of the many controversies that still surround the battle of Isandlwana, none is more enduring than the failure or otherwise of the ammunition supply to the British firing line; and whether or not the construction of the ammunition boxes was wholly or partly to blame.

At the height of the battle there were, in fact, three firing lines, separated from each other by considerable distances:

1. The Nyokana *donga*

This position was manned by the Hlubi and Edendale Troops of the NNH, commanded by Colonel Durnford, totalling approximately 100 mounted men and supported in the later stages of the battle by as many as fifty mounted colonials. As already described, this force, having made a fighting retreat for several miles, was short of ammunition when it took up its final stand in the *donga*. Black troopers were dispatched to the camp a mile away for replenishments, but as Durnford's own wagons were yet to arrive, the troopers sought ammunition from the imperial quartermasters of the British infantry. The troopers were refused: either through cussedness because they were black; or because the quartermasters were, in the circumstances, mistakenly nurturing their own stocks; or because there was difficulty in opening the ammunition boxes thus causing a pile-up of runners at the point of distribution.

When the troopers returned to the *donga* empty handed, at least two white officers of the NNH, Davies and Henderson, galloped to the camp but were no more successful than the troopers had been. It is interesting to speculate why Lieutenant Cochrane, the only imperial officer attached to the NNH and who was in the *donga* with Davies, was not sent as he would have been able to exert far more authority on the imperial quartermasters than the colonials. Finally, running out of ammunition and having been denied more, both troops were forced to abandon the *donga* and, perhaps in disdain of their treatment, abandoned the battlefield altogether. On their way through the camp at least some of the troopers encountered the late, but opportune, arrival of their own column's wagons and replenished their empty bandoliers. However, by that time the camp had been overrun from all sides and the Edendale Troop rode on to Fugitives' Drift where, without the disciplined conduct of its troopers, it is unlikely that the many fugitives who followed in their wake would have survived. As Trooper Clarke subsequently wrote:

> 'When we caught up [with] C. Raw... his mounted Basutos were already on the Natal side of the river, and had it not been for the Basutos I doubt if a single white man would have escaped by Fugitives' Drift, as they kept the Zulus in check while the few escaped.'

2. The Tahelane Ridge

This position was held by Mostyn's and Cavaye's companies joined by Raw's and Roberts' troops of the NNH. They were supported by Younghusband's company in reserve below, and soon to be reinforced by Vause's troop of the NNH plus Stafford's company of the NNC. Thus there would have been many more troops in this location than there ever would be in the so-called 'firing line' to the front of the camp:

Three companies of 24th	approximately 250 men
Three troops NNH	approximately 150 men
Total:	400 men *

All armed with breech-loading rifles

One company of Stafford's NNC	120 men
Total:	520 men

Their scattered position on the ridge, over steep and broken ground, was 1–1½ miles from the centre of the camp, and 1¼–2 miles from Durnford's position in the Nyokana *donga*, and from the 'firing line' ¾ mile, distances which would have fluctuated as the battle ebbed and flowed. The NNH had been conducting a fighting retreat and the infantry companies had been firing away for some while at elements of the Zulu right horn passing their position at 800 yards. Both units had used a considerable amount of ammunition. Shortly thereafter they were ordered to retire on the camp. As they did so they were pursued by overwhelming numbers of the enemy and Lieutenant Essex, advised that ammunition was running low, returned to the camp where he organised, 'bandsmen, cooks and et cetera', under the charge of an officer, to carry boxes of ammunition to the line. He also mentioned loading a mule cart with the intention of taking it to the line himself but, before he could do so, he was distracted by the appearance of the enemy entering the camp from the rear.

Just at the moment that Essex was distracted, Bloomfield the quartermaster of the 2/24th, was shot dead and Essex found that the Zulus had closed to within 200 yards of the line which had been retreating ever since Essex had left to get ammunition. It therefore seems questionable as to whether ammunition ever got to the line in time to be of any use. More likely, that the unarmed bandsmen and cooks with so many elements fleeing the camp and seeing the oncoming mass of the enemy, dropped their seventy-eight pound burdens and ran.

Essex made no reference to the ammunition boxes of the 2/24th being difficult to open and as far as Essex's evidence is concerned, there is no reason to assume that they were. On the balance of probability, the line ran short of ammunition but for no other reason than that no reserve had been taken out initially and so when the need arose, the line was too far from the camp, or too difficult to reach, to be replenished in time.

A further consideration is that, when engaged in vigorous activities such as fighting or doubling, the men were, through faulty equipment, subject to loosing some of their ammunition.[9] Each infantry man had an ammunition pouch on either side of his waist belt but the majority of his full issue was carried in a ball-bag (an archaic term which was still in use describing a cartridge bag). Major-General E. Newdigate, commander of the 2nd Division, wrote, 'Complaints were made about the ball-bags; the weight of the cartridges made the bags open, and when the men doubled the cartridges fell out.' Major A.R.P. Woodgate who was prominent in leading a bayonet charge at the Battle of Kambula, was equally condemning, 'with the ball-bags much ammunition was lost.' Colonel C.M. Clarke who led the 57th Regiment at the Battle of Gingindlovu wrote, 'the ball-bag was universally condemned: after a few days' wet it required constant repair.' Thus as Mostyn's and Cavaye's men fought up and down the Tahelane Ridge, much ammunition must have spilt to the ground as, no doubt, would have been the case in other sections of the battlefield. There were no 'firing line' survivors to report these losses.

3. The 'firing line'
The troops manning this position faced the chest of the Zulu Army and were the last to become engaged. Their location was approximately ⅓ mile north-east of the NNC lines, over ¾ mile from the 1/24th's lines and its ammunition supply, and approximately ¼ mile east of Mostyn's and Cavaye's companies at the moment they were overwhelmed.

The 'firing line' consisted of the two Royal Artillery 7-pounder cannon and three infantry companies, those of Wardell and Porteous of the 1/24th, and Pope's company of the 2/24th, totalling approximately 250 imperial infantry, and further supported by poorly armed elements of the NNC, many of whom fled as the tide of warriors approached.

Despite being the last to come into action, the 'firing line' had a target that could not be missed and which no doubt induced rapid fire on the part of the infantry. Had they been firing at a rate of say one round per ten seconds, seventy rounds would have been expended in less than twelve minutes, causing either Pulleine or Degacher to send runners to the 1/24th lines at an early stage for additional supplies.

Privates Williams and Bickley of the 1/24th, who survived, later mentioned ammunition being taken to the 'firing line':

> 'The companies out skirmishing were now apparently getting short of ammunition, and it was being carried out to them by bandsmen and wagon drivers and other unarmed people about the camp... Meanwhile [the 'firing line'] were firing volleys into the Zulus, who were only 100 to 150 yards distant from them. They kept this up till they got short of ammunition... the men in the camp – bandsmen and men on guard, and et cetera, were trying to take ammunition to the companies, but the greater part never got there, as I saw horses and mules with ammunition on their backs, galloping about the camp a short time afterwards.'

Private Wilson, a bandsman of the 1/24th, noticed ammunition being taken to the 'firing line' only ten minutes after the companies had been positioned in front of the camp. All these observations were in respect of ammunition being dispatched from the camp of the 1/24th and not from that of the 2/24th, several hundred yards away, where Essex had obtained ammunition a little earlier.

Again on the balance of probability, it is likely that a great portion of the ammunition en route to the 'firing line,' never reached its destination – and not only because of bolting pack horses and mules. With a wall of warriors only a few hundred yards beyond the 'firing line', the unarmed ammunition carriers must have been most reluctant to venture in that direction. Indeed they could not have failed to have seen the Hlubi and Edendale Troops, and numerous other people, fleeing the camp. Thus during their ¾ mile journey from the 1/24th's lines, either struggling with fractious animals or with a seventy-eight pound load, they most likely abandoned their duty and fled. It does not go unnoticed that Privates Williams, Bickley and Wilson, who fitted the criteria for ammunition carriers, managed to avoid being roped in for such duty and wisely escaped at the first opportunity.

There was undoubtedly a further hitch in the ammunition supply. For whatever reason at least some boxes were found difficult or impossible to open. Although Smith-Dorrien's famous story of the difficulties he experienced was not recounted until twenty-eight years later, this is hardly a reason to disbelieve a man of his calibre. He recalled: 'with thousands of rounds in the wagons 400 yards in the rear, there was none in the firing line, all had been used up.' He also recalled rounding up all the camp stragglers he could find, including the sick and artillery men in charge of spare horses, and setting them to work breaking open ammunition boxes 'as fast as we could and kept sending out packets to the firing line.'

As we have seen Essex did not experience a similar problem and the difficulties encountered in opening the 1/24th's boxes could have been due to climatic conditions that they had endured. The 1/24th had served far longer in Africa than had its more recently arrived sister battalion, and the brass screws that secured the lids of their boxes might well have become fast in their seatings, and impossible to move with an issue screwdriver. Or, alternatively, the necessary screwdriver could have been lost or mislaid. Thus the only way to get to the ammunition may have been to break the box open – easier said than done, it being of anything but puny construction.

Made either of teak or mahogany, the ⅞-inch thick planks, dovetailed or screwed into position were bound all round with two brass or copper bands, fastened every 2½ inches by brass screws. The box was made to withstand the roughest treatment and to protect the 600 rounds contained within its tin lining against any mishap. Access could only be gained by a tongue-and-groove sliding lid, often wedge shaped, located on top of the box and taking up about half its length. The sliding lid was secured by a single 2-inch brass screw which penetrated down into the front planking.

The only way of opening the box was by removing the screw or, in an emergency, smashing open the lid by brute force. At Isandlwana, for whatever cause, it became expedient to break open some of the boxes and so meet the difficulties related by Smith-Dorrien. The War Office, no doubt wishing to exonerate itself from any implication that the design of its box had contributed to the defeat, soon replaced the single screw with a quick release split-pin fastening and announced that the box in any event 'on emergency' could be opened by 'a good kick or a blow with a stone.' (It further justified the split-pin replacement by stating that the old screw fastening 'occasioned loss of time and even more serious consequences'; surely an oblique reference to Isandlwana?)

However, there remains a puzzle: in his description of breaking open the ammunition boxes Smith-Dorrien recounted the following conversation:

> 'Whilst I had been at it for some time, and when the 24th had fallen back to where we were, and the Zulus close behind them, Bloomfield, the quartermaster of the 2/24th said to me, "for heaven's sake don't take that man, for it belongs to our battalion" and I replied, "Hang it all, you don't want a requisition now do you?"'

It seems clear from Smith-Dorrien's account that, when he wrote of the 24th having 'fallen back to where we were', he was referring to the 'firing line', it being composed in the main by Wardell and Porteous' companies of the 1/24th – hence Bloomfield's reluctance to hand over 2/24th ammunition. Yet, according to Essex, by this time Bloomfield had been shot dead. After twenty-eight years, perhaps Smith-Dorrien had got Bloomfield mixed up with Quartermaster James Pullen of the 1/24th? The alternative is that Smith-Dorrien was talking to Bloomfield before Bloomfield was shot and the firing line referred to was that composed of the remnants of Cavaye's and Mostyn's companies. If that were the case, though, Smith-Dorrien would not have seen the end of the 'firing line', having already made his escape.

It seems, however, that Lord Chelmsford for one was unaware of the simple expedient of kicking open the box as, on 26 March 1879, he issued the following orders,

> 'Each wagon and cart with the convoy must have some ammunition boxes placed on it in such a position as to be easily got at. The regimental reserve boxes must have the screw of the lid taken out, and each wagon or cart will have a screw driver attached to one of the boxes so that it may be ready for opening when the screw has not been taken out.'

Whether or not a box could be opened by a blow from a stone, a boot or a rifle butt is a contentious subject that has been frequently debated by historians and battlefield buffs. Some years ago, believing that the box was not designed to be opened by a kick or blow, nor ever could be, the writer constructed a mock-up of a box using ¾-inch teak planking and securing the 'sliding lid' with a 2-inch brass screw. Kicking the lid produced no movement and it took forty blows, alternating a 4-pound hammer with a rock of the same weight, before the screw finally erupted through the side of the box, being bent in the process, and carrying a large chunk of the front planking with it.

The sliding lids of the original ammunition boxes had butt joints contained within the tongue and groove slides which prevented the lid from being carried right across the box to fall off the other side. Thus, because of the butt joints, the lid could only be opened one way, that is over the side of the box on which the securing screw was located. If the box was to be opened by force, the lid had to be pounded at the opposite end to the securing screw. It was, therefore, without a screwdriver, no easy task to access the ammunition. There is a surviving ammunition box, reportedly recovered from Isandlwana, in the Warriors Gate Museum, Durban. The photographs on page 128 give evidence of its robust construction and refute the War Office statement that the box could be opened with a good kick or blow with a stone. This in turn gave rise to the hoary old myth, that is still given credence to this day, that an amminition box could be opened with a single blow from a rifle butt under pressing circumstances.

There can be little doubt that the ammunition supply to the British firing lines, for whatever reason was found wanting. Whether or not an efficient distribution would have made any difference to the outcome of the battle is doubtful for nothing could have countered the inexpedient deployment of the scattered defenders.

Bibliography

Unpublished Sources and Private Information
Brenthurst Library, Johannesburg
Alison, Sir Archibald, Autograph Letters, 6 March 1878 – 26 October 1881. MS 165.
Harness, Arthur, Autograph Letters, 4 January 1878 – 2 October 1879. MS 158.
Killie Campbell Africana Library (KCAL) Durban
Manuscripts and papers of: James Brickhill, William James Clarke, T. H. Cunningham,
Henry F. Fynn, Ashley Thomas Goatham, Charles Rawden Maclean, W. Stafford, Frederick
Symons, Sir Evelyn Wood.
Natal Archives, Pietermaritzburg
Sir Evelyn Wood Papers.
Public Records Office, Kew
Various papers reference PRO and PRO/WO.
The Royal Archives, Windsor
Various papers, as enumerated in the notes, by gracious permission of Her Majesty Queen
Elizabeth II.
Royal Engineers Museum, Chatham
Durnford papers.
Private Papers
Vause, R. *The Vause Diaries and Papers* – property of Robin Stayt, Durban.
Diary of Sgt Major Cheffins – property of Lindsay Reyburn, Pretoria.

Newspapers, Journals and Periodicals
South Africa
*The Bloemfontein and Free State Gazette, The Cape Argus, The Farmer's Weekly News, The Friend, The
Natal Mercury, The Natal Witness, The Port Elizabeth Telegraph and Eastern Province Standard, The
Times of Natal.*
United Kingdom
*Fraser's Magazine, The Graphic, The Illustrated London News, The London Gazette, Oldham Weekly
Chronicle, The Times* (London), *The Times Weekly Edition, Soldiers of the Queen* (Journal of the
Victorian Military Society), *The Anglo-Zulu War Research Society Journal, The Anglo-Zulu War
Historical Society Journal, Military Illustrated, The Society for Army Historical Research Journal,
Medal News.*

Published Sources
Notes on Transport, Pamphlet published by the 2nd Battalion, Oxford Light Infantry (Revised
1897)
Regulations Field Forces South Africa 1878, example consulted courtesy of Professor John
Laband, University of Natal, Pietermaritzburg.
Abbot, P.E., and Tamplin, J.M.A., *British Gallantry Awards*. London, 1971.
Ashe, Major, and Wyatt-Edgell, E.V., *The Story of the Zulu Campaign*. London, 1880.
Bancroft, James W., *The Zulu War VCs*. Liverpool, 1992.
Barthorp, Michael, *The Zulu War: A Pictorial History*. Poole, 1980.

Bennett, Ian, *A Rain of Lead: The Siege and Surrender of the British at Potchefstroom*. London, 2001.

Binns, C.T., *The Warrior People*. London, 1975.

Binns, C.T., *The Last Zulu King – The Life and Death of Cetshwayo*. London, 1963.

Brooks, E.H. and Webb, C. de B., *A History of Natal*. Natal, 1965.

Bulpin T.V., *Discovering South Africa*. South Africa, 1970.

Buthelezi, oMntwana Mangosuthu G., *The Anglo-Zulu War – A Centennial Reappraisal, "The Bias of Historical Analysis."* Durban, 1979.

Child, D (ed.), *The Zulu War Diary of Col. Henry Harford*. Pietermaritzburg, 1978.

Clarke, Sonia, *Zululand at War, 1879*. Johannesburg, 1984.

Clarke, Sonia, *Invasion of Zululand*. Johannesburg, 1979.

Clarke, Sub-Inspector W., *A Record of the Services of the Natal Mounted Police*, Pietermaritzburg, n.d.

Clements, W.H., *The Glamour and Tragedy of the Zulu War*. London, 1936.

Coghlan, Mark, *Pro Patria* [History of the Natal Carbineers 1945–95]. Pietermaritzburg, n.d.

Colenso, E.F., assisted by Lt.Col. E. Durnford, *History of the Zulu War and its Origins*.

Coupland, Reginald, *Zulu Battle Piece – Isandhlwana*. London, 1948.

Dawnay, Guy C., *Campaigns: Zulu 1879, Egypt 1882, Suakin 1885*. Cambridge, 1989.

Droogleever, R.W.F., *The Road to Isandhlwana: Colonel Anthony Durnford in Natal and Zululand, 1873–1879*. London, 1992.

Durnford, Edward, *A Soldier's Life and Work in South Africa 1872 to 1879. A Memoir of the Late Colonel A.W. Durnford, Royal Engineers*. London, 1882.

Edgerton, Robert B., *Like Lions They Fought*. New York and London, 1988.

Ellis, Peter Berresford, *H. Rider Haggard, A Voice from the Infinite*, London 1978.

Emery, Frank, *Marching Over Africa*. London, 1986.

Emery, Frank, *The Red Soldier*. London, 1977.

Featherstone, Donald, *Victorian and Colonial Warfare*. London, 1992.

Filter, H. and Bourquin, S., *Paulina Dlamini*. Pietermaritzburg, 1986.

Forbes, Archibald, *Barracks, Bivouacs and Battles*. London, 1892.

Forsyth, D.R., *Medal Roll, The Colonials, South African General Service Medal*, Johannesburg, 1978.

French, Major The Hon. G., *Lord Chelmsford and the Zulu War*. London, 1939.

Furneaux, Rupert, *The Zulu War: Isandlwana and Rorke's Drift*. London, 1963.

Fynn, Henry Francis, *My Recollections of a Famous Campaign and a Great Disaster*, M/S KCAL, Durban.

Fynney, F.B., *The Zulu Army*. M/S Pietermaritzburg, 1878.

Gon, Philip, *The Road to Isandlwana*. Johannesburg, 1979.

Guy, Jeff, *The Destruction of the Zulu Kingdom*. Johannesburg, 1979.

Hallam Parr, Henry, *A Sketch of the Kaffir and Zulu Wars*. London, n.d.

Hamilton-Browne, Col. G., *A Lost Legionary in South Africa*. London, 1912.

Hattersley, Alan F., *Carbineer; The History of the Royal Natal Carbineers*. Aldershot, 1950.

Holt, H.P., *The Mounted Police of Natal*. London, 1913.

Jackson, F.W.D., 'The 1/24th Regiment, Marches to Isandlwana', *Soldiers of the Queen*. February 1979.

Knight, Ian, *Great Zulu Commanders*. London, 1999.

Krige, Eileen Jensen, *The Social System of the Zulus*. Pietermaritzburg, 1957.

Laband, J.P. (ed.), *Lord Chelmsford's Zululand Campaign, 1878–1879*. Stroud, Gloucestershire, 1994.

Laband, J.P., *Rope of Sand*. Johannesburg, 1995.

Laband, J.P., and Knight, Ian, (eds.), *Archives of Zululand: The Anglo-Zulu War 1879*. London, 2000.

Laband, J.P., and Thompson, P.S., with Henderson, Shiela, *The Buffalo Border Guard, 1879*. Durban, 1983.

Laband, J.P., and Thompson, P.S., *Field Guide to the War in Zululand*. Pietermaritzburg, 1979

Laband, J.P., and Thompson, P.S., *Kingdom and Colony at War*. Pietermaritzburg, 1990.

Laband, John, and Mathews, Jeff, *Isandlwana*. Pietermaritzburg, 1991.

Lehmann, Joseph H., *All Sir Garnet*. London, 1969.

Lock, Ron, *Blood on the Painted Mountain*. London, 1995.

Lock, Ron, 'Britain's Tribesmen on Horseback', *Military Illustrated*, January 1997.

Lock, Ron, 'The Making of the Peace', *Military Illustrated*, May 1997.

Lock, Ron, and Quantrill, Peter, *The Red Book. Natal newspaper reports on the Anglo-Zulu War, 1879*, Compilation. Pinetown, kwaZulu-Natal, 2000.

Low, Charles Rathbone, *Soldiers of the Victorian Age*, London, 1880.

McKay, James, *Reminiscences of the Last Kaffir War*. Cape Town, 1970.

Mackinnon, J.P., and Shadbolt, Sydney, *The South African Campaign, 1879*. London, 1880; reprinted London, 1995.

Maxwell, J., *Reminiscences of the Zulu War*. Cape Town, 1979.

Milton, John, *The Edge of War*. Cape Town, 1983.

Mitford, Bertram, *Through the Zulu Country*. London, 1883; reprinted London, 1988.

Moodie, Duncan Campbell Francis, *The History of the Battles and Adventures of the British, the Boers and the Zulus, etc. in Southern Africa from the Time of the Pharaoh Necho to 1880*. Cape Town, 1888.

Morris, Donald R., *The Washing of the Spears*. London, 1966.

Nicholls, Brenda, *Francis Ellen Colenso and the Zulu War*. Paper undated, *circa* 1979.

Norris-Newman, Charles L., *In Zululand with the British Throughout the War of 1879*. London, 1889; reprinted London, 1988.

Newark, George and Christopher, *Kipling's Soldiers*. Romford, 1993.

Preston, Adrian (ed.), *Sir Garnet Wolseley's South African Journal, 1879–80*. Cape Town, 1973.

Ritter, E.A., *Shaka Zulu: The Rise of the Zulu Empire*. London 1957; reprinted London, 1990.

Roberts, Brian, *The Zulu Kings*. London, 1974.

Samuelson, L.H., *Zululand its Traditions, Legends, Customs and Folklore*, Durban, 1974.

Samuelson, R.C.A., *Long, Long Ago*. Durban, 1929.

Schiel, Adolf, *23 Jahre Sturm und Sonneshein in Süd Afrika* (Twenty-three Years Storm and Sunshine in South Africa). Liepzig, 1902.

Smith-Dorrien, Horace, *Memories of Forty-Eight Years' Service*. London, 1925.

Stalker, J., *The Natal Carbineers: History of the Regiment from its Foundation 15 January 1855 to 30 June 1911*, Pietermaritzburg 1912.

Stuart, James and Malcolm D., *The Diary of Henry Francis Fynn*. Pietermaritzburg, 1986.

Taylor, Stella, *Shaka's Children*. London, 1994.

Thompson, P.S., *The Natal Native Contingent in the Anglo-Zulu War, 1879*. Pietermaritzburg 1997.

Tomasson, W.H., *With the Irregulars in the Transvaal and Zululand*. London, 1881.

Tylden, G., *The Armed Forces of South Africa 1659–1954*. Johannesburg, 1954.

Unterhalter, Elaine, *Confronting Imperialism: The People of Nqutu and the 1879 Invasion of Zululand*. Durban 1979.

van Warmelo, N.J., (ed.), *History of Matiwane and the amaNgwane Tribe*. Pretoria, 1938.

Vijn, Cornelius, *Cetshwayo's Dutchman*. London, 1880; reprinted London, 1988.

von Kehrhahan, J., *Das Filter-Larsen Denkmal*. South Africa, 1938.

War Office, *Narrative of the Field Operations Connected with the Zulu War of 1879* (Compiled by J.S. Rothwell). London, 1881; reprinted London, 1907 and 1989.

War Office, *Precis of Information Concerning Zululand*. London, 1895.

Webb, C. de B., and Wright, J.B., *A Zulu King Speaks*. Pietermaritzburg, 1978.

Whybra, Julian, 'The Ten Gunners', *Soldiers of the Queen*, January 1990.

Wood, Evelyn, *From Midshipman to Field Marshal*. London, 1906.

Wood, Evelyn, *Winnowed Memories*. London, 1918.

Wright, John B., *Bushmen Raiders of the Drakensberg 1840–1870*. Pietermaritzburg, 1971.

Wright, John, and Manson, Andrew, *The Hlubi Chiefdom*. South Africa, 1983.

Young, John, *They Fell Like Stones; Battles and Casualties of the Zulu War, 1879*. London, 1991.

Index

Page references in *italics* refer to map and illustration captions.

Active, HMS, 36
Adendorff, Lt, 175, 180, 212, 231
Aldershot, 268, 300
Alison, Lady Jane, 72,
Alison, Maj-Gen Sir Archibald, 72, 245, 251, 268
amaChunu Tribe, 43, 44, 168, 172, 180, 181, 186, 187, 189, 223, 224
AMAFA (aKwaZulu-Natali, Heritage Council), 10, 11, 296
amaHlubi Tribe, 22, 42, 93
amaNgwane Tribe, 92, 93, *122*, 186, 187, 189, 190
amaPondo Tribe, 52, 57, 315
amaXimba Tribe, 92
Anderson, Drummer John, 229
Anstey, Capt T.H., *156*
Anstey, Lt Edgar O., 168, 172, 185
Ashanti Ring, 247, 265
Ashanti War, 72, 265
Avery, Lt A., 138

Babanango, 67, 130, 131
Bambata kaMancinza, Zulu chief, 289
Banister, Lt George, 283, 306
Barker, Tpr William Walwyn, *88*, *115*, 165, 168, 169, 170, 187, 188, 190, 205, 213, 221, 294, 295, 308
Barry, Capt A.J., 168, 172, 173, 175, 180, 181, 185, 186, 187, 189, *200*, 205, 298
Barton, Capt Robert, 76
Barton, Capt William, *152*, 174, 181, 185, 187, 195, *197*, 199, 209, 214
Basuto ponies, 189
Basutoland, 22, 93, 294
Batlokwa Tribe, 93
Batshe River, 94, 132, 241
Beach, Sir Michael Hicks, 316
Beaumont, William, 162
Bellairs, Lt-Col W., 265, 268, 269, 271, 273, 278, 292
Bemba's Kop, 78
Bengough, Maj Harcourt, 91, *88*, *99*, *139*, 140, 149, 162, 163, 182
Bickley, Pte J., 172, 193, 291, 324, 325
Biggarsberg Mountains, 16, 66, 67, 68, 72, 73, 77, 129, 164, 178
Black Umfolozi River, *18*
Black, Maj Wilsone, 80, 215, 216, 224, 227, 240, 241, 242, 254, 279, 292

Black's Koppie, 94, 167, *200*, 213, 217, 227, *234*, 274, 292
Blood River (Ncome), Battle of, *18*, 54, 56, 58, 95, 75, 148, 315
Bloomfield, QM Edward, 209, 323, 326
Boer, Hans, 171
Boers, 19, 20, 21, 23, 24, 29, 46, 53, 54, 55, 56, 57, 58, 60, 65, 68, 75, 92, 129, 148, 315, 316
Boundary Commission, 31, 32, 33
Brackenbury, Maj Henry, 247
Bradstreet, Capt C.B., 174, 204, 213
Brickhill, J.A., 71, *111*, 171, 174, 175, 194, 204, 210, 213, 214, 220, *222*, 283
British Naval Brigade, *32*, *71*
British Regiments
see also Colonial units
Cavalry
  12th Lancers, 72, *116*
  14th Hussars, 71, 179
  17th Lancers, 241, 294, 297
Royal Artillery (RA), 36, 41, 148, 172, 191, 192, 195, *200*, 227, *234*, 251, 252, *258*, 324
  N Battery, No 5 Brigade, 41, 70, 179, 252
  Rocket Battery (11th Battery, 7th Brigade), 86, 91, *152*, 161, 173, 176, 181, 182, 187, 188, 190, *201*, 202, 213, 220, *234*, 237, 241
Royal Engineers (RE), 10, 235, 238, 242, 251, *270*
  5th Field Company, 41, 76, 163, 179
Infantry
  3rd Regiment (The Buffs), 30, 36
  4th Regiment, 264, 284, 292
  13th Light Infantry (LI), 31, 71, 147
  24th Regiment, 8, 15, 36, 37, 49, *120*, *123*, *125*, 144, 193, 236, 240, 244, 269, *260*
  1/24th Regiment (2nd Warwicks), 15, 27, 30; service in South Africa prior to Anglo-Zulu War, 31, 36–8 *passim*; 41, 49, 67; crosses Buffalo into Zululand, 69, 71, 72, 74, 77, 79; 86;134, 141, 142, 144, 147; at the Battle of Isandlwana, 165, 166, 167, 171, 172, 181, 182, 187, 190, 192–5 *passim*; *197*, 206, 211, 212, 217, 224, 231, *234*, 240, 241, 269, 274, 275, 282, 290, 291, 293, 297, 308, 318; and

ammunition controversy 324–6 *passim*
2/24th Regiment (2nd Warwicks), 70, 76; crosses Buffalo into Zululand, 77–81 *passim*; 94, 134, 141, 144, 147, 148, 150, 155, 159, 163; at the Battle of Isandlwana, 167, 172, 177, 179, 192, 193, *200*, 206, 209, 215, 217, 225–31 *passim*; *234*, 236, 240, 241, 244; *258*, 278, 279, 282, 283, 290, 298, 318, 319; and ammunition controversy, 323–6 *passim*
27th Regiment, 58
32nd Regiment, 71, *127*, 174
34th Regiment, 244
54th Regiment, 71
60th Regiment, 298
75th Regiment, 172
80th Regiment, 69, 31, *119*, *126*, 222, 284
90th Light Infantry (LI), 31, 36
95th Regiment, 49, 71, 149, 236, 237
99th Regiment, 31, 77, 298
104th Regiment, 163, 269
Imperial Mounted Infantry (IMI) (No. 1 Squadron), 8, 36, 41, 42, 70, 72, 79, 80, 94, 95, *116*, *126*, 147, 148, 155, 177, 178, 179, 183, 198, 213, 214, 222, 223, 224, 226
Royal Regiment of Wales (RRW), 10, 11, 290
South Wales Borderers (SWB), 292
Supporting forces
  Army Service Corps (ASC), 41, 46, 241, 298
  Commissariat Staff, 41, 46, 50, 28, 66, 70, 74, 95, 96, 150, 163, 181, 299
  Army Hospital Corps (AHC), 41
Britain, 15, 19, 23, 26, 39, 42, 55, 58, 65, 221, 265
Bromhead, Lt Gonville, 163, 269, 270
Browne, Lt Edward, 72, 141, 275, 317
Brownlee, Hon Charles, 32
Buckingham, Fort, 24, 31
Buffalo River, 7, 16, *18*, 24, 32, 36, 43, 55, 58, 66, 67, 68, 73, 74, 75, 76, 82, *88*, 96, *102*, *126*, 129, 148, *152*, *200*, 212, 214, 219, 220, 235, 236, *258*, *259*, 267, 269, 270, 297, 302, 316

Buller, Capt Ernest, 71, 139, 140, 159, 254, 264, 299, 300
Buller, Lt-Col Redvers, 285, 292
Bullock, QM Sgt John, *116*, 174, 205
Bulwer, Sir Henry, 249, 250
Bunting, George, 296
Burma, 192
Bushman's Pass, 96, 219, 316

caffres, 9, 50, 281
Cambridge, Duke of, C-in-C of the British Army, 27, 35, 47, 72, 143, 236, 240, 255, 256, 262, 263, 264, 265
Campbell, Lt W.D., 177, 178
Canada, 69, 181, 192
Cape Town, 56, 166, 167, 247, 255, 256, 283, 287, 299
Carnarvon, Lord, 26
Cavaye, Lt Charles, 6, 8, *101*, *123*, 192, 195, 196, *197*, *200*, 202, 203, 205, 208, 209, 211, 212, 231, 282, 317, 318, 323, 324, 326
Centane, Battle of, 37, 148, 191
Cetshwayo kaMpande, King, 7, 8, 12, 13; his early life and coronation 19–27 *passim*; receives Ultimatum 31, 33, 34; 48, 51, 52, 53; involvement with invading Boers, becomes king 56–65 *passim*; 67, 74, 77, 79; assembles Zulu Army 82–5 *passim*; 86, 87, 96, *105*, *106*, *107*, *116*, *120*, *121*, 202, 210, 229, 256, 283; capture and exile 287, 288; 315, 316, 321
Chadwick, George, 296
Chard, Lt John, 163, 172, 173, *200*, 270, 317
Chatham Ridges, 268
Cheffins, Sgt-Maj F.W., 58
Chelmsford, Lt-Gen, Lord (Frederic Augustus Thesiger), 9–18 *passim*; issues Ultimatum and plans invasion of Zululand *18*, 19–35 *passim*; description of forces under his command 36–50 *passim*; 55, 59, 64, 65; invades Zululand 66–83 *passim*; 86, 87, *88*, 90–6 *passim*; arrives at Isandlwana, reconnaissance into Zululand *98*, *99*, *105*, *109*, *111*, *115*, *121*, *123*, 129–43 *passim*; despatches Dartnell's patrol, splits his force and proceeds to seek the Zulu Army 145–59 *passim*; receives note that camp is under attack 160; 161–82 *passim*; 183, 184, 189, 192–5 *passim*; 198, 199, 202, 204, 211–4 *passim*; is finally convinced camp has been attacked 215–7; returns to camp 224–9 *passim*; proceeds to Rorke's Drift 230–2 *passim*; 235–9 *passim*; plans court of inquiry and returns to Pietermaritzburg 240–255;

parliamentary criticism of 256–63 *passim*; interrogation by Horse Guards 259, 260, 261, 264–79 *passim*; receives C-in-C's criticism 280–3 *passim*; 284, 285, 288–93 *passim*; returns to England 299–300 *passim*; 301, 304, 306, 308–19 *passim*; 326
Chillianwalla, Battle of, 74
China, 292
Church, Capt H.B., 252
Clarke, Sir Andrew, 247
Clarke Tpr W.J., 7, 67, 70, *112*, 132, 133, 146, 185, 226, 227, 230, 231, 294, 323, 324
Clery, Maj Cornelius Francis, 10, 71, 72, *127*, 132, 133, 140, 141, 147, 148, 160, 168, 170, 178, 215, 216, 226, 235, 236, 238, 240, 243, 244, 245, 246, 248, 251, 254, 255, 263, 268, 271, 276, 278, 279, 291, 292, 293, 299
Coate's Ferry Hotel, *111*
Cochrane, Lt Francis Dundonald, 174, 176, 193, 205, 245, 254, 283, 292, 322
Coghill, Lt Nevill, 8, 10, 132, 67, 71, *126*, 132, 169, 171, 212, 214, 218, 222, 223, 291, 294, 295, 296, 297
Colenso, Bishop J.W., 246, 257
Colenso, family, 14, 246
Colenso, Frances, 246
Colonial Units
 Alexander Mounted Rifles, 31
 Baker's Horse, 31
 Border Guard, 7, *109*
 Border Horse, 31
 Buffalo Border Guard (BBG), 31, 42, 43
 Carrington's Horse, 41
 Durban Mounted Rifles, 29, 31
 Durban Volunteer Artillery, 8, 21, *119*
 Frontier Light Horse (FLH), 31, 76, 166, 168
 Karkloof Carbineers, 22, 42, 173
 M'Fengu Levy (Eastern Cape), 30
 Maritzburg Rifles, 298
 Natal Carbineers (NC), 10, 31, 42, 69, 73, *108*, *115*, *116*, 164, *201*, 241, 289, 294, 298, 317
 Natal Hussars, 8, *124*
 Natal Mounted Police (NMP), 31, 36, 42, *109*, *112*, *125*, *201*, *234*, *258*, 289, 293
 Natal Native Border Police, 24
 Natal Native Contingent (NNC), 9, 28, 29, 30, 31, 43, 44, 45, 46, 63, 68, 77, 79, 80, 81, 86, 87, 90, 91, 94, *108*, *113*, 130, 132, 133, 136, 137, 138, 139, 142, 145, 146, 147, 148, 150, 154, 155, 158, 159, 161, 162, 163, 164, 167, 168, 172, 173, 174, 175,

176, 177, 180, 181, 182, 185, 186, 189, 190, 192, 193, 195, 198, 199, *200*, 205, 206, 209, 210, 215, 222–6 *passim*, 227, 230, 231, *234*, 248, 249, 250, 251, 256, 257, *258*, *260*, *261*, 273, 274, 275, 279, 276, 295, 298, 317, 319, 323, 324
 Natal Native Horse (NNH), 30, 36, 92, 93, 96, *108*, *113*, *114*, *116*, *123*, *124*, 173, 174, 178, 181, 185–95 *passim*, 197–205 *passim*, 208, 209, 211, 289, 292, 294, 317, 318, 322, 323
  Edendale Troop, 92, 93, 174, 188, 189, *200*, 205, 206, 213, 223, 292, 322
  Hlubi Troop, 92, 188, 189, *200*, 206, 208, 213, 288
  Jantee's Horse, 92, 173
  Zikali Troops, 93, 176, 185, 189, 192, 195, 205, *207*, 209, 214, 224
 Newcastle Mounted Rifles (NMR), 31, 42, 43, 194, 204
 Pulleine's Rangers, 166
 Raaff's Rangers, 31, 58
 South Africa Native Labour Continent (SANLC), 290
 Stanger Mounted Rifles, 32
 Victoria Mounted Rifles, 31
 Zululand Reserve Territory Carbineers, 294
Conical Hill, *88*, *101*, *152*, *156*, 164, 165, 168, 169, 170, 171, 172, 175, 176, 180, 187, 190, 191, 216, *234*, 275, 317, 318
Crealock Lt-Col John North, 10, 71, 72, *109*, *123*, 129, 134, 137, 140, 149, 154, 160, 161, 162, 163, 198, 216, 217, 232, 235–9 *passim*, 240, 243, 245, 246, 247, 251, 252, 254, 255, 263, 266, 268, 269, 271, 273, 274, 282, 290, 291, 292, 299
Cunynghame, Lt-Gen Sir Arthur, 192, 237
Curling, Lt Henry, 8, *119*, 172, 254, 283, 291

Dabulamanzi kaMpande, Prince, 210, 298
Daly, Lt J.P., 217
Dartnell, Maj John, 7, 42, 69, 72, 73, 81, *88*, *109*, *112*, 132, 137–42 *passim*, 145, 147, 148, 149, 150, 151, 154, 163, 164, 174, 227, 230, 236, 241, 244, 254, 273–7 *passim*, 279, 293, 294, 317, 318, 319
Davey, Lt, 145, 147
Davies, Lt Harry, 174, 188, 190, 205, 208, 322
Day, Tpr, 226, 227
De Jager, Gert, 95
Degacher, Capt William, 74, 167, 195, 202, 203, 212, 217, 324
Degacher, Col Henry, 70, 167, 279

Delagoa Bay, 52
Develin, Capt, 214, 215, 224
Devil's Pass, 285
Dilke, Sir Charles, 262, 263
Dingane kaMpande, King, 53–7
    passim, 59, 75, 92, 93, 315, 320,
    321
Dinuzulu kaCetshwayo, Prince,
    288
Disraeli, Benjamin, 233, 265, 266,
    299
Dixon, Tpr Arthur, 74
Dlamini, Paulina, 60, 61, 64
Domba, Zulu chief, 250
Drummond, the Hon William, 47,
    48, 71, 136, 138, 139, 140, 160,
    171, 184
Dubois, Edmond, 47
Dubois, Robert, 47
Dunbar, Maj W.N., 94, 134
Dundee, *18*, 66, 69, 75, 257
Dunn, John, 20, 22, 31, 33, 34, 48,
    60, 62, 65, 82, 83, 288
Dunscombe, Capt R., 80
Durban, 8, 10, 29, 31, 32, 36, 38,
    44, 53, 76, 78, 95, 165, 173, 193,
    194, 296, 297, 315, 327
Durnford, Col Anthony William, 7,
    8, 10, 14, 22, 29, 30, 42, 46, 47,
    86, 87, 90, 91, 92, 93, 96, *101*,
    115, *116*, 149, *153*, 160, 161, 162,
    163, 173–99 *passim*, *200*, 205, 206,
    208, 212, 213, 215, 216, 218, 219,
    221, 223, *234*, 235–51 *passim*, 254,
    256, 257, *258*, *261*, 262, 265, 266,
    267, 272, 273, 274, 280, 281, 282,
    288, 292, 297, 298, 300, 317, 318,
    322, 323
Durnford, Lt-Col Edward, 6, 7,
    234, 235, 239, 242, 246, 247, 254,
    273
Dyer, Lt H.J., 179, 217
Dyson, Lt Edward, *125*, 196, *197*,
    200, 203

East London, 45, 145
Eastern Cape, 15, 25, 29, 31, 37,
    41, 71, 80, 166
Edwards, Capt F.I., 255
Edwards, Tpr W., *115*
Elandskraal, 149, 162
Ellice, Sir Charles, 255, 266, 267,
    268, 270, 280
Ellis, Pte Owen, 86, 142
emaKhosini Valley, 83,
Empandleni, *18*
Entumeni, *18*
Erskine, Capt. W., 168, 221
Eshowe, *18*, 48, 86, 87, 284, 285,
    287, 288
Essex, Capt Edward, 172, 193, 202,
    203, 208, 209, 212, 221, 254, 283,
    323, 325, 326
Ethiopia, 59

Fairbridge, Charles, 247

Fannin, John Eustace, 64
First Fruits Ceremony, 25, 26, 62,
    80, 82
Foley (wagon conductor), 171, 193
Forbes, Archibald, 255, 274
Fort Napier, 298
French, Maj the Hon Gerald, 256,
    260
Frere, Lady Catherine, 256, 257
Frere, Mary, 51, 210, 256, 257
Frere, Sir Bartle, 7, 19, 23, 24, 28,
    29, 31, 34, 43, 46, 55, 58, 65, 67,
    70, 71, 73, 78, 81, 83, 87, 90, 95,
    96, *105*, 129, 232, 240, 247, 249,
    256, 257, 266, 277, 288, 293, 296,
    316
Frontier War, The 9th, 25, 27, 29,
    30, 37, 49, 148, 166, 167, 192, 252
Fugitives' Drift, 7, *88*, *102*, *115*,
    126, *152*, 219, 223, *234*, 294, 295,
    322, 323
Fugitives' Trail, *88*, *152*, 220, 301
Fynn, Henry Francis, Jnr, 26, 32,
    44, 48, 68, 71, 75, 76, 81, 96, *99*,
    109, *129*, 132, 133, 139, 140, 148,
    151, 216, 217, 223, 227, 228, 235,
    274
Fynn, Henry Francis, Snr, 32, 60
Fynney, F.B., 32, 33, 34, 59, 60, 63,
    320

Gabangaye, NNC chief, 43, 168,
    223, 224, 227
Gamble, Band-Sgt D., 220, 222,
    228
Gamdana kaXongo, Zulu chief,
    139, 140, 141, 174, 181, 223, 275,
    276
Gardner, Capt. Alan, 71, 179, 193,
    195, 198, 204, 205, 206, 213, 217,
    218, 254, 283, 292, 293, 318, 319
Gates of Natal, *18*, 86, 87, 91
Gcaleka tribesmen, 191
Gebule, Zulu chief, 33
German South-West Africa, 294
Gibraltar, 192
Gingindlovu, 33
Gladstone, Prime Minister, W.E.,
    287
Glyn, Col Richard, 36, 47, 48, 49,
    66, 67, 70, 71, 72, 75, 77, 79, 80,
    96, *127*, 129, 134, 136, 139, 147,
    148, 149, 150, 155, 159, 160, 162,
    166, 169, 171, 211, 212, 213, 215,
    216, 220, 225, 226, 235, 236, 237,
    238, 243, 244, 245, 246, 248, 249,
    254, 255, 266, 267, 268, 269, 270,
    271, 272, 274, 276, 277, 278, 279,
    282, 292, 296
Goatham, Pte, 36
Godwin-Austen, Lt F., 217
Gort, Viscount, 168
Gossett, Maj Matthew, 71, 139,
    140, 145, 147, 215, 217, 225, 253,
    254, 292
Grant, Pte H., 188, 213

Great Kei River, 192
Green, Tpr H., 133
Greytown, *18*, 24, 43, 66, 68, 69, 70
Griffiths, Lt T.L.G., 179
Gun War of 1880, 294

Haggard, H. Rider, 48, 64
Hallam Parr, Capt Henry, 71, 150,
    155, 160, 225, 293
Hamer, J.H., 174, 181, 186, 187,
    205, 209, 220
Hamilton-Browne, Cmdt G., 15,
    80, 81, *88*, 137, 141, 146, *153*,
    177, 178, 179, 195, 198, 199, 214,
    215, 224, 225, 248, 252, 276, 277,
    284, 319
Harford, Lt Henry, 77, 80, 147,
    154, 158, 174
Harman, Col George, 244
Harness, Lt-Col Arthur, *113*, 150,
    158, 177, 179, 193, 214, 216, 224,
    225, 241, 244, 252, 253, 254, 277,
    283, 319
Harrismith, 69
Harvey, Capt J.J., 252, 298
Hassard, Col Fairfax, 251, 254
Havelock, Gen H., 262
Hawkins, Sir John, 188
Hawkins, Tpr Villiers Caesar, *88*,
    165, 168, 169, 170, 187, 188, 190,
    205, 213, 295
Helpmekaar, *18*, 31, 36, 38, 43, 64,
    66, 67–73 *passim*, 80, 91, 96,
    247–54 *passim*, 269, 292
Henderson, Lt Alfred, *114*, 161,
    174, 208, 294, 295, 322
Higginson, Lt Walter, 175, 180,
    181, 182, 188, 189, 222, 294, 295,
    296
Hlazakazi, Mountain or Hill, 76,
    88, *129*, 137, 138, 141, 164, 273,
    276
Hlobane Mountain, 284, 285, 292,
    294
Hlongwane Tribe, 93
Holcroft, Lt F., 138
Holmes, Drummer, John, 299
Hong Kong, 292
Horse Guards, 236, 247, 257, 262–7
    passim, 270, 272, 280, 281, 297,
    300
Hough, Pte J., 211

Inanda Location, 44
Indian Mutiny, 49, 69, 237, 262,
    265
Indian Ocean, *18*, 20, 32, 68
Inkatha, 12, 26
Ireland, 165, 192, 244, 292, 295
Isandlwana, 3, 4, 7–16 *passim*, *18*,
    23, 29, 30, 32, 35, 38–43 *passim*,
    47, 55, 61, 64, 67, 72, 73, 76, 83,
    88, 91, 94–6 *passim*, *102*, *104*, *112*,
    114, *115*, *116*, 120–5 *passim*, *128*,
    129–39 *passim*, 144, 145, 146, 147,
    150–6 *passim*, 160–199 *passim*,

200, 208–17 *passim*, 221–31
passim, 235, 236, 239–45 *passim*,
249, 250, 251, 252, 256, 264–72
passim, 275, 282, 284, 285,
288–302 *passim*, 316, 317, 318,
319, 322, 325–7 *passim*
Isipesi Hill, *18*, 94, 95, *97*, 178, 275
IsiXepi Military Barracks, 130
iThusi Hill, *88*, *99*, *100*, 141, *153*,
201
iZigqoza Clan, 12, 20, 44, 77, 168,
180, 195, 199, 210

James, Lt Walter, *112*, 256, *258*,
259, *260*, *261*
Jarvis, Captain Henry, 55, 56
Jekyl, Maj, 239
Jenkins, E., 257, 262, 263
Johnson, Pte D., 188, 190, 213
Jones, Tpr S.B., 137

Kambula, 39, 58, 63, 282, 285, 292,
294
Kambule, Elijah, 92
Kambule, Job, 290
Kambule, Sgt-Maj Simeon, 92, 93,
213, 218, 289, 290
Keate's Drift, *18*, 68
Kimberley, 22, 161, 174
King Edward VII, 292, 297
King Williams Town, 30, 165
Kipling, Rudyard, 40
kiSwahili, 59
Knox, Alfred, 29
Konigkramer, Arthur, 9, 10
Kranskop, *18*, 24, 86, 87, 90, 91, 93,
94
Krige, Dr Eileen, 59
Krohn, Capt, 168, 175, 206, 298,
312
Kwa Mahamba Drift, *88*, *99*, 162,
182, 249

Ladysmith, *18*, 66, 247, 296
Laing's Nek, 294
Landman, Willem, 95
Landman's Drift, *18*
Langalibalele kaMthimkhulu,
Hlubi Chief, 22
Law, Lt-Col F.A., 251, 252
Limpopo River, 78
Lloyd, James, *105*
Lloyd, Llewellyn, 48
Lloyd, Lt W.W., 37
Lloyd, Maj-Gen, 250
Lock, Ron, 9, 11, 13, 14, 34
London, William QM, 8, *116*, 174,
187, 205, 209
Longcast, Henry William, 48, 71,
184, 215, 287
Longhurst, Sgt S., 242, 243
Lonsdale, Capt James, 168, 180,
195, 199, *200*, 202, 210, 298
Lonsdale, Cmdt Rupert, 7, 16, 30,
80, *88*, *89*, *111*, 136, 137, 138,
139, 145, 147, 148, 163, 168, 225,

248, 249, 254, 267, 277, 317, 319
Lowe, Col Drury, 241
Lower Drift, 31, 36, 68, 83
Lower Tugela, 66
Luard, Col C.E., 242, 243
Lukhwazi, Zulu commander, 223,
224
Luneberg, 284
Lysons, Maj-Gen Sir Daniel, 255
Lytton, Lord, 299

Mabaso Hill, *89*, *153*, *156*, *157*
Mabilwana kaMhlanganisa, Zulu
commander, 33
MacLeod of MacLeod, 48
Magaga Knoll, *88*, *101*, 133, 142,
144, *152*, 164, 168, 172, 175, 180,
181, 186, 196, *197*, *200*, 202, 210,
275
Magdala, 49
Magogo Hill, *89*, *113*, 137, 138,
144, 215
Mahlabathini Plain, 82
Mahubulwana kaDumisela, Zulu
commander, 33, *106*
Mainwaring, Lt Henry, 76, 77, 141,
142, 150, 214, 224, 293
Malakatha Hills, *88*, 136
Malta, 28, 181, 192
Mandalakazi, Zulu clan, 183, 210
Mangeni Falls, *18*, *89*, *99*, 149, 158,
159, 177, 179, 204, 216, 235, 252,
272, 273, 279, 284, 302, 317, 318,
319
Mangeni Valley, *88*, 129, 133, 136,
148, 149, 151, 162, 302
Mangosuthu Buthelezi, Prince, 11,
13, 14
Mansel, Insp George, 69, 132, 133,
134, 138, 154, 158, 177, 215, 219,
230, 231, *234*, 235, 254, 276, 294
Manzimnyama Stream, *88*, 134,
197, *200*, 217, 219
Marshall, Gen Frederick, 241, 242
Martini-Henry rifle, 37, 40, 148,
155, 186, 191, 196, 209, 284, 291,
292, 301
Masiphula kaMamba, Zulu
commander, 21
Masotsheni ('Place of the
Soldiers'), 78
Massowah, 49
Master, Col, 242
Matiwane kaMasumpa, Ngwane
chief, 93, 186
Matshana kaMondisa, Zulu chief,
129, 131, 132, 136, 137, 139, 146,
148, 158, 159, 162, 171, 177, 275
Matshana's Stronghold, *89*
Mauritius, 28, 165, 192
Mavumengwana kaNdlela Ntuli,
Zulu commander, 130, 183
Maxwell, Lt John, 155, 227, 228
Mbuyazi kaMpande, Prince, 12, 20,
21, 22, 44, 168, 288
McDougall, Lt, 179

McEwan, Boy Soldier, Joseph, 229
Meerut, 242
Mehlokazulu kaSihayo, Zulu
commander, 24, 219, 223, 289
Melvill, Charles William, 297
Melvill, Lt Teignmouth, *126*, 134,
166, 171, 181, 195, 203, 212, 214,
217, *222*, 223, 235, 236, 291, 294,
295, 296, 297, 318
Mfunzi, *106*
Mfecane Horde, 92
Mgana, Zulu chief, 250
Mgungundhlovu, *18*
Mhlatuze River, *18*, 51, 87
Middle Drift, *18*, 24, 27, 56, 64, 86,
90, 91
Milne, Lt Archibald Berkeley, 71,
140, 141, 148, 151, 177, 178, 179,
293
Mitchel, Gen Sir John, 50
Mitford, Bertram, 58, 301
Mkhandumba kaButhelezi, Prince,
13
Mkhosana kaMvundlana, Zulu
commander, 211
Mntumengana kaButhelezi, Prince,
13
Mnyamana kaNgqengelele
Buthelezi, Prince and Zulu
general, 130, 288
Molife, Sgt-Maj Jabez, 188, 206,
207, 218, 288, 289, 298
Mome Gorge, 288
Mons, 292
Mooi River, *18*, 67, 70
Morris, Donald, 294, 295
Mostyn, Capt William, *101*, *123*,
134, 135, 168, 192, 195, *197*, *200*,
202, 203, 205, 208, 209, 211, 212,
231, 282, 318, 323, 324, 326
Mpande kaSenzangakhona Zulu,
King, 4, 19, 20, 21, 53–60 *passim*,
130, 131, 315, 316, 320, 321
M'singa (Umsinga), *18*, 32, 44, 45,
48, 66, 68, 86, 91, 96, 249
Mthonga kaMpande, Prince, 77
Müller, Carl, 29, 58
Murray, Capt Orlando, 137, 168,
206, 276, 298
Mvubi, NNC chief, 248
Mzimvubu River, 52
Mzinyathi River, 129

Napoleon, Prince Louis (The
Prince Imperial), 285
Natal Colonist (newspaper), 29
Natal government, 19, 21, 22, 42,
65, 69, 75, 92, 96, 289
Natal, British Colony of, 19, 55
Natalia, Republic of, 56
National Monuments Council, 296
Ncome (Blood) River, 36, 54
Ndabuko kaMpande, Prince, 8, *121*
nDondakusuka, Battle of, 12, 20,
53, *120*, 202, 210, 288
Ndwandwe, tribe, 51, 52, 154

Nelson, Tpr W., *125*
New Zealand Infantry Brigade, 297
Newcastle, *18*, 43, 162
Newdigate, Maj-Gen Edward, 241
Nguni, people, 51, 52, 59
Ngwebini Valley, *89*, 140, 141, 151, 153, *156*, *157*, 164, 165, 169, 184, 185, 189, 226, *229*
Nicholson, Gen, 239
niggers, 45
Ninth (9th) Frontier War, 25, 27, 29, 30, 37, 49, 148, 166, 167, 192, 252
Nkabane Hill, *89*, 158
Nkandla Forest, *18*, 87
No. 1 Column, 36, *18*, 78, 86, 87, *124*, 181, 264
No. 2 Column, *18*, 86, 87, 90, 91, *115*, 139, 160, 161, 162, 174, 208
No. 3 Column, *18*, 36, 37, 41, 43, 44, 47, 48, 49, 66, 68, 69, 71, 73, 75, 76, 78, 83, 86, 93, 96, *111*, *125*, 149, 162, 172, 179, 183, 243, 264, 266, 269, 270, 282, 292, 293, 316
No. 4 Column, 36, 48, 78, *18*, *119*, 243, 252, 264, 284, 292
No. 5 Column, *18*
Nodwengu, Zulu barracks, 82, 129
Norris-Newman, Charles, 67, 70, 72, 147, 158, 159, 183, 195, 210, 216, 241
Northern Cape, 41
Norwegian Mission, 25, 62
Notch, The, *152*, 187, 189, 191, 199, *201*
Nourse, Capt Cracroft, 182, 187, 188, 190, 254
Nqutu, *18*, *101*
Nqutu Ridge/Plateau, *88*, *97*, 133, 140, 141, 142, *152*, *156*, 164, 165, 170–5 *passim*, 180, 181, 185, 195, 203, 205, 209, 220, 226, *234*, 254, 274
Ntshingwayo kaMahole, Zulu general, *121*, 130, 131, 151, 162, 169, 170, 183, 184, 185, 199, 203, 210, 284, 288, 301, 318
Ntuzwa kaNhlaka, Zulu commander, 130
Nubia, 292
Nyanda, Sgt-Maj, 93, 186, 214
Nyazane, Battle of, *124*
Nyezi Hill, *89*, *153*, 165, 169
Nyokana *donga*, *88*, 91, *152*, *200*, 205, 206, 208, 217, 318, 322, 323
Nyoni Heights/Ridge, *88*, *152*, 180, *200*, 275

Omdurman, Battle of, 292
Ondini, 12, 22, 26, 34
Orange Free State, 69, 78
Osborne House, 194
Osborne, Sir Melmoth, 288
Oskarberg, 16, 74, 161, 164, 230
Oude Molen, 287

Parsons, Lt, 215, 216
Parsons, Tpr, 138
Paterson, Pieter, 250
Pearson, Col Charles, 36, 86, 240, 264, 284
Pearson, Fort, *18*, 30, 31
Peel, Sir Robert, 257, 263
Penn Symons, Capt William, 177
Penrose, Lt C., *156*, 185
Phakade, chief of the amaChunu, NNC, 43
Phillips, F.L. Sub-Insp, 133, 134, 276
Phindo Hills, *89*, 155, 162, 177, 284
Pietermaritzburg, 7, 10, *18*, 22, 28, 30, 36, 42, 64–9 *passim*, 73, 92, 95, *107*, 134, 142, 165, 188, 232, 240, 242, 246, 247, 248, 256, 271, 298, 301
Pinetown, *18*
Pitts, Pte S., 232
Pohl, Lt B., 178, 179, 198
Polela River, 92
Pongola (Phongola) River, 20, 57
Ponsonby, Gen Sir H., 51, 255, 256, 290
Poole, Capt R., 287
Pope, Lt Charles, *125*, 142, 150, 167, 171, 193, 195, *200*, 206, 209, 241, 317, 318, 324
Port Elizabeth, 30
Port Natal, 53, 55, 56
Porteous, Lt Francis, 192, 195, *200*, 206, 209, 324, 326
Potspruit, 29, 31
Potter, Charlie, 48
Pretoria, 64
Pretorius, Comdt-Gen Andries, 54, 58, 75, 76
Price, Pte John, 159
Prince of Wales, Edward, 72, 257
Pritchard, Lt, 137
Pulleine, Lt-Col, Henry Burmester, 8, 15, *114*, *121*, 141, 142, 149, 160, 165–95 *passim*, 199, 202–6 *passim*, 212, 213, 217, 218, 236, 238, 244, 245, 246, 248, 255, 265, 267, 272, 276, 277, 282, 283, 284, 291, 293, 298, 317, 318, 319, 324
Pullen, QM James, 212, 213, 326

Quantrill, Peter, 9, 13, 14, *113*
Quartermaine, Allan, 48
Qudeni Forest, *18*, 87, 94, 139, 151
Qudeni Track, *89*, 137, 145, 150, 151, *153*, 154, 155, 163, 177, 190
Qwabe Ridge, *88*, *153*, *156*, *157*, 169

Rainforth, Capt T., 269
Raw, Lt Charles, *116*, *152*, 173, 181, 185, 186, 195, *197*, 199, 209, 214, 292, 294, 295, 323
Red Book, The, 300
Regulations Field Forces South Africa 1878, 45, 271, 278, 279

Retief, Piet, 75, 93, 131
Reuters, 255
Richie, Rev M.R., 298
Richmond, *18*
Robben Island, 22
Roberts, Lord, 293, 299
Roberts, Lt J.A., 8, *124*, *152*, 173, 181, 185, 195, 292, 323
Robinson, Sir Hercules, 287
Robson, Field Cornet, 24
Rorke, James, 43, 74, 75,
Rorke's Drift, 7, 16, *18*, 24, 31, 32, 36, 40, 45, 64, 66, 68, 73, 74, 75, 78, 79, 86, *88*, *89*, 90, 91, 94, 96, *97*, *129*, 131, 134, 139, 140, 149, 150, *152*, 160, 162, 163, 167, 172, 173, 175, *207*, 208, 212, 223, 225, 230, 231, 232, *234*, 235, 237, 238, 240–51 *passim*, 254, *258*, 267–72 *passim*, 278–83 *passim*, 293, 297, 302, 319
Royal Laboratory Woolwich, 1*28*
Russell, Col Baker, 39
Russell, Lt-Col John Cecil, 72, 73, 80, 81, *89*, 94, *116*, 131, 137, 183, 198, 199, 216, 224, 226, 253, 254, 273, 277, 292
Russell, Maj Francis Broadfoot, 187, 190

Samuelson, R.C., 287
Sand Spruit, 45, 68
Sandhurst, 162, 166, 243
Schiel, Col Adolf, 298
Schreuder, Bishop, 25, 90
Scott, Lt Frederick, 164, 165, 167, 169, 170, 171, 176, 182, 185, 188, 189, 190, *201*, 205
Second Sikh War, 74
Secunderabad, 165
Sekhukhune, 41, 71
Senzangakhona kaJama, Zulu chief, 51, 56
Shaka kaSenzangakhona, King, 51–6 *passim*, 59, 60, 93, 151, 199, 300, 315, 320
Shepherd, Surgeon-Maj Peter, 212
Shepstone, Capt George, 8, 96, *116*, 139, 140, *152*, 161, 163, 173, 181, 185, 186, 187, 191, *200*, 204, 205, 208, 220, 294, 318
Shepstone, John Wesley, 32, 34, 46, 62, 131, 159
Shepstone, Sir Theophilus, 17, 21, 23, 26, 27, 32, 48, 65, 72, 95, 132, 134, 243, 316
Shepstone, Capt Theophilus 'Offy', 72, 73, 137, 159, 241, 242, 243, 247, 294
Shingana kaMpande, Prince, 8, *120*
Shiyane Hill, 74
Sigcwelegecwele kaMhlekehleke, Zulu commander, 62, *120*, 210, 223
Sihayo kaXongo, Zulu chief, 24, 27, 34, 73, 79, 81, 82, 86, 95, 130,

139, 148, 158, 163, 219, 249, 275, 302, 316

Sikhota kaMpande, NNC chief, 77

Silutshana Hill, *89*, 154, 164, 177

Simmons, Gen Sir Linton, 239

Sitheku kaMpande, Prince, 210

Smith, Capt Thomas Charlton, 58

Smith, Maj Stuart, 179, 193, 206, 211, 220, 221

Smith, Mr (surveyor), 25, 34

Smith-Dorrien, Lt H., 7, 67, *111*, 149, 160, 161, 163, 167, 174, 193, 212, 221, 232, 254, 283, 292, 325, 326

Sokexe, stronghold of Sihayo, 79

South Africa, 10, 11, 13, 14, 26, 28, 37, 39, 41, 50, 58, 165, 174, 181, 192, 226, 238, 243, 246, 255, 256, 302

South African Defence Force (121 Battalion), 290

Spalding, Maj Henry, 163, 269, 270

St Helena, 192

St Paul's, *18*

St Vincent's Church, 301

Stafford, Capt W., 29, 176, 205, 208, 209, 221, 323

Stanger, *18*, 24, 30, 32, 66

Stanley, Col Fred, 194, 238, 255, 256, 262, 263

Stevens, Tpr Richard, 191

Stewart, Lt-Col H., 298

Stimson, Tpr, 230

Storr-Lister, J., 287

Strathallan, Viscount, 48

Strickland, Commissary-General, 95

Sudan, 52, 292

Sullivan, Commodore, F.W., 230, 293

Swazi, 20, 52, 55, 57, 65, 264

Swaziland, 55, 65

Swedish Mission, 74, 75

Swift, Tpr K., 170

Swinburne-Henry carbine, 42, 92

Symons, Capt W. Penn, 159

Symons, Tpr Fred, 69, 81, 137, 138, 146, 159, 215, 216, 224, 226, 253, 294

Tahelane Ridge, *88*, *101*, *152*, 175, 195, 196, *197*, *200*, 202, 203, 205, 208, 323, 324

Tanzania, 59

Tarboton, Tpr W., 295

Theodore, King of Abyssinia, 49, 148

Thirteen chiefdoms, 185, *286*, 287, 288

Thorns, The, *18*, 68, 69, 70

Thring's Post, 31

Tlokwa Tribe, 93

Tommy Atkins, 37

Torrens, Lt-Gen H., 243

Trainer, Pte J., 188, 213

Transkei, 166

Transvaal, Republic, 19, 23, 28, 29, 31, 32, 90, 93, 95, 161, 134, 292, 298, 316

Tugela Ferry, *18*, 68

Tugela (Thukela) River, 7, *18*, 19, 20, 22, 24, 30–6, 43, 53–8 *passim*, 67, 68, 69, 78, 82, 86, 87, 93, *111*, 202, 211, 289, 315, 316

Turner, Sgt, 198, 199

udibi boys, 12, 61, 130, 131, 224

Uganda, 59,

Ultimatum, the, 7, 19, 27, 31, 32, 33, 34, 65, 76, 82, 83, 316

Ultimatum Tree, the, *106*, *107*

Ulundi, 11, 12, *18*, *43*, 55, 64, 67, 75, 79, 82, 94, 133, 141, *259*, *261*, 267, 280, 281, 283, 285, 289, 293, 294, 299, 300

Umgeni, *18*

Umdloti River, *18*

Umkungo, NNC Chief, 250

Umlazi River, *18*

Umqwe, chief of the Maqatini Clan, 44

Umvoti River, *18*

Upper Sind, 181

Utrecht, 36, 90, 292

Uys, J.J., 95

Vant's Drift, *18*

Vause, Lt Richard Wyatt, *123*, 173, 176, 194, 205, 208, 209, 221, 222, 249, 294, 323

Vereker, Lt the Hon Standish, 168, 180, 185, 186, 187, 189, 298

Vermaak's farm, 91, 96

Verulam, 66

Victoria Cross, *115*, *126*, 166, 222, 295, 297

Victoria, Fort, 56

Victoria, Queen, 21, 42, 58, 80, 194, 236, 255, 256, 262, 277, 287, 289, 299

Victorian Empire, 23, 25, 28, 42, 80, 165, 290, 293

Vijn, Cornelius, 299

Voortrekkers, 53, 54, 66

Vumandaba kaNtati, Zulu commander, 33

Walker, Col Forestier, 32

Walsh, Lt Henry, 147, 148

Walsh, Sgt, 194

Wardell, Capt George, 192, 195, *200*, 206, 209, 217, 324, 326

Warriors Gate Museum, 8, *128*, 327

Wassall, Pte S.*126*, 222

Weenen, 250

White Mfolozi River, *18*, 67, 75, 93

White, Maj Francis, 211

Whitelaw, Tpr, *89*, 165, 168, 169, 170, 171, 188

Williams, Pte John, 171, 172, 193, 211, 212, 213, 220, 324, 325

Williams, Sgt-Maj, 175, 180, 189

Wilson, Pte E., 193, 325

Witt, Otto, 74, 75, 163

Wolfe, C/Sgt, F.H., 217

Wolseley, Gen Sir Garnet, 13, 72, 90, *121*, 249, 265, 266, 285, *286*, 288, 289, 290, 291, 297, 299, 300

Wood, Col Evelyn, 36, 39, 40, 63, 75, 76, 78, 83, 86, 90, 96, 174, 218, 243, 252, 264, 282, 283, 284, 285, 292, 295, 299

Woodruffe, Mr, 47

Woolwich, 252

World War II, 61

Wylde, Atherton, 246

Younghusband, Capt Reginald, *125*, *192*, 195, *200*, 202, 203, 205, 208, 209, 211, 223, 224, 282, 318, 323

Zibhebhu kaMaphitha, Zulu chief, 1*22*

Zulu Dawn, 108

Zulu army, *8*, 32, 35, *98*, *121*, *156*, *201*, *258*, 320, 321, 324

Zulu army bivouac, *153*, *157*

Zulu kingdom, 6, 14, 19, 22, 23, 26, 28, 30, 31, 53, 55, 57, 58, 131, *286*, 289, 315, 316

Zulu regiments
See also Appendix B, pages 320–1
abaQulusi Clan/Regiment, 33, *106*, 285
Falaza Regiment, 60
Iowa/iQwa Regiment, 59
Khandempemvu Regiment, 185, *201*
mCijo Regiment, 33, 185, *201*, 202, 275
Mkisimana Guild/Regiment (female), 60
nDluyengwe Regiment, 62
Ngwekwe Regiment, 60, 320
Nkobamakosi/nGobamakhosi Regiment, 59, 60, 62, *120*, 184, 191, *201*, 208, 210, 219, 223
Tulwana/uThulwana Regiment, 59, *201*
uDududu Regiment, 184, *201*, 208
uMbonambi Regiment, 59, *106*, 184 191, *201*, 208, 210
Umkusi Regiment, 59, 321
Undi Corps, 185, *201*
uNodwengu Regiment, 184, 196, *201*, 208
uNokhenke Regiment, 184, 185, 196, *201*, 202, 203, 208
uVe Regiment, *107*, 184, 191, *201*, 208
Zululand, Resident of, 78
Zwide kaLanga, Zulu chief, 51